The Broken Circle

Also by David P. Bridges

The Bridges of Washington County: Spanning Work and Nature

The Best Coal Company In All Chicago, and How It Got That Way

Fighting With JEB Stuart: Major James Breathed and the Confederate Horse Artillery

The Broken Circle

David P. Bridges

RESOURCE *Publications* · Eugene, Oregon

THE BROKEN CIRCLE

Resource Publications
An Imprint of Wipf and Stock Publishers
199 W. 8th Ave., Suite 3
Eugene, OR 97401

www.wipfandstock.com

ISBN 13: 978-1-62564-152-6

Manufactured in the U.S.A.

This is a work of fiction. Names, characters, places, and incidents are used factually or are the product of the author's imagination.

Back cover photo provided by Gordon Valentine.

Dedicated to:
My parents
Shelby Powell Bridges

&

Barbara Best Bridges
Along with all my family

&

My English Setter bird dogs
Angel, Bella, & Rosey

&

The Men of
The Stuart Horse Artillery
Confederate States of America

&

My Twenty-five
Confederate Ancestors
Who Fought for their Southland

Acknowledgments

I WOULD LIKE TO thank the following people for their academic influence and development of my writing of historical fiction. Without them I could have never developed the skills to write any novel, including this one. Thanks to Professor Amanda Cockrell, Hollins University; Professor Mark Farrington and Tim Wendell, the Johns Hopkins University Writing Program; Dr. Martin Marty, Professor Emeritus of the University of Chicago, Divinity School; Dr. Don Livingston, Professor Emeritus of Emory University and the Abbeville Institute; Dr. Welford D. Taylor, Professor Emeritus of the University of Richmond; and Mr. Robert Trout, author, for his consulting with me on horse artillery.

I was fortunate to have interested a number of people in this novel. These individuals became my unofficial and voluntary editorial staff. Without their thoughts and skills I could have never completed the novel. Thanks to Lieutenant Colonel John Zebelen (retired), U.S.A.F. in the Vietnam War; Bill (retired), U.S. Army in the Vietnam War; Jane Perry; Reverend David Miller (retired), Presbyterian Church U.S.A.; and Polly Miller.

Others I wish to thank are Mr. Waite Rawls III; Jim Flanigan; Francis O'Neil; Dan Toomey, author/historian extraordinaire of Maryland, Michael Lucas, and Dr. Tom Strong. I must thank Gordon Valentine for the photograph that appears on the back cover of this book. Thanks also to my neighbor Hartwig Balke and my two nieces, Tori and Emily Bridges.

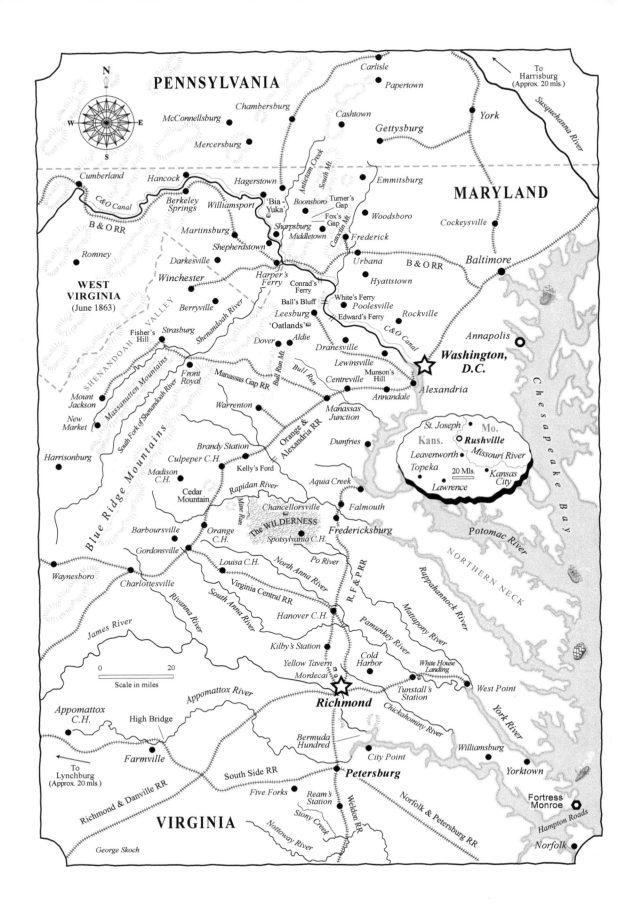

School of Medicine

Baltimore, Maryland

Autumn 1859

CAREFREE TO BE AND to live, for James was blessed to take control of it, he felt, as he led his colleagues, Ed McCullough, Frank Wooten, and Johnny Cochran to Davidge Hall of The University of Maryland, School of Medicine. They walked up the steps of the white columned building with its rotunda domed structure. James opened the tall wooden door for his friends, and they ambled up another flight of stairs and entered into the Anatomical Hall.

They sat together on the polished wooden circular seating. He observed the rotunda, which had a beautifully designed oval ceiling with sky-lights and a golden chandelier hanging from the center of the oval. The seating angled down to a lectern that was on the floor in the middle of the circle. He listened to the loud chatter as an excitement filled the hall in anticipation of the lecture to be presented by the newest professor on the School of Medicine's faculty.

He had met Dr. William A. Hammond, U.S. Army, on campus. The doctor told him in passing he would be lecturing on the anatomical parts of the lung from *Elements of Anatomy* by Quain, Sharpey, and Wilson, and on Horner's *Treatise on Special and General Anatomy*. He had pored through these books in preparation for the day's lecture.

He scrutinized Dr. Hammond, a robust man with a balding head, slightly slanted eyes, and a full beard and moustache. James watched him and thought he was rather intimidating and bet he did not suffer fools. The doctor stood next to Dean G. W. Miltenberger behind the lectern as they exchanged pleasantries. The dean raised his hands over his head and brought them down to his side a few times to quiet the students.

The dean cleared his throat, "Hume, humeeee." Then he began, "Mental power and culture cannot be imparted by pouring knowledge into vacant and inactive minds. The results of a medical education depend upon the quantity and quality of the instruction given and the ability of the instructors who give it. Also, and in a much larger measure, upon the character of the pupils, who they are by nature, and what they have been made by the training, good or evil, to which they were subjected before they entered the hallowed halls of the School of Medicine."

James listened to this rhetoric a few minutes, and then the dean shook the hand of Dr. Hammond, introducing him to the class. Dr. Hammond started directly into his lecture: "The word 'pneumonia' is applied to inflammation of the substance of the lungs. It is therefore a disease in which the eye fails and the touch cannot guide us to its true condition. Then what have we left but the ear to give us some information reflecting the nature of this great disease? First, it becomes necessary for us to understand the anatomical characters which give rise to the auscultatory signs by which we are able to discover the condition of the lungs at the time we examine them."

James eagerly took notes along with his other colleagues as he was anxious to learn more of what Dr. Hammond had to say because he had chosen pneumonia as the subject for his graduation thesis. He knew Dr. Hammond was as well known as a contributor to various medical journals as he was for his lectures on anatomy.

Dr. Hammond continued: "We generally find these very well-masked changes which the lungs undergo during the course of this disease. The first is congestion, the second hepatization, and the third and last change is that of purulent infiltration. It is curious, but a well-known fact, that the right lung is greatly more subject to attacks of this disease than the left. Why this is true we do not know. Again the lower lobes are a great deal more subject to the disease than the upper and, here again, science has deserted and left us ignorant, for we know not why it is. Such changes as we have described certainly must give signals by which we are able to discover the important processes which are going on within the cavity of the thorax. Therefore, if the ear can be applied to the chest, and the lungs are at this time in the first stage of inflammation, what do we hear?"

Dr. Hammond paused and lifted his head up from his notes.

James grasped his black French-style goatee in a fidgety manner and spoke up cheerfully, "A very peculiar sound, which resembles the rubbing of one's hair between his fingers or the wind that passes through the branches of the trees in autumn. I have learned the term *rales* in relation to the sound. This is diagnosed as a result of thumping the chest, called percussion."

"What is your name, young man?"

"James Breathed."

"How did you come to this diagnosis, Mr. Breathed?"

"This peculiar sound is termed by Dr. Lannec as crepitant rhonchus. He believes this is the most important symptom, for it gives us the first, sure intimation that inflammation has begun and consequently life must be lost unless the disease is quickly arrested by powerful remedies."

"Very good," Dr. Hammond said. "Anything else you'd like to add?"

"Well, it's universally acknowledged, I believe, that it proceeds from the very smallest of the bronchial tubes and from the air vesicles themselves. The belief among men of science is that the sound is caused by the formation and bursting of little air bubbles. By the difference in the sounds, diagnosis is possible. When the ear is applied to the chest we no longer hear crepitant rhonchus but, instead, we hear the bronchial respiration, which resembles the cooing of a dove or the sound produced by blowing through a quill," he said as he finished confidently.

James felt his knowledge of the subject might have taken Dr. Hammond by surprise. The professor's round mouth hung slightly open before he looked back down at his notes and then up at his students saying, "The lung at this stage has become solid and therefore admits no air into vesicles and small tubes, from which this peculiar blowing sound is heard. At this stage, the voice is also changed. It is much more resonant than in health and the patient talks indistinctly. This sound is called bronchial voice or bronchophony. The cause is the same as bronchial breathing. It is impossible to know the exact condition of the lungs in the third stage. But sometimes doctors can discover the condition of the lungs from a portion of their being expectorated."

James was seated between Frank and Johnny. They were all intensely absorbed in the lecture. He poked Frank in the ribs with his finger.

"Quit!" Frank said in an irritated tone.

James smiled at Johnny as the lecture came to an end.

Dr. Hammond called out, "Sir, may I speak with you a moment?"

James climbed down the steps of the lecture hall and walked over toward the lectern to greet the doctor.

"You seem to have a strong grasp of the subject matter, young man. Do you have a particular interest in this subject?"

He explained to the new professor that his final examinations were to take place before faculty, and that the public examinations as a candidate promised to be rigorous. He would have to defend his thesis on pneumonia, and he understood, in order to graduate, he would need a majority vote in the affirmative from the faculty. "A student can be failed by four professors out of seven on the panel."

"I assume you're so knowledgeable on the lung because you've to defend your thesis on the subject?"

"Yes, Doctor. I've spent a year and a half here, and by February fourteenth of next year my thesis will be due for review. I aim to pass my oral examination on my thesis of pneumonia," he shared with emotional enthusiasm.

"You're on your way, sir! It sounds to me like you've got a strong understanding of the lung and the calamities that affect the lung. I look forward to hearing the defense of your thesis this spring. Godspeed to you and your endeavors in medicine."

James looked around and saw that his close colleagues had gathered on the floor of Anatomical Hall, and they had listened intently to his and Dr. Hammond's conversation.

James turned with a smile on his face to Ed, Frank, and Johnny. They left Anatomical Hall and spun their way around the outer stairs to the outside of Davidge Hall. He and his colleagues walked over to the shade of an immense oak in the courtyard and sat for a while to reflect upon the lecture. Their conversation soon wandered onto the subject of war.

"During the War of 1812, from a ship in Baltimore Harbor, Francis Scott Key observed 'bombs bursting in air' over Fort McHenry. In that direction," James explained, "you can almost see the Fort." He had heard that the oak was actually hit by a cannon ball during the war, but he was unsure of the reliability of the yarn.

James stood after a time of conversation and, as usual, walked in the lead. His three friends crossed the street with him and walked toward his residence in the infirmary. The three stories of the university hospital, which housed the infirmary, had a wide sidewalk in front of it that wrapped around the side of the complex. He noticed doctors in their white cloaks kibitzing on the sidewalk.

James was one of two infirmary residents and was paid $300 per year, in addition to his board, room, and laundry. He accompanied professors on their rounds and read histories on patients admitted since the physician's previous visit. He attended instruction in the practice of surgery under the direction of Dr. Smith, which was his favorite class. His infirmary home, away from his Western Maryland home at Bai-Yuka Plantation, had over 150 beds and received patients with every variety of acute and chronic disease.

The long day of lectures and laboratories had started early in the morning for him. He had done his clinical rounds with Professor Nathan Rhino Smith. He looked forward to a good hot meal, a few hours of study, and a good night's sleep.

James knocked on the door of the infirmary. He and his friends were met by a stern trio of Dr. Butler, who was the resident physician and an austere, handsome man, Dr. Wagner, the short and stumpy clinical reporter, and a Nun who stood watch over the entrance like a guard dog.

"How was your lecture today?" Sister Mary Ann, the Sister Superior asked. She was a wisp of a woman, and her habit always neat and clean. He had known from her brogue that she was an Irishwoman, and it had been made clear to him that she had been in charge in the "Old Country." She always had the first good word to say to him, as she seemed to favor him over the other residents.

"We had a very fine lecture from Dr. Hammond, the new 'prof' on the faculty," he answered as the other two professors listened in on the conversation.

"What would he be lecturin' about on this fine, beautiful fall afternoon?"

"He talked my game today. He spoke of the lungs and pneumonia, the very thesis I'm working on."

"And, as usual, James was very knowledgeable, perhaps overly so," Frank injected as he jabbed James in the ribs with retribution in his eyes.

"I just shared with Dr. Hammond some of my research knowledge. I'll have to defend my thesis before him come this spring. I hope he'll remember me from Anatomy class and will be favorably inclined toward me. I do want to graduate out of this place with honorable promptitude."

"James seems to think he's not learned enough to graduate. A meritorious student with such a serious cast of mind; he is a real doubting Thomas. He worries that he may not graduate from this institution in his lifetime," Ed observed with a trace of humor.

"Jest not. I'll graduate in good time. I hope to go to the West and practice. The West is where the real action is in America today. I mean, Sister, it's not that this old infirmary is not exciting, but the border between Kansas and Missouri is a hotbed of fighting. Where there is fighting, a doctor is certain of a brisk profession. From what my cousin Lige White said when he was out there in '52 with the army, there'll continue to be a brisk conflict along the Kansas-Missouri border, particularly if Kansas is admitted as a 'free' state. War has not started here yet, but it's already under way out West. I aim to get away from here where there are already so many newly minted doctors and go west to learn firsthand the type of skills I fear will soon be needed along the borders, north and south, between Southern Cavalier and New England Puritan states."

"That's all and well, but you'll likely get shot at by those hotheaded secessionists, and we may never hear from you again," Johnny concluded. He was the solemn one of the bunch and could always put a damper on conversation, interjecting a bit of reality.

"I think I've more to fear from 'old Ossawattomie John Brown' and his ilk than from the slavery advocates," he riposted to Johnny.

James was not shy when it came to politics. He often boasted of his strong Southern sympathies, as he had been known, when provoked, to "breathe a little fire" on the topic of states' rights. He had had a medical apprenticeship with his uncle Dr. Charles Macgill prior to attending the University of Maryland, School of Medicine. His apprenticeship consisted of three years in Hagerstown during which time he observed his uncle's office practice, accompanied the doctor on calls, read the doctor's shelf of books, served as a technician, performed menial tasks, and emulated his mentor. He often reflected on Dr. Macgill's thought that the best way to have the whole slave and anti-slave issue worked out was to give a gun to every white man in America and have them shoot it out. His uncle believed it would come to this eventually and James frequently quoted him.

"I know the secessionists will not be shooting at me, for I'm on their side. I know you've other ways of thinking, Johnny, but I feel certain they'll know one of their persuasion when I arrive out West," he continued.

"Son, if you go west you'll carry with you the reputation of this School of Medicine, and you'll not be going to fight," Dr. Butler said. "You'll be a doctor with the

Hippocratic oath as your guide. It'd serve you well to look up this oath once again. For what you really fight for is life."

"Furthermore, gentlemen, you shouldn't be divided amongst yourselves," Dr. Wagner added. "We're all Americans here and there is no room in this hospital for partisan agitation. Mr. Breathed, if you ever want to become a doctor, you should apply yourself to your books; the other three of you might do the same. None of you'll ever make it through this School of Medicine on hot air."

James thought the two doctors were correct and he bid adieu to them all. He walked down the dimly gas lit corridor to his room to do exactly what the doctors had just suggested he do, study.

2

No Place Like Home

JAMES STOOD ON THE train platform and thought about what he had accomplished in this last year of his life in Rushville, outside of St. Joseph, Missouri. In May of '60 he had graduated meritoriously with his thesis on pneumonia from the School of Medicine. He had found correct his calculations that there were too many doctors back East; besides, he knew, the action in America was in the West. So west he had gone. With Kansas recently admitted as a free state, he had seen guerilla fighting in the Border War. He had been surrounded by Southerners in Buchanan County, and he was comfortable as his heritage was mainly Southern.

He pondered his past and future while waiting to catch the train from St. Joseph back East. His parents had requested he return home and, as the firstborn, he felt he had to oblige them. What he had seen on the frontier enforced what he knew in relation to war. War was about to explode back East, and he wanted to be there to play a man's part in whatever developed in Maryland. According to a *Harper's Weekly* article he had recently read, President Lincoln was on his soapbox of preserving the union.

The mist was so thick on the platform that other people seemed ghostly to him. Fog shrouded them and then moved away only to envelop them again. He glanced over his right shoulder and noticed a soldier in a blue Federal uniform with his family. The balmy mist floated around the soldier and gave him a holy presence. With an inviting smile on the soldier's face he walked over to James.

"Good day to you, sir. My name is Lieutenant Jeb Stuart."

"And a good day to you, Lieutenant. And hello to your charming family. I'm Dr. James Breathed from Maryland," he responded, bowing slightly and noticing the rank on the uniform.

"Allow me to present my family. This is my wife, Flora Cooke Stuart," Stuart replied. Mrs. Stuart curtseyed at the appropriate moment and graciously smiled. "And this is little Flora and my baby son, Philip," Stuart said pointing first to young Flora peeking from behind her mother's wide hooped skirt.

"Your manner of speech and demeanor proclaim you a Southern gentleman and, if I'm not mistaken, a native of Virginia. This is also my native state," James responded, smiling warmly at the Stuarts.

"We both find ourselves a long way from home, Doctor. Do we not?"

"Indeed. But in such times as these I feel called back to my home to perform a man's part if need be."

"I take it, then, you honor the call of your native state to stand by her in what will soon be her hour of greatest need?"

"What else could gentlemen from the Old Dominion or the Old Line states do, consistent with honor?"

He received Stuart's hand to shake it and Stuart patted him on the shoulder.

"I see your values are cut from the same cloth as mine. I, too, feel honor bound to see my family safe to Richmond. Then my duty is with Virginia. For her honor I've ever striven. Perhaps you'll ride with us on our journey home. I feel we've much to share in these troubled times."

"I'd be greatly honored in sharing such genteel company."

While they were speaking together the train had rolled up to the platform and had stopped to unload passengers and freight.

Suddenly they heard the conductor holler, "All aboard who's going aboard!"

He watched as Stuart took the hand of little Flora and grabbed the hand rail going up the rear passenger car entrance. Flora cradled baby Philip and followed. James followed close behind the Stuarts. They worked their way to the middle of the train car to be seated. He heard the whistle blow as the engines' wheels spun out on the tracks. The wood-burning engine spewed ashes and smoke over the passenger cars, wafting its way back to the open car windows adjacent to where they all sat. The mist and cold morning air had Stuart dressed in his U.S. uniform with his blue frock coat for warmth. James admired the pretty dresses of Flora and their little daughter.

He and Stuart sat directly across the aisle from each other, separated by a few feet. Their conversation quickly moved past the *bon ami* pleasantries of strangers and settled onto the pressing issues of the day.

"Do you have an opinion on Virginia's current crisis of secession?" Stuart asked.

"I was born a Virginian in Berkeley Springs and see myself as a Virginian who grew up from age ten in Maryland. It seems as though the South has already spoken, with so many states having left the Union. There's tension mounting by the day in Charleston. I'm afraid our hotheaded South Carolinian brothers may be the people to get hostilities started."

He saw Stuart shake his head affirming his thoughts and then he unbuttoned his blue frock coat.

"If my home state follows suit with the other Confederate States, I'll have to remain loyal to my state first. I've served the United States since I graduated from West Point, but now it's time for my true loyalties to show. My first duty is to Virginia."

They spoke in hushed voices, as Stuart still wore the uniform of the United States Army. He understood that people had been arrested for such secessionist talk. He trusted Stuart from the moment they met on the train platform, feeling that he had a sincere countenance and a demeanor which elicited trust. It was this sincerity, along with his professionalism as a trained soldier that enabled him to trust the officer.

"I think I'll serve my home state of Virginia," James confided. "If Virginia secedes I think I'll offer her my medical training and serve in the Medical Corps. I've so many years invested in medicine it seems a waste not to serve the cause in this capacity."

James fidgeted with his pocket watch and looked to catch the time. The conversation made him a bit nervous; after all he was talking to a man dressed in a blue Federal army uniform.

"That seems logical," Stuart immediately responded. "I'm sure there're other important ways that you can serve her. You seem to have other aptitudes that might be better employed in, let's say, the cavalry. You're certainly a leader of men and not a follower; I sense this about you. You're certain I can't count on you to enlist and fight under my command, whatever that might be?"

James reflected for a moment before giving his response. He was an excellent horseman, capable of shooting a revolver from horseback at a dead run after the wolves and coyotes that pestered sheep and cattle on the Bai-Yuka Plantation. But Stuart was suggesting fighting and killing. He thought the medical Hippocratic oath was about saving life, not taking it. It seemed too much to contemplate now with a man he had just met.

"You've given me something to think about," James allowed. "There's no doubt in my mind I'll be loyal to my native state of Virginia, for her cause is just. But I was sure the Medical Corps would be the place for me to serve."

"There're many ways to serve. I need good men of stature and intelligence to serve under my command. You've both these attributes. I implore you to rethink your position on the Medical Corps. Consider what your response would be if the sacred soil of Virginia were invaded by a Northern army."

"In such case I'd enlist in Martinsburg with the cavalrymen from my home county of Morgan. The adjoining county of Berkeley would also have men enlisting that I've known growing up. Maryland may not go with the South, so there is no certainty that I could find a Maryland unit around Hagerstown where, I'm ashamed to say, there's much Federal sentiment. My best bet is to go where I'll know other men and join up with them."

"Now you're thinking like a trooper. Fight with men you know, trust, and have hometown loyalties with and you'll be much happier. You're right about Maryland.

Besides, Virginia is your home state by birth. If I may make a personal observation—it's also by moral sentiment!"

⌘

Their train continued east across the state of Missouri. They continued to talk about the crisis of the Union. James parted from his new friends after the smoky train ride ended in St. Louis. He traveled from St. Louis south on a Mississippi River steamer to Memphis and from there by train to Chambersburg, Pennsylvania.

His train ride from Memphis to Chambersburg was arduous. He had to change trains several times before boarding the Cumberland Valley Railroad passenger train that would take him on the last leg of his journey to Hagerstown. He providentially sat next to a freed Negro who wore a clerical collar. He observed that the reverend was a middle-aged man, thin as a rail, wiry, with a nose resembling the beak of a falcon. The reverend's intelligent eyes, half buried under long bushy eyebrows, twinkled like two celestial orbs. His mouth was large and he smiled; his expression was outstandingly benevolent. He was clad in severe black, and he presented himself as a pious and peaceable civilian.

Although James was exhausted by his travels, he did enjoy good conversation and his mind wandered when he felt overtired. He reached into his black frock coat pocket and brought out a small Bible that he carried with him. He had been given it while attending the College of St. James. As he read the Bible he inquisitively eyed the reverend. He placed the Bible on his knee and struck up a conversation.

"Hello, I'm Dr. James Breathed."

"Greetings, I'm Reverend Daniel Ridout."

"What denomination do you serve?"

"I'm a Methodist Episcopal minister. I live with my family on the east side of South Mountain."

"I studied theology at the College of St. James across the road from my plantation home. I relish the opportunity to discuss theology. Are you very learned on the subject?"

"Yes, a Wesleyan, with Calvinist influences; I'm learned."

"Well then, you know that Calvin believed that God's 'secret plan' is the basis which gives rise to providence. Calvin thought that the universe was ruled by God's secret plan, but anyone who has been taught by Christ's lips that all the hairs on his head are numbered will look for God's cause. I believe that all events are governed by God's secret plan."

He had just read this verse pertaining to Christ in his Bible.

"God's providence can be summed up by defining general providence. This aspect of the nature of God relates more to the big picture events that take place in the creation such as: war, famine, disease, natural disasters, and so on," said the reverend.

He was taken aback by such wisdom with which Reverend Ridout responded. A puzzled look came to his countenance as he pondered what the reverend had said.

"I believe that God, witnessed to in Scriptures, is teaching that humans don't understand God's wider purposes in events in history," James said, "whatever they may be. It's God's intention that they take place, and through these events God is working out his benevolent secret plan."

"If I follow your reasoning, the impending war is a part of the general providence of God. Consequently, God, in his secret plan, knows that this war will take place and that many lives will be sacrificed upon the altar of war. What kind of God do you think would have such a war to benefit his own purposes? What are these purposes in your opinion?" Reverend Ridout asked, looking James directly in the eyes.

James scratched his head and paused for a moment to squarely reflect on the questions he had been asked. He reflected back to his theological schooling at college recalling a particular text that he had read that inspired him to speak in an oratory fashion. Grasping hold of the bench to his front, James turned to speak face-to-face with the learned reverend.

"The concept of providence in American history and its leadership is deep-seated," James said. "The Confederate soldier will look back to the Revolutionary War to justify their purpose in fighting. It was General George Washington's trust in the providence of God that allowed him to be the man he was, and to achieve what he did. Washington's God was there at the darkest days of the founding of our nation. Washington seldom missed an opportunity to give thanks to God's providence and to beg God to continue favoring our nation."

"You're correct about our Founding Fathers' will to have an independent and sovereign nation under God," Reverend Ridout said. "But how does that relate to the purposes of God in this war?"

"The South will become an independent sovereign nation under God. We'll not be ruled by the tyrannical North. This is God's purpose for this war. To solve the issues of our sovereign Southern states, letting Southerners live how we want to live. If we're to be ruled by a higher power it shall be God, not a powerful central government, which is what the Yankees desire," he emphatically responded.

He felt the train pulling into the Hagerstown Station; they had to end their conversation in order to disembark from the train. They shook hands, and James stepped into the aisle in front of the reverend. As new friends, they had agreed to keep in touch, having exchanged addresses.

As they stepped from the train car onto the plank boardwalk, a robust and haughty United States sergeant stopped Reverend Ridout dead in his tracks. The sergeant deliberately blew a puff of his nasty cigar in the direction of the reverend.

"Hey, boy, do you have your papers? Why are you so handsomely dressed? Shouldn't you be on the plantation pickin' cotton?"

James noticed that his new friend was visibly disturbed and agitated by the comment.

"Excuse me, sir," the reverend replied, "but I'm a freed man. I ask for your respect as a fellow free man!"

"You're all alike once you get your freedom—uppity!"

James stepped in between the sergeant and Reverend Ridout. James had respect for the uniform and authority but also had respect for his new acquaintance, and he was not going to let this bully push around his new friend.

"Pardon me, but this is my friend. He has his freedman's papers. Reverend Ridout, take them out."

The reverend pulled out his papers and presented them to the Federal sergeant. The sergeant's face turned beet red. He grabbed the papers from the reverend's hand and opened them up with contempt.

"Okay, you're free to move on," the sergeant said as he glanced through the papers. "You sir," he said to James, "I want to check your baggage. Go and get it off the train and bring it here to me immediately!"

"Yes, Sergeant," James coldly responded.

James walked to the baggage car and off loaded his trunk of belongings. He pulled them down to the sergeant and was ordered to open the trunk.

"Slave lovers like you belong on the plantation with them."

James watched the sergeant begin to pull out all of his belonging. He threw them onto the plank boards, distressing him.

"So you're a doctor. Your caring about uppity darkies is such a waste of your time. After you clean up your mess you're free to go. Stay on the plantation and do not come North again!"

"Yes, Sergeant."

James put his belonging back into the trunk and closed the lock. He left the Hagerstown train platform with a bitter feeling in his gut. He thought there was no reason for the search. Nor should the sergeant have been so rude to his new friend. He reflected on the irony of the injustices he had just witnessed. He thought if that Yankee sergeant was an abolitionist, then God help all free Negroes.

James expected his younger brother John Jr. to be waiting for his train's arrival at the Hagerstown train terminal. John Jr. would have ridden from Bai-Yuka Plantation, located a few miles south of town, to meet him with a horse and wagon to make the journey home. When he first saw his brother, he was whittling on a stick. John Jr. looked up to greet him with a smile and came to help him load his trunk into the wagon.

"Brother, it's so good to have you back home," John Jr. said as he shook his older brother's hand.

"It's fine to be home after a year away from the family. It was a long and exhausting trip from Rushville."

"What is it like out West?" John Jr. asked. "Are there really Indians at your back door at night shooting arrows at you?"

"There're Indians around, but the ones I knew were friendly," James replied as he climbed aboard the wagon.

The brothers happily rode off together, exchanging stories and catching up on each others' lives.

They reached the plantation and turned down the tree-lined drive to the big house. James noticed that the April sky was clear and the trees were beginning to bud along the lane to the house. His home plantation, Bai-Yuka, was named after an old Indian word meaning; "fountain rock." The pillared front of the home beckoned him as the porch majestically wrapped around to one side of the Greek Revival style domicile. It seemed like an eternity since he had seen his parents or any of his ten brothers and sisters.

As the wagon appeared, the family flocked out. He felt a warm feeling, as he knew he was back in the bosom of his loving family. Willie and Sarah, the married house servants following his family, were waving their hands in the air with excitement. He was greeted by the whole family with open arms.

"Welcome home, my boy," Judge John Breathed said.

He climbed down from the wagon as the judge reached out and clasped his eldest son on the shoulder. James gave his father a firm handshake, kissed his mother on the cheek, and then moved around and hugged his brothers and sisters, giving a kiss on the cheek to his favorite sister, Priscilla.

"Father, it's good to see you. I was searched at the rail station as if I were some kind of common criminal. What has gotten into the Yankees?"

"Ever since that *rail splitter* was elected, nothing has been the same. That's why we felt it best for you to come home to the safety of your family. Enough talk of politics; stable your horses and come in the house."

He and his brother remounted the wagon and rode as faithful disciples to the stable, for they both worshipped their father. They removed the traces and saddles from the horses and together, walked back toward the house.

Suddenly, James made a turn for the servant quarters.

"I'll see you in a few minutes," he said.

He made his way behind Bai-Yuka and found his way to a number of small buildings, which were the quarters. When he knocked on the door of one of the cabins he heard a familiar female voice.

"Who's it, please come," Mae said.

"It's James. I've returned from the West and wanted to see how you'll were doing."

"Mr. James, do's come in. It's so good to see ya after all dis time. How your medical practice a sittin' out West?"

"I'm afraid I've left it behind. I've made some new plans for my life."

"And what mightin' they be?"

"I've not shared this with anyone yet, but I'm going to join the cavalry. I met an officer by the name of James Ewell Brown Stuart. His friends call him Jeb. He has personally invited me to serve under his Virginia command, whatever it might be!"

He turned to see the Breathed servant Jimmie walking into the quarters and greeted him. Jimmie had always been amongst his closest confidants. He was about the same age and build, both about five feet ten. They had been raised from infancy together, and he trusted Jimmie like a brother. Jimmie walked across the room and hugged him.

"Mr. James is gonna jine the cavalry, what do you think of that, Jimmie?" Mae said, with a strange look on her tar-black face. "Doesn't that mean you'll have to be killin' peoples, Mr. James?"

"I'll have to do whatever my commander tells me to do. I'll not think about it, but just do it. That's how things work in the military."

"But, you're a doctor and you're to be saving lives and not a kill'em," Mae ruefully pointed out to him.

"Mr. James, pay no heed to her. How ya doing? Can ya tell me about the West?" Jimmie asked.

"I will. But first I must return to the house. I need to get cleaned up for our quail hunt and Saturday supper. I think Mother has a fine meal prepared for my homecoming."

"After church in the morning there gonna be a big homecoming party and all the neighbors are invited," Jimmie announced.

"Well, that'll be fine. I'll look forward to seeing everyone after church at St. Mark's. Now I must say good-bye. I'll see you later."

He parted from his two friends and went across the open lawn to the house. It was time for his favorite pastime on the back forty. He knew the plantation had always been blessed with an abundance of quail. He had been dreaming of the quail hunt ever since he left St. Louis. He was twelve the first time the judge had let him shoot, and he quickly became a crack shot with a double barreled shotgun.

He knew the judge would have lined up a Saturday afternoon hunt with some of their neighbors. This day would be different than most he thought, as his skin still crawled with anger at what the Yankee sergeant had done to him at the train station. He was now fired up enough that he might well see blue uniforms on the quail.

⁓⊙⊛⊙⁓

James, the judge, Dr. Charles Macgill, John Jr., and neighbors Mr. Hezekiah Clagett and Reverend Clarksmoore walked out the front door of the house and climbed into the rickety horse-drawn wagon. They rode the short distance to the back forty where the hunting was the sportiest. James thought about having a cigar as the men puffed on them, but he had never taken a strong liking to them. They sat in the wagon and talked of the impending crisis.

"James, did you have a chance to practice medicine to the fullest out West?" Dr. Macgill asked.

"I think I had a good run of it. I saw a lot of pneumonia, cases of typhoid and scarlet fever. I only wish there was more I could've done for many of my patients. I did a few amputations in the St. Josephs' Infirmary. The procedures seemed far more difficult than I remembered them being on cadavers at the School of Medicine."

"Isn't it hard to deal with all the blood when you do operations?" John Jr. innocently asked.

"No, thanks to all the fine intern years I've had with Dr. Charles and my experiences at school. I've become comfortable with all the blood. It no longer bothers me."

"Young man, where're you on the current crisis?" Dr. Charles asked.

"Well, I've been meaning to talk about this with you and Father. I know how much time and money you put into my education, but I've some new ideas."

They bumped along the old dusty dirt road toward the back forty. He had known the time would come when he would have to divulge his new career path. What he would say had occupied his thoughts ever since Stuart had proposed a new path for his life.

He held the side of the wagon as Willie drove the horses to a clump of trees and pulled over. They stepped down from the back of the wagon and Willie handed each of them a shotgun. The five men walked off into the high brush. Willie went to the kennels, opened the gate and patted each of the two English Setters. Then he cut them loose of their kennels. The beautiful setters running through the field harkened James back to fond memories of his youth. The dogs ran headlong into the brush, eagerly roaming back and forth until they found a covey of quail. They locked on point. He and the group of hunters eased their way closer to the setters.

"Careful, James," Dr. Charles said. "They could flush in any direction. Be ready Judge; it looks like they'll break toward you."

"We're ready," James and John Jr. simultaneously responded.

James sensed the moment, pregnant with the hunter's wild expectation. The quail exploded before him in every direction as twenty of the birds came battering out from the underbrush. He shouldered his gun and fired twice. Each time a quail came to the ground. The judge turned behind him and fired, missing with the first shot and connecting with the second. Dr. Charles had the majority of the birds come toward him. Dr. Charles got off two quick shots, both kills. James heard the blasts of the neighbors and John Jr. They were not as successful, but did drop two birds from the three guns. He saw the setters come off point and go into retrieval mode. They quickly gathered up the fallen prey and brought the birds back on Willie's commands.

"Nice shots!" responded Hezekiah Clagett.

"Gentlemen, I commend you on your excellent shooting! James, you shot with vengeance as if you felt a passion in your shooting. Is there something you would like to share with your family and friends?" Reverend Clarksmoore inquired.

James walked toward the setter and retrieved one of the quail from its mouth, the bird struggling and kicking in his hand. He quickly wrang its neck to put it out of its misery, and the bird's blood stained his hands.

He knew the time was right, so with a smile on his face, he blissfully proclaimed, "I'm joining the Virginia Cavalry if the state leaves the Union!"

"James, what about your medical oath?" Dr. Charles asked.

"James, you're sure we couldn't sit and talk about this decision—you must have thought long and hard about it?" The judge asked in stunned disbelief.

"I knew you looked different when I saw you on the road today. You want to kill Yankees!" John Jr. excitedly exclaimed.

"James, you know I passed up a West Point appointment in my youth. I lament your decision to leave medicine. Couldn't you serve in the Medical Corps?" The judge asked.

The questions barraged him, and they overwhelmed and perplexed his thoughts. He reasoned a response, then, at that moment, Willie hollered out, "Point!"

They all moved toward Willie, the majestic setters on solid point, their white feathered tails extended straight up in the air, their right front paws held up off the ground. The dogs stood solidly like stone walls. Both dogs stared into the brush where the next covey hid.

There was more concentration in this moment than he had had since he made the decision to join the cavalry. Despite all his elders' cautions, James was confirmed in his belief that the best purpose for his life would be to join the cavalry. Stuart had had his influence and now it was time to act upon his own conviction. He was determined not to be dissuaded. Even his younger brother was elated with his decision to fight the Federals.

3

The Homecoming Gala

EARLY SUNDAY MORNING JAMES was up and about the plantation in a reminiscent state of mind after the wonderful quail hunt and dinner from the night before. The question of his medical or military service had been avoided due to Willie and his well-trained setters. He had watched the setters move rapidly from one quail covey to the next the rest of the afternoon, leaving little to no time for conversations. He believed the question lingered in everyone's mind; the issue was in the open, but no one approached the subject.

He was elated to begin this beautiful spring morning with church services at the Saint Mark's Episcopal Church. His father had founded the church and wanted to educate his family at the College of St. James. He and his mother had desired that their children's hearts be educated as to the meaning of Jesus the Christ. James had grown up attending this beautiful gray stone church with a small steeple. It was only a few miles from Sharpsburg, Maryland. They could take two large carriages filled with family from Bai-Yuka to the church in a few minutes. His brothers had education in religion at Saint Mark's and academics at the college, which too was near at hand; his sisters were home schooled.

"Morning, Judge. I'm grateful as always to have you here this morning for church services," Reverend Clarksmoore greeted.

"It's a fine morning when I get to worship and hear your thoughtful homily, Reverend. It has been a year or more since James has been here to worship. Aren't you happy to be back, James?" his father said.

"Yes, sir. I did miss worship at St. Mark's. I've wonderful memories of this church."

"Nice shooting, James. I think you shot most of the quail dinner last night," Mr. Clagett observed.

"Thank you, sir. You did a fair job of wing shooting yourself. Will you be coming to join us for dinner after church today?" he asked.

"Yes, you can count on me and my family coming to your homecoming event. We have been talking about it for weeks now. I understand your cousin Mollie Macgill will be coming as well," Mr. Clagett said.

"Yes, Dr. Charles assured me that she will be in attendance. I know she wasn't due back until late last night from her trip to Galveston. She was out farther west than I. It's taken her even longer to return. I look forward to seeing her very much."

He and his neighboring congregates gathered in the sanctuary and sat together for the worship service. James spent a great deal of the time thinking about Mollie. He had not seen her for over a year. Their letter writing had kept them connected. However that was not the same as seeing her face to face.

⋘⊙⊙⋙

A joyful spirit permeated the air as James and his family exited Saint Mark's Church. To the front of the church on the other side of the stone wall James saw Lappon's Crossroad, which led to the Breathedsville Mill on the corner.

"I'll be joining you shortly," Reverend Clarksmoore said to the judge as they clasped hands. "We've much celebrating to do with James back on the plantation."

"We've two pigs a-roasting in a pit since last night; it'll be grand. All the church is invited and all our neighbors: the Rowlands, Mrs. Grimes, Dr. Rench, the Emmerts, the Malotts, the Clagetts, Mr. Kennedy, and George Shafer will be coming over. We've the fatted calf slaughtered and the fine china prepared, music too."

"Fine, fine," Reverend Clarksmoore said as James's mother, Ann Macgill Breathed, shook the reverend's hand while holding two-year-old Edward in her arms.

James and all his brothers and sisters went through the church door.

"Well good morning, James, and Priscilla, and Jane, and Isaac, and Wilbur, and John, and little Elizabeth. See you soon," Reverend Clarksmoore said as he grasped each of their hands in succession.

They all followed their mother and father like a clutch of swaddling swans. After shaking Reverend Clarksmoore's hand at the door, his family and their neighbors gathered inside the stone wall on the lawn. They then filed past the congregants to their carriages, climbed in to make the drive back to Bai-Yuka for final preparations of the homecoming gala.

⋘⊙⊙⋙

James stood in front of his home in the early afternoon. He watched carriages, buggies, three-seat spring wagons, and Conestoga wagons all drift up the plantation lane. He observed on the front porch fiddlers, a bass player, a guitar player, and a banjo picker strumming away making happy mountain music. His servant friends had set tables around the front yard with under-glazed blue floral patterned Wedgwood china and silver. Chairs were placed in circles throughout the yard. A dance floor of wood had been assembled in front of the pickers.

James smelled the fermented apple cider and watched the youngsters play games of hopscotch and jump rope while the adults chatted and exchanged stories. Willie and Sarah directed their children to attend to the needs of the throng of guests. His childhood friends, Jimmie and Mae, were clad with white gloves and dressed for the occasion in their finest garments. They served the apple cider in silver goblets while their four younger brothers and sisters collected empty goblets in the yard.

While making small talk with some friends, James spotted a fine ornate black carriage coming toward the house. He recognized Dr. Charles Macgill and his wife Mary Ragan. Their coachman, Alfred, drove them up the lane. He could not hide his excitement as his mentor approached. His anticipation grew as Alfred directed the four-up team of fine horses to the side circle at the right of the house. As the carriage turned, he noticed in the back seats his cousins, Barlow, Davidge, James, and Mollie.

Mollie smiled and waved to James. When she exited the carriage, she extended her parasol and walked toward him. She was outfitted in her finest silk day dress that featured a beautiful floral pattern with purple irises. Her hair was confined at the nape of her neck in a bun and covered by a bonnet. Dr. Charles, with his firm austere countenance greeted James first.

"Hello, Doctor Breathed."

"How do you do, sir?"

Mollie stepped from behind her father.

"Why, James Breathed, it has been so long," she gleefully said.

"Yes," James said as he reached for her exquisite hand and pulled her to him. They exchanged a warm hug, and he kissed her on her flushed pink cheek. She had always been of the finest etiquette and charm. He also gave her mother a peck on the cheek. He shook the hands of Barlow, Davidge, and James.

"Gentlemen, you're keeping yourselves fit and strong, I see," James said as others in his family walked over to greet the Macgills.

"Of course," Barlow said. "We may need our strength and our wits about us, as the Yankees seem to be pressing us beyond our tolerance."

His father led their relatives to the table of cider. Jimmie gave a goblet to Dr. Charles.

"Good ta-see-ya again, suh," Jimmie said.

He quickly filled more goblets for the others.

"Mollie, would you like a cider?" James asked.

"Why of course, James. Thank you, Jimmie."

"Daddy tells me you've made quite a change of plans for your life. Do tell us how you made this decision."

James stood amongst his cousins who wanted to know all about what he was thinking of doing. They, too, had been contemplating what he had shared yesterday at the quail hunt. His home state of Maryland had not yet harkened to the call of their Southern brethren. He smelled the smoke from the roasting pit as it drifted over the guests. All the excitement of the Macgills' arrival had almost overtaken his thoughts of food.

When he was about to speak, Willie and Sarah came around from the back of the house with silver platters piled to the sky with pulled pork. James's mother rang the old family dinner bell from the front porch signaling to all the hour to dine had arrived.

"James, your mother is calling us to sit. Why don't you escort Mollie to the front table where you're both the honored guests," the judge said.

"Yes, sir," he said as he reached his arm out, elbow bent, for Mollie to hold.

"James, I'm unsure who is more honored here today, you or me."

"We're both deemed worthy of our family's seat of honor. I'll sit at the head and you to my right. How shall that suit you, Mollie?"

"That'll be splendid."

He walked her across the front yard to the table just off the front porch. Her radiant beauty had always made him feel special in her company. He admired the jet black hair that curled into a bun, her beaming blue eyes that sparkled with delight. He pulled the chair out for her, and she sat like an elegant lady of the gentry class. When all the guests were settled at the tables and chairs, the judge came to the front porch and overlooked all his neighbors and friends.

"We're honored to have such fine folks as you to be our friends and neighbors. The Macgills and the Breatheds are so thankful to have James and Mollie home again, safe within our loving family circle. Let's show our young folks our appreciation with a warm round of applause!"

When the cheering concluded he heard his father ask Reverend Clarksmoore to return thanks.

"Let us bow our heads in gratitude to Almighty God," Reverend Clarksmoore intoned. "Let us pray. Heavenly Father, from whom all our bounty flows, we give thanks this fine Sabbath day. We're especially mindful of the safe passage you've granted to thy humble servants James and Mollie. Bless them with your guiding hands as they endeavor to do thy will. Father, in these troubling times of the prospect of war, we ask for thy providence to reveal itself, such that we may drive the Yankees from our peaceful lands! Amen."

James heard the exuberant cheers that went up from the Southerners as Reverend Clarksmoore stepped down from the porch. Then he listened to the pickers break out into a chorus so familiar to them all. They all sang loudly and with gusto:

> *I wish I was in the land of cotton,*
> *Old times there are not forgotten;*
> *Look away! Look away! Look away, Dixie Land!*
> *In Dixie Land where I was born in,*
> *Early on one frosty morning,*
> *Look away! Look away! Look away, Dixie Land!*

Conversations started among the guests upon the conclusion of the supper meal. They stood around the dance floor watching the children gaily dance around in a state of bliss as if there wasn't a looming dark cloud of war on the horizon. James observed that the gentlemen had their cigars, while some of the farming folk pulled long and hard on their corncob pipes. He held a snifter of brandy, which had replaced the apple cider and engaged the younger neighborhood gentlemen from farms and the college who puffed their cigars, pipes, and their egos. They were an eclectic group who all seemed to have a taste for the coming war, eager to join up and fight.

"James, we've not been enlightened with your opinion on the late unpleasantness. What say you, a cavalryman to be?" Davidge inquired.

"I'll soon be leaving Bai-Yuka. I had hoped for peace, but we've been insulted to the point that our chivalry has been jeopardized by the Yankees," James said as he quickly told the story of the Yankee sergeant at the train station. "If Virginia fights, I'll go with her."

"Everyone knows Southern gentlemen can fight better than any rabble immigrant from the North. I bet it would take five of them to bring me down. I, too, will whip Yanks by the bushel full," Barlow said as he stood by and puffed on his cigar with vengeance in his eyes.

James and the young men had by this time moved to the shade of a tree. They milled around, kicking the dirt with their boots and brogans.

"No Yankee's going to tell these proud men how to live and run our plantations," Davidge said.

Their conversation began to escalate as Barlow waved his arms about, impassioned with emotion. "James, you already aim to fight. You've met this Stuart officer fellow, and he has made it clear you're welcome to come with him. How about the rest of us? We've no contacts like you," Barlow said.

"You're only sixteen, Barlow. You need to grow up before you take up arms. I hear the Marylanders might form their own company of cavalry. Maybe it might pay to look into this," James said.

They conversed as smoke hovered over their heads. James thought the drum beat of war loomed on the horizon as many states had already seceded from the Union.

"Age and wisdom before youth," Mr. Joseph Duble said to them as he walked over to join their conversation. "War's risky and dangerous business, gentlemen. I hate to mollify your heroism, but I must advance my opinion. It all seems to be so glorious to young lads like yourself. You know nothing of the hardships of war, the disease, the dysentery, the hunger. It's not the bullets which scared me most in the Mexican War, but the other infirmities of war that got to me."

Mr. Duble told them that the Confederates did not have the industry in the South to fight the North on equal footing. "We've cotton and tobacco, but that does not make guns and cannon to win wars. The Yankees will first blockade Southern ports, and their revenue from these products will dry up. Confederates need money to fight a war, and the Yankees have plenty more of that than the Confederates do."

A calm came over them all. James thought the wisdom of his elder had spoken about things of war which he knew little about. He had known of the myriad rumors about Mr. Duble. The gruff old man was missing a few fingers on his right hand attributed to his having been a cannoneer and gripping a ramrod too tightly while plunging the charge down the tube when the cannon fired prematurely taking his fingers with the ramrod sailing through the air. The old vet really did know the perils of war he thought.

"Passionate young men like you will run to war and be slaughtered by the thousands," Mr. Duble said as he inhaled his pipe. "I saw your types go down in the last war; but pay no attention to an old veteran like me."

James looked up to see his cousin Mollie and his sister Priscilla strolling over toward him. They quickly discovered that the conversation which engaged all men was at hand—war.

"James, it's so pleasant to have you home. I beg you to enjoy being with your family and friends," Priscilla said. She was his closest sibling, in whom he often confided. "Come and enjoy the gala, James. The war will be here tomorrow and you can discuss it later."

"Yes, sister. I understand. You're right, we must live now. "Carpe diem," he said.

"Nothing but war, even at our homecoming. Come, James, we must dance and enjoy ourselves at our gala," Mollie insisted.

She took him by the arm to the dance floor. They danced a galop, creating a storm indicative of the mood of the Southerners. He noticed that the crowd had gathered to watch them enjoy their own festivity. After a few songs of great bliss, the two excused themselves from the dance floor and sat together under a shade tree in front of the house. Bai-Yuka held many memories for them.

"What a beautiful sunset. I so love this time of the evening at Bai-Yuka. I recalled it often in Missouri," James said. "This is what life is all about, family, friends, good food, and my home."

"What was your experience of the West?" Mollie asked.

"It's a wild place full of Indians and frontiersmen, 'sodbusters' and cattlemen, who're working out their dominance. They struggle to determine their own traditions. Often times 'might makes right' and the gun has the final word in disputes. In my practice I treated the outcome of these arguments."

"James, you're really going to fight? I mean Daddy has spent so many years educating you for medicine and all. You're so gifted at what you do. You really mean to give it all up for a war?"

"I can stay here under the safety of Bai-Yuka," James said as he reached to hold her hand. "Or I could . . ."

4

The Reality of War

SHORTLY AFTER THE HOMECOMING gala, James enlisted at Martinsburg, Virginia, as a private with the Berkeley Troopers, Virginia Cavalry. He became part of Company B of the 1st Virginia Cavalry under the command of his friend Stuart, who had by that time become a colonel in the Confederate Army due to his resignation from the U.S. Army in order to wear the gray. They were part of the Provisional Army of Virginia now moving toward Harper's Ferry.

Some months had passed since James had enlisted; the reality of the war was setting in for him as he had witnessed a few skirmishes and seen some enemies killed. He had been serving Company B as a scout along the Potomac River. The land he was familiar with had gentle rolling terrain with fenced cultivated fields, woods, and full of apple orchards. His 1st Virginia Cavalry was comprised of 334 troopers and they were ready to fight.

He did reconnaissance work from Leesburg to Shepherdstown, and west to Falling Waters, Virginia. It was his and his scouting comrades' responsibility to report any Federal movements back to Stuart in a timely fashion.

He routinely rode more than thirty miles in a day covering his territory around Falling Waters. His home was a few miles north on the other side of the river. His family was surrounded and monitored by Federals. He and the scouts sheltered at Camp Stephens, four miles north of Martinsburg, with the majority of the cavalry. His reconnaissance found him watching the infantry of the Federal Major General Robert Patterson's forces.

"Can you see any movement from where you sit, Thomas?" James asked.

He studied his companion's dark complexion and black hair. Thomas House was from Harper's Ferry. He was a serious academic type who had been heading to

Harvard to study history and politics before the war kept him from matriculating. They knew the terrain better than most of the other privates in their Company B.

"I don't see much. I'm sure those Yankees are lookin' to force our hand soon and cross the Potomac into Virginia. They say Patterson is lookin' to get a fight going."

"Well if a fight is what they're looking for, we're the men to give it to them. We might be outnumbered two to one, but that is an even fight," James said with an air that indicated he was stating an obvious fact.

"They look settled for now; best we start back toward camp before it gets too late."

They turned their horses from the river and headed toward the camp. James knew they would not make it back by nightfall, as the sun was beginning to set. They encountered two other scouts on their ride back to Camp Stephens: George McClarey, a good Irishman, and Daniel Cushwa, a local boy. They all decided to bivouac for the night.

George was a farmer with a florid complexion and flaming red hair that seemed to always be scruffy and in disarray. He had been born in Ireland and had a thick Irish brogue. George was five years James's senior and often led James to believe, his superior. Daniel was a neighbor to James and was a thick muscular boy, younger than him, with a physique of iron. His family of millers and farmers had land on the Potomac in Williamsport, Maryland, not a stone's throw from Bai-Yuka. Daniel and James had known each other from an early age, as they both were from prominent land holding families.

"It's good to see you, boys. Are you out on a joy ride?" James teased.

"No, but we understand y'all were picnicking on duty. They sent us to spy out any real Yankee troop movement," Daniel said.

"Not much chance for a picnic," James laughed. "What with riding all day up and down this river, getting shot at by the Yankee pickets on the other side, it's a might dangerous for a picnic."

"Where you boys intend to bivouac for the night?"

"I suspect we'd stay close enough to the river so that we can see the Yankee campfires around Williamsport and hear any splashing at the ford if they come our way. It seems as though their main body is just across from us," George said as he pointed in the Federal's direction.

"They look restless. I doubt they'll do anything tonight. They're simply learning how to play soldier. I think they're trying to build up the courage to have at us if Patterson has a mind to let'em," James said.

They decided to camp south of the Potomac River near a toll house along the Valley Turnpike. They chose a spot on a hill with a bald clear of trees. They could see the Federal camp fires across the river as the sun set in the radiant western sky. It would be a restless night, James thought.

After a dinner of salted pork back and hardtack, they gathered around the small fire. James had always been thoughtful, and he spoke first as the darkness enveloped them.

"The South has been imposed upon beyond rational reasonability. We're a big fat bullfrog getting ready to be swallowed up by a Northern black snake," he said, poking the fire with a stick.

Daniel chewed on his tobacco wad and said, "All we want is to be left alone; this war is about the submission of the South. The South is and has been mistreated and wronged by the North in relation to tariffs for over forty years. This war will rectify these injustices."

"We've the cash crop of cotton and the North simply has industry and sweat shops," James said. "They work their wives and children as we do our slaves. We've our issues with slavery and they've their issues with child labor. Which is the greater evil?"

"There're a series of political issues leading up to the war of our quest for independence," Thomas said, ever the astute student. "The idea of secession was given birth by President Jefferson in his two Kentucky Resolutions."

"New England was talking about secession from the rest of the United States in 1803 and the South Carolinians wanted to secede over the Nullification Acts during the Jackson administration," Daniel emphatically said.

"I'd no idea you were so conversant in these issues of politics and history, Thomas. Would you speak further on these issues?" James asked.

"New England also was on the verge of secession during the War of 1812. They even held the Hartford Convention to consider it. The Missouri Compromise question brought to the forefront the politics of secession for further thought. Finally, here we're at war in 1861. It's all taken a certain track to a train wreck of disastrous proportions," Thomas said.

James heard a rider approaching in the darkness. All four of them grabbed for their revolvers. James saw the rider move in closer, and he observed the apparent gray uniform and his tension dropped. First Corporal James Cunningham, a thin, brown haired farmer, gestured that he was one of them.

"Gentlemen, I'm your commander, no need for the guns; they're a less than charitable way to welcome an officer into your camp. What do you know of the enemy across the river?" Cunningham asked as he dismounted his horse.

"We watched them all day," James said. "And they seem to be amassing across the river in Williamsport. We decided that it was best to bivouac here for the night so that we could keep a close eye on the Federals' movements."

"Very good, gentlemen," Cunningham said. "I'll camp with you tonight. Did I interrupt some conversation?"

"We were talking about the causes of the war," Thomas said. "Might you've something to add to our conversation in relation to why we're fighting the Yankees?"

"Control is their goal. Don't touch the Yankee pocketbooks," Cunningham proclaimed as he swaggered over to the campfire after tying off his horse. "Everything in the North is at right angles. Look at their streets, all to right angles. We're people that follow the streams, animal paths, and ridges to demark boundaries in our cities. Nothing is straight or at right angles."

James and the other cavaliers settled in closer to the fire; the green acrid algae smell from the river wafted through his nostrils. He could also sense the restlessness of the Yankees. He felt the night air begin to cool off which made it more bearable from the oppressive heat.

"We're Scots-Irish people whose place and lore keep our identity," George said. "Traditional Southerners share a common heritage."

"The Yankees are money grubbing snakes and they want to destroy our way of life, take our slaves and our lands. The abolitionists ain't above taking our darkies to use as cheap labor in their mills. Our people didn't come over on the Mayflower, we came to Jamestown and don't you forget it. I reckon the Puritan Yankee ain't knowin' nothin' about Southerners," Daniel said.

"The New Englanders from Rhode Island hauled the darkies from Africa and sold them to the South. Now the North puts all the blame for slavery on the South," James said. "They profited from slavery and now they want to take away my friends, Jimmie and Mae, since they can't make money off slaving anymore," he said.

"Nathaniel Hawthorne wrote that nature for the Puritans was feared and the red men lived out there with the devil," Cunningham said. "They only have their right angles which represent Puritan control. It was only a matter of time before the Southerner was considered the demon to replace the red man. It was only a matter of time before Virginians knew that a large Federal government would exploit the South. We're firm believers in our individual states' sovereignty, not a powerful central government."

"The Puritan believes as if he is God. They look to reason and not to an enlightened God," Thomas said. "This is a war to prevent our independence and take from us the rights we won in the Revolutionary War. The South is a result of a struggle that had begun across the ocean many years ago. Northern and Southern ideology and identity are so different that it was only a matter of time before the Union began to divide over all these issues."

"The novelist William Gilmore Simms knew that the signers of the Declaration, Edward and John Rutledge, were sons of Ireland. Simms viewed the Scots-Irish as the center of a vibrant way of life in the South. Our way of life includes mirth and song, which the Puritan Yankee has come to destroy. Why can't the Yankees let us be ourselves, have our plantations, our darkies and stop meddling in our business? It's about our cultural identity," James said.

Daniel, who had been quiet, finally decided to speak. "I haven't had the education to keep up with you boys. Hell, I'm just a tolerable prosperous Maryland plantation farmer. I don't grow cotton. The land's too poor to grow tobaccy any more. I got a few slaves, but they are more like family than anything else. This nice talkin' guy from the Colonization Society came by and talked about freein' his slaves so they could go back to Africa. He was a good Christian. He had asked the slaves if they wanted to go. The slaves fell on their knees and begged him never to do that. They said they would rather be slaves here than go back to the place where the bad tribes killed their family, burned their villages, stole their cattle, and then sold their parents off to slave traders. My Daddy fought with General Dan Morgan to keep oppressors from invadin' Virginia. I intend to do the same thing. They may call themselves Union men, but they act like Redcoats."

"It's time to end this conversation and get some sleep. We never know what the Yankees might be up to in the morning. Have a good night and don't forget to douse the fire; we don't want to let the Yankees see our position any sooner than it's necessary," James said after a period of silence with nothing but the cicadas chirping in the trees.

⌘

James had a restless night under the clear Virginia sky. It was cool and the smells from the river wafted over him the whole night. He awoke by four o'clock in the morning and stood with his binoculars looking over the Potomac into the town of Williamsport. He was star struck as the sky at four-thirty was lightened by a comet. He thought it was an omen predisposing victory for the Confederate's side. He could see the movement of lights and a long line of men coming straight at him.

"Commander, Daniel, George, Thomas! Get up! Get saddled. We've got company comin' our way!" James exclaimed as perspiration ran off his face.

"What—What?" Daniel said as he came to his senses.

"Over yonder, the Yankees are on the move!" George excitedly said.

"Thomas, gather your bedroll—get your horse!" James said.

James watched as, in a matter of minutes, the men gathered their horses from the trees and saddled them.

"Hurry, George!" Cunningham shouted. "Get mounted and let's ride!"

"Hup, hup, move out!" James cried out as he frantically spurred his horse.

They rode eight miles at breakneck speed rearward to Camp Stephens. James leapt from his saddle and ran to alert Stuart. They had done their jobs effectively, he thought; it was now up to the higher commands to take over and do their jobs.

He stayed at Camp Stephens and fell into order with the lead element of Company B. His captain, John Blair Hoge, was now in command of Company B. He observed that Hoge was clad in full-dress gray uniform, haughty and swarthy; his boots decorated with large spurs. He was armed with an immense sabre and a brace of revolvers in black leather holsters.

While at Camp Stephens, James saw Colonel Jackson give orders to Colonel Kenton Harper's 5th Virginia Infantry. Harper's infantrymen marched by him with four artillery pieces. James had had many theological discussions with Pendleton, an Episcopal minister and West Pointer, who was now in command of one of the four guns from the 1st Rockbridge Artillery. He had heard that the four guns had been named in Reverend Pendleton's honor, Matthew, Mark, Luke and John.

"There goes Luke," James said as Matthew, Mark, and John stayed in the reserve.

༄༅༅

Stuart's cavalrymen encountered a Federal company of infantry. James watched Stuart emerge from the woods and saw the vulnerable soldiers behind a fence rail that faced a side road. He sat his horse and watched in amazement as Stuart, dressed in his blue uniform, began working his persuasive mind, instead of gunfire.

James was not a student of war and he had no experience at it. He was good with people and did not realize that war could be so diplomatic, as Stuart exemplified before his eyes. Stuart enterprisingly rode up to the Yankee infantrymen and asked them to throw the fence rails to the ground. The resting infantrymen with their weapons stacked mistook Stuart and his men for Federal troopers, James guessed.

"Throw down your arms or you're dead men," Stuart demanded of the Federals. "Come forward and send your commanding officer over to speak with me immediately."

James sat his horse, Billy, positioned in front of the ranks. He could feel the tension in the air, and he was fascinated with the boldness and the audacity of Stuart. James was mounted next to John Beatty Seibert, the 1st Sergeant of Company B.

"Do you really think they'll come forward and listen to Stuart?" James asked John. "This is a bluff and Stuart could easily be shot for his audacity."

"I think Stuart knows it. Draw revolvers and be ready if they don't follow his orders," John responded.

He knew that in a few moments the bluff would either work or there would be open firing from both sides. James drew his pistol as the tension mounted, pointing it in the direction of the Federals. Then he saw the commanding officer of the 15th Pennsylvania come forward to speak with Stuart.

James's horse began to stir. "I think it's working. Stuart has pulled it off!" he softly exclaimed to John.

A brief conversation between Stuart and the Federal ensued. The Federal officer threw up his arms. James heard the order that the infantrymen do the same, and saw that most of the men dropped their guns.

Suddenly, three Federals opened fire on the Confederate troopers. James pointed his revolver at one of them and fired; he had hit his target in blue. He noticed, after firing, that one of the most aggressive troopers to fire was a darky next to him in the ranks by the name of James Humbles, Company C.

In the aftermath James saw three Federals had fallen to the ground mortally wounded. He had shot one of the three men. He had seen the elephant of battle for the first time and was no longer a virgin of the war. He dismounted his horse, as the other

Confederate troopers were corralling up the prisoners and walked across the open field to the man he had shot.

James observed that the ball had struck the infantryman's chest above his heart; the hole in the blue uniform oozed blood. He knelt down and grasped the hand of the dying lad. The infantryman was even younger than him. He realized what he had done; he felt he had done his duty. As the mortally wounded soldier coughed up blood and wheezed his final breath, James simply reached forward and closed the soldier's eyes as the commotion went on around them. After all, he thought, the soldier was a Yankee, and war gave a license to kill, legally.

James touched the bullet hole and the blood covered his fingers. He knew he had now become a warrior. He had done it now; he had killed a man for the first time. He had taken an oath to save life and now he had taken one. What would the people at the School of Medicine think of him now? How would God judge him for what he had done?

His metamorphosis was now complete from saver of life to taker of life. The only difference between the School of Medicine and the battlefield, he pondered, was that blood was on his revolver and not his scalpel.

5

Meditation along the Potomac

BEFORE SUNSET JAMES AND the men of the 1st Virginia Cavalry settled into camp not far from Darkesville, in the shadows of Washington City. James looked out to see a vast number of shelters that dotted the landscape, varying in color, well-ordered in lines like spokes of a wheel emanating from centrally located campfire hubs. His long picket line for the horses paralleled the spokes of the shelters of his comrades. He and his horse, Billy, were inseparable.

James sat with Thomas, George, and Daniel around the campfire. He felt a warm hearted kindred spirit with these troopers. They had become brothers to him. They had enlisted together, ridden together, shared stories, and had the common bond of being Marylanders. The comradeship of war had united his spirit uniquely with theirs, a truth only a fellow soldier could possibly grasp. He sang *Dixie* with an assertive confidence along with them, and in their company he enjoyed corn pone and a piece of bacon for supper. He never felt he was above his comrades in arms for they all served a mutual cause.

He knew that Federal General Patterson was occupying Martinsburg. James had been relocated with General Jackson and his entire command to Darkesville after the battle at Falling Waters, Virginia. He felt the nearness of the enemy, stirring in his consciousness, only a few miles from his camp. He had heard that the Federals were cleaning up the B & O Railroad catastrophe that General Jackson had left in his wake of destruction.

His mind was playing tricks on him. If he tilted his head in the enemy's direction, beyond the whistling of the wind through the trees, he thought he could hear the echoes of the Federals' conversations. Their distant presence made him feel an uncomfortable tension in his gut. He kept one eye on the campfire and one on his revolver that hung at his shelter.

"James, you appear to be deep in thought. You're not still thinkin' about that Yankee you killed?" Thomas asked as he poked the fire with a stick.

"No. I'm thinkin' about how Stuart was so composed amidst certain danger that day."

He wanted nothing to do with the subject Thomas was so determined to discuss. His mind incessantly pondered it. He stared into the fire and saw the face of the lad he had shot, moments before the boy's life had slipped away. He recalled the small open field where they encountered the regiment of Federals relaxing with their arms stacked. He had replayed the scenario in his head numerous times. The lad was a picket with a shouldered musket, he thought, and had unexpectedly mounted the musket and pointed the weapon toward the Confederate troopers.

James heard a loud pop from the fire and held his breath for a moment, remembering the sound of his own revolver firing before the lad fell to the ground. He could not rid his mind of the anguish he felt from that day. It was plaguing him.

"Stuart was a sight to marvel, was he not? I'd hardly believe he was able to get the entire horde of Yankees to surrender with hardly a shot fired," Daniel said, casting a furtive glance at James.

James pulled at his black goatee and chewed on his bacon while gazing mindlessly off into the starry night. He felt the urge to flee as if he might be able to escape from the black cloak of turmoil that loomed within his soul. Noticing the moon coming up over the hills outside the camp, he felt it beckoning him as if the celestial orb could mysteriously resolve his troubles. He was not certain if he had committed murder or if he had simply been doing his duty, and he wondered if God would forgive him if the killing was in vain. Why did he feel so guilty?

His gaze finally settled on the shelter pole where the revolver hung ready for action at a moment's notice. Feeling an anxious sense of self-preservation, he gazed to see campfires dotted throughout the environs spurting tall, defiant flames. At last he shed his coat and slouch hat and finally took the appearance like most of the other men. He found that their attire for the night was comfortable and relaxed.

First Corporal James Cunningham stepped into the ring of light cast by the fire, "Boys, are ya'll getting your fill'o corn pone and bacon? Good vittles are always cookin' at the 1st Virginia. Them boys over yonder shot themselves a turkey and have it roastin' on a spit. I reckon it should be done a-perfect soon."

"Corporal, we're just chatterin' about Stuart. He seemsta' know how to handle himself with the Yankees. He has no fear of the enemy, handles 'em like a mama bear movin' around her cubs," George offered as he whittled a stick.

"Well, he's a-been with the injuns out West before all this started back East," the corporal recalled, kicking a stick back into the fire. "He surely knows war and fightin', and he knows all about Yankees."

"Yeah, I know. We came back together on a train from the West. That's what got me in this cavalry unit," James said as the men drew nearer to him.

"What? You mean you know'd him before the war broke out?" Daniel said with a hint of admiration.

"Yes. After we figured out we were on the same side, we talked at great length about how I might serve if Virginia seceded from the Union. I thought I would use my training in the Medical Corps," he shared as he swallowed the last of his corn pone.

"What did ya see and do that made you feel this way?" Thomas asked, standing next to him.

"The irregular pro-slavery forces in Kansas were fighting over the border outside Rushville, and I was sympathetic to their cause. I had been taking care of their wounded men and was getting an ear-full of the conflict before this war ever began in the East," James responded as the men listened intently to his story.

He thought that he had wanted to do more for the gunshot patients, but didn't know exactly what to do. Many a day he had ridden out to see the aftermath of the conflicts. He was moved by the idea of fighting and he naively itched to be involved.

"So that explains why you're now fighting instead of practicing medicine," the corporal said. "I couldn't figure you out, James. A doctor gone to fightin' didn't make much sense to me."

"Me neither," Daniel interjected.

"Well, I'm hardly the sort of man who sits out history while it's being made in my midst."

James thought that Lieutenant Stuart capitalized on his vulnerability. His recruitment was made easy for the lieutenant due to their bond, both of them being men of action and having somewhat high-minded aristocratic ideals.

"There, now you have my story," James concluded.

He felt anxious to leave the conversations, so he shoved the last bit of bacon into his mouth and abruptly turned from the campfire, taking leave of his comrades. He walked over to his shelter and strapped on his revolver, and then headed over to the horses on the picket line where Billy quietly chomped on some hay that he had put out earlier. After tightening the girth strap under Billy, he rebridled him and moved to the creek where Billy drank his fill of cold stream water.

Walking past the campfire, one of his friends hollered out, "Where ya going at this time-a-night?"

"Getting a little fresh air, clearing my head a bit," he said as he swung his leg over the saddle. "We'll be back soon."

He rode off to the hills outside the camp. The full moon glistened ahead of him as he headed straight for it, casting a long shadow behind horse and rider. The open hillsides smelled of fresh grasses and hemlock trees that bordered the terrain. Above the whole valley, indeed, the sky was heavy with effervescent vapors of campfire smoke and the smell of horses. He rode until he was out of sight of the campfires, nothing but the refreshing Virginia air to keep him company.

His mind drifted as he began to focus on what was bothering him; even his friends knew it still gnawed at his soul. He was coming to terms with the fact that he was a soldier in the 1st Virginia. By the providence of God he had met Stuart on the train. Did God intend this? Perhaps God had wanted them to meet. He had already made some good friends since he had joined up in Martinsburg, men he felt he had known his whole life.

What did they think of him? He was a doctor who had killed a man. He wondered if he was a hypocrite or just a soldier doing his duty. For that matter he did not know what to think of himself. Was he too quick to fire, too eager to kill a man?

A breeze blew by him and seemed to slap him in the face. Billy was loose reined and seemed to know where he was going up the hill ahead.

James thought he was only protecting the boys and the others, but only a few of them had fired. Why had he fired so quickly? Were the boys just too slow? He had looked into the eyes of the dying lad and felt his stomach ache with anguish. It was like the blood of the lad was on his revolver. He never feared blood, but doctors are to be about the business of saving and giving life. He took that life in an instant with the snap of his trigger. What would all the other School of Medicine professors think of him now? Why was he not doing something for the Confederate Medical Corps?

Suddenly, he was caught off guard by the caw of a black crow sitting in a tree over his shoulder. He grabbed for his revolver and swung it around in the air in search of a target. The crow flew off in front of him like a black demon, heading directly into the full moon. An eerie image settled into his mind as his nerves calmed. It had startled him and broken his train of thought. He looked up at the full moon as the crow flew toward it. The image of the crow stirred his emotions. He felt teary eyed at recalling the memory of the soldier he had killed. He wiped his eyes and patted Billy on the shoulder, "It's okay, Billy. We'll survive this war together, you and I."

He considered that maybe this demon-like image was a sign from God that he had done wrong. But did God use crows to send men messages? No, that was foolishness. He had done nothing wrong; this was war. There was no room for sentiment and emotions in relation to the Federal lad he had killed. Kill or be killed, he must remember this if he was going to survive this war.

He thought it was a nice speech he had just made to himself, but if all that was true, why did he feel so glad when he saw the Federal fall? He had to admit it; he was proud that he had fired fast and true. What would have happened if he hadn't fired? Would that soldier have killed Stuart? Or Tom? Or Daniel? That's what it came down to in war. He believed he needed to shoot the enemy before his enemy could shoot his brother, and he knew his brothers were thinking the same way. He killed the Yankee because he had to. He guessed he would keep on killing like that. He just prayed to God he would never start killing for any other reason.

He sat proud in his saddle, his back rigid and straight. He was fighting for his family, his way of life, Bai-Yuka, Jimmie and Mae, and for his brothers-in-arms. His Southern high-minded cause was just, and repelling invaders warranted killing. God must understand this and surely be on the side of the Confederacy. The Old Testament was full of Holy Wars and this was certainly a Holy War. The Yankees had invaded, come to force his people back into the Union. *Who wants to be coerced into a Union? Damn them Yankees to Hell!* He would whip the Yankees and drive them back above the Potomac if it took all he had, maybe even his life.

He crested the hill and watched the moonlight fill the valley. His thoughts not yet still, he pondered how beautiful the Virginia hills were in the shadows of the moon. Not twenty miles from this very spot, he had studied at the College of St. James. On nights such as this, he had rested from parsing his Greek and watched the moon shadows from Bai-Yuka. He remembered his Herodotus, and recalled accounts of the endless ancient war of Leonidas at Thermopylae. He wondered if his people were like the Greeks against the Persians. Would he cower with the Thebans or stand with the Spartans? Outnumbered and poorly equipped, would he someday stand at his Thermopylae?

He turned Billy and started slowly down the hill. He didn't know how long he had been wandering in the moonlight. He noticed that his shadow wasn't nearly so long now. He took the reins and spurred Billy with alacrity down the hill at a cantor. He and Billy were soul mates, rider and steed; they darted over the open hills back to camp. He felt satisfied in his newly developed beliefs, for now.

6

Dearest James

ON SATURDAY, THE MAIL came and James received a letter from Hagerstown. He opened it with haste and read it:

Hagerstown, Md., July 12, 1861

Dearest James,

I received and read with much gratification your letter of the 6th inst. I know you did what you had to do when confronted with the enemy. Now that you are entwined in this war I pray for your safety daily and admirably think of your happy countenance. You are indeed fortunate to be under the command of such a brave and gallant officer as Colonel Stuart. My brother James of Co. K, 1st Virginia Cavalry is well and I pray for him, too. Davidge and Barlow have not yet enlisted.

My father holds you in high esteem and asks about you frequently. He has said you are the finest doctor he has ever trained. Have you had any call for your medical expertise in the field? You have a sordid calling in this war; I know God certainly has blessed you with numerous gifts and talents. Use them for the good as I know you will.

The reciprocal hatred of the North & South now is too deep, too ineradicable to hope for a swift end to this scourge upon our land. What is dearest to our hearts is the Southern Cause for which you now fight. The Cause I refer to is that of liberty and freedom to live as we wish and to become a sovereign nation. We are oppressed by the Yankee soldiers who have taken up residence in and around Hagerstown. Their surveillance is intrusive into our daily lives and I resent it. It is not a safe place for a Dixie girl, such as I am.

The Yankees' unsavory comments towards me are crude and mischievous to the point of insult. I heard one mutter under his breath, 'There goes a real Southern Belle, I wonder if she has a beau?' The other day one of them spat on the ground before me and laughed in my face. No Southern gentleman would stand for such treatment of ladies, be they friend or foe. I celebrate our Cause and wish only strife and misfortune upon these cursed Yankee soldiers who distress my family and me.

Our every move is watched by the infernal Yankees. Father can scarcely practice medicine without being questioned as to his intentions. He leaves in the morning on his rounds and they want to know where he is going, who he sees and when he will return home. As their numbers increase, we hear the clanking of fresh chains around our feet. Can we yield? The women of the land say stand fast! The high-spirited and gallant cannot relent. The Southland and their Spartan mothers have positioned the sabre in the hands of their beloved sons and implored them to fight for their sovereign country.

They say women are lucky to remain safe and removed from the conflict's center, but I find myself envying your position of action. Day by day, we wait for some news from the front or a favorable development. I am so tired of waiting! I wish to serve my country and my Cause as you and your men do every day. I have not found my opportunity yet, but continue to seek out any way I may contribute. I have gifts and talents, and father's contacts in Baltimore City I shall certainly find to our advantage in this war.

James, I vow to you that I, too, shall fight for our Southern Cause in ways which I do not yet know. The days will come when I shall brandish the sabre of liberty for the just Cause of my beloved Maryland and the Southland. As Jael outwitted and slew Sisera so shall I rise up for my country. With faith in God and the Southern Cause, I shall vanquish our enemies as if they were the unrighteous enemies of Zion. God will provide me with the tent nail and teach my hand to hammer.

Be safe and take pride in your endeavors as a soldier of the 1st Virginia Cavalry. I think of you often. You are on the right side with our God at the throne of righteousness and justice.

Very Truly,
Mollie

James closed the letter and wondered how she had gotten the letter through the Federal's line. He pondered; she had always been clever. He smiled, musing on her determination. Thomas and the boys had stood around him as he read the letter. They tried to peer over his shoulder as he read.

"Who was that from?" Thomas asked him as he quit trying to see the salutation on the letter.

"Oh, no one in particular; someone I know back in Hagerstown," he said.

"Come on, James, you ain't let on that you've a special friend to all of us. Is there someone you'd like to tell us about? Come on and admit it, James, you're sweet on this gal, ain't you?" Daniel said with a gentle poke to his ribs.

James flushed crimson and turned from his comrades as the call rang out from Corporal Cunningham, "Boots and saddles!"

James looked up and said, "Drill, drill, drill from early mornin' to night. Well boys it's time to earn our keep."

He sauntered over to his shelter which he shared with Thomas, put on his coat, strapped on his sabre belt and lashed the leather piece over his shoulder. He felt his mood change to one of anger as he realized what she was being subjected to by the Yankee soldiers. He shuddered briefly, thinking of what any Yankee Sisera could expect from the mercy of his Mollie. He placed the revolver belt around his waist with cap and cartridge boxes on the belt. He picked up the smoothbore carbine sling and slung it over his shoulder. He clipped the smoothbore to his shoulder and pointed it into an open field, and then clicked the trigger. He thought to himself, a dead Yankee, the very one who taunted her. He grabbed his slouch hat, canteen, and gauntlets and walked over to Billy. As he walked away he felt Thomas was grinning at him.

"You'll have to come clean with your friends. You're saved by the call, but we'll not let it go that easy," Thomas said with a grin as he had simultaneously dressed the part of a trooper with him.

⁂

James felt the crisp morning air as the hot July sun began to appear over the trees that surrounded the campground. He looked at fleecy piles of clouds majestically towering in the distance. He viewed the other troopers around the camp getting all their battle gear and arranging it on themselves. He fitted and adjusted Billy's tack; it would likely be a long day.

James never knew if the call to arms was a drill or the real thing, he always prepared as if he were to meet the blue demon on the field of battle. The monotony of the drill always pressed at him. He supposed perhaps he didn't truly comprehend the importance of the drill, for he had not been in a full scale battle. They had all become bored with the drilling; he guessed they all wanted to see some real action.

He led Billy to the drill field. He was apprehensive and did not want to voice his doubt that he had acknowledged only to God, himself, and Billy. He was afraid to openly share his dilemma with his comrades. He had learned as a young boy to keep his emotions private and safe. He often played soldier as a young boy at Bai-Yuka with his friends. One day he was hurt by a "Redcoat" friend and his revolutionary ardor was crushed. His father told him that men are rational and stoic like real Revolutionary soldiers who freed America from the British, twice. He vowed to fight heroically when he played, and from then on Redcoats would not get the better of him. Only

God and Billy would know of his inner confession, but none of his comrades would see him vulnerable.

"Form Company B," Captain John Blair Hoge yelled out with his chest extended, sitting high on his stallion. James knew Hoge was a confident soldier, the model of a stalwart partisan, with many years of law practice in Martinsburg. James had learned the Federals occupied Hoge's hometown, and was certain that the captain was ready to throw them out with retribution.

He reflected that Hoge looked as if a part of his soul was occupied with evil feelings. Hoge had learned that the Federals had marched by his home and his law office as if they had a rightful reason for being there. James knew through many prior conversations with Hoge that this infuriated him. Hoge's wife and family were held captive in their own hometown. Something seemed skewed about this scenario, for James understood how Hoge felt because the Macgill family and his own family were in the same occupied situation.

James eyed the troopers coming out of the camp and into an open field adjacent to the camp. He had been taught through previous experiences that punctuality was an important trait in the 1st Virginia Cavalry; if he were late to the forming of his company, the corporal Cunningham would let him know it.

"Form company—Stand to horse," 1st Lieutenant George Newkirk Hammond barked out as 1st Sergeant John Beatty Seibert and 1st Corporal James Cunningham echoed the captain.

"Mount the company," the captain commanded. "Open order."

James and the troopers had numbered off, while standing to horse, one through four. James numbered off as a three and moved forward four paces along with the troopers numbered as ones. They lead their horses by the bridle reins.

"Prepare to mount," Lieutenant Hammond called out.

"Mount—Close order—March!" the noncommissioned officers bellowed.

"Captain, sir, company formed. Ready for orders!" Lieutenant Hammond thundered out.

Once mounted, James thought the troopers looked a marvel as they stood at serious attention. The whole company was assembled in rows like a perfectly planted cornfield. He and the troopers were knee to knee in their ordered rows, gray uniforms, some with raggedy britches and coats of various colors. Their shiny tack and weapons sparkled in the sun. James was surrounded by his comrades: Daniel, Thomas, and George, and he suspected the chatting that had earlier begun in camp would follow him into the ranks. He gazed over at the color-bearers carrying the Confederate national flag and the Virginia State flag as they moved forward six paces. The unfurled flags snapped in the wind.

Captain Hoge hollered, "Company—By fours—Move out to the left—Walk!"

The captain saluted the flags with a patriotic reverence as the formation passed by. James heard the noncommissioned officers and Lieutenant Hammond again echo the command of the captain.

"March!" Lieutenant Hammond yelled out. James struck spur to Billy, patting him on the neck.

He and Billy had formed a symbiotic relationship; they understood each other as if they were one, and were in harmony with the ordered universe. By fours the formation stoically marched out to the national flag and turned methodically to the left. James became the soldier, transformed into a cog in the machine of war. He and the column of horses formed into a long line of troopers. His column of horses moved alongside a tall row of trees next to the open field.

"Keep your intervals; keep your files," Corporal Cunningham nagged at the troopers like an old mother hen.

He, Daniel, Thomas, and George rode four abreast within the column. The dust created by the horses' hooves flew all about them as the sun warmed the morning air. Grit got in his mouth and he could feel it like sandpaper in between his teeth.

"James, we're all ears, my comrade. You don't have to kiss and tell, but we want to know. Who is this young gal you smile so fervently about after reading her letter?" Thomas inquired, a tent mate who felt slighted by his having kept a secret.

"Boys, I know you won't let this die, so I'll explain everything you want to know to your burning ears' desire," James said as he moved tranquilly forward in the column.

They were all warriors now, young men who knew the gravity of the business before them. He noticed a scar on Daniel's neck that he had not seen before. Then he saw a hole in the coat of the uniform of the trooper in front of him.

"Yes, do tell all," Daniel eagerly said as he reached over and patted James on the shoulder.

"I trained under the tutelage of her father, Dr. Charles Macgill of Hagerstown, before I went to the School of Medicine."

James didn't want to talk about the exact nature of the relationship—he was not at all that sure himself what it would be. He told them that Mollie was his age and that she was a "kissin' cousin" of his. They had grown up only a short distance apart. He expounded that she was from one of the best families in the state, a woman of fine character, well-educated, well-traveled, very beautiful, of charming manners, and with an iron will to get into the war and serve the cause. He moved with the column down a ravine into the shade of the trees.

"James, she sounds like a real beauty. Have you ever thought of making a commitment to her?" Thomas asked, now satisfied there were no secrets between them.

"I've always been fond of her and she of me. In her letter she speaks of the growing numbers of Yankees who are harassing her and her father, suspecting them of Southern sympathies. I know him well and over his dead body will he take the Yankee 'oath' of allegiance to the 'rail-splitter'!"

"Why've you never mentioned her to us?" Daniel said.

"I fear for her safety and don't want to implicate her as a Southerner by association through me. She often takes trips to Baltimore City and sees her friends who called themselves the 'Monument Street Girls' who're ardent Southern sympathizers."

He told them she stayed at the Barnum's Hotel. He did not know her friends but believed the Federals watched everyone closely in Baltimore City.

He and his comrades came near a stream at the bottom of the ravine. Ever vigilant, he surveyed the thick woods looking for movement.

"Keep your intervals—No talking," Corporal Cunningham said, with a stern look toward him.

"Company!" Captain Hoge roared.

"Company!" the NCOs hollered.

"Front into line—Trot!" Captain Hoge ordered.

"Front into line—Trot!" Lieutenant Hammond echoed.

"March!" Captain Hoge growled.

James and the horsemen moved from columns of four into rank and file order. The long line of troopers awaited the next command. Sweat poured off their faces. He and the troopers came out of the ravine and into an open hay field bordered by tall pines. Billy was clinking his hooves on the loose, shingly rocks. The mass of horseflesh was a powerful cavalcade of fighting strength, James mused.

"Front into line—Right wheel—March!" the Captain barked.

James beheld the great mass of men moving gracefully in a clockwise cavalry wheel in the open field. He and the boys were circling in perfect harmony with the others. While he breathed in the sweet smell of the grasses, he daydreamed. The smells reminded him of pleasant days gone by and the hay harvest season at Bai-Yuka. His father and siblings worked hard during the harvest. He remembered the calluses on his hands and his aching back by the end of those days.

"Front!" Captain Hoge commanded as precision was executed by the troopers. James moved forward again, Billy not missing a beat at the cadence of hooves striding forward.

James stared at an officer emerging from the woods on his horse. He recognized the officer to be his friend Stuart as the officer swung in front of the troopers next to Captain Hoge. Stuart wore a rough looking blue undress coat of the United States Army. James saw around Stuart's waist a black leather belt from which hung a holstered revolver on his right, and on his left a sabre with a basket hilt. Stuart's brown moustache mingled with a huge beard reaching to his breast. His uniform was impeccable, completed with his signature plumed hat.

"Excellent," Colonel Stuart said. "Now we're gonna see what superior troopers can do," James overheard Stuart saying to Hoge while drawing his sabre.

Stuart took over command. He had the cavaliers move back into columns of four and led them north toward the Potomac River. James heard grumbling up and down the ranks. He had his own misgivings, but would never utter them out loud.

It was then that James realized Stuart was heading directly for the enemy's position.

James rode onward through luxuriant pine groves, sullen streams hidden under the pine needles, a peaceful scene, he reflected, as if the brothers Jacob and Wilhelm Grimm had depicted it in a fairytale. He remembered that these tales concluded with evil prevailing; all was not as serene as the Brothers Grimm led one to believe. He was following Stuart but was leery that lurking along the perilous route was the possibility of hidden Federals.

Suddenly, James saw on the road before them, at one thousand yards, a regiment of Federal infantrymen. He could see the column of blue on the road, bunched in between looming shade trees. He stirred anxiously in his saddle and gripped the reins tightly. But instead of engaging the enemy directly, Stuart halted the troopers and ordered them to dismount in a field of lush clover. James was perplexed. Billy's hooves crushed the vegetation, and Billy, along with other horses, frantically pranced and whinnied. A chaotic scene of pandemonium erupted. James struggled to control Billy. Horses all around him kicked their hooves in the air, and his comrades struggled to soothe the terrified animals.

"Fight as skirmishers," Stuart commanded as he flailed his plumed hat in his hand as if orchestrating directions to the chaotic menagerie of horses and cavaliers.

With a shaky hand, James hooked Billy's link strap to George's horse's halter. He saw Thomas and Daniel do the same. James grabbed his smooth bore carbine hanging to his side on the sling, and then rushed forward into a line of battle in the open clover field. He stared at the Federals as they deployed off the road and entered into the field directly in front of the cavaliers, closing the gap between the forces.

He saw that the Yankees were advancing quickly toward him, snaking into a line of battle. Sweat soaked his leather gauntlets like a dish towel. Three hundred yards to his front the Federals were marching in battle lines with muskets shouldered. He watched them move with synchronicity like a blue machine set on the destruction of anything in its path. He could hear the commands from their officers, "Fire!"

A volley from the infantry whistled by him as the blue-clad soldiers stood in the clover field, muskets pointed at him, blue-gray puffs of smoke billowing forward. He knelt in the clover and listened for the order to fire, while keeping his eye on the blue. He felt the tension as it grasped his throat as if an invisible hand clasped his Adam's apple.

"Fire!" Corporal Cunningham bawled out. "Reload!"

James squeezed off a round, and then he quickly reached behind his back to the cartridge box pulling out another round. He couldn't keep his hands from shaking as he poured the powder down the muzzle and then loaded the ball. His mind was in a haze as he shoved the ramrod down the muzzle. The percussions were deafening to him. He felt frantic energy in the air. The yelling of the cavaliers reverberated up and down the line that stretched to his right and left. He experienced an ethereal sensation and a sudden dizziness. He stood and wobbled a bit before he came back to the reality of the moment. He fell back while keeping his face toward the enemy.

The dismounted cavalry line to his rear fired as he passed by them.

"James! You all right?" Thomas asked as he kneeled in the soft clover.

"Yeah," he said. "Give 'em hell, Thomas!"

He knelt again in the clover and a blue-gray hue of smoke drifted in a cloud and enveloped him. His nostrils were permeated by the acrid smell of sulphur. He sneezed. After a number of rounds had been dispensed, the dismounted cavalrymen steadily fell back. The shock of their fire seemed to halt the Federals in their tracks. He noticed that gaps in the Federal lines were quickly filled by blue clad soldiers.

"Withdraw—March!" Stuart commanded with discretion. "Keep your faces forward to the Yanks, men—steady!"

James noticed that Stuart remained a stalwart figure on his steed, calm in the face of fire, as he rode behind the dismounted skirmishers. He witnessed Stuart, sure and confident, as the commander rode back to where the horse holders stood. He ruminated that Stuart ordered the withdraw because there was nothing to be gained from further skirmishing other than more dead Federals, which was good, but at the cost of how many more good Southern boys.

James finally made it back to Billy. He was breathing heavily as the excitement of the moment began to overtake his fear of the enemy. His tongue cleaved to the roof of his mouth, perspiration ran off his forehead, his eyes felt like metallic orbs that bulged from their sockets. He heard minie balls *zzzz-ip! zzzzzz-ip!* by him, singing like bees in his ears. He was at a pitched fever point, aware that death hovered, beckoning him to its lair.

His fellow cavalryman George was holding three jumpy horses in the rear. The irritated horses were moved in circles with George following them, working to keep control. James unhooked the link strap and expeditiously mounted Billy. He scrutinized Stuart who was reforming the men with a cool bravado. Branches snapped and fell to the ground as the blue demons' bullets smacked into trees and brush. Stuart seemed to never lose control of his emotions in the wake of fire. He regally pranced around his troopers, shepherding them like King David in a desert of confusion. The troopers remounted while the wounded got extra attention and care from Stuart.

"Trot—March!" Stuart ordered the cavalcade. When they were out of sight of the Federals, back down the road they had ridden earlier, he saw Stuart pull in his reins.

"Company—Halt!" Stuart exclaimed. "You were brave and sage troopers in the line of fire. However, you're uninformed of this nature of warfare."

Stuart told them to always remember to trot away from the enemy. He told them that, as brave soldiers, their honor was more prized to them than all else in the world. When they went into battle, Stuart said, they were to gallop, grit their teeth, and strike fear into the enemies hearts. He wanted them to remember that a superior trooper with a strong horse could never be caught out, provided that they put the fear of God into the hearts of their enemies.

Stuart paused his speech just as the whining of an artillery shell overhead shrieked into the woods behind him and exploded out of range. James was impressed with how Stuart had handled the skirmish. He felt a need to shine in the presence of Stuart, but knew he was not noticed by him.

"Relax, men," Stuart calmly said. "I wanted you to hear the sound of artillery firsthand. I've been expecting this. I knew they would shoot too far overhead; they always do. Now you've heard what an artillery round sounds like; take note of it."

Another round cleared above their heads. He heard it make a sound like a swarm of bees in a fury.

"Men, you must become hardened to this noise and stay focused on the enemy. When you lose your focus is when the Yanks will take you by surprise. Always listen for the 'Rally' bugle and watch for the flags to reform in battle. Don't think; react to the situation—with instinct—and you'll do fine in battle," Stuart said as he turned his horse back toward camp.

"Forward—March."

⸎

During the next few days Stuart continued to school them. He ran them into skirmishes and near artillery fire. James and the boys were beginning to learn from a seasoned veteran of war. James admired Stuart's ability to get his troopers in and out of dangerous situations without a scratch. He learned from Stuart to appraise the topography in an instant and utilize it to his advantage in every scenario.

He knew of Stuart's reputation for recklessness, but he was convinced that one of his secrets to leading men was putting himself in harm's way. He saw Stuart out front when they confronted the infantrymen on the ride. Stuart would not send men where he himself was not willing to go. He had noted that Stuart always intermixed with his men in the fight; was always with them in body and spirit on the field of battle.

This impressed James and he began to develop an unquestionable devotion to Stuart. He wanted to learn more about how to command. James found ways to be near Stuart in camp without making himself intrusive. He listened to Stuart tell his stories of Indian fights, tales of his past that fascinated him. His confidence as a warrior was beginning to grow, and he had Stuart to thank.

7

The Lord Is My Shepherd

The First Great Battle of the War

THE SUN CLIMBED INTO a cloudless sky while gnats hovered around James's eyes. The gnats hung in the air in front of him no matter how many times he tried to swat them away. Mosquitoes the size of bees danced around his ears. A horsefly pestered Billy's rump before James finally reached back and swatted it dead.

He thought about the scenarios which might lie ahead. He determined to fight hard for the cause, no matter what the outcome. His cause was no longer about the sovereignty of states. He simply desired to live at Bai-Yuka in the manner in which he was raised there.

His commander, Stuart, oversaw the squadron comprised of four cavalry companies on the ride to Manassas Junction. He and the boys were heading toward their encounter with the Federals. The day's objective was a pass that would lead them to Manassas Junction in time for the confrontation. He had journeyed through Ashby Gap previously on trips east with his father and was familiar with the terrain. He and the boys rode together in columns of four chatting away. The dirt kicked up by the horses on the road made him dirty and grimy.

"We'll soon be in our first battle," James said assuredly, looking down the row of his comrades. "You boys ready to see the elephant?"

"James, is ya afraid o' dying in battle?" George asked. "I mean we're gonna face the whole of the Federal Army—I just want to know your thinkin' on the subject."

"You needn't be trying to dodge shot or shell or minie," he responded to George with an air of confidence.

"James, you're educated beyond your own capacity. You know you gotta be smarter than the mule to drive the mule, Doc," Daniel reminded him, looking over his horse's neck.

"Yeah, yeah," James said. "Every one of these missiles of death strikes just where God permits 'em to strike, and nowhere else. You're perfectly safe where they fly thickest until God permits you be stricken."

"What's the use of ducking, that what you mean?" Daniel asked. "If a minie's goin' to hit ya, it's goin' to hit ya. Right, James?"

"Something along those lines," James said as he took a swig from his canteen.

His squadron had been traveling east for some time now. They had ridden through Berryville and were approaching the Shenandoah River. He realized it was time for the hourly ten minute break to water and rest Billy. His faithful steed was lathered and was ready for some water.

"Halt—Dismount!" Corporal Cunningham commanded. "Water your horses at the creek, return back into order; we've a long way to get and there're Yankees waitin' for us."

They dismounted and walked their horses to the creek for water. A few of his comrades pulled out their corncob pipes and pouches of tobacco and had a smoke. He saw others spit out their plugs of tobacco for a cool drink of water from the creek.

He reflected on his student years spent at the College of St. James, recollecting that he had gone to chapel every day, studied Aristotle, Plato, Saint Augustine, John Calvin, and many other great thinkers. Desiring to explain his thoughts to the boys so that they could better understand what he had learned as a Calvinist, his mind pondered on his past lectures of theology and then it hit him, the perfect parable to illustrate his point. After watering Billy he led him back to the column and stood, reins in hand.

"Remount," Corporal Cunningham commanded. "Forward—March!"

Their column moved out at a walk, and he continued the thought he had started before watering the horses. "God has special providence in relation to an individual man's death as to when he shall die and how he'll die," James explained. He pointed his finger at the boys abreast of him. "A merchant, entering a wood with a company of faithful men, had unwisely wandered away from his companions. In his wandering he came upon a robber's den. He fell among thieves and was slain. His death was not only foreseen by God's eye, but nothing took place without God's deliberation."

"When we're directed to find shelter behind trees or a stone wall by a commander, putting these things before us to shield us from a minie, how do you understand this?" George asked with a quizzical smirk.

"Why, George, God governs heaven and earth. You don't understand the doctrine of providence. I look upon those trees and that stone wall as 'special providence' for me at that moment. I'm simply acting on the doctrine when a commander directs me to avail myself of these objects of providence," James replied with a smile.

He gazed at Thomas as he pulled a trickler full of corn liquor from his pocket. "James, you've always been too profound for me. I thought you were a doctor. Here, have a nip."

"Don't mind if I do," James said as he tipped up the container. "Thanks."

"I suspect we're as safe in our shelters as on the battlefield," Daniel said. "Hell, a log could fall from a tree and kill me asleepin' if'n God meant it to. Right, James?"

"That's right, Daniel. I bet you'll not put your shelter under a tree tonight," he laughed.

James and the squadron rode into the shadowy uncertain darkness as the first day was coming to a close, the heat subsiding and the sun setting through the trees. Comfortable in the saddle, James dozed for short periods. He reasoned the arduous journey seemed ironic; he suffered the ride through beautiful mountainous terrain only to subject himself to possible death. The warm mountain air coursed through his nostrils and he smelled the acrid odor of a skunk. The odor awakened his senses to the sweet smells of pine needles mixed with leaves. He savored the familiar odors. He thought about the perils of war in which he would soon face the possibility of his own demise.

In his mind, fears began to race as the column pressed forward; thoughts of his own demise had never entered his thinking before this lonely night. He did not know if his theological example had pacified his comrades, though it certainly helped ease his mind. He mused he was thankful for the teachers he had had, as their wisdom had formed his beliefs. He believed he had to surrender to his own theology and God's providence; his survival might depend upon it.

Pleasant thoughts returned to him. He reflected on the last time he had seen Mollie at Bai-Yuka. He had always been taken by her beauty: her green eyes, her long dark hair, and her supple, creamy skin. He fretted for his family and always thought about their safety. His year of doctoring in Missouri had been a long time away from his family and her. There seemed to be some chemistry bonding them, yet over the years nothing had ever happened between them. He warmly recalled when he last held her soft hands at Bai-Yuka, days before his enlistment. Their last dance together remained indelibly etched in his memory, holding her body close to his on the dance floor. Maybe, he surmised, he did not want to cloud his relationship with his mentor, Dr. Charles Macgill. He was uncertain why he had not pursued her. However, his feelings for her were beginning to blossom. He missed her.

He rode along as Billy followed the horse in front. The gentle rocking motion caused him to fall in and out of sleep. Throughout the course of the night, Bible verses came to him periodically from, he thought, a divine mystical messenger: *The Lord is my shepherd; I shall not want. . . .* He was aware of an inner security. He knew that God was always with him, guiding, protecting, and caring for him. He believed he would fight under the shield of God. His anxiety and fear of death on the battlefield diminished as he reflected upon his faith.

He stared into the night sky and picked out the constellation Orion. The stars making up the great hunter inspired him to think of Virgil's *Aeneid* and the twelve books of poems he had read at the College of St. James. He recalled the story of Aeneas and his wandering from Troy to Italy. *O Muse, recount to me the causes . . .* he thought.

Then, he pondered, in the battle that lay ahead would the Confederate "Trojans" have the same victory as Aeneas? *I sing of arms and of the man . . .* he thought.

The great battle before him awaited an outcome. His fears were placed in God's hands. At last he and the other troopers finally arrived at the battle site. They bivouacked on Bull Run, a mile or so from the Stone Bridge that led over the Warrenton Turnpike. He guessed that he had ridden sixty miles in a day and a half. He was tired and needed time to rest.

⁂

The crackling sound of musketry awakened him at sunrise around five. Reveille sounded. He and the boys responded to the clarion call and quickly ate their rations of hardtack, salt pork, and cornmeal, which they had prepared in utter exhaustion the night before. He noted, ironically, that the day of the war's first battle was on a peaceful Sabbath day. He took note that the weather was bright and beautiful under an alabaster sky; it was perfectly clear, and the air was deathly still.

"Boots and saddles!" James heard the call ring out.

He arranged his carbine, two revolvers, and sabre; checked his spare revolver cylinders and carbine ammunition; then tightened Billy's girth strap and rebridled him. Billy pawed at the ground, manifesting his adrenaline that seemed to be in sync with James's restless and dreamless night. He led Billy into the cool water of Bull Run, and then headed toward the open field along a creek. He had been issued an extra blanket before they departed, for he had left sick. He rid his thoughts of illness and bolstered his masculine energy for the fight.

He surveyed the field adjacent to the creek. It was filled with a mass of horseflesh and cavalrymen leading their mounts by the reins, trying to find their position amidst so many Southern partisans. Prebattle tension filled the air. He and the boys fell in with the Berkeley Troopers taking their place in the front row. They were the most skillful cavalrymen in the regiment. However, this also meant they would be the first to take fire from the enemy.

"Captain, Company B is formed, ready for orders," Lieutenant Hammond announced.

James heard the lieutenants of the other three companies echo Hammond. He saw that Captain Hoge was with the other three Captains, all mounted and gathered close to Stuart at the front of the four companies. He noticed Stuart with his signature long beard and plumed slouch hat. His contagious excitement spread like wildfire amongst all of them.

Mounted in the front row, he could hear Stuart clear as a bell. "Captain Hoge, I want you, Loudon and Newtown companies to head around this creek behind Henry Hill to Bald Hill. Use the woods for concealment and give yourselves a good observation point so you can see the infantry movements to the front on the left flank of the

Confederate line. The Howard Dragoons are to stay where they are in reserve. Captain, call out four men to come with me to do reconnaissance behind enemy lines."

"Privates Breathed, House, McClarey, Cushwa, forward and fall in with Colonel Stuart," the captain growled.

The four men broke rank and rode to the side of Stuart. Beside Stuart was his Adjutant, First Lieutenant William Blackford. James thought he was a stern looking professional soldier with a bushy moustache and eyes set deep under his brow; his clean-cut facial features made him stand out as an intelligent man. Blackford was to accompany them on the scouting mission. They rode forward and soon were behind the Confederate line. James observed the infantrymen formed along the run with muskets pointed toward the enemy's advancing line. Billy's hooves spewed dust into the air as he and the boys came up to the Stone Bridge over Bull Run.

"Men, there'll be no shots fired at the enemy. We don't want to give away our position, is that understood?" Blackford demanded.

"Yes, sir," James replied with the boys in unison.

They crossed the Warrenton Turnpike with revolvers drawn. Stuart motioned them to his side; he heard the musketry, which was hot and heavy. They paused.

"Good morning, privates. Splendid day for a battle. Private Breathed, you appear a little anxious. Ready for a brawl with the Yankees?" Stuart rhetorically asked as he pulled out his field glasses and took a look around. "I suspect they'll continue to come on line across Bull Run to our right, and ahead at the bend in the run. Once they've crossed they'll push us yonder to that hill and try to flank us on the left. When Jackson arrives, we'll be on his left ready for orders."

"Sir, I agree. They'll try to push us over that stream and up the hill. We'll be ready to pounce on them with our cavalry," Blackford responded as he wiped the sweat from his brow and viewed the scene with his field glasses.

The night before James had heard rumors that Stuart had ridden the terrain. "I've seen the top of the hill where there is a plateau with deep gullies running across it. On Henry Hill, close in the middle of the plateau, is an old farmhouse. Young's Branch nearly encircled the front of the farmhouse toward the bottom of the hill. Beyond it, on the right flank, is another house," Stuart said.

Stuart peered through the field glasses. "Private Breathed, do you see the house to the west?"

"Yes, sir."

"The Yankees will come from that direction, and we'll be ready for them."

Dull orange flashes burst out before him from the Federal artillery, the belching blue-white powder smoke rolled out from the guns in the calm air. To his ear came the thunderous sound of the percussion, *Boom! Boom! Boom!* as the artillery fire waxed and waned.

A shell exploded over them and shrapnel rained down upon them, but none of the assembled were hit. James held himself with the stalwart strength of Aeneas and mused that the hell's kitchen in the Federal's mess was now serving shards of shrapnel with no fixin's. But he was tense, in a trance, viewing the battlefield from a panoramic perspective. He had a hard time understanding how commanders could make sense of all the movements of soldiers, when to his eye there was confusion everywhere. He looked at wave after wave of blue infantry advancing online. He sensed the rifles and cannon were filling the air with deadly minies and artillery shells. He saw the lines push forward and back, then forward again as wagons overturned in between the two fighting lines of blue and gray. He could smell the burning straw and broomsedge mixed with the sulphurous smell of burnt black powder.

James rightly assumed the exploded shells convinced Stuart it was time to end the observation, and the scouting party returned to the safety of their lines. He, Stuart, Blackford, and the boys rejoined Company B in the thicket of pines on Bald Hill. He viewed the open fields to the front of the hill, smelled the scent of the sweet pines, and noticed a road a short distance away. He stood with Billy and pulled out his pocket watch to notice it was 11:30 am. He was close enough to Stuart to overhear his conversation with Blackford.

"Those Yankees are attacking Henry Hill and breaking Evans's, Bee's, and Bartow's lines across Young's Branch. Jackson's Virginia Brigade needs to get in position soon or the Yankees might push them over Henry Hill. Jackson told me to support the endangered left."

Impatient, they all waited for the direct orders to engage the enemy.

James looked on as the infantry fought before them. He heard thousands of muskets pop, and the smoke drifted as infantrymen on both sides fell. He could plainly observe Stuart's agitation. He stood impatiently next to his horse while awaiting orders from Stuart. *Where were they?* he thought.

"I've never seen so many infantry in one place before. If this is the elephant then I'm ready to conquer it face to face," James said.

"Hold your horse and be ready. We'll soon enough have our part in this battle. If'n I know Stuart, like I know myself, he's always ready for a fight," George said, standing next to him.

Realizing the fighting was at a critical stage, James took note of a mounted staff officer who had come charging up to the pines, horse and rider out of breath, "Colonel Stuart, with compliments from General Beauregard. He directs you to bring your command into action at once. Attack where the firing is hottest."

He saw the officer salute Stuart, turn his horse, and gallop back down the hill.

"Mount!" Stuart commanded.

James climbed into the saddle. The color bearer moved forward from under the pines. James was excited. His thoughts were focused on the enemy. He rechecked all his weapons and capped off the carbine.

He and the three companies came down the hill and out onto the road. They moved forward to the greatest need on the high ground below Young's Branch. One hundred yards away the smoke lifted and James saw a company of infantry straining forward, marching in double-quick step down the road. He thought the oddly dressed Zouave infantry in their fez hats, short jackets, baggy red pants, and white gaiters were funny looking. He perceived they were preparing to probe into Jackson's rear on the left flank.

"Front into line!" Stuart ordered. "Charge!"

The 1st Virginia's colors flew ahead of James; the sound of their bugles elevated his blood. His horse's gait changed to a canter. He heard the thundering hooves and braying bugles reverberating through the air. He shouted and spurred Billy. He saw the colors flapping as the cavalrymen's cadence unleashed its ferocity into a gallop. They came up the road like dammed waters let loose.

James and the boys were halfway to their foes when hundreds of rifles opened on them. Troopers fell from their saddles. He heard the whizzing minies buzz by his head and saw more troopers fall. He focused his whole being on the enemy line to his front as he leaned forward in the saddle; his mind engaged in the ethos of mortal combat. Cavalrymen ahead of him were blown from their mounts backward over their horses rumps. Horses tumbled earthward, neck first, into the road and the field upon which they were charging. He saw arms flailing into the air torn asunder by the whistling minies. He watched freed weapons fly through the dust and hit the ground. Cavalrymen numbers were being decimated, as deadly fire vacated many a saddle before they had even reached the infantry's line.

Suddenly a trooper went crashing down into the dust next to him. The riderless horse turned, galloped to the rear. Much to his horror, he glanced over to see George trampled under the stampede of hooves. He wiped the sweat from his brow. "Yaai, Yai. . . . Yaai, Yaai, Yai . . . Yaai!" he yelled out as he drew his revolver.

He heard sounds of many cavalrymen yelling, terrifying shrieks and confusion abound everywhere. He opened fire at the infantrymen, firing off six quick shots; each winners of his wrath. Many of the infantrymen fell to the ground a few yards to his front. He and Billy darted into the melee between infantrymen who were overwhelmed by the stampede of horses. He pulled his second revolver as Federals stood wide-eyed all around him.

"For George, you Yankee sumbitch!" *Pop! Pop! Pop!* His revolver flashed sparks from the barrel.

In the chaos, he continued to look for targets. He had discharged both of his revolvers so close to soldiers the spark blasts marked their jackets. He reached for his carbine. An infantryman had grabbed hold of his weapon. The whites of the soldier's eyes flashed before him for a moment. He kicked the soldier square in the face causing the soldier to stumble backward and fall to the ground. He lifted the carbine and pointed down at the soldier on the ground and snapped the trigger.

He saw Stuart, standing in his stirrups rounding the base of the hill, chanting his commands, "Rally to the colors! Rally!"

James rode to the colors and reloaded two new cylinders into his revolvers. While the Zouaves were reloading, Stuart turned to his men, and the troopers charged the infantrymen again.

He rode Billy into the sea of two tides, like great gale force ocean waves, the waters colliding in rough seas of thunderous shock. He saw more cavalrymen slam to the ground. His horse reared as he and the other troopers struggled to regain control and balance. He heard weapons popped as dust charged the air. He smashed into their line shouting and cursing the enemy. There followed a wild fracas, and he experienced a sense of cotton mouth to the point he could not spit. He was tarnished with powder smoke that gave off a poisonous odor.

He could have drummed time to the rhythm of the fight as the roar of the un-dammed waves of cavaliers created a clamor. It rose and declined as the groaning, shouting, breathing of men was heard while they grasped defiantly for life. James heard horses in a panic, sounding louder and louder as the thunder of their hooves came down, trampling those who had already fallen.

The smell of sweat and powder wafted around him, hot sabre metal clanged with each blow, and rifle percussion whistled through the air. He was running at a high-spirited pitch. Action surged in every direction, blood spilling and bones shattering with every minie strike and sabre slash. He felt an assault of nausea, but kept on fighting with resurgence. He and his comrades were gaining the upper hand. Rage and battle ecstasy enveloped him, causing him dizziness that invoked a delirium, making the whole fight seem a twisted blur of horses and Federals in a whirlwind of sheer madness.

He realized the infantrymen had no time to reload their muskets, so they, instead, presented fixed bayonets. As he and Billy flashed by, the desperate infantrymen thrust their blades of sharp, pointed steel at the two. They had become one, a dynamic fight-ing machine. Billy was now cut on his rump, bleeding profusely, but the faithful steed fought on as James, a mighty warrior, whirled to and fro in the saddle. Every muscle in his body strained to keep him in the fight as he gasped desperately for breath.

James and his fellow cavalrymen were gaining ground and pushing the Federals back up the road. He pulled his sabre and began slashing at one of them, piercing his shoulder and breaking his collar bone. The miscreant crumpled to the ground grabbing his wound. James spurred Billy on into the melee to find quarry who dared to stand before his blade. He felt the tide had turned in favor of the insurmountable cavalrymen as the Federals scattered in every direction, fleeing on the road north toward the ford. He watched the soldiers plunging across Young's Branch as they tossed equipment, cut traces from artillery horses, and mounted the horses to flee the Confederates, completely demoralized, no longer able to withstand the horse assault.

He heard the whining artillery guns firing north up the turnpike. He thought of the damage it inflicted on the scattered soldiers! The artillery action made a lasting impression on him as the smoke from the guns drifted down to the battlefield. He thought of Major Samuel Ringgold in the Mexican War. The major had grown up at

Bai-Yuka; his boyhood home was the homeplace of an American hero. He knew of his flying artillery techniques that had won the first battle of the war at Palo Alto. A West Pointer, the father of flying artillery had won the battle with skillful horse artillery maneuvers that had inspired him in his youth.

James thought, today he had fought with that same spirit of his boyhood hero, Ringgold. The major would be proud of him!

Late in the day Stuart took James and his 1st Virginians on to harass the terror-stricken, retreating Federals. He, Daniel, and Thomas took a side road. They attacked the retreating Federal soldiers' flank. He was part of two companies under Stuart's command, charging against the western end of the Federal's retreating column. He observed pandemonium breaking loose as the Yankees, in total defeat, made haste for Washington.

"I hope they got what they came to see," James said to Thomas.

"We've routed them and now we're escorting them back to Washington where they belong, off of Virginia soil," Thomas replied.

James saw a terrific jam of overturned wagons, fright-stricken mules, and heard teamsters shouting out cuss words.

"Move on, mule, or you'll feel the lash of this goddamned whip," a desperate Federal driver yelled out.

James continued to wage war. Many prisoners fell into his hands, which required Stuart to detach him and a few other men back to confine their prisoners.

After James had deposited their prisoners, thunder and lightning broke toward the evening, and pouring rains swept over the battlefield. He and the 1st Virginia bivouacked at Sudley Farm, and Stuart made headquarters there for the night.

⌒⌒⌒

The next day James was caught in a torrent of rain much of the time, and it fell in hard horizontal pelts upon him. He observed the panorama of the battlefield with soldiers lying in awkward poses, some headless, others missing arms and legs; a shifting spectacle of once fighting men scattered far and wide, motionless on the rain-drenched earth.

He thought of them as grapes that had fallen from the vine of war. He saw drivers maneuvering their ambulances around the battlefield, slogging through the mud in an attempt to save life. He was emotionally stricken as he helplessly watched men filling ambulances with the wounded and dying soldiers.

He saw a horse struggling and kicking on its side as it tried to get up. Its right front leg was missing from the knee down. He pulled his revolver and shot it in the head. At least it would not suffer, he thought, as he gazed out over the battlefield at the mass of suffering humanity. So many men in blue and gray; it was a sight he would not soon forget.

In the pouring rain, he felt compelled to administer medicine and aid. But as others went about the business of burying the dead, James mounted Billy and rode down Sudley Road toward the scene of the battle with the Zouaves. He noticed the men in the burying parties stripping the dead of clothes and boots. He reined Billy off the road and traversed from his intended course over to the burying party.

"Hey, those dead Yankees have souls, you know. Strip 'em, but leave the gold. It's not right to desecrate their bodies," he said as he peered down on them. He spoke with a voice of divine authority.

"Who're you, soldier? Tend to your own affairs! We're gettin' rich off these dead Yanks," the rough edged man said as the pouring rain splattered his pant legs and boots with a combination of blood and mud.

"I'm also a trained doctor. Some of these men may appear dead to you, but they might be saved. They like to have their teeth and the gold in them if they survive."

"They's all Yankee bastards. If'n they ain't yet dead, we'll make 'em dead sure enough," the man said as he gave a yank on the tooth and then stood with the bloody tooth in the palm of his hand. "Takin' this one right to the bank."

He picked the tooth from his palm and showed its gold filling to James.

"Make sure they're dead before you take their teeth," James said as he reined Billy back to Sudley Road with a disgusted look on his face.

"Like I said, Doc, if'n they ain't dead, they'll be when we're finished droppin' 'em in the grave. Good day to you, Doc," the man said to James's backside. He looked down at the Federal he had taken the tooth from and kicked the body over into the grave.

James reached the battlefield where he had fought the Zouaves. He dismounted Billy, studied the bayonet gash on his horse's flank, and decided to tend to it later. He then walked out among the many wounded and dead. He spotted his friend George, the Irishman, who lay in a pool of his own watered-down blood, shot in the head. He knelt down beside his lost comrade. George's revolver lay close to where he had fallen. George had died happy, James thought. He had love for the fight, a feisty Irishman. God had had a minie with his name on it. George was in God's hands now, eternally. James reflected upon the parable he had told George on the long ride to the battle. It could have been him lying dead in the rain. Why had God spared him and taken George?

James took hold of George's arms and crossed them over his chest. He solemnly looked into George's open eyes and closed them. James uncovered his head and delivered a brief prayer before the burial party arrived. He would send the revolver home to George's parents with a note telling how George had died bravely fighting for his country.

He remounted Billy and tried to close out of his mind the cries from the wounded and all the suffering injured. He beheld so many painfully wounded soldiers: shattered leg bones, some with entrails lying on the ground beside their body, head wounds, so many of gray and blue in terrible medical condition. His heart was conflicted. He wanted to help them all, but he was a cavalryman now. He was no longer a doctor.

8

Let Baltimore be held, with a gentle but firm and certain hand.

—*Abraham Lincoln*

MOLLIE'S CLANDESTINE JOURNEY TO Baltimore City began in Hagerstown with Alfred at the helm of the landau carriage. It was a beautiful mid-September afternoon as they neared the outskirts of Baltimore City. Her carriage ride east on the National Pike was long and arduous. She had found Baltimore to be a peculiar town socially, though she believed there was more actual culture to the square block than could be found in Boston.

She had learned, through her correspondences with her Baltimorean friends, that the Federal naval ship, *Harriet Lane*, had docked at the Calvert Street wharf and had trained its guns on the Inner Harbor and the city's business district. She had also learned that the Federals occupied Baltimore City with a firm and certain hand. She believed this sent a message to Southern sympathizers that Pratt Street type riots would no longer be tolerated.

She had read in the Hagerstown *Herald and Torch Light* newspaper that on September 4th, in Baltimore City, Major General Dix had issued an order prohibiting the display or sale of secession badges, flags, pictures, song sheets, photographs, infants' socks, or any emblem of the Confederacy. She was saddened by the lack of Southern emblems as she and Alfred made their way through the city streets. They saw no compassionate people for the cause, and the omnipresent feeling of the Federal occupation permeated the city streets.

She felt as if she had done something wrong. She was an innocent citizen, other than her sympathizing beliefs. Her covert agenda to meet and begin to conspire would soon change her guilty feelings into a jeopardizing reality. She felt the tension as if she were perpetrating a crime. She knew the decisive Confederate victory at Manassas had left reverberating tensions in Baltimore City soaring northward like a great gray raptor with talons of attack stretched before it. Despite the oppressive mood on the streets, she knew the interchange of news between Richmond and Baltimore was a daily occurrence.

⸛⊙⸰

Mollie and Alfred trotted up in the carriage to the southwest side of Calvert and Fayette Streets to David Barnum's Hotel. She thought it was the grandest hostelry in Baltimore City, a classic building on the order of Boston's elegant Tremont House. She saw Barnum's delicate engravings of the Jacksonian period that showed a restrained elegance of style and architectural beauty. She mused that the proper look was like some aging dowager with its bulging iron balconies. Catty-corner to the hotel she saw the Middle Department Commander Dix's 8th Army Corps building. Austere Federal guards posted as sentinels at the building's entrance created a bit of anxiety for her.

Alfred unloaded her trunk and gave it to the bellhop. Mollie was dressed in a fashionable skirt, which was solid burgundy in color; it was very full with knife pleats used to fold the bulky fabric into a smooth line at her waist. Her bodice had a center front opening, which used hooks and eyes to close it. Her neckline featured a white collar with a brooch pinned to it positioned at her throat. Alfred remained with the carriage as Mollie entered the hotel. She felt the eyes of the Federal detectives in the lobby of the hotel follow her. She understood that she and Alfred would be under this kind of watchful surveillance and that this put her in peril.

She made her way to the elegant marble front desk to check in for a few nights.

"Miss Macgill, so good to see you again," the hotel clerk welcomed her.

"I always enjoy my time here at the Barnum's Hotel," she said. "Can you see that I have my usual suite?" Her usual suite provided her the view of the War of 1812 Battle Monument. The hustle and bustle of Monument Square was exhilarating to her, although she had never become accustomed to city life. Even so, she always enjoyed every minute of her time in Baltimore City.

"Yes, Madam."

She took the suite key as the bellhop moved the bags to her suite. She then walked upon stylish oriental rugs to take a considered turn through the lobby. She felt as if a queen had preceded her in those very footsteps; possibly one had. The grandfather clock, bronze statues of John Calhoun and other notables, and the dark woodwork gave her a feel of being in the company of royalty. She heard guests chatting around the lobby under the watchful eye of posted Federal soldiers and unbeknownst Federal detectives. These men ruined her reveries, for she felt that they watched her every move.

She was delighted to see her dear family friends across the lobby. She waved her glove-covered hand and flitted across the room to greet them.

"Miss Jennie and Hetty Cary, so pleasant to see you both," she said.

"It certainly is our treat to see you, Mollie. How is your father? He is such a loyal friend of the Cary family," Hetty said. She was known to be a "Monument Street Girl" and was now keeping a low profile during her frequent visits to the city.

Mollie had always thought Hetty was one of the most beautiful ladies of the southland with her pearly white complexion and long red hair, brown eyes, perfect facial features, and shapely figure.

"He's doing wonderfully. Why don't we move into the Library Room for a bit of tea? Ladies, will you join this 'Dixie girl' for some refreshment?" Mollie said defiantly so that the soldiers lingering nearby could plainly hear her words.

The soldiers were talking amongst themselves as she and her two friends walked by them toward the Library Room. Mollie accidentally dropped her white handkerchief on the floor, which had been tucked in her sleeve. One of the gawking soldiers picked it up and returned it to her with a gentle smile on his lips. With a quick grasp, she took it back and then dropped it into the trash receptacle at the entrance to the Library Room. She was all the while watching out the corner of her eye, surveying the soldiers who followed her every move in the hotel. The soldiers so darkened the mood of this otherwise festive place.

Mrs. Mary Sawyer, Mrs. Key Howard, Miss Martha Dungan, and Mrs. Lily Mackall, also discrete "Monument Street Girls" who were also present in the lobby, had followed Mollie and her friends to the Library Room for tea. To Mollie, the lobby had taken on a gloomy tint. The women sat posed around a circular table set with a beautiful floral arrangement as the darkies in white gloves served them their afternoon tea.

"I understand our Maryland legislators have an important vote on September 17 in Frederick City, only a few days away," Mollie said.

"Yes, for secession of our fine state to the Confederacy. Let us pray for God's will and the Southern cause, as our elected officials dictate our home state's future in this triumphal war," Hetty replied.

She knew the Cary family was aristocratic, educated, and decidedly Southern, and they preached secession among the young ladies of her class. Thomas Jefferson was a relative through both lines of the family.

"I fear those legislators, who don't vote to remain in the Union, will end up in Fort McHenry, our 'American bastille,'" Mollie jokingly said.

"The rumors floating around the Maryland Club suggest that this time around, Maryland will vote to secede from the Union. I believe there is nothing that Abraham Lincoln can do to stop this state from following our Southern brothers and sisters who have already left the Union," Mrs. Howard said, fanning herself with an oriental antique.

⋙☙⋘

After their conversation had gone on a while, one of the darkies serving them appeared with a teapot to refill their tea cups. The women continued to discuss the war. Mollie sipped the fine Chinese tea, which to her tasted better than Southern tea. She was making mental notes as to the information being shared amongst these ladies of Baltimore City's aristocratic elite.

"Mollie, it's time to carry on to dinner at my home on North Eutaw Street, as we discussed in our last missive," Hetty said with her usual witty, outspoken, and fearless attitude.

Mollie had learned that Hetty was now living in Southern Maryland due to the threat of arrest in Baltimore City.

"Certainly, I'm famished; it'd be my pleasure to dine now. Alfred is out front with the carriage. Shall I have the bellhop tell him to bring the carriage up to the front door?"

"Yes, that would be splendid."

"I'll run to the room and powder my nose and meet you at the front door."

Mollie went to her room to freshen up, and then returned to Alfred and her carriage. Hetty joined her as Alfred opened the carriage door for them. He then climbed into the driver's seat and whipped the horses into action. The carriage pulled away from the front of Barnum's and went north on Calvert Street. Mollie saw the Battle Monument in the square in front of the Gilmore House on Calvert Street, and she noticed that men in long black coats who wore stovepipe top hats were walking around the monument. Despite the war and the anti-Southern sentiments she perceived the people milling around seemed nonchalant as they always did on every other trip she had taken to Baltimore City.

She felt the air to be cool and pleasant for a carriage ride. They turned left on to Lexington Street's cobblestones, continuing west across Park Street. She knew the city streets well, and she noticed the facades of the buildings that lined the street were sooty from the coal smoke.

"What a wonderful night," Hetty quickly said as she moved into more intimate conversation. "I've some friends I want you to meet. They're going to get you information that will help our cause. I've a close-knit group of special friends who're a part of my network in Baltimore. You can trust them to help you."

"I, too, have a friend I want you to meet. He said he would come to your home tonight. Lige Viers White is his name, and he is from Poolesville. He has been working undercover in Maryland and Baltimore City since the war broke out."

"Yes, I'm most eager to meet him. I have heard he does excellent work for the cause. How do you know him?"

"He's a cousin way back through my paternal line. In '55 he lived in Missouri fighting as a U.S. soldier in the Border Wars with Kansas. He seems to believe that the Yankees are going to move across the Potomac and invade Leesburg."

"Very well. He'll fit in well with my friends awaiting us at home," Hetty said, almost whispering with her hand to her mouth as if to protect the secretiveness of her conversation.

They passed by Bird & Company Foreign & Domestic Dry Goods store on the corner of Howard and Lexington Streets. A few blocks farther, they came to the Lexington Market, and the carriage came to a halt on the corner of Eutaw Street and Lexington. Then they turned left and traveled down to the Young Women's Seminary at 233 North Eutaw Street. They exited the carriage, and there to greet them was Lige White. He stood under a cupola over the set of stairs that led to the front door.

"Ladies, so fine to see you both," Lige said with a smile.

"Lige, this is Hetty Cary. I told her on the way over from Barnum's you might be here," Mollie said.

"I've heard about you, Mr. White. Please join us for dinner at my parents' table."

"Most certainly! I'd be honored."

Entering the house, Hetty invited them directly into the dining room. Mollie looked around at the interior, which was nicely decorated with two oil-painted landscapes. On the fireplace mantel sat an antique clock and double candle holders on each side of it. Two vases with patterned floral designs were positioned at the ends of the mantle. A mirror with gold wooden trim hung above the mantle. A sideboard set into the wall had the silver service upon it. A chandelier hung from the ceiling over the dinner table with four globes for the gasolier fixture. The wooden floors were polished, surrounded by mahogany paneled walls. The tablecloth draped over the table to the floor. The home was ornate and stylish as people of this caliber should have it, she thought. Mr. and Mrs. Cary were not at home for the dinner; Hetty had explained that they were away at an important Baltimore City political event.

As Mollie sat, Lige pushed in her chair; he sat between them. She looked at him, thin as a rail in stature with a saintly countenance. His brown hair, which waved back over his forehead, was trimmed to perfection. He had never been a muscular man, but exuded an air of confidence, she recalled. They all were feeling more comfortable being in the privacy of the Cary home.

"I understand from Mollie that you're concerned with Federal troop movements along the Potomac," Hetty stated with a low tone of voice.

"Yes, rather. I'm sure they're up to something, maybe even an attack on Leesburg," Lige answered. "Mollie, your cousins, the Williams, have a home on the grounds of Federal Camp Benton outside Poolesville. I have learned General Charles Stone is commanding the camp. How might you discover what's going on inside there?" he asked.

"Well, I think I might be able to make a trip over to see my cousins Mary Florence and Sarah when I return from Baltimore City," Mollie said.

"They'd let you on the property since you are related to the plantation owners—I should think?" Hetty suggested.

"Most definitely! You'd need to take them some important information that only a family member would know. If you're successful in getting to them, I believe they or their darkies might know what is going on. Word travels openly and rapidly around the camps as soldiers get restless and talk amongst themselves. If we can discover what Stone is planning to do in relation to taking Leesburg, we'll be able to confront him as he comes over the Potomac River," Lige said.

"I'm sure I'll think of something," said Mollie.

Let Baltimore be held, with a gentle but firm and certain hand.

"When you've the information, I'll meet you at the west end of the Spring House at Stoney Castle. There's a large oak there where we can meet and not be seen by the Yankees," Lige said as the "yellow scarf" of intrigue was now in place.

They ate dinner on fine Wedgwood china. As the night lingered on, Mollie, Lige, and Hetty continued planning how best to secure vital information needed by the Confederates at Leesburg. Mollie was convinced the best hope for espionage pointed to infiltrating Camp Benton. She knew she was the person who could get into the camp. However, she had to contrive a good reason to see her cousins so that the Federals would believe it important enough to let her into the environs of the camp.

After dinner, on the ride home to Barnum's, Mollie was invigorated by the thought of becoming a spy. She had been dreaming of how she might help the cause. Her dreams of aiding Maryland and the southland had come true. She thought of James, how proud he would be of her intentions to spy.

9

Legendary Artillerist Dream

JAMES SLEPT IN HIS tent a long time. Encamped with the 1st Virginia Cavalry he was visited by a strong dream. He dreamt of Bai-Yuka.

Walking down the stairs into the parlor . . . he could see a casket with white chrysanthemums, white peace lilies and white orchids all around the parlor and the casket. He felt uneasy . . . walking toward the casket, wanting to know who was in it. Lifting the lid of the casket . . . suddenly a soldier was peering at him . . . he, jumping back . . . the soldier sitting up. . . . It was Major Samuel Ringgold, his boyhood hero of the Mexican War, dressed in his uniform with sabre at his side.

He, turning and scurrying to the stairs . . . while the major was climbing out of the casket. . . . It was a terrifying vision. He running up the stairs just as the major was walking out the front door of Bai-Yuka. He racing to his room . . . immediately drawn to the window.

To his amazement he could see stands of small spiny mesquite. Everywhere were waist-high sharp pointy grasses that covered the field next to Bai-Yuka . . . a virtual desert enveloped the landscape . . . an eerie fog wafting across the open battlefield with shallow depressions and an old river meandering, obscuring a resaca; and on the other side of it, a mile long line of Mexican soldiers. Their infantrymen's bayonets and dragoons with lance heads glinting in the sunlight with pennons on the lances. Mexican and American flags rippling in the breeze . . . the Mexican soldiers dressed in blue uniforms indistinguishable from Federal blue uniforms.

In his front yard, he could see the 8th, 7th, and Light Dragoons regiments' guidons . . . the dragoons posing for a charge . . . their guidons flapping in the wind . . . Farther down the line were infantrymen standing at attention. . . . In front of them, appearing like a ghost, Major Ringgold walking through the columns of troopers toward his two batteries of "flying artillery." The major mounting a horse . . . walking his horse up to the cannon . . . raising his hand . . . bringing it down . . . the cannon belching forth light-blue clouds adding to the fog wafting over the field. The cannon shells racking holes in the Mexican-American lines. . . . He jumping up and down at the window . . . he could hardly contain his excitement.

The gunners were stripping off their coats . . . rolling up their sleeves . . . tying their suspenders around their waists . . . wearing red flannel shirts; the sun glistening off the sweat on their foreheads and muscular arms. He, watching them limbering and unlimbering . . . firing a few shots . . . dashing through the smoke . . . firing again with lightning-like rapidity . . . partly hidden from view by the dense clouds of dust and smoke. The major atop his horse commanding the gunners . . . the flag bearer riding along with him . . . an unfurling Confederate Saint Andrews battle flag blowing in the gusting wind. To his right were the lines of troopers mounting . . . ready to charge.

The Mexican-Americans returning cannon fire . . . he seeing the shells in mid-air coming directly for Bai-Yuka . . . the shells passing by the house . . . others falling to the ground in front of the window . . . never exploding . . . as if the house and he have a protective shield from the missiles' destruction. The dragoons charging forward passing the major's cannon . . . the Mexican-Americans advancing toward the major's Confederate line of artillery.

The major looking backward to the house signaling to him to come down to the battlefield . . . It was all exciting to him . . . turning from the window . . . running down the stairs and out the front door . . . running to Major Ringgold on his horse. The major holding a lanyard in his hand . . . he approaching him gleefully . . . reaching out his hand grasping the lanyard. The major saluting him . . . raising his hand . . . lowering it . . . he pulling the lanyard . . . firing the cannon.

Suddenly, he hearing a Mexican-American solid copper cannon ball whistling through the air and striking the major . . . hitting him first in the right thigh, passing through the holsters and upper part of the horse's shoulder, and then striking the major's left thigh as it passed out the horse's other shoulder . . . the major tumbling from the horse . . . the horse flinching and buckling at its knees, crumbling on top of the major.

James awakened from the dream in a cold sweat, grabbed Thomas who lay nearby him in the tent, "Where am I?"

"James, you're dreaming, wake up, you're at Munson's Hill in Virginia," Thomas replied.

"Strange dream!"

"What was it about?"

"I thought I was home at Bai-Yuka as a boy. I saw Ringgold in a coffin," he said with a puzzled look on his face. He stood up and looked around to assure himself he was not on the desert battlefield.

"Who's Ringgold?"

"You know, the Mexican War hero who grew up at Bai-Yuka. He created a horse artillery tactics manual. At the Battle of Palo Alto he was shot from his horse by a cannon ball and died a few days later."

"Oh, that Ringgold. I've read a piece written by some guy named Randall called *Maryland, My Maryland*. He refers to him."

"What does he say about Ringgold? I'd like to read it; do you have a copy?"

"No, but I'll keep an eye out for it. Come on; let's water the horses and then get some vittles."

They walked over to their horses on the picket line. He observed the early morning fog densely hanging around the horses; a long line of many horses' lead straps were lashed on the line. He pulled Billy's lead rope and led him to the stream.

"Mornin', Daniel," he said as Billy's head gracefully bowed to take a drink.

"Mornin', James."

"I miss George. He always had something funny to say," James somberly said.

"Yeah, he was a good fellow."

"He rode right next to me in that charge. Never could understand why he got it, leaving me to tell about it."

"Yeah, I remember. I was on the other side of him when he hit the ground. I suspect he never knew what happened. I want to go like that if I get it. Did you send off his revolver to his parents?"

"Sure did," he said while pulling up Billy's head from the stream.

James and the boys walked back to the picket line. They headed for the mess table and had some bacon and corn pone. He smelled bacon and horse manure, a robust smell that he had become accustomed to.

After breakfast he and the boys returned to their horses, gathering them up for reconnaissance and picket assignments. He noticed, out of the corner of his eye, a courier ride into the camp and approach Corporal Cunningham, saluting him.

He was near enough to them that he heard the courier say, "I need to speak with Private Breathed."

"Private Breathed, front and center," Corporal Cunningham commanded.

James guided Billy by the reins out of the ranks a few yards over to the courier.

"Private Breathed?" the courier asked with a stern look on his face.

"Sir," James saluted, knowing he had been watched, but did not think he had done anything wrong.

"Come with me, Private Breathed. General Stuart wishes a word with you."

They rode through cavalry camps en route to headquarters. They arrived at the headquarters tent with the 1st Virginia guidon blowing on a staff in a gentle wind. He noticed the Virginia State flag was positioned next to the guidon. The general was seated under a fly that extended from the opening of the tent ten feet out, supported by poles at each corner in order to give shade to him while sitting at his field desk.

James dismounted, handing Billy's lead strap to a guard posted for the protection of the general. Stuart stood up from his desk and approached him in the open air.

"Private Breathed, my regards," Stuart said reaching out his hand.

"Sir, you called for me?" he said as he reached to shake the general's hand. "Congratulations are in order I believe. Word of your promotion to brigadier general has made its way around the camps."

"Thank you. How has the cavalry been for you? I know you've missed your calling of medicine. I assume there has been much of this needed practice to keep you busy?"

"I've done what I could for the men," James said as they walked back under the shade of the fly.

"Allow me to introduce Assistant Adjutant General John Esten Cooke, a rather fine novelist before the war, and now an excellent aid in camp!"

"Private, or should I refer to you as Doctor?" Cooke said with a salute.

They sat under the fly as Cooke produced a notebook, and then sharpened his pencil with a knife.

"I've petitioned Governor Letcher for cannon. I'd like you to recruit and train artillerists for my new 1st Stuart Horse Artillery. I need your talents and intelligence in this Confederate Army to expand into another important arm of service. You may call it my 'Long Arm'; for I need to develop artillery in conjunction with my cavalry," Stuart said with a concerned look.

"Sir, I'm honored that you'd have presented me with this challenge. I certainly saw what Lieutenant Beckham's guns did at Manassas. May I share with you a personal point of interest relevant to this service?" he said with a ghostly stare of amazement toward Stuart, his face white as if Stuart had a premonition and knew of his dream.

"Please, Doctor. What's on your mind?"

James was sitting forward in his chair, unsure of himself, wringing his hands. He began to recall the dream in detail, both of the men listening intently as he told the dream sequence.

"I believe we've our answer," Cooke said. "Truth is stranger than fiction. I could hardly have created such truth as was shared by you in your dream."

"Certainly Doctor, you understand as well as I do, that to which God is calling you." Stuart said. "You've been handed the artillerist's lanyard. It's up to you to take hold of it and embrace your destiny. I've in mind a West Point man to take over-all command of my horse artillery. You'll be working with an able Alabamian, 1st Lieutenant John Pelham. The two of you should work well together. I'm certain of this; Ringgold would have had it no other way."

Stillness came over James. He sat back in his chair, relieved that his dream story was well received. He heard Billy whinnying and saw him pawing the ground. The guard tried to control the restless horse.

"Even your horse is excited at the prospect of artillery," Cooke said.

The meeting came to a close and Stuart stood, reaching out to him to shake hands. James shook his hand with a firm grip of confidence; Stuart affirmed him with a pat on the back.

"You'll make a fine artillerist, Doctor! Artillery requires intelligent, quick thinking soldiers in command. You're capable, as I surmised from our first encounter on the train platform. I'll keep you informed on the development of my First Stuart Horse Artillery. Let's get back to the business of the war. We'll speak again soon."

James mounted Billy and rode off to his camp. He thought he had been well received; he would now prepare for his new calling, horse artillery. He felt confident he would do well. He believed Ringgold had sealed his destiny as a potentially great horse artillerist of this war.

10

The Wind is Sown

MOLLIE HAD BEEN OUT riding side saddle, here and yonder, on her horse Sadie, dressed in her feminine riding habit consisting of a tailored burgundy jacket and skirt of light wool. When she came around the corner, a block from home, she spied forty or more Federal soldiers outside her family's house. The soldiers mingled together on South Potomac Street. She reached the soldiers, dismounted, tied her horse, and snatched her riding whip from the satchel.

"What in God's name is going on here?"

Mollie walked through the ranks of sweaty soldiers to the front stoop where Captain Saul was knocking.

"We're here for the arrest of Dr. Charles Macgill," the captain said. "Stand aside if you know what's good for you, little missy."

Mollie watched the door open and her brother, and father's namesake, Charles Griffith appeared, grim faced, as he viewed the soldiers who had gathered. A disgusted look crept onto his face.

"Sir, I order you to stand aside," the captain ordered as he forced his way into the house, a paper in his hand.

"What's the meaning of this? We've done nothing wrong," Charles Griffith said.

"I'm here for the arrest of Dr. Charles Macgill," the captain said as the band of ill-disciplined militia looked on. He stepped into the parlor of the house.

The parlor was exquisitely furnished with oriental rugs, velvet sofas, and finely crafted dark wood furniture. The walls were covered with commissioned oil paintings that were reproductions of a bygone era of European masterpieces.

Mollie's father, Dr. Macgill, stood in the parlor near the staircase, arms crossed. He was a stout man, broad shouldered. His features, full and forceful, were suggestive of an iron will and the courage to enforce it. His family gathered around him. Mollie held her riding whip, with the tail curled on the floor.

"Dr. Macgill, you're my prisoner," the captain said. "I order you to come with me."

"By whose order?" Dr. Macgill asked with a stern voice.

"By order of Colonel Kenly who has instructions from the Honorable Secretary of State, William Seward," the captain responded as he walked across the parlor and handed him the warrant. Dr. Macgill received the letter and read it aloud:

Headquarters
Darnestown, 29 September, 1861
Confidential
Colonel Kenly
1st Maryland Regt.

Sir,
You are authorized and directed to arrest Doctor Charles McGill of Hagerstown, Maryland. When arrested he will be sent to Fort McHenry and thence to Fort Lafayette. Do not let the arrest fail of speedy execution for which this shall be your warrant.

Very Truly Yours
As Always
(signed) N. P. Banks
M. G. C. Division
True Copy
Fred C. Tarr
Adjutants 1st Md. Regs.

"I was a major general of the Twenty-fourth Maryland Militia appointed by Governor Ligon. I've served this country faithfully," Dr. Macgill proclaimed. "General Patterson ordered me to care for his soldiers after they were injured in an accident. I attend to soldiers at the Female Academy here in Hagerstown. How dare you serve me such an insipid letter."

"You'll come with me. We can do this peacefully and respectfully if you submit," the captain said with an increasingly irritated tone.

Mollie observed her father's countenance turn stoic.

"Very well. But first I must see to my ill wife, who is upstairs. If you'll excuse me for a moment, sir," Dr. Macgill said as he proceeded up the stairs.

"Stop him. He's not to leave this room," the captain ordered.

Mollie stared down two soldiers who tried to grab Dr. Macgill by the arms. Dr. Macgill turned about quickly, gave them a push, and knocked them down the stairs.

Charles Griffith came to his father's aid and a struggle broke out in the parlor. Mollie raised her ivory-handled riding whip and snapped it violently at the soldiers. In response, a soldier drew his sabre, which nicked her brother on the neck, drawing blood. Charles Griffith fell back and grasped the bloody scratch.

Other soldiers drew revolvers, some pointed at Mollie as she defiantly snapped the whip again.

"I beseech you all to leave my father be. Leave this house immediately," Mollie shouted as she moved between the soldiers and her wounded brother.

"I demand order! There'll be no more violence," the captain hollered. "Step away from Dr. Macgill. And quit that whip cracking, little missy, now!"

Mollie coiled her whip, signaling her capitulation to the captain's demand, and the tussle ceased. Two soldiers moved swiftly toward Dr. Macgill and forcefully directed him to the front door. He left without a word, but the soldiers kept their revolvers drawn as they exited the front door. Once outside, the captain motioned for the spare horse to be brought forward, accompanied by a full guard of mounted troopers. In the street, Dr. Macgill mounted the horse, as did the captain. Dr. Macgill's family gathered on the front steps to watch.

"Arrest that man as well! He tried to attack a Federal soldier; that is warrant enough to bring him along," the captain said pointing to Mollie's wounded brother.

"Arrested just like John Merryman of Cockeysville. Lincoln has become a despot who thinks he's beyond the laws of the land and the Constitution itself!" Charles Griffith said as he was being directed to mount a horse next to his father's.

"Where're you taking them?" Mollie inquired as she held her riding whip firmly.

"They'll be incarcerated at Camp Banks near Williamsport. They'll then be transported to Fort McHenry in Baltimore. You, missy, had better learn to control your temper if you know what's good for you," the captain said.

Mollie watched the troopers ride south, and the dismounted soldiers followed. She sat dumbfounded on the front steps of the house.

"How can they barge into our peaceful home, arrest father, wound Charles, and simply ride away with them? This war has become personal. I'm no longer going to take it sitting around here doing nothing. These people think they can step on the Macgills and get away with it. There'll be a reckoning for this!" she exclaimed as she gathered herself and started issuing orders to both siblings and house servants, her hands flailing in the air. "James, go and find Barlow and Pat and let them know what's happened. Alice, go and tell mother what's taken place. Alfred, I want you to ready the carriage for a trip to Poolesville."

⌘

After spending the night at her good friends, the Trails, in Frederick City, Mollie and Alfred had driven through the town of Poolesville en route to the Williams's plantation. They headed out the Edwards Ferry Road toward the plantation house. Her cousins, Mary Florence and Sarah Poole, would not be expecting her; Lige would have gotten the word of her possible visit to Richard Walter Williams, who was James Breathed's uncle.

Looking forward at the fork to the Williams plantation, Mollie viewed across the fields to her right and saw the imposing side view of Stoney Castle, with its stone facade and high portico. Her family often visited her cousins, the Whites, for elegant dances in the Stoney Castle ballroom of the Tidewater-like manor. She reminisced how Lige had danced the Virginia Reel with her into the wee hours of the morning on her last visit.

No sooner had they passed the entrance road to Stoney Castle than the fork to the Williams's plantation branched off to the left. Alfred turned the horse down the fork, but the carriage was immediately halted by two pickets in well-tailored uniforms.

"Hold up a minute, boy," a soldier said to Alfred. Then directing his attention to Mollie, he asked, "Pardon me, ma'am, but it's my duty to inquire of all who pass why they wish to do so."

Mollie could tell from his accent and his mode of speech that he was both from New England and somewhat of a gentleman. "To answer your question, sir, I'm on the way to visit my cousins Sarah and Florence. If you would be so kind, please send up to the house and ask the master if Miss Mollie Macgill isn't expected, bringing good news from his sister."

She heard orders given, and the second picket went down the lane. The first picket continued to make light conversation with her with deference due a lady. "I trust this delay will not inconvenience you too long. But should you be admitted to our camp without warning, I would not be performing my duty. You may even be subject to indignities which are easily avoided by this brief delay."

"Do your duty, sir. I understand. But these are strange times in Maryland. From your speech and bearing I'd speculate that you weren't raised for your present calling, but for a higher station."

"You'd be surprised," the soldier replied, "at the number of well-educated gentlemen we've in the ranks of the 20th Massachusetts. We're mostly Harvard men fresh from the Yard, and of good families. We've Abbotts, and Lawrences, and even Wendell Holmes, son of the poet."

The talk continued in this fashion, with the soldier doing most of the talking and she looking earnestly at the talker, until the second picket came back up the road and reported, "Richard Williams was expecting his cousin." They were allowed to proceed to the house; the door was ajar in relation to her plans, she surmised.

⚬⚬⚬⚬

The house they approached looked nothing like Stoney Castle. It was clearly a Piedmont plantation house. As they moved forward she saw four chimneys of different shapes and uneven height, and a number of outbuildings, including a few slave cabins. The whole complex was situated on the top of a hill, just as she remembered it being.

As they approached the house, Mollie noticed that a few Federal soldiers were walking on the road. It wasn't until she got almost to the carriage loop that she gasped:

She beheld before her, in the lowlands that fell off to the south and west, was a vast sea of tents.

A passing soldier moved closer to the carriage and spoke, "Can I be of any assistance, ma'am?"

Mollie could see he wore the same uniform as the pickets; she quickly smiled at him.

"Why all this takes one's breath away! The last time I visited my cousins there were cattle down there. I've never seen so many soldiers in a camp! And to think, all this on one of my family's plantations."

Her amazement, which was surreal, provoked thoughts that cautioned her to be even tempered in order to calm what she believed were the soldier's suspicions.

"In truth, ma'am, you see but a part of it. This area in front is Camp Benton, with thousands of sons of New England and New York. And over there is Camp Stone with thousands more soldiers from Minnesota and Wisconsin. So, as you see, this part of Maryland is well protected."

"Thank you for your kind interest in my momentary distress. If all the soldiers are as polite as you and the pickets I met coming in, I'm sure Maryland is both well and gently protected."

Alfred jolted the carriage toward the front door of the Williams House before the soldier could reply to her.

As Mollie approached the front door, she saw a six-foot-long black snake lurking along the wall of the dark stone cellar staircase, seeking prey in the shadows. She had heard many farmers say that black snakes were friends that slid through the walls to kill mice and rats. There was no doubt in her mind that the Williams plantation was infested with rats, but now of the two-legged blue variety. She thought of herself as a powerful and stealthy snake that had come to the plantation to deal with the Federals. Although she had calmed down to some degree, she was still angry about the arrest of her father and brother.

She knocked and waited patiently for the door to open. She was still feeling nervous, and was startled when a house servant suddenly opened the door.

"Miss Mollie, come in. Marse Richard is expecting you. I'll call for Miss Mary Florence."

Mollie gazed past the servant to see Mary Florence, wearing a floral day dress, walk through the parlor across round coiled rugs.

"Why, cousin Mollie, what a pleasant surprise."

As Mollie handed her travel wrapper to the Williams's house servant, she inhaled the rustic smell of cedar logs from the fireplace and noticed purple irises mixed with lilies posed in a vase on a table by the window.

"Thank you, cousin. Alfred, bring my trunk along, see to the horse, and then you're free to visit with the other darkies."

She directed Alfred to place the trunk in a room off the parlor.

"To what do we owe this out of the blue visit?" Mary Florence asked.

Before Mollie could answer, in walked her cousin Sarah Poole and uncle Richard.

She walked across the parlor's wooden floors, past the old piano, and gave a hug to her uncle and a sisterly kiss to her cousin. Mollie moved over to the window and looked out over the flower vase. She saw Federal pickets walking only a hundred yards from the window. Behind the wooden fences she could see many Federal soldiers stationed in a large field down the hill. At the bottom of the hill she saw a photo salon comprised of two large tents where the soldiers were having their photographs taken. She saw a myriad of white tents and a small log cabin with a thatched roof and a sign that read "Hospital" on the door. In the wheat field, not fifty yards from the house, she saw a notched log building she thought to be the headquarters of the 20th Massachusetts Regiment.

"The Yankees have arrested father and Charles Griffith. They're on their way to Fort McHenry as we speak," Mollie said as she turned from the window with an anguished face.

"I can't believe that. On what pretext?" Richard asked.

"They gave no reason. That bedeviled Lincoln has suspended habeas corpus. Others have been arrested and imprisoned with no explanation," Mollie said with clenched fists. "There's no longer a constitutional government, only a despot who believes he's above the laws of the land."

Mollie moved to the sofa and sat down. Her hair was in a bun and her dress a little dirty from the forty-five mile trip to Poolesville. She pulled off her white gloves and drew a handkerchief from her dress sleeve to wipe her face. The house servant brought cool lemonade on a tray and served each of them a glass. Mollie waited for the servant to exit the room before she spoke again.

"I met with our cousin Lige White in Baltimore a few weeks past. I've not been involved in this cruel war, but now I plan to place myself amidst it," she said with an angry look on her face.

"Do tell," Sarah Poole said. "We've become friends with the Yankees. The plantation darkies bake pies and cakes, and we let them sell their baked goods to the Yankees."

"Tell Mollie what you've gone and done," Mary Florence said. "She's sweet on a Private Whittemore, a sharpshooter with the Second Massachusetts. Isn't that the truth Sarah, fraternizing with the enemy, aren't you?"

"Well, he's a nice boy. He hasn't ever met a Southern woman. I know I've never met a New Englander before," Sarah Poole said with a grin as her face brightened. "And you know what? Those Harvard men hate the abolitionists as much as our fire-eater secessionists Yancey and Wigfall! They told me so!"

"New Englanders are the worst kind of Yankee," Richard said. "They all think they're so superior to us simple Southern plantation folks."

"Sarah, you may be able to help me. The outside darkies may also be able to help," Mollie said as she started forming a plan of action.

"What's it that you're after, Mollie?" Mary Florence questioned.

"It's dinner time," Richard said, glancing meaningfully at Sarah. "Maybe we should continue this conversation after we've eaten."

Richard stood and Mollie and her two cousins followed him to the dinner table; Richard's other children joined them. Mollie smiled at the house servants who brought out fresh salads with plump, red, juicy tomatoes from the garden. A wonderful pork loin was served with green beans and mashed potatoes. After dinner Tyler pie was served, and she learned why the Federals were buying so many pies. She knew it was a Williams's family specialty and that it took prizes at the fair year after year.

At the conclusion of the meal, Mary Florence sent Sarah on an errand that would keep her busy for quite a while and, over coffee, Mollie continued to develop a plan with the Williams family to gather information to deliver to Lige White.

"Lige told me he believed the Yankees planned to attack Leesburg in the near future, but he didn't know when or where General Charles Stone was planning the attack," Mollie said. "Camp Benton is the center of what they call the corps of observation, with outposts on every ford and ferry between Georgetown and Harper's Ferry. Stone has many more troops available to him than General Evans has to defend Leesburg. However, they're all spread out north of the Potomac. If the Yankees start concentrating forces at one of the crossings that threaten Leesburg, we'll know something is up."

"They've about six thousand troops here at Camp Benton and Camp Stone," Richard spoke up with a sense of glee. "But they'll need more to take Leesburg from Shanks Evans. Colonel Baker is up by the mouth of the Monocacy with his California regiments. General Banks has more troops at Darnestown, but Lincoln is still too afraid of Johnston marching on Washington to move them. The extra troops would probably come from Camp Baker."

"How easy is it to get notice of troop movements?" Mollie asked.

"It's right dangerous to be caught any farther south and west of Poolesville than this. Even the residents need passes to go to the Edwards Ferry stores. But I don't think the Yankees would attack Leesburg by the ferries or fords. Evans has them too heavily picketed. But the Yankees will have to attack before the end of October or forget it. Once the leaves are off the trees there would be no cover."

"Lige said something similar," Mollie said. "He thinks the Yankees could be stopped if they try to use the Edwards Ferry ford, even though it is fordable and there is a sluice gate from the canal to get boats into the water. That's why Shanks has put his fort where he can respond to an attack from Goose Creek or Edwards Ferry."

"Mollie, you know how dangerous it'll be for you if you're caught moving military information to the Confederates?" Mary Florence cautioned.

"If James can fight, so can I. I promised him I, too, would do my part to stop Lincoln and his merry band of Yankee marauders."

"Well, the Yankees would be dumb to try to attack between Conrad's Ferry and White's Ferry. Granted they'd have good cover since no one ever cleared the timber off

Ball's Bluff, but that bluff is steep and they'd have to cross Harrison Island. This McClellan is a bear for organizing. He strikes me as a might shy about fighting," Richard replied.

"Well, considering how dumb the Yankees have been so far, we can't overlook any possibility," Mollie responded.

"We can help get you the information. Sarah can certainly get the Yankee to talk, although we had best keep her in the dark since she can't keep her silly mouth shut. The darkies are all reliable and can certainly get information while selling pies and cakes," Richard said. "I think we've a solid plan."

Mollie assumed she could stay with Richard and her cousins until something developed one way or the other. Then, after a prearranged signal, she would go to Stoney Castle where Lige would meet her at the west side of the spring house.

～⊙～

A few weeks had passed since Mollie had arrived at the plantation. She had integrated herself with her cousins in the house and occupied her time with needlework, reading, and riding the blooded horses on the plantation. She observed the Federal forces as they used the road to Edward's Ferry that ran in front of the plantation house. Couriers were continually reporting on horseback from the various outposts of the corps of observation, as she had expected.

One day she noticed patrols and supplies moving in and out of Camp Benton; detachments, watching the fords and ferries, were changed from time to time. But she alleged nothing big seemed to be materializing.

By now the Federals were used to her presence, especially her morning rides. The outside darkies continued to make money selling pies, cakes, and other treats to the Federal troops, but reported to her only hearing the usual griping of soldiers.

As October idled away Mollie witnessed some interesting changes in routines, such as an observation balloon, the building of a tall signal tower on the hill east of the orchard, the making of ovens for baking bread, and the building of log huts with "California" chimneys. She imagined Stone's command had grown to over ten thousand, still there was no evidence of a serious attack south of the Potomac.

～⊙～

"Good morning, Alfred; fine cool twentieth day of October!" Mollie exclaimed. "Would you saddle one of the horses in the pasture and bring him to the house for me to take my morning ride? I'll meet you here at the house after my breakfast."

"Oh! Yes, Miss Mollie. Marse Williams haz me fetch de saddle and I ketch 'em up earlier tis mornin."

"Good, bring him to the front circle."

Mollie was dressed in her black wool riding jacket and skirt. She felt she looked smart. Her slightly racy, small, ostrich feather-trimmed porkpie hat gave her an aristocratic appearance.

"Thank you, Alfred. I'll return before dinner," she said as she tucked her ivory handled riding whip into the satchel bag.

She thought her riding whip had come in handy when she had previously encountered Federals. She would not hesitate to use it again if the occasion arose, particularly with some of those New York Tammany riffraff boys, who were no gentlemen, like the Massachusetts men.

She rode off sidesaddle, down the hill, toward Camp Benton, always staying to the north among the wheat fields down by the branch. She went as far as the lone tree visible from Stoney Castle to make certain there was no sign in the window there. On her way back to the house she was rode past the headquarters house of the 20th Massachusetts and noticed a young man about her age with a sketch pad sitting under a shade tree. She rode over to him and smiled.

"How do you do, Miss? Allow me to introduce myself. I'm Winslow Homer, an artist for *Harper's Weekly*."

"Good day to you, Mr. Homer. A pleasure to make your acquaintance. My name is Mollie Macgill. I'm here visiting my cousins, the Williams. I'm from Hagerstown, where my house is securely guarded by Federal soldiers intent on making us safe from the rebels," she said as she patted her horse on the neck.

"I grew up in Cambridge outside of Boston," Winslow said as he sharpened his pencil with a razor. "I'm making sketches of the soldier's uniforms, weapons, and the camp headquarters to submit to the *Weekly* as illustrations for the magazine's articles."

"I believe Harvard College is in Cambridge."

"Yes, you're correct. Many of the soldiers from the 20th Massachusetts in the camp are Harvard men; all fine gentlemen, smart too."

"Well, I certainly hope they can end this awful strife and restore our country to the solid Union it once was."

"I certainly hope so, too. We've been having some fine pies and cakes from darkies at the farm house. Do tell them how much we've enjoyed their cooking," Winslow said as he sketched the headquarters building on the pad.

"There seems to be a lot of excitement around the camp," Mollie said as she admired Winslow's sketch.

"I don't know what's going on," Winslow said. "I'm just waiting here to make a portrait of Senator Baker for *Harpers*. He was supposed to meet me here early, but he got sudden orders to move his men down river. In the meantime, I sit here sketching this rather boring building."

"I haven't met many gentlemen artists from the North. My father is a doctor in Hagerstown. He has been treating a fair number of wounded soldiers since this conflict broke out; a lot of them have been local militia. But I prate on, keeping you from your work."

"On the contrary, your visit has been the most pleasant experience I've enjoyed since I came to Maryland."

She blushed, "Why thank you, Mr. Homer. Maybe we'll talk again on one of my morning rides. But the family will be waiting for me, so I must be off," she said as she reined her horse to turn toward the stables.

"Be careful. Don't ride around the back of the camp. The target range is over in that direction. I wouldn't want you or your horse to catch a ricochet," Winslow said as he went back to sketching the headquarters building.

"Have a blessed day, Mr. Homer. I know we'll meet again."

She rode on toward the back of the stables. She suspected that Homer's remark about Baker getting orders was significant; she needed confirmation. Alfred greeted her at the barn and took the horse into the stable. She walked to the house with an appetite for food and for more information. She thought of James and how proud he would be of her for discovering what the Yankees had in mind.

"Hello, Uncle. Am I in time for dinner?" she asked as she walked onto the front porch.

"You most certainly are, Mollie. Do come in," Richard said.

She and the Williams family sat around the table as the house servants filled their glasses with lemonade. Richard asked her to bless the food and then motioned to the servants to bring the meal.

"I met a fine young artist in the field this morning named Mr. Homer. He told me that Senator Baker received sudden orders this morning that have kept him from coming to be sketched as planned," Mollie said with an excited, puzzled look on her face.

Suddenly she saw old Timothy, with skin black as tar, come into the room in a state of great excitement; Richard bade him to proceed.

"It's lak dis. I'se been sellin' pies down at Conrad's Ferry when I heard some powerful angry words from dat Gen'l Baker. Seems like his soldiers done come down dere, but the canal boats with all dey things went to Edwards Ferry. Ole Baker said dat he need dos boats powerful bad. Some odder soldyer says dey still has a few boats, but that jus make Baker madder. He says he's got to cross two places."

"Can't they bring the boats back up the canal?" Richard asked after he had thought for a few moments.

"No, suh. Leastwise not til tomorry. But Baker say dat too late."

After Timothy left, Mollie, Richard, and Mary Florence sat around the table looking at each other.

"Two sets of boats mean two crossings, probably at an island," Richard said, "The closest island is Harrison's Island. I would guess the Yankees were counting on barges to cross from the Maryland side to the island, then from the island to the Virginia side to stage an attack on Leesburg over Ball's Bluff. With only half the barges available, they'll have to improvise. I doubt they can get all their men over very fast. They sure can't get 'em back very fast if they need to."

Mollie beheld Sarah entering the room as lightly as usual.

"My friend Private Whittemore told me he has been drilling with the California soldiers from Camp Baker this morning. Then George tells me they aren't from California at all, but come from Philadelphia. Why would Pennsylvania men say they came from California? Anyway, George is plum worn out from sitting on some island all night waiting for a scouting party to return from Virginia," Sarah explained and then quickly departed the room.

"The other darkies who've been selling their pies and cakes inside the camp tell me they've seen a lot more wagons of supplies arriving lately. They seemed to believe that in the last few days the excitement level has risen at the camp," Mary Florence added.

"Oh, and Mr. Homer said they've really enjoyed the pies and cakes," Mollie said.

"Good," Richard said. "If that keeps our darkies going to the inside of the camp and looking around for us, then we'll give them all the pies and cakes they can possibly desire to eat."

Mollie stood up and paced about the room.

"I believe they plan their attack on the morrow at Ball's Bluff and maybe Edwards Ferry, since they kept the boats there. However, if they attack with insufficient barges at Harrison's Island, they'll have a problem with transportation. I must get word to Lige White tonight."

She had Alfred saddle a fresh horse. She rode off into the failing light to the signal tree; the yellow scarf in place, she thought, as her horse approached the spring house behind Stoney Castle after a short ride.

"Good evening, Mollie. You look well," Corporal Lige White said as he stood next to the spring house.

She dismounted.

"I'm well indeed. I've information for you," she said smiling and taking Lige's extended hand as he kissed it and motioned her to sit on the low wall.

"I'm scouting for General Evans. He'll be most interested in what you may have learned from your stay at the Williams's plantation," Lige said.

"Well, to begin with a man named Winslow Homer . . ."

11

Sweet Retribution

Late November 1861

Centreville, Virginia

James and his new congenial comrades spent the cool November morning building small log cabins laid out in rows near the village of Centreville. He worked diligently to replace his tent of linen cloth with a warm newly built cabin in preparation for winter weather. Many times he had walked around the village, which was comprised of a white stone church and a number of houses on either side of the main dirt road. He liked the citizens who told him they hoped the road would become a thoroughfare from Washington City, a short distance east of the village, to points west.

He had bid adieu a few weeks past to the 1st Virginia cavalrymen and had been warmly welcomed by the Stuart Horse Artillery boys when he took the responsibilities as 1st lieutenant. Maryland laid claim to Major Samuel Ringgold, and James was following in his legendary limber tracks. His new band of brothers came from different parts of the Southland.

James had learned that the men of the Beauregard Rifles came from a regiment of Virginia Artillery. A number of Louisianan Creoles also responded to the call and found their way into his burgeoning unit. Filling out their muster rolls were mountain men from Floyd County, Virginia. He admired their physical stoutness: strong and able with the axe, they had traded their metal axes for tubes of iron cannon.

James and the artillerists had responded to the noble call of Brigadier General Stuart and 1st Lieutenant John Pelham to form the Stuart Horse Artillery. They had all enthusiastically enlisted in order to take part in the pageantry of glorious horse artillery service.

James stood with some of his artillery comrades next to the church, leaning on its stone wall, pulling on his three-inch-long black goatee. He looked away from the village perched upon the raised ground to see the slightly hilly barren plains. He observed the artillerymen leading horses to the four cannon placed in a row; the gunners helped the lead, swing, and wheel drivers position the teams of six-up horses into their harnesses. He also saw the gunners adjust the black leather traces that held the animals in the cannon teams and the artillerymen, seventeen yards behind the cannon, working to place their six-up team of horses in front of the limber and caisson. He viewed the men checking the shinny cooper boxes to make sure they were filled with shell, shot, canister, tools, and fuses ready to fire in the afternoon drill.

"The two twelve-pounders are fine pieces. We need to replace the two six-pounder mountain howitzers," James said as he gestured toward the four guns pointed toward Washington City.

"I agree," Henry said standing next to him. "Lieutenant Pelham has been talking about two batteries of splendid twelve-pounder brass guns, soon coming up from Richmond."

His friend Private Henry Haw Matthews was oddly shaped. He resembled a penguin, but lean instead of fat. His arms were short and hung like wings to his side. He wore a tattered gray coat with holes in the arms. James thought Henry's long neck was crane-like; his mouth stretched seemingly from ear to ear, his nose like a duckbill. Like himself, Henry was from Maryland, and they both had the blood of the "Old Line State" coursing through their veins.

"Lookin' forward to keep'em ladies shining so they sparkle in the sun," Robert said as he strolled over to him while kicking a rock with his boot.

James looked at Private Robert McGill Mackall who had a full gray beard and a moustache sprinkled with the gray hairs of age and dignity. His skin was tanned dark and was weather-worn from a lifetime of farming the Floyd County soil. Robert spoke with a pleasant Virginian accent; his serious nature reflected a chivalric demeanor of an older true Southern gentleman.

"I saw two of those guns commanded by Lieutenant Beckham fired at Manassas. He did well by them to run the Yankees up Sudley Road, all the way to Washington, as we harassed their retreating army," James said as a peculiar-looking short artillerist walked into their midst.

"Gents. Good day," John Bollman said.

They had not been issued their uniforms, yet. James wondered why Private Bollman tried to distinguish himself by his gray top hat with a black band around it. He mused the Creole had a peculiar look to him regardless, what with his curly shoulder-length black hair, only one tooth in the front upper grouping of incisor teeth, and eyes that were squinty under slanted brows.

James noticed the Creole stroke his moustache and goatee. Bollman was constantly drinking in the camp from a flask he kept hidden in his jacket pocket, which made him an irascible character. Frequently Bollman dawdled around the campfire and told entertaining stories from the Louisiana low country.

"What's this here gatherin'?" Creole inquired.

"We're justa waitin' for the bugle. Afternoon drill," Robert responded.

"Well, you'll best get to your'n horses. I seen Lieutenant Pelham fixin' his stallion. Reckon we be drillin' soon," Creole surmised as he turned and walked off toward the picket line.

James looked after Creole, puzzled, for he thought he was an inbred, strange man.

When Creole was a good distance away from them, their conversation commenced.

"He's a scrapper for such a short man. I heard he once took to fightin' his own father. He beat the tar out of him over a disagreement. Bloodied him up something awful," Henry said.

"Yeah, from the looks of him, missing all them teeth, I'd stay clear of him after he's been a drinkin' and up to tomfoolery. Bet he fights dirty, too," Robert said.

James heard the bugle sound, which alerted them to prepare for afternoon drill. He looked over his shoulder to see Lieutenant Pelham on his horse coming down the row of half erected cabins.

"I suspect we best get ready for drill," he said as he walked toward Billy on the picket line.

❧☙

Mounted on Billy, James waited for commands from Emmett Shaw and William Hoxton, the acting sergeants, or chiefs of pieces. James was second in command to Pelham, also a chief of piece for drill purposes. He gazed toward Pelham at the front of a myriad of mounted artillerymen. They were both twenty-three years old, but Pelham with his golden boyish locks of hair and ordinary athletic stature, was remarkably handsome.

They had talked about his West Point training; they were both skilled horseman. He believed Pelham admired him as a schooled doctor, for Pelham's father was a country doctor. He had heard about Pelham's handling of his guns at Manassas; he knew this had caught Stuart's eye. James knew Stuart considered him for the command due to his medical degree, but he did not get the nod because, he felt, he lacked military training.

"Attention—Battery!" Pelham hollered out.

"Attention—Section!" Shaw and Hoxton echoed.

"Battery forward—March!" Pelham commanded.

James gently spurred Billy into motion as he peered over his right shoulder to see four six-up teams pulling their cannon. He viewed behind the cannon teams the four muzzles pointed backward at ten mounted artillerymen in two rows of five each. At the rear of the mounted men, another set of four six-up teams pulled the limbers and caissons.

"Battery—Right wheel!" Pelham commanded.

"To the right—Forward—March!" the four chiefs of pieces cried out.

James noticed Private Bollman showing his top hat to Private Mackall. Bollman was prideful of the top hat.

"Private Bollman! Attention in the ranks!" James hollered, looking sternly at Creole.

"Yeah. You ain't nothin' but a private," Creole jested, ignoring him, while spitting his dark brown 'bacca juices on the ground.

James turned back in his saddle at the same time the battery moved to the right on the open plains. He noted Creole's insubordination. He had no rank over Creole. He had only been appointed acting chief of piece by Pelham a day ago. Though he had the responsibilities of 1st lieutenant, he was still officially only a private.

"Pay no attention to zat crazy voodoo artillerist," Shaw said from the position of chief of piece adjacent to him. "He'll get his come-upins soon enough."

James nodded his head, agreeing with Shaw. His friend Emmett Shaw, with his distinguished German-style curled moustache and goatee, was austere in his expressions. James had noticed that Shaw's deep blue eyes were constantly lit with a rage of fire, and that he carried himself in an upright manner, a slender, physically strong first generation Virginian with Irish and German ancestry. His fearsome broken German-English accent made James believe one would fare better to corner a mama bear and her cubs in a dark cave than to have to cross the ominous German.

"Front into line—March!" Pelham commanded as the four guns turned forward. He was riding before the artillerymen on the plains sitting up in the saddle, his back straight as an arrow. "Form sections—March!"

James watched his gun being pulled forward with another six-pounder as he rode alongside the team lead driver who was driving the first two horses in the team.

"In sections—March!" Pelham ordered as the artillerymen came to a stop after their cannon was in position.

James studied the gunners as they dismounted and clipped their lead straps to the halters of the two horse holders who then led the eight horses to the rear of the caissons and limbers.

"Drivers, drive on!" James commanded.

"Wheels clear!" the drivers barked out.

James watched as the drivers turned hard right several yards and did a half figure eight loop around to the spot he had marked for the cannon placement.

"Unlimber," James cried out when the drivers had the cannon in place to his satisfaction.

James marveled at the drivers as they faced to the rear with the cannon muzzles, which were pointed toward the open plains. The gunners unhooked the cannon from the team of horses and placed the trail of the cannon on the ground. The drivers then systematically drove the horses in another half figure-eight and came in behind the stationary cannon, with the limber and caisson to their rear.

"Chiefs of pieces, take command of your gun," Pelham hollered as the dust was flying and clouding the horses, guns, and artillerists.

"Load—Come to the ready," he cried out to Shaw and Hoxton.

"Shell, six hundred yards," Pelham said as the number nine gunner, standing behind the lid of the cooper limber box, cut a fuse.

James, mounted on Billy next to the limber box, watched the gunners to the front swab the tube, plunge the tube to dry it, while another gunner thumbed the vent. He then saw the artillerists load the shell and prick and prime the cannon tube while gunner number four held the lanyard at the ready.

Pelham rode his horse between the limbers and the caissons observing, "Good artillerists should be able to get off three to four rounds in a minute! Battery—Two second intervals. Battery—Fire!"

Boom! Boom! Boom! Boom! James heard the cannon erupt down the row, sending plumes of smoke skyward.

"Reload—Double-quick!" Pelham commanded.

James could see a few cavalrymen in the distance coming toward them from the east. As the gunners worked to reload a second round, he saw General Stuart appear in the distance. He watched Stuart and his entourage ride up next to Pelham as two more rounds were fired from the row of cannon.

"Halt—Firing," Stuart said as he and Pelham rode between the guns and the limbers and caissons. "Bully! Bully! A fine demonstration of artillery fire. Must be able to work these guns under counter battery fire."

James, Stuart, and Pelham continued to teach the nuances of artillery tactics and they drilled the artillerymen until late afternoon.

⋞⊚⊚⋟

Long days of artillery drilling exhausted James. He pulled off his coat and shirt as he walked from the picket line back to his tent. He was hot and sweaty, ready to relax and unwind. He came to his tent and threw back the white linen flaps of the fly to let the breeze blow through to cool him off. He lay on top of his blankets on the ground and placed his wet shirt to the side and reached for a dry one, which he placed across his belt at his waist. He dozed off.

After only a few minutes he was startled awake. He wearily lifted his dry shirt straight up, draping it over his chest. Suddenly, a black sticklike object, about three feet long, struck his shirt. The black object bounced to the side and slithered out the side of the tent. James quickly sat up and put his shirt on. He stood up and came out of the tent, pulling his suspenders over his shoulders.

In front of his tent, Creole stood with his arms crossed grinning.

"Welcome to Artillery Hell, Private Chief of Piece, pleasant dreams?" Creole said as he walked away hilariously laughing, pulling his flask and taking a nip.

James hid his dismay as he lifted his coat off the tent pole and put it on. Privates Matthews and Mackall walked over to him.

"If'n that happened to me I'd knock his block off. I hate snakes!" Henry said as other artillerymen joined the circle around him.

"James, I wouldn't let 'em get away with it. Report him to Captain Pelham," Robert said as he respectfully patted James on the shoulder.

"Ah, what comes around goes around," James said, turning toward his tent to retrieve his supper bowl and cup, intentionally leaving his spoon. His comrades also went to their tents for dinnerware. They followed him to their mess table and stood around the tables at their respective mess locations waiting to be served supper. He looked over and saw Creole hilariously laughing and talking to other artillerymen at his mess table. He noticed that Creole was not wearing his top hat.

"Hold these, Robert. I forgot something in my tent," James said as he slipped out from around the table and walked back toward his tent.

He went past his tent to Creole's tent. The scalawag's top hat was on the ground inside the tent. James reached in the tent and grabbed the hat. He walked amongst the tent rows toward the picket line of horses and went behind a horse that had laid a fresh pile of manure on the ground. Smelling its fragrance as it steamed in the cool night air, he reached down and scooped some of the manure into his hand. Holding the hat in his forearm against his body he carefully reached inside the top hat with his other hand and peeled back the inner rim of the hat. Then he stuffed warm manure under the rim and folded it back, delicately, to insure that Creole would not notice it.

He walked back to Creole's tent, placed the top hat exactly where he had found it in the tent, then wiped his hand on the grasses to clean off the manure. He strolled back to his tent and took out his canteen, and poured water over his dirty hand, and then picked up his spoon and went back to his mess table.

"Forgot my spoon," he said to Robert. "Thanks for holding my bowl and cup."

"No problem, James," Robert said as he passed back the mess gear.

James filled his bowl with beans and beef stew, while taking some corn bread. He filled his cup with water and sat down on a log between Henry and Robert. Creole waved his hand at him and grinned ear to ear from where he sat with his messmates. James looked over to Creole, smiled a smile of sweet retribution, and waved back to him.

12

Firstborn Heroics

August 26th, 1848

James and his artillerymen were relocating to a new camp. They crossed a deep tributary. When he got to the middle of the crossing, Billy stumbled on rocks, and James was thrown from him. He splashed into the water and when he came up, unhurt, he found himself in the company of a memory from his boyhood.

His neighborhood chums had come over to Fruit Hill Manor above his hometown of Berkeley Springs, Virginia, to go fishing. James usually spent his days with his four siblings, playing around the front yard and swimming in the pond below the manor. He liked to lead his two sisters, Jane and Priscilla, and the other neighboring children in games of "kick the can" and "hide and go seek." His newborn brother, Francis Wilbur, required that he stay close to home so he could help his mother tend to him.

He felt very happy on that day for he had gotten permission to ride with his friends, Frank and Billy, to the Potomac River to fish. He eagerly watched the boys ride down the lane and into the yard.

"Help me get saddled up," James said to them. "Father told me this morning this would be the last time I could go fishing and gigging before we move to Maryland. I bet the black bass are bitin' hard!"

"Gee, James, could I come?" Priscilla asked.

"No, this's for us boys only. Besides you need to stay here and help mother with chores and taking care of little Francis."

"Awe, you're always gettin' to have all the fun," Priscilla said as she turned toward the front door of the manor.

"Frank and Billy, come with me and help me get saddled up," he said to his two fifteen-year-old neighbors.

They lashed their horses to the hitching post and walked with him from the front yard to the Breatheds' stable, over the hill. He asked Frank to walk through the stable and catch Sadie in the back corral.

"Get the blanket from the tack room," Frank said, and James turned and scampered off to get the blanket.

"Now place it up high on his mane and pull it back to where you want it, somewhere about here," Frank pointed to the appropriate placement of the blanket.

"Billy, go to the tack room and bring a bridle and an English riding saddle from one of the saddle trees. Whoa, Sadie," James said. "Let me have the bridle. I can do it."

James brought over a round metal bucket and placed it below Sadie's head. He stepped up on the bucket with the bridle in hand and placed the bit in the mare's mouth. He lowered Sadie's ears under the leather head straps, and then used his small fingers to eye the holed leather chin strap into the buckle and tightened it. He jumped down off the bucket as Billy reached for the girth strap and pulled it through the buckle, tightening it.

"All ready to ride," Billy said.

"I'll get my frog gigging spear and pole. I bet we get some five pound black bass today!" James exclaimed.

They followed James as he led Sadie up the hill from the stable to the front yard. He took the bridle reins and lashed them to a post next to their horses. They proceeded into the manor where his mother met them.

"James, you be careful on the river today. It's been raining a lot recently and the currents will be running swiftly. They may be dangerous, so don't wade in too deep after the frogs."

"Mother, we'll be fine. Billy and Frank are good swimmers. Besides we're going to fish at Hancock and the river is shallower there than at Sir Johns Run. Bye, Priscilla. Have fun at home. I'll bring home supper, whopper black bass," James declared as he reached for his gigging spear and pole.

They went out the front door, untied the reins from the pole, and led their horses to the mounting stone block. James tied the spear and the pole to a strap at the rear of the saddle so that his tackle stood straight up in the air. He climbed on the stone and mounted Sadie. Frank and Billy did the same, and they rode out to Cornelius Road and down the steep grade into town.

"Boys, we need to swing by Father's Mercantile to get our bait," James declared while looking back at his friends. "Follow me."

"Right behind you, James," Frank said as he kicked his horse to catch up to him.

When they got to the bottom of the grade they came to Wilkes Street and James reined Sadie to the right. They passed by old homes along both sides of the street, simple in style, housing the local mountain folks of Berkeley Springs.

"That's Mr. Cutchins' house. He works for the Pavilion, kisses ass to the wealthy planters, politicians, and well-to-do who came to Berkeley Springs for the spas. You know our town invented the Quarter Horse race. Folks around here love cockfighting and gambling. When was the last time you boys saw a cockfight?"

"I never seen one," Billy answered.

"Me neither," Frank said.

James came to the end of Wilkes Street and saw directly in from of him the buildings that housed the spa baths, which had been built on a small quarter acre plot of land. He viewed the nearly completed Pavilion Hotel with its four stories and columned encompassed front porch that faced the baths' buildings.

"You know Lord Fairfax himself bathed here and sixteen-year-old George Washington was a surveyor in town," he arrogantly told his neighbors who were much less schooled than he was.

"You're always so smart, James. Where do you get all this learnin'?" Billy inquired.

"Pa teaches me, and I got a special tutor."

"Good for you. I'd rather be hunting and fishing than be doing all that learnin'," Frank said.

James reined to the left on to Fairfax Street and rode half a block to the Breathed Mercantile Company.

"Tie 'em up here," he said leaping from Sadie's back. "Come on in and say hello to Father."

James tied Sadie to the rail and stepped onto the board sidewalk. He observed many more people than usual strolling on the sidewalks that wound around the baths.

"Something must be going on today. I've never seen so many people walking around the baths as there're here now," he said to Frank.

Frank opened the door of the mercantile and strolled in. James had helped load the aisles of shelves with dry goods, jars of tobacco, and burlap bags of flour—every conceivable good known to man.

"Mornin', boys," James's father said from behind the counter. "Come for the bait you need to catch them whoppers you've been telling me about?"

"Yes, sir," Billy said. "We need some big juicy crawlers and crickets. We're going to Hancock. I gotta great secret hole a little ways up the Potomac."

"Sir, can I help you find something," Mr. Breathed asked of a well-dressed gentleman who had just entered the mercantile.

"I could not help but overhear the excitement in the voices of the boys about going fishing. I'm Harry Pennington of the New Jersey Penningtons. This is Alexander C. M. Pennington Junior. We're from Newark, here today to see President Polk."

"I read something in the *Constitution* newspaper about the president's visit today. When is he expected?"

"He's to arrive on the B&O Railroad at noon. He's coming from Cumberland and taking the stage from Sir Johns Run."

"I'm also in a stagecoach partnership with Colonel Strother. We own the stock and interest in Dandy Jack Stage Line, and we run from the hotel to the B&O Railroad at Hancock. If you need a ride back that direction let me know. I'll be glad to service your needs" Mr. Breathed said.

"Thank you for the offer of your services. Tell me something of the history of your town? I've never been here before."

"Well, the Indians came here for the medicinal value of the warm springs. Today we're a tourist town for people from all up and down the eastern seaboard who come here to cure what ails them. The fire of '44 destroyed my mercantile and a good many buildings in the commercial district in town. Colonel Strother's Pavilion Hotel, where I'd guess you're lodging, is the best servicing the seaboard."

"Very interesting history. There might be something you could help me out with. My nephew here, Alexander, is your son's age, and he's not so interested in seeing the president. He's more an outdoors type and he loves to fish. Might it be asking too much to have him go fishing with your boy and his two friends for the day?"

"Certainly not, if the boys are willing; it's fine with me. James loves the outdoors, too."

"Be great to have him along," James said. "He can ride on the back of Sadie with me."

"James, grab a cane pole from the barrel and fix up Alexander with tackle."

"What do I owe you for the pole?"

"It's on the house. I served in our state legislature last year. I recall the name Pennington from New Jersey. Governor William Pennington I believe?"

"Yes, he was governor until '43. Also, William Sanford Pennington was governor from 1813 through 1815. Alexander's father served in the state general assembly in '37 in the Whig Party. He's a West Point man of the class of '28. We hope Alexander might consider West Point when the time comes."

"I was appointed to West Point by my uncle, Governor John Breathitt of Kentucky, but I declined to enroll. I've more of an acumen for business than the military. I don't much care for fighting and killing, anyhow. My hopes are that James considers medicine, although he does have a powerful theological mind as well. Clergy don't get paid much. I don't want him to struggle financially. His uncle, Dr. Charles Macgill, is a fine doctor in Hagerstown. In fact his wife and three daughters are visiting today and are at the Pavilion."

"Well, I understand I'm amongst fine Virginia gentry here at your Mercantile Company."

"I'll not be here much longer. I'm moving the family to Maryland. I want to get James started in formal education at the College of St. James near Hagerstown. It's the finest Episcopal Seminary training school around these parts. We're enrolling James this fall. This will be his last fishing trip because we start the move next week," James's father said while he finished placing the tackle on the pole standing next the counter.

"You didn't tell me cousin Mollie was in town. How long are they to be here?" James asked.

"Don't worry, James. You take Alexander with you and enjoy yourself fishing. They'll be here when you get back. You can say hello to your cousin Mollie and her sisters then," his father said walking from behind the counter to shake Mr. Pennington's hand while patting Alexander on the head.

"You boys get along now. Have a great time—catch some whoppers!" Mr. Pennington encouraged as he ushered the boys out the front door to their horses tied to the hitching post.

James and the boys mounted their horses as Mr. Pennington helped his nephew onto the back of Sadie behind the saddle. Mr. Pennington then tied Alexander's pole to the saddle. Alexander grabbed James around the waist with both hands clinched tight. James perceived Alexander's uncomfortableness on the horse.

"You do much riding up in New Jersey?" he asked Alexander as he rode Sadie back up Fairfax Street towards Wilkes Street.

"No, I'm a city boy. Newark is a good-sized city. We mostly have servants who drive us around in carriages when we need to go out."

"Well, hold on tight then. We're heading out the Hancock Grade toward the river. It's about six miles to the river from here. Come on, Frank and Billy, let's get it!"

James trotted his horse around the corner of Fairfax and Wilkes Streets heading back across Cornelius Road, and then went straight up Wilkes Street trotting onto the Hancock Grade. As he rode along he thought Berkeley Springs to be a most beautiful mountainous area. He loved the wild and romantic country threaded with horseback and carriage drives in all directions, breezy mountain tops that he often explored, and mineral waters bubbling out of the ground.

A few miles outside of town James noticed a rockslide that had fallen from Warm Springs Ridge. The white rocks, which had come down close to the Hancock Grade, had cascaded in all directions at the bottom of the ridge. He obliquely rode forward toward the fallen rocks. When he came close to them he marveled at the glistening white sand piles that had come down with the rockslide.

"Hold up here a minute, boys. I want to see what this rockslide has brought down with it," he said sliding off Sadie's back onto the ground.

He scooped up a handful of granulated white sand, as pure as sugar.

"This looks like you could put it on your porridge in the mornin'. I wonder what you could make with it."

He put the handful in a satchel bag attached to the saddle.

"Let's get going, James. You always have to investigate everything," Billy chastised.

James remounted by climbing onto one of the big white rocks that had come down off the ridge. Alexander gave him a hand up onto Sadie's back. They rode four miles out of town past Orrick's Spring.

"Lover's go up there to kiss," Frank said to Alexander. "It's called Lover's Leap. Wonder if you've to jump over after you kiss the girl?"

"Don't be silly, Frank. I suspect you're supposed to jump and leap for joy after you kiss a girl, not kill yourself," James retorted.

"How would you know, James? You never kissed a girl have you?"

"No, but I've a cousin here in town tonight who I'd like to kiss. She's real pretty."

⌒⊙⌒

They rode by Brosius Heights to their right and traveled down into the flat alluvial flood plain area below the Heights. As he descended to the river he could see the Baltimore and Ohio Railroad tracks, the ferry to Hancock, the Potomac River, and a canal boat being pulled by a mule along the Chesapeake and Ohio Canal. They turned their horses westward up the river to the fishing hole Billy had spoken of, with the town of Hancock on the other side of the river. They dismounted at the hole and fastened their lead straps around tree trunks.

James heard the sound of a steam whistle approaching on the B&O tracks. Billy's fishing hole was close to the tracks.

"I bet that's the president's train coming toward us after dropping the president at Sir Johns Run!" James exclaimed.

"Could be!" Alexander said. "Maybe we should wave in case he has decided to get off at Hancock."

"Y'all can wave all day. I'm goin' fishing," Billy said.

James heard the reverberating thunder come around the bend as the steam train suddenly appeared, coming toward them blasting the whistle. They all waved, just in case Alexander was right, as the train screeched by on the rails.

"Let's fish and gig," he said. "The president will be in town when we get back. I promised supper for my family tonight. I don't want to let Father down. He always reminds me I'm the 'firstborn'. That means I've extra duty in the family because of it."

They walked to the fishing hole and prepared their hooks with large worms. James carefully observed Alexander, as he seemed to know exactly how to bait the line. He had assured James on the ride to the river that he had expert New Jersey-learned talents as a fisherman. Alexander seemed to be as smart as he was. They took a liking to each other. They talked about living in the North as opposed to living in the South. They talked about their families, realizing they were quite similar in aristocratic terms, both being part of the established ruling class. Alexander informed him that New Jersey had slaves, too. He told him that some slaves lived next door to him in Newark and that he was friends with them.

⌒⊙⌒

A few hours passed and the sun was descending in the sky, settling over the ridge behind them. James had amassed a pile of black bass. He noticed Alexander getting restless as he sat on a rock in the river.

"James, I'm not having as much luck as you're having. Maybe I could try my hand at gigging frogs," Alexander said.

"Sure thing, Alexander. Come over here. I'll show you how to gig frogs," he said.

James gave him a few lessons with the spear before Alexander waded into the swift currents of muddy water. James knew the current was running fast, and thought the color of the water was brown from all the mud washing down into the river.

"Be careful," James cautioned. "The currents can pull you in quickly if you lose your footing."

"You sound like my father, always telling me what to do. I'm fine; go back to your fishing."

James had seen Frank and Billy move down stream earlier. He felt comfortable with knowing the older and stronger boys would protect Alexander from harm's way. He picked up his pole and went back to fishing.

Suddenly, James saw his gigging spear fly up in the air and Alexander's body being pulled under the brown water by the swift current. He stood on his rock, dropped his pole and he yelled downstream.

"Frank, Billy! Alexander has gone down! Save him!"

James saw Alexander's arms flailing as his head bobbed in and out of the wild currents that had caught him, pulling him under. The currents moved Alexander farther out toward the middle of the river. James ran downstream after him, passed Frank and Billy who stood paralyzed with their poles in hand, and watched Alexander struggle to keep his head above the water.

"Come on, boys, he's drowning!" James shouted, running out of breath.

James came to a pool along the bank. He sat down and quickly pulled off his shoes and shirt. He recklessly jumped into the Potomac's muddy waters. The currents drew him out toward Alexander. James struggled to keep his head above the water as the powerful undertow was pulling him down, too. James did not fight the current, but used it as he swam toward Alexander, spitting out the dirty water that tasted like algae.

He reached Alexander just as he felt the boy's strength giving out. James grabbed him by the scruff of his shirt neck and paddled with his other arm toward the shore.

"Don't fight me, Alexander! I've got you now!" James assured, aggressively stroking the waters and using the currents to draw closer and closer to shore.

He was near exhaustion when he spied a large tree that had fallen into the river up ahead. He dragged Alexander behind him like a sack of potatoes, dead weight in the water. He reached out and grabbed a branch from the fallen tree and pulled with all his strength, working his way toward the main trunk of the tree. He managed to lodge Alexander up against the trunk as the current rushed by. Through sheer will power, James inched along the trunk until he could feel the rocks beneath his feet, never letting go of Alexander's shirt collar. The slippery rocks on the bottom, mixed with the mud, made it difficult for him to regain his footing.

"Alexander, are you all right?" James said as he steadied his footing on the round rocks of the river bed; there was no reply.

He firmly hit Alexander on his back with his open hand and Alexander coughed up muddy water.

"You're okay now! Cough up the water."

"Yes, I got a mouthful," Alexander sputtered; "thought I was going to drown."

"Walk with me, you're fine now. I've got you. Steady. Frank, Billy, help him out," James called as Frank and Billy waded into the river, out of breath.

"Alexander, I've got you! That musta been a big frog to knock you over. Did ya get your spear in him?" Frank asked, making light of the situation.

"I didn't see what knocked me off my feet, but I know it wasn't a frog," Alexander replied.

James and the boys walked back upstream to the spot where he had shed his shoes and shirt. They all sat down to catch their breath. James put his shoes and shirt back on. The boys then continued back to the fishing hole and the horses. James, always the responsible one, collected his stringer of fish and secured them to Sadie's saddle. They rode back to town as the sun set behind Warm Springs Ridge.

ตจงอ

The crowd of spa visitors gathered around James and the boys on the front porch of the Pavilion Hotel. Mr. Pennington stood next to Alexander with his arm over both his and James's shoulders as Colonel Strother stood next to him and listened to the story. The Maryland aristocrat-politician and novelist John Pendleton Kennedy also listened attentively as Frank shared their adventure of the day. Mary Ragan Macgill and her three daughters listened eagerly, Mollie standing next to him. Frank and Billy told the story to the crowd of James's brave rescue of Alexander.

"I should think the president would like to hear of such gallant behavior," said John Blair Hoge, an accomplished lawyer from Martinsburg who stood in the crowd.

"Yes indeed, I'll summon him at once," said Captain William E. Bowie, a Marylander.

James saw President Polk appear on the porch after a few minutes, and the story was told again by the boys. James remained quiet. He looked toward his new friend Alexander, while Mollie stared admiringly at him. She thought he was her gallant and brave cousin.

13

Yuletide and the Wild Hunt

JAMES AWAKENED CHRISTMAS MORNING with high winds howling across the plains of Centreville and battering against his cabin door. Visions of his past Christmases swirled through his thoughts, blowing pleasant memories in and out of his half-asleep mind. His rustic cabin confines hardly reminded him of Bai-Yuka. He rolled off the bunk and placed pine kindling and a cedar log on the embers of the fire. He could see his breath in the cabin as he set his bare feet down on the compacted dirt floor, and the cold sensation sent chills up his legs. He felt a decided absence of Christmas warmth and joyous spirit.

"Henry, Bill, Robert, wake up everyone, it's Christmas Day. Old Santa Claus has been here and left me coals for the fireplace. You all must not have been good this year, since all you got was green pine," James laughed as he stood shivering in his red skivvies looking around the cabin at his eight fellow artillerists.

Bill Clem rolled over in the top bunk above his bed. James thought Bill was a rather odd-looking man, robust as a pear, with a fair complexion, light colored short hair, round face with goatee and moustache. Bill did not bother to place his spherical glasses on over his hazel eyes, which stared annoyingly at James.

"In my Maryland home we didn't give no count to your Santa Claus. Christmas was just another day. Go back to sleep, James. It's too cold to be up and botherin' your cabinmates," Bill proclaimed as he rolled his back against the mud chinked cabin logs.

"You fellas are no fun. Guess I'll write a letter to Mollie," James declared, pulling a stool closer to the radiant heat now swelling from the primitive fireplace.

Feeling shunned by his cabinmate, Bill, he picked up his pen, warmed the ceramic inkwell and began to write. He figured at least Mollie would like to know he was thinking of her on Christmas Day:

Centreville, Va., December 25, 1861

Dearest Mollie,

I have pressed pen, ink, and paper into service this Christmas Day, and am cheered knowing that when all other enjoyments, save that of thinking and dreaming of the dear ones I have left behind, are taken away from me by the wild excitement of this military life, I can huddle next to a warm fire and write to you.

I fondly remember the cedar Christmas tree, the little colored glass lamps having been lighted among its branches, with the gifts spread under its lower branches. The stockings hung from the mantle, filled with balls, knives, and thimbles; dolls in boxes and eye-catching books. How we crouched at the entrances of the parlor, behind the doors, beneath the stairs or wherever else our bodies found snug anchorage until Father let us loose upon the gifts. I recall my brothers and sisters taking down the well-stuffed stockings with glee. Father would proclaim, "Merry Christmas, James"; "Merry Christmas, Uncle"; "Merry Christmas, Grandpa." We would salute him with affectionate cries of "Merry Christmas, Father."

The egg-noggin had passed from room to room during the morning. When Mother rang the dinner bell, merriment was in the hearts of us all. For us, the lion and the lamb were at peace, symbolized by the two groaning dining tables. More family had arrived to join in the feast spread over the tables with every delicacy imaginable. We all awaited the moment when Willie, our old faithful servant, came in with a colossal platter with the boar's head.

In this Spartan camp, I miss our Breathed traditional "Old English Yuletide Wild Hunt" on South Mountain. Nor will I see, this season, the fruits of the Hunt, the boar's head with an enormous apple in his gaping mouth, encircled in bay leaves and rosemary, set down before us on our Christmas Day table by Willie. My ears burn now with the sound of carols we sang as Willie placed the boar's head before Father. Father always tells of the Old English tradition of the Wild Hunt and the legend of Hereward the Wake. We Breatheds would lift our glasses to toast the Boar's Head. He had given his life so that we could make merry on Christmas Day. Our Old Scottish English fathers celebrated the Hunt and we toasted them. We toasted the "Lord of Chrystmasse," for we are Scottish, not Dutch.

After dinner Father delivered gifts of love to the adults, and they all shared hugs and kisses. The presents of gold, myrrh, and frankincense given to the baby Jesus historically were shared by all.

Knowing the pain you must feel with the cruel absence of your Father, I am in hopes these lines may find you and yours enjoying your health, trusting that God will protect the good doctor. You were the love of my boyhood, the hopeless love of my early manhood, and my affection for you deepens yet.

Our 1st Lieutenant Pelham is a fine Alabamian and a West Point man. He is beloved by the whole Stuart Horse Artillery and praised by everybody else.

The "High Command" has placed vanward in the Southern Confederacy soldiers capable and eager to lead the valiant states onward to conquer and to triumph over our despotic foes. The artillerymen are bronzed, strapping, sinewy, and it will not take such men of stout body and mind long to inflict terror into the Yankee hearts. We are a fine band of men, like Sir Walter Scott's Highland Chieftain Mac-Ibor Vich Ian Vohr of Glennaquoich. As George Washington's Cincinnatus did many years ago, we will deliver our Country and return to our farms and to our loved ones. I'm content my destiny is in the omniscient hands of a merciful God who has so favored the Southern States. I trust His mysterious Providence is with me and will preserve me for a meaningful life in His service.

I rode with Stuart at Lewinsville, Annandale, and Dranesville. Lieutenant Colonel Fitzhugh Lee is now with the 1st Virginia. He is a rotund, blue eyed, far-gazing soldier with a bold eagle nose. I rode with him on Billy, my Chevalier Bayard, on the forage to Dranesville outside of Washington City. Our squadron arrived mid-morning from the east on two roads and by afternoon the fight to protect our forage wagons began. By chance the town was occupied by many Yankees with their artillery set on hilltops over-looking the town. The Sumter Flying Artillery battery opened the engagement, but it had a caisson blown up. We had to abandon another limber and caisson in the face of superior numbers. Our Infantry retreated after a two hour encounter. My cavalry comrades and I were ordered to protect the wagons, which we had safely bivouacked five miles away. The next morning we rode back to bury our dead and see to the wounded. War is not as glorious as the novelists and politicians would have us believe. I have great reason, Mollie, to be thankful to God for preserving my life through the dreadful conflict of Dranesville. I did not receive a scratch.

I heard about our boys whipping the Yankees at the Battle of Ball's Bluff last Fall. The newspaper accounts I have read reported a "turkey shot" as the Yankees tried to escape back across the Potomac, but had forgotten to bring enough boats. I certainly hope our Williams cousins in Poolesville are all safe. Do you hear anything from them about the Battle? It is always good to hear about our victories!

I would like to see you. I can get leave of absence and see you at Oatlands Plantation outside of Leesburg. If you are so inclined and able, I would walk through deep snow to see you there on January 9th. I am friends with George Carter, whose family owns Oatlands. He is supplying us with good horses. He will give us rooms and meals while we stay. I know getting from Hagerstown to Oatlands will not be easy, but cousin Lige White reckons he can get it done.

If you can come, please see if you can find a copy of John Esten Cooke's novel, "The Last of the Foresters: Humors on the Borders, A Story Of The Old Virginia Frontier." I met Cooke and would like to read his work. I have been reading William Gilham's "Authorized Cavalry Tactics, U.S.A.: Manual of Instruction" and also "Manual of Instruction for the Volunteers and Militia of the Confederate

States" published in Richmond earlier this year. However, this Manual reading is heavy work and I would enjoy a novel.

Now I have written you a long prosy letter. Give my love to all my cousins. I shall count the days and the hours until the day I see you again. Take good care of yourself.

Merry Christmas,
Jas

James folded the letter carefully and enclosed it in an envelope. He noticed that his cabin mates were now up and about. He dressed in his Thomas jeans, put on his coat, and went out. He gave the envelope to one of Lige's scouts who said he would give it to Lige directly, shaking his hand. James then walked toward a huge Christmas bonfire around which many of his artillerist comrades had gathered.

"Merry Christmas, Breathed," Pelham said. "We're just sharing our family Christmas traditions. Would you like to tell yours?"

"Come on, Breathed, regale us with a tradition or two from Old Maryland," 3rd Lieutenant William Hoxton said.

He looked at this Fauquier County gentleman, a William and Mary man who rated a Lieutenant's commission, a commission he had eschewed in order to enlist in the ranks. Bill, Robert, and Henry emerged from the cabin and rubbed their hands together against the cold. Soon they had all gathered closer to the fire.

"Our celebration of the season always begins with the 'wild hunt,' which was an Old English tradition," James replied. "My father and I'd ride east on National Road, a few days before Christmas, to Mountain House at Turner's Gap in South Mountain and spend the night. Early the next morning our servant Willie would drive the wagon and the hounds to Fox's Gap on the mountain to hunt the elusive and dangerous boar. I carried my trusty .50 caliber Hawken rifle."

James told them how he and his father would ride out from Fox's Gap following the hounds until their howls signaled the hunt was on. The hounds would surround and exhaust the boar. Last year it was his honor to pull his Hawken and take steady aim for a killing shot behind the boar's front leg. He shot from his horse and as soon as the great beast tumbled to the ground his father yelled excitedly, "Kill the boar! Cut the beast's throat! Kill it!"

James told them that he calmly dismounted and retrieved his hunting knife from the satchel. After calling off the hounds, he walked over to the kicking and struggling boar. He grabbed the boar by the ear, careful to avoid its long, razor-sharp tusks, and thrust the knife into the flesh of the beast's throat. The blood rushed out onto the ground as the boar breathed and kicked its last.

Creole, who stood across the fire from him, was somewhat taken aback by the "Christmas tradition" of Maryland gentlemen.

Creole shared, "Hey Breathed, after all, we aren't savages really. We are soldiers who are paid to kill Yankees. But, you seem to enjoy killing."

"Let him continue, Creole," Lieutenant Hoxton interjected, annoyed by the interruption.

Taking no notice of the interruption, James continued, "My father came over to the boar and shook my hand and said to me, 'Merry Christmas, son.' Father and I tied the hind legs of the fallen boar with a rope, swung the rope over a tree limb and fastened the rope to the saddle. Father led the horse forward and the beast came off the ground and hung in the air."

He told them how he had used surgical knives to cut the head from the boar's body, and how he had sawed the spinal cord and severed the head from the beast with precision so that the Christmas platter would contain a work of art. He had then held up the head toward the sky and thanked God for another successful "wild hunt," as the warm blood of the beast dripped upon his arms and clothes. Lastly, he told of how he had butchered the boar, alone in the forest, as his father rode back to get Willie and the wagon to load the meat for the Christmas Day feast.

"Breathed, did the end of your innocence begin with your first wild hunt'?" Pelham inquired. "Breathed family 'Old English' traditions seem a bit grim."

James looked up from the fire for the first time, looking at Pelham with a slightly puzzled expression. After a few seconds of silence, Pelham quickly went on, "How does your tradition end on Christmas Day?"

"Bai-Yuka, my home outside of Hagerstown, was always lovingly decorated to the hilt by my mother and sisters. Christmas Day culminated with the dinner and tables of delicious food. Family came from all around to celebrate the birth of Christ with us. At the appropriate hour, Willie was summoned to have the honor of the presentation of the boar's head, which he always did solemnly and with great pride. He would place the boar's head on a platter before my father and we'd toast it!" he said looking around the fire at the trancelike silence into which his comrades had fallen.

For a few moments no one moved or took their eyes off of James.

Finally, Pelham said, "Would anyone else like to share their family Christmas Day traditions?"

14

A Virginia Tryst

THE MORNING WAS BITTERLY cold as Mollie and Alfred departed the Macgill home. The wheels of the black landau coach crackled against the frozen surface of South Potomac Street as they traveled to the home of Colonel Jacob Hollingsworth. Mollie had dressed warmly in a black cape with slits for her arms. She wore a black bonnet with a wide cloth ribbon to keep her ears warm and in her lap a fur muff for hand warmth. She had told Alfred to layer his clothes, for he would face the elements without the protection of the coach.

She had always known Jacob to be a man of prominence in the Hagerstown community. She saw him standing at the door of his house, smoking a pipe while waiting for her to arrive. He wore a three-piece suit with his vest tightly buttoned and the white collar of an Episcopal priest. He stood a lanky six feet tall, had a long narrow face, a speckled thin-cut beard, and moustache. He warmly greeted Mollie as he climbed up into the carriage.

Jacob was not an ordained priest, nor even a deacon, but he had been on the vestry of Saint John's Episcopal Church in Hagerstown with her father for many years. Mollie had always admired that he was well versed in the current Episcopalian politics and the ways of the clergy; he knew the Macgill family well. She had previously alerted him to the nature of the trip into Virginia and had discussed with the sage seventy-two-year-old Southern gentleman the objective. He had informed her that his ruse of "Father" would pay dividends in getting past the watchful Yankees. She understood he had unsettled business with anyone who proclaimed themselves a Yankee.

She chatted with Jacob as Alfred drove the two-up team of horses south on the Valley Turnpike toward Williamsport and the Potomac River. Their surreptitious journey on Valley Pike was encumbered by numerous mandated stops by Federal horsemen. Their rhetoric of "official church business" with clergy in Winchester seemed to mollify the skepticism of the soldiers.

They arrived at the Williamsport Ferry, and she looked around to see that it was well protected. A great many Federal troops were milling up and down the river. She looked out her window to see that the tall and sturdy pole of the ferry was anchored by two metal cable lines that spread in a V formation from its apex to the ground. The cable crossed to the Virginia side of the Potomac River through the round house wheel. It was anchored on Virginia soil in the same fashion as on the Maryland side. They rode to the loading dock and nonchalantly halted the team.

"Let me see your papers," a gruff blue-coated Federal corporal demanded.

Her anxiety level rose as several well-armed privates surrounded the coach.

"You most certainly may," Jacob said. "I'm Father Jacob Hollingsworth from the Saint John's Church in Hagerstown. I'm accompanying Miss Mollie Johnston here to Winchester. We've official Episcopal Church business to attend to at Christ Church in Winchester. Her sister in that parish is seriously ill and declining fast."

"I'm sorry to learn of your sister's infirmity, Miss Johnston," the Federal picket said as he returned the pass Jacob had handed him.

"Thank you for your kind words," she said tearfully sitting with her black skirt draped over the coach seat.

With one hand she handed her "Lige White" authenticated papers to the picket and with her other hand she felt under the coach seat for her five-shot Colt patent revolver.

"Through your affiliation with my church, for I, too, am Episcopalian, I believe I can trust a man of the cloth! If not a brother Episcopalian, then who can I trust? Darky, drive on to the ferry," the Federal picket said, returning the papers to her as he waved Alfred forward.

⇛

Her stamina was tried on the jarring journey south on the Valley Pike. The stress of the encounter at the ferry and the extreme cold caused her to shiver. She wondered at times if her hasty, ill-defined mission was going to be worth it, but she was ready to risk anything for the cause. To keep her mind off the cold, she explained to Jacob her role in the gathering of information for Lige White. Her work had influenced the outcome of the Battle of Ball's Bluff.

Mollie felt comfortable sharing her experience, now that they were in friendly territory. Jacob was a long-standing friend of both the Macgill and Breathed families; she knew he could be trusted.

They reached Winchester late that night, and she discovered General Thomas J. Jackson's rearguard occupied the town. Getting past the Confederate pickets was easily done when she produced the signed pass Lige had prepared, in his own handwriting, ordering that all assistance be given her.

A picket approached the coach, "Sir, can you inform my driver as to how to find Commander Peter Gip's headquarters?" Mollie asked.

"Yes, I'll do so straightaway. Here are your papers."

They arrived at the headquarters and exited the coach to speak to the commander.

"Miss, I understand you are kin to Lige White. He wrote and told me to expect you," the commander said as he warmly greeted them.

"How do you do, sir." Mollie responded.

"My name is Colonel Jacob Hollingsworth. I'm escorting Miss Macgill on her mission, a family friend you understand."

"I certainly do, a pleasure. I'm in charge of White's underground network line of couriers. We've been rather successful in collecting intelligence from his large network of agents and speeding it to General D. H. Hill's headquarters. I understand the importance of you both getting to Oatlands. I've arranged for food and warm lodgings. I've a soldier who will show you the way to the house, free from the prying eyes of Federal spies. I've also arranged for housing for your coachman."

"Very well, Commander. We're grateful for your assistance," she responded.

"In the morning, Peter will guide you to Berryville. Joseph Conner will meet you there and guide you to Castleman's Ferry, C. C. Wenner will take you to Round Hill. Frank Myers will take you to Hamilton, and William Luckett will get you safely to Kate Coleman's at Leesburg where you'll spend the night."

"You've done a lot of planning. Thank you so much. If you don't mind, we're exhausted and need some food and rest," Jacob said as he shook the commander's hand and bid him adieu.

"Good evening, sir. Thank you," Mollie said, and then turned toward the door.

❧☙

After another long day's journey, they finally arrived at Leesburg to be warmly greeted by Kate Coleman. The next morning, well refreshed, Mollie, Kate, and Jacob joined Lige for breakfast.

"Lige, so good to see you," Mollie said as she kissed him on the check.

"Always a pleasure to see you, Mollie. I hope your travels were safe and uneventful," Lige remarked as he pulled out her chair and seated her at the table.

"This is Colonel Jacob Hollingsworth, a long time friend of the family."

"Colonel, a pleasure," Lige said as he shook his hand. "I assume you've had some time to talk with Kate."

"Not much, we arrived very late last night."

"I got them a meal and to bed as quick as I could last night," Kate said as Jacob pulled her chair and seated her.

"Kate, when did you last speak with Laura Ratcliffe?" Lige asked.

"Why just the other day. She let me know to expect Mollie and Jacob."

"Laura has been doing fine work in providing intelligence to Jeb Stuart. The general has been very complimentary of her efforts."

"Kate, I understand you've never been to George Carter's Oatlands Plantation. He has proven to be quite a partisan for our cause," Mollie said.

"I do look forward to meeting him today. We should eat and move on down the Carolina Road. It'll be rather brisk this morning," Kate replied.

"Certainly," Lige responded as he began to eat his breakfast.

⤷◌◌⤶

James tucked his chin down into his greatcoat, riding along the Old Carolina Road on Billy, approaching the end of his twenty-five mile journey from Centreville to Oatlands Plantation. Strong winds whipped around rider and steed, who had become one for the sake of warmth. The light snow on the ground melted as temperatures inched above freezing. The prospect of seeing Mollie again, if she did make the journey, kept his spirits high.

He rode the Old Carolina Road, which was a direct route from Centreville to Oatlands Plantation. Turning off the road onto Plantation Lane with plenty of light left in the day, he turned Billy left onto the circle in front of the Oatlands Plantation manor. He knew George Carter II was the sole resident proprietor of the Oatlands House; his mother owned Oatlands.

He marveled at the front porch with its four columns two stories high with ornately carved leaf patterns at the top. He could feel the influence of "King" Carter from the Colonial period in the stately manor. A slave came around from the back of the home and took Billy's reins from him as he dismounted.

James looked up when his feet hit the ground and there Mollie stood on the front porch smiling at him. He was no longer cold. His warmth of spirit radiated over to her, and words at this moment could not express their feelings.

"Welcome to Oatlands," George said with a gracious smile while standing next to Mollie on the red stone porch. "Feel free to take a stroll in the garden before supper. I'm sure you two have a lot of catching up to do from what Mollie has told me."

James smiled back at George who was dressed as a proper country gentleman, with an off-white frock coat that came to just above his knees. The collar of the coat was black and it matched his neatly tied cravat. His vest was black and buttoned to the top.

James maneuvered around the mounting block and walked up the porch steps with a lightness that belied his stiff limbs. He smartly grasped George's hand and greeted him warmly, and then he placed his right hand on his waist making an elbow into which Mollie could slide her arm. He turned with her securely in tow and they stepped down from the porch. He suddenly felt a sensation of warmth in contrast to the harsh, winter weather. They preceded toward the brick pillars of the garden gate.

"It's so good to see you, Mollie. You've been my constant thought since I last saw you at Bai-Yuka," he said as they continued through the garden gate, turned right and took the first series of stone steps down into the garden. The huge boxwoods along the path sheltered them from the wind.

"James, there's so much to tell you that I scarcely know where to begin," she said as he dropped his elbow and reached to hold her hand.

"I want to hear all about what you have been doing. But first, what news of your father?"

"None," she said in a sober voice. "The Yankees have him shut up tightly in Fort Warren and will allow us no communications. Our house is watched constantly by Yankee agents. They seem to fear him more than Johnston's army. They've no legal grounds for holding him. We've heard that he refuses all loyalty oaths and, with his status as a hero of Maryland, they fear his influence on Maryland politics if he's released."

He could sense the pride in her voice as she talked of her father.

"As well they might. He's the most honorable man I've ever known. He's known to be such, even by Marylanders of Union sentiments. One of his stirring speeches would be worth a division of Southern infantry."

She grew quiet as they walked farther into the garden.

"What of your mother and sisters?" he asked. "How're they taking this?"

"Mother's health is not good, but she rarely complains. My sisters are bitter, especially Alice, but we're Macgills, so we do what we can to dissuade our persecutors," she sighed with anguish.

They had come down three flights of stone steps, and some distance in front of them was a waist-high stone wall that enclosed the whole garden. They crossed a terrace until they approached a well of stone that rested on four stone blocks. It looked as if it was from the medieval period. He noticed an ornate metal piece resembling nothing so much as a horseshoe over the well, as he quietly took her other gloved hand.

"Mollie, your hands are so cold! Your trip must have been an ordeal."

Before she could reply, he squeezed her hands in order to warm them.

"James, I've something I'd like you to know about. In one of my letters to you I promised I'd get involved in this war. I've done so. After they arrested Father, I went to our Williams cousins' plantation to try to get some knowledge of the Yankees' plans for the troops stationed there at Camp Benton and Camp Stone," she said without withdrawing her hands from his.

She proceeded to relate the piecing together of what intelligence she and the Williams family collected, and then explained how she passed the information to Lige. She believed the information was terribly important, particularly the part about the Yankees' lack of boats. She told him that Lige rode off to inform General Evans.

"Mollie, you've done a great service to our country."

"Later, Lige told me that my information resulted in our victory at Ball's Bluff. I've become one of his agents."

As he listened to her tale, his look went from that of interest to astonishment. He suddenly saw her in a whole new light. He suddenly realized that this determined young woman, whom he still considered just a young girl, had been responsible for killing more Yankees than he had; more importantly, she secured a Southern victory. His deeds of arms suddenly seemed insignificant. After she finished her tale, he couldn't restrain himself. He looked into her eyes for a moment with a dozen conflicting emotions lighting up his face. He spontaneously kissed her on the cheek. She, far from being shocked, stared deeply back into his eyes. He kissed her again, this time on the lips. Again she did not shy away, but only slowly pulled back with a strange light in her eyes. After a timeless moment, with his heart racing, he let go of her now warm hands.

"Mollie, I apologize for taking such a liberty. Please forgive my impulsiveness."

"There's nothing to forgive, James. I admit I wasn't expecting your passion. The look on your face was such as a woman usually only dreams of seeing but once in a lifetime."

Her response left him speechless. For a few seconds only cupid could tell the tale of their hearts from the pattern of their breath that hung in the frosty air. She turned slowly and made a tentative step back toward Oatlands.

"This information shouldn't be shared, even at the table tonight. Your safety is in silence. If you're caught, you could end up in a cell like your father . . . or worse," he said, falling in beside her as they began the walk back to the manor.

In silence, they moved through the darkness that engulfed them, arm in arm. They walked back up the three series of stone steps and through the entrance gate, each wrapped in their own thoughts. Had they but known, but were afraid to acknowledge, they had both just seen their own reflection in the other, like in a mirror, sparked by a kiss. They walked the short distance to the Oatlands manor, climbed the front porch steps, opened the front door and entered the great room.

He looked around the room and took note of the tall case clock, which he had just heard chime seven times. His eyes gazed at fine oil portraits and commissioned copies in oil of great masterpieces hanging on the walls. The ceiling molding around the room was exquisitely carved, probably by German masters, he thought. A trophy elk head had just caught his eye when George entered the great room from beneath its muzzle.

"Woodrow, please help my guests with their coats," George said to the house servant as he helped Mollie out of her black cloak. She handed her bonnet to Woodrow and George gave him her cloak and James's greatcoat. He still wore his 1st Virginia Cavalry uniform, which had kept him warm on the journey to Oatlands.

"Business before pleasure," James said. "I've the requisition papers signed by 1st Lieutenant Pelham for the twenty horses you so generously offered to the Stuart Horse Artillery. Will you be accompanying me on the ride back to Centreville in the early morning?"

He handed over the papers to George.

"Certainly, Doctor, or should I call you James?"

"James will be fine. I remember our first meeting years ago in front of the School of Medicine. A lot has happened since then, but none of it diminishes the pleasure of seeing you again, George."

Out of the corner of his eye he noticed Lige, Jacob, and Kate walking into the great room. The smells from the kitchen wafted through his nostrils. With the soft, courteous voice peculiar to a Virginia gentleman, George invited them to the dining room.

"George, that's a unique canteen of cutlery on the beautiful sideboard," Mollie said. "I love the vases by the clock. What vintage is the clock over the fireplace?"

"The clock belonged to King Carter, from whom I had the honor to descend a few generations back. The College of William and Mary gave him the clock for his many years of service as a trustee."

James surveyed the table, which he thought could seat ten, but this night was set for six. Although the dinner was formal, the seating was not. George did not sit at the head of the table, as James had expected he would; rather George seated himself on the kitchen side of the table. Across from him sat Jacob; Kate was seated on George's right, beside Jacob. Lige took his place next to Kate, and James was seated next to Mollie on his other side.

Mollie felt like a queen as she looked at the blue and white Canton ware set on the white table cloth. White napkins and fine silverware were set, and candle après and other larger Canton ware pieces were at the center of the table. The arrangement resembled that of her own family's table set.

George summoned the liveried house servants, and the first course of oysters from Alexandria were placed before them. When James was served he asked the colonel to return thanks and bless the food.

"George, if you'd be so kind, tell us about the operation of your plantation. I grew up on a small plantation, though nothing like the size of Oatlands," James said, speaking up after the blessing.

He listened as George modestly described his stock, crops, yields, and all in such detail that it was apparent that he was no absentee landlord or the owner of a struggling agrarian enterprise.

As course followed course, James enjoyed the conversation at the table, which ranged from George's relating highlights of his European trip, through the writings of Karl Marx, the latest works of Dickens, and the new theory of Charles Darwin's on human beings having evolved from apes.

After the servants had cleared away the remains of dinner and served the nuts, the little group lapsed into silence, preparatory to the conversation taking a more serious turn.

"George, in regards to your tour of Europe, I'd be indebted if you would share your observations on what the Europeans make of our oppression by our would-be masters, particularly as regards to their sympathy for the righteousness of our cause," Jacob said, breaking the silence.

"I toured Paris, Munich, and Liverpool, with many side excursions along the way. As to sympathy for our cause, I found little. Bismarck has his eyes on lands in

Poland and Denmark; England and France have their eyes on Bismarck," George replied frowning slightly for a moment.

"But surely with its dependence on Southern cotton for its factories, the English cannot leave the Yankee blockade long in place without ruining their economy," Jacob replied.

"The English saw this coming. Both '59 and '60 were bumper years for cotton in the Deep South. The English bought a record number of bales at a goodly price. I saw this on my '60 tour as the docks at Liverpool unloaded a seemingly endless mountain of cotton bales, ship after ship, with more ships at anchor waiting their turn. The cotton warehouses of England are full to bursting. They feel no economic hardship at this time."

James thought about George's observations, not knowing exactly how to respond.

"Maybe that's so for now. However if the war goes on, England may yet feel the pinch." Jacob somewhat emphatically responded.

"It's not just cotton," George replied. "The grain harvests of Europe have been poor for two years. Without Yankee grain exports, England and France could face starvation among the working classes. Then there's Bismarck. Europe has still not recovered from the affects of the Crimean War, and I believe Bismarck is determined to get land from his neighbors for a new German state. England won't bring on another conflict with the Union while things are so unsettled on the Continent. Then there's Canada. If England intervenes openly and precipitates war with the Federals, Canada would be an easy prize for the Yankees to take."

"Very interesting observations, George," James said.

"It's deeper than that," said George. "While the nobility of England support the South, the masses do not. Prime Minister Palmerston dare not force war in the face of opposition from Mill, Bright, and Cobden. As long as the South maintains slavery, the masses will be cold to her."

"What about France?" Lige asked, finally speaking up.

"Emperor Napoleon is not to be trusted. He schemes and dreams. He promises one thing to you and the opposite thing to your foe. God save us from depending on France," George replied with a sneer.

"I've heard that phrenology is all the medical rage in Paris," Jacob said.

"I believe it's simply 'pseudoscience,'" James piped as he felt the guests were beginning to look depressed.

George looked up and began speaking in a more cheerful vein. "What the South needs is victories at arms. Inflict a stunning defeat on the Yankees and we'll have all the European allies we need."

"Well, we can't have a victory unless we have a battle," Lige spoke up again. "When will McClellan come out from behind his fortifications and fight? My agents can only find conflicting rumors. Lincoln wants Little Mac to attack, but Little Mac ignores him. The two most persistent rumors are that Mac will attack Johnston at Manassas or that he'll sail his army down the bay and attack Richmond from the water. But where? And when? Johnston must know so he can maneuver."

James observed Lige glancing around the table, but there were no answers to his questions. What Lige saw was a remarkably quiet James Breathed glance briefly at Mollie, and then become lost in thought. Kate looked across at James as if she would speak, but received no encouragement. James noticed Jacob looking rather tired, nodding off after a fine supper; George looked a bit ill at ease that he had depressed his guests. Mollie had a strange look on her face, glancing up at Lige with some determination.

"Mollie, what news of your father?" Lige asked.

It took Mollie a few moments to collect her thoughts. "I constantly wonder how he is doing, imprisoned with no warrant, no right of habeas corpus. I think he's now at Fort Warren in Boston."

James perceived that Lige's words seemed to alert Jacob.

"Mollie, I feel for you and your father," Jacob said. "He is a close friend and we've served the church together since '43. I know he's taking care of his comrades jailed with him, and probably his jailers too. He's a man of true virtue and admirable character. As some of you may not be aware, I lost one of my best friends to the infernal abolitionists in Carlisle, Pennsylvania, in '47."

James listened as Jacob told them that James Kennedy had gone north to get his twelve runaway slaves back. The abolitionists ended up murdering Kennedy. No trial, no investigation ensued after the crime. Jacob had never gotten over his death, and to this day he blamed those abolitionist Yankees.

"You know, James, I sold Bai-Yuka Plantation to your father. The judge is a good man. With John Jr. and you serving the Confederacy, I'm surprised they have not come for your father," Jacob said.

James quickly changed the topic of conversation from his father.

"The question we all need to address is, under McClellan's command, what is the Federal army going to do next? Where and when?" James smiled briefly at Kate. "Kate, I know you've been doing your part, for I remember seeing you helping with the wounded at Frying Pan after Dranesville. Lige informed me you serve with Laura Ratcliffe and her Fairfax County network."

Kate returned a demure smile as James turned to her.

"I learned this afternoon that Mollie did her share to bring about our victory at the Battle of Ball's Bluff," James said.

Lige nodded in polite acknowledgement of his comment about Mollie, his eyes fixed on her. James noticed Lige's fixation with the two of them, and thought his cousin might have something else for her in the world of espionage.

James saw that, by everyone's mutual consent, the dinner began to break up. It had been a long day for them all and the prospect of rest beckoned; George raised his glass to toast.

"To our Southern cause, our Southern women, and to all my friends gathered here to expedite our course to victory! Here—Here!" George said as glasses were clinked all around.

Everyone departed from the table and lingered around the great room. Mollie bid Lige to follow her into the card room so that they could discuss matters in privacy.

"Our cousin is a Methodist Episcopal minister in Baltimore, as you well know," Mollie said. "John Augustus Williams is a protégé of Charles Baker of Baker Brothers & Company. Mr. Baker regularly imports and exports out of Baltimore Harbor. If McClellan is coming by water he'll need every ship in Chesapeake Bay he can get his hands on. Charles Baker will know all about the shipping in Baltimore City. Lige, if you could get a letter from me to John Williams announcing I'm coming for a 'family visit,' I'm certain Cousin John will introduce me properly to Mr. Baker. I may be able to pick up something of interest."

"If you write a letter to John, I'll see it's delivered by the fastest means possible," Lige said.

"I'll do so immediately and give it to you in the morning," Mollie said. "Tomorrow I'll head back to Hagerstown, then get myself to Baltimore City as fast as I can."

"I'll have a courier at Barnum's Hotel. You can get the information to him."

The next morning James was up early seeing to the horses, which took longer than he had anticipated. Mollie was gone by the time he got back to the manor from the stables. He regretted not being able to say good-bye to her. He alleged that in such times as the present the call of duty was understood between them, and superseded personal matters.

On the cold ride back to his camp, his mind was still unsettled. He knew now that she was of much greater depth than he had previously acknowledged. To win her love would take more than being a Maryland gentleman, and more than being a doctor. He would have to become a soldier worthy of her hand.

As he stared down the long, cold Old Carolina Road, herding the twenty horses, he vowed that his service to the South would be such that she would respect him as much as he respected her.

15

Two if by Sea

FEBRUARY 1862

ON THIS COLD DAY of late February Mollie and her cousin Reverend John Augustus Williams were guests in residence at the home of Charles and Elizabeth Baker. Mollie was attired splendidly in a silken, heavy and fine purple paisley day dress. She was warmly attired, as she never knew what sort of blustery weather might arrive off the Chesapeake Bay in late February. She looked around the opulent parlor of the Bakers' home at 66 Paca Street and admired its twelve-foot tall windows and burgundy drapes, through which the afternoon sun glimmered onto a large oriental carpet. A gasolier hung from the center beam of the spacious, well furnished, and comfortable room. Overhead, intricately carved oak beams completed the picture of wealth and strength, she thought.

Mollie knew John had lived with the Bakers for almost a year, after he had graduated from Dickinson College. John had been appointed to serve as minister of the fledgling Chatsworth Methodist Episcopal Church. John and James had attended grammar school together at the College of St. James, both destined to take holy orders, she recollected.

She guessed John was as tall as James Breathed, but there, except for equally penetrating voices, the comparison ended. John was thin and suffered from chronically poor health. In contrast to James' fierce stare, John had sleepy eyelids, although beneath those lids were bright, intelligent, and sympathetic eyes. Where James was given to blunt, profane language, John was of gentle, courteous, and pious speech. James's masculine strength could appeal to strong women, but John would set no hearts aflutter. One trait of John's that particularly endeared him to the Bakers was his way with children, of which the Bakers had seven.

Mollie was immediately struck by Charles's stern countenance as they all chatted in the parlor. He had a pronounced forehead beneath thick, black hair combed back in natural waves; his intelligent, penetrating stare bestowed the businessman with a commanding presence. His acknowledged position as a pillar of Methodism had enabled his rapid rise in Baltimore City politics. Now president of the second branch of the Baltimore City Council and ex officio mayor, Mollie could have been intimidated by him, but was not.

She was a new acquaintance of the Bakers, having come from Hagerstown with a letter of introduction from a trusted business associate, asking Charles to give her every assistance. She felt that once Charles had learned she was the daughter of Dr. Charles Macgill, he would be determined to help her in any way he could.

Mollie eyed the folding doors between the parlor and the hall as the Irishwoman house servant tightly closed them upon departing. Charles and Elizabeth sat in red, leather-backed chairs, while Mollie seated herself on the love seat as John leaned on the mantle.

Mollie and John talked with their hosts. Their talk sometimes strayed to family matters, but always meandered back to the war. Mollie told of how she felt that the war had gripped Maryland so firmly and seemingly for so long that it had marked every door from Western Maryland to the Eastern Shore. While she spoke, she remembered the expressions on some faces that the war had touched and changed forever.

"John, you're the genealogist," Charles stated. "How're you two cousins related?"

"Well, Mr. Baker, Mollie, James Breathed, and myself are all great-great-grandchildren of Reverend James McGill. Elijah White, whom we call Lige, is descended from the Reverend McGill's brother."

Mollie observed Charles thinking a few seconds, and then he changed the subject. "Mollie, I'm sorry the Federals have imprisoned your father. Do you know his whereabouts?"

"Sir, we're not sure, but think he might be at Fort Warren in Boston's Harbor."

"You may call me Charles, my dear. In the '50s your father and I were deeply involved in Maryland politics. We worked hard to overthrow the Know Nothing party's control in our state. Those Know Nothings are against the Jews, Catholics, Free Negroes, and anybody they deem not directly descended from Jamestown and Plymouth. I think America has outgrown this narrow way of thinking."

"What do you feel is the view of most Baltimoreans these days?" Mollie asked while looking at her cousin John. "How is this occupied city coping with the Federals?"

"I feel the unrest of my congregants as we struggle to make Chatsworth a church a Methodist could attend without having to adhere to the Buffalo abolition resolution. Their loyalties are torn. We didn't join the Methodist Episcopal South in '44, although many now wish we had. We cannot in good conscience support the M.E. North abolitionists. None of us like having the heavy-handed Federal martial law in Baltimore City," John said.

"I'd agree with John," Elizabeth said. "We've grown restless with the Federals watching our every move and constantly questioning Charles's allegiance. He is doing his best to run the city despite martial law. It's not easy for him to keep his Southern sympathies off his coat sleeves."

Mollie admired Charles's dapper dress, which looked to her like a penguin in a three-piece suit and smoking his pipe, waving away each puff of smoke before drawing and blowing another. He stood from his leather-back chair and walked across the spacious parlor toward her. She understood his actions to mean he had something on his mind that he wanted to share in secret.

"The Federals are up to something," Charles confided, "but we haven't figured it out yet. The Army Quartermaster Department has chartered steamers from Old Bay Line, Weems Line, Eastern Shore Steamboat Company, and Baltimore & Eastern Shore Steamboat Company. I've used some of these ships to transport my glasswares. I'm sure that they're stockpiling steamers and schooners, but whether it is for supply or soldier transport is not clear. I've observed that up and down Locust Point there is a great concentration of supplying the ships as the vessels at anchor await their turn to dock. I see more activity than usual and the Basin's docks are bustling," Charles said as he turned away from her and walked diagonally across the parlor in a well-worn path toward the hearth.

"Mr. and Mrs. Baker and John, what I've to tell you must be kept in the greatest of confidence because lives depend on it!" Mollie announced as she anxiously stood to pace the floor with Charles. "What I want to share concerns thwarting our oppressors. It also may influence whether James makes it through this war alive. If what I'm about to say becomes known, my father may never be released. I've done some scouting for the Confederates. The Battle of Ball's Bluff was won by our men thanks in part to information I got to Lige White, who then took the information to General Evans. I'm now tasked to find out what General McClellan's next move will be with the Army of the Potomac, and when he might move his Army."

John moved from the mantle over to his cousin. Looking her intently in the eyes, he placed his hands on her right arm, over the ruffles on the sleeves, and tightly grasped her arm.

"Mollie, I know you're concerned for James and your father, but putting your life at stake through spying is serious business," John emphatically stated. "Are you sure you know what you're getting yourself into, cousin?"

"Yes, I know! And I know my father is imprisoned because he won't take that cursed oath! Also, it may interest you to know, John, that your father and sister are involved in the same business I am," she hotly replied. "But, pardon me; that was cruel."

John was clearly shaken by her tone, but a wry smile played across his face as he returned to face the mantle. He and his group of Southern clergy were doing similar service for cousin Lige; evidently she had no idea, and Charles's imperturbable face gave her no clues.

"Mollie, why doesn't your father take the oath?" John asked. "God knows he's too old to take the field of battle. Judge Breathed and Mr. Baker took the oath, yet still work to thwart the Federal efforts to tyrannize us."

"John, since you and James grew up together, I think you'd be well advised not to raise that question around him. Judge Breathed took the oath readily, but I see little that he has done to oppose the Federals. James is furious with his father. Charles, I know your situation is different, since by taking the oath and remaining in office you do all you can to blunt the Federal tyranny."

Charles gazed out the window at the threatening clouds and spoke, "Mollie, I fear that oath or no oath, men of Southern sentiment, such as myself, will soon all be forced from power. But Maryland is my state; I'm proud of her. Maryland should be the model for every slave state in the Union. Besides, this war is not about slavery, it's about race relations. No other state has dealt with this truth better than Maryland. We've as many free darkies as slaves, and more than any other state in the Union. We opened our own colony in Africa to repatriate freed slaves; it became the model for Liberia. The abolitionists want to end slavery, but could care less about the poor darkies who are despised in the North worse than in the South. Thanks to men like your father, Mollie, Maryland has regained popular sovereignty. We were just getting rid of the Know Nothings when this war was thrust upon us. Now our rights are naught. We're occupied by a brutal army captained by unscrupulous politicians and incompetent generals. My place is here, my fight is here, and my enemy is Yankee aggression. I took the oath for Maryland. For Maryland's sake your father did not take the oath. But I've talked long enough. What's your mission, Mollie, and how can we help?"

"I vowed to James I was going to fight this war from home and that I will! I need to know what the Federals' intentions are for all these steamers, schooners, and other transport vessels in the harbor. Charles, how do we find out?"

⁂

Mollie heard the shutter slam so hard outside her window in the Baker home that the howling wind tore it from its hinges and crashed it to the ground. Startled from a fitful sleep, she took a moment to collect herself. She knew that a gale was raging outside as she lit the candle next to her bed, then propped herself up with her pillows, and pulled the covers up to her chin. The flickering candle provided enough light to allow her to see that the hands on the dresser clock stood at two in the morning.

She had dreamed that Federal soldiers had come to arrest her, and the sound of shattering wood and glass seemed to make the dream more real. She began to dress. She heard children crying somewhere in the house. Something was clearly amiss, she thought as she heard a soft knock on the door.

"Mollie, are you all right?" Elizabeth asked, standing outside the door. "May I enter?"

"Just a moment," Mollie responded as she got into a sturdy robe and stepped into her slippers.

She opened the door carefully. Seeing that Elizabeth was alone, she opened it wider to admit her, saying, "It was thoughtful of you to call. What's going on?"

"A terrible storm. Your shutter has blown to the ground, that's all, my dear. But I fear we'll get no more sleep this night. The police have already sent for Charles. There seems to be much damage all over Baltimore City."

"Thank you, Mrs. Baker. I'm all right now."

"Why don't you finish getting dressed, then come downstairs to the parlor? The cook is already up fixing coffee for Charles. We can get some tea. I must go back to the children."

"I'll be right down," Mollie said as Elizabeth turned and left the room.

She went over to the washbasin, poured cold water from the pitcher into the basin and splashed some on her face. Fully awake, she finished dressing. As she walked down the staircase to the second floor, John emerged from his room in his pastoral garments.

They entered the parlor, which was now toasty warm from the Irishwoman's stoking of the hearth earlier. She saw Elizabeth already seated by the fire, with baby Francis in her arms. Charles was dressed for the heavy weather, and she saw that he was downing a large mug of steaming coffee. The house servant soon approached with the tea tray, the pot steaming.

"Good morning," Charles said as he rose from his chair. "Beastly night. I fear I must prove a poor host; I must go out and inspect the damage. Worst storm I can remember for a February without snow, that is. Here, Mollie, take my chair."

"Thank you."

Mollie discerned Charles was clearly tense as he paced the floor waiting for the patrol wagon to take him around Baltimore City. "Before I go, I've something more to say on this war, so you'll understand my position." Charles moved to the hearth, and stared intensely into a deep bed of coals above which flames still played. "George Washington said a wise thing that has always stuck with me, '*In war we should treat our enemies as if one day they might be our friends.*' I wonder what he would think of this nation today. In the first council meeting this year, I quoted Henry Clay, '*Whenever the most valuable elements of union, mutual kindness, reciprocal feelings, equal rights, and frustrated bonds, which now happily unite us, shall be destroyed, all hope for the future of our country shall be extinguished forever.*' I'll oppose tyranny, but not with hate. Whoever wins this war, we'll still have to live next to each other, whether the boundary is a state line or a national border. And we Marylanders don't know on which side of such a border we might find ourselves." A loud pounding on the door announced the arrival of the patrol wagon to take the vice-mayor of Baltimore City on his inspection duties. "I must go. I'll be back as soon as I can, but do not expect me before dawn."

Soon Charles had gone in the patrol wagon. Mollie, John, and Elizabeth sipped their tea.

"I wasn't expecting the Federals to come to your house so late at night," Mollie said. "I must've been in the midst of a dream, being chased by Yankees through the streets of Baltimore City when the shutter fell to the ground and awoke me in a fright."

"You're amongst friends, Mollie, and you need not feel threatened here. If the Yankees come for anyone, it'll be Charles. But I don't think they'll do that, leastwise, not for a while. The way this war is going, the Union is going to need all the medicine bottles Baker Brothers can make. I wouldn't be surprised if our window glass line picks up tomorrow, too."

They consumed their tea slowly while the wind continued to howl outside.

After a while, John spoke up. "I've not been home to the farm in Poolesville in a great many months. Tell me the news of the farm and family."

Mollie replied, "Your father and sisters are doing about as well as can be expected with six thousand Yankees camped on the property. The slaves are getting rich selling food to the soldiers. Seems like the wealthy Yankees sent their sons to Poolesville. One whole regiment came right out of Harvard. They got shot up pretty bad at the Leesburg battle. They even carried Dr. Holmes's son up to the house, shot in the chest. Last I heard he lived. Sarah seems to have taken a fancy to a Yankee soldier from Massachusetts. His name is George Whittemore. I suspect he's a respectable Yankee, if there is such a person. Seems George is quite talkative and Sarah never could keep a secret, so we always know what the Yankees are up to. They've got a telegraph line right from the farm to Washington. They even have an aerial balloon there. The Yankees now call the place the 'Corps of Observation.' Most of the soldiers have moved out into the Shenandoah Valley, but they don't seem to be doing much, or so Sarah tells me in her letters."

"How is it that you get mail so readily?" Elizabeth asked with a skeptical look on her face.

"My cousin, Lige, has a special mail network all along the Potomac," Mollie stated. "It stretches all the way to this city. I hope to get a message to send to Lige when we've learned something of McClellan's plans. John, do you know of James's whereabouts? I was hoping to find out how the Stuart Horse Artillery is getting along in Centreville. He writes me on occasion, but each letter we exchange gets more dangerous."

"I do exchange epistles with Aunt Ann Macgill. She doesn't seem to know much about James. Most of James's siblings are Southern. As soon as one of his brothers gets old enough, sometimes before, he runs off to join up with the Confederate cavalry," John said.

Mollie replied, "Your Aunt Ann Macgill is not doing well and, in fact, is very ill. I also heard that James's sister, Jane, is taken sick as well. The doctors of Hagerstown are puzzled by what might be wrong with them. If my father were home to look after them he might determine their maladies, but that isn't to be."

"I trust that God will watch over them," John said. "James always thought more of your father than his own, and holds his father to his uncle's higher standard. Until Dr. Macgill is released and healthy, I fear there'll be no reconciliation between father and son, if then."

Mollie watched Elizabeth exit the room to look in on the children again. Toward dawn the winds began to abate. They retired to their separate rooms, each with their separate thoughts.

⋘⋙

Mollie was happy that the last day of February dawned calm. She learned of reports of tremendous wind damage all over the city and that ships limped into the basin, which told of damage all over the Chesapeake Bay, including ships foundered and beached by the storm.

She picked up the *Baltimore Sun* and read that Captain Shellhorn, a Philadelphian, and his two sons suffered from the wind and the cold as they were marooned in their ship overnight. The schooner *Alexander* had run ashore as ten-foot waves broke over the vessel. Two dead bodies were taken from the vessel. She also read that ten schooners were blown ashore at Wharton Creek alone, and church steeples were down all over the city.

Charles suggested that Mollie not start back to Hagerstown yet, as the roads were impassible from the thousands of fallen trees. She accepted the Bakers' gracious invitation to stay in residence. Besides, her work was not done.

Charles, busy trying to put the city back in order, was in and out with news over the next few days of her stay. Mollie saw John come and go a good deal while making pastoral calls and meeting with fellow clergy. Meanwhile, Mollie stayed mostly in the Baker house, helping Elizabeth with the children. It was on the 4th of March when Charles reported to them that the Federal agents were frantic to get ships repaired and back in service.

⋘⋙

Mollie marveled at the Bakers' black social landau, which was also well suited to business, with its facing, richly upholstered bench seats. Two large lanterns were set parallel to the coachman's seat, with four-in-hand reins held in the grip of the competent Irish coachman. The coachman patiently awaited those who emerged from the residence. All dressed warmly because of the snow and freezing rain that was now striking Baltimore City.

The owner of the coach appeared through large carved paneled doors, which opened outward. An Irish house servant in white gloves moved aside as Mollie, John, Charles, and Elizabeth walked out through the door and down the steps.

The coachman stepped down from his perch and opened the coach door, and then, with his white gloved right hand, swept it from left to right, bidding them to enter the coach. Mollie and Elizabeth entered first, followed by Charles and John

Augustus. With a click, the coachman closed the door securely, remounted his perch, and picked up the four-in-hand reins.

"Tally-ho," the Irishman hollered as the team dashed off south out of the residential district and into the busy Baltimore City streets toward The Baker Brothers & Company's two commodious warehouses.

Farther east from the warehouses on South Charles Street, Mollie saw Pratt Street and the docks that had held the magnitude of ships. She noticed the storm had left the docks in disarray. Something would have to be done, she knew; business would have to go on for Charles Baker.

As the coach approached the warehouses, she saw a sign that was in big black bold letters "Baker Brothers Co." and below the fourth story row of six windows were the large letters "Window Glass"; below the six third floor windows was another set of large letters that read "Glass Ware." The three-story building, attached to the right of the main building, had big letters on it as well. Above the seven columns of this building she observed two sets of the name "R. J. Baker."

Mollie felt the coach slow as the driver guided the landau coach to a halt between a four-wheeled wagon and a two-wheeled cart. The Irishman leapt from his high perch to the ground to open the coach door for the passengers.

"Top of the mornin' to you, Mr. and Mrs. Baker," Mr. Stone greeted. He was standing in front of the red bricked Baker Brothers warehouses at 32 and 34 South Charles Street.

"Good day to you, Mr. Stone," Charles said as he tipped his black top hat in the general direction of Mr. Stone. "Please come in and join us in my office."

Mollie, John, Elizabeth, and Mr. Stone followed Charles to his office. Mollie pulled up a chair close to a warm fire to thaw. The luxurious office measured twenty-five by twenty-five feet. The wood panels of choice mahogany bounded the room. Each corner featured columns that were squared off and paneled with hardwood. On the left column, facing Charles's cherry desk, hung a three-foot tall chiming clock with a bold white face and ornate hands. On the right hand column hung a narrow lithograph of Fort McHenry. She read the words of the Star Spangled Banner, which hung under the lithograph next to a framed etching of Francis Scott Key. Two paneled beams were centered in the room, detailed with elaborate wood carving, ornately and meticulously done, she thought.

"Mr. Baker, last night I was at a shipyard at Locust Point and the Federals were working frantically to get the ships that were battered from the storm back into readiness. The *Sun* has been keeping a close eye on what ships and steamers are coming and going. The pace of action is frightening, something like this port has never seen before. Ships are anchored two and three deep to get loaded with war supplies," Mr. Stone reported.

Charles picked up the conversation, "I've noticed that ever more ships are being requisitioned from under my nose, ships I already had under contract to move my products. As the vice president of the *Seaman's Mission Bethel*, I know many of the sailors and dock workers are exhausted from what the Federals are demanding they do to get their ships loaded here at the docks."

Mr. Stone continued, "I've also heard that any ships that can't be repaired by March 15th should be set aside. Only ships that can be repaired before this deadline are being worked on."

"Captain W. B. Kirwan of the steamer *William Selden* of the Old Bay Line has told me he can no longer move my product to Fredericksburg. He's solely working for the government at $1,500 a day. I was paying him $1,200, so it looks like Mr. Lincoln has outbid me on transportation," Charles seethed as he paced his office floor.

There was a brief silence. Mollie thought about what she had just heard.

Charles said, "That's all, Mr. Stone. Your information is invaluable. You're excused."

"Sir, it's been my pleasure to do what I can for the cause. Have a good rest of your day," Mr. Stone replied as he tipped his hat to all in the room and started for the door. "Oh, one other thing, for some reason a number of the ferries have been ordered to Annapolis, empty."

Charles turned rapidly and fixed Mr. Stone in his gaze, "Empty! Ferry boats! I thank you again, Stone." Mr. Stone left. Charles watched out the window until he was certain that Mr. Stone was gone, and then turned to them. "This could only mean one thing. Those ferries will be hauling soldiers from the Annapolis railhead. Come, Mollie, we must talk to Captain Kirwan."

⋯⊙⊙⋯

At Locust Point Mollie observed a great concentration of supply vessels that were anchored, waiting turns at the docks. She read in the *Sun* about the number and names of strange steamers in the harbor; their own familiar steamboats were also reported on. The report also acknowledged when popular excursion and bay steamers were used for war purposes.

"There's not a company that hasn't been affected by whatever the federal government is up to: The Baltimore Steam Packet Company, or the Old Bay Line, Merchants & Miners Transportation Company, Eastern Shore Steamboat Company, Baltimore & Eastern Shore Steamboat Company, Slaughter's Line, The Powhatan Steamboat Company, and The Weems Line, the oldest of them all, which is owned by Confederate sympathizers," Charles said.

"Very interesting, Charles, what do you make of it?"

"I don't know. I bet Captain Kirwan can tell us."

They made for the Old Bay Line docks where Charles had conducted much business.

Mollie saw the old friends step up next to a boiler undergoing noisy repairs and have a very private conversation. A half hour later Mollie and Charles were driven back to his office.

"I feel, Mollie, we've conclusive evidence that the Federals will be moving a large expeditionary force to the Northern Neck of the Rappahannock on the morning of the fifteenth. According to Kirwan, the only place on the Rappahannock that can land a force as large as McClellan's is Urbana. Above Urbana the river gets too narrow to maneuver that many ships," Charles reported as he got out a large-scale chart of the Rappahannock area and unrolled it on his desk. "Here is Urbana. Evidently McClellan wants to cut off Johnston from Richmond. The supplies will come mostly from Baltimore City. The troops will probably load at Annapolis and Washington."

After studying the map a moment, she jumped to her feet. "General Johnston must be warned at once. If the Confederate army is cut off from Richmond, it'll be destroyed," she concluded, looking directly at Charles. "Please have your coachman take me immediately to Christian Emmerich's shop at 18 South Street."

Charles walked to the door, "Coachman, bring the coach!" Charles looked puzzled as she continued, "Christian Emmerich is a good deal more than a fashionable shoe and boot maker for the bon ton of Baltimore City. I've already arranged to meet Charles Langley there. He'll carry the information to one of Lige White's couriers, who will take it directly to General Johnston at Manassas Junction. We've no time to tarry!"

She was determined as ever to get her information into the right hands. She left in the luxurious coach to get a new pair of boots.

16

Bring Up! The Stuart Horse Artillery!

Battle outside Williamsburg, Virginia

MAY 5TH, 1862

JAMES STARED OUT IN the early dawn rain on the tranquil waters of the historic York River at Bigler's Wharf, seven miles northeast of Williamsburg. The shadow of an osprey, skimming low on the river, spread its mighty wings and turned toward the bank. He watched it strike, and felt a sense of awe for its power. There was a splash, a shrill piercing scream, and then the osprey ascended into the air. The osprey beat hard against the weight of the flailing fish, its wings snapping at the air. The bird rose again in the twilight of the dawn and glided with its catch toward the dark line of trees along the opposite bank.

"Good mahnin," William said as he opened his slumberous eyes. "Step out of the rain. I have a question for you 1st Lieutenant."

"What'd that be on this fine rainy mornin'?" James asked. He looked away from the river and stepped under the fly of the tent.

"Tell me something about Captain Pelham. Now that we've been voted first and second lieutenants under his command, I'd like to know about his leadership style. I've not been in the unit as long as you, and I don't know how he thinks," William M. McGregor mused.

James had learned that McGregor was a year younger than him, and had been schooled in a log cabin in Talladega, Alabama, and then went on to East Alabama College at Auburn and studied law in Jacksonville.

He had taken note that William was not tall, but strongly made. William had a thick dark moustache and goatee upon his bold, squarely cut face. James thought William stood very straight, was an earnest intellectual and a formidable warrior.

"In some things he's like iron, unyielding in his discipline. He'll tolerate no shade of insubordination or disobedience, or neglect of duty in relation to commanding the First and Second Stuart Horse Artillery Batteries," James said.

"We saw no action at Dam Number Two near Yorktown. He has over one hundred and forty men and eight guns under his command. I wonder how he'll react in battle when the Yankees put him under fire?" William replied with a puzzled look on his face.

"We've seen no Yankee ships for three days on the river. I believe the Yanks are coming inland. I suspect you'll be seeing Captain Pelham in action today," James observed, taking his kepi off his head and smoothing his black hair back off his receding hair line.

James saw the camp stirring, the rain turning into larger pelting drops bouncing off the linen tents. He sat himself on a log stump under the fly and William sat across from him. They were of equal intelligence, and they respected one another. James was often guarded about whom he shared with on a more personal level, yet he took a chance with William.

"You'd go home to Alabama any time you please, with leave of course, to see family and friends. I, on the other hand, can't go home to Maryland. I feel like a Jew in Babylon. Like the Israelites, I'm forced into exile from my home as they were from Jerusalem for four hundred years. The Yankees, like King Nebuchadnezzar, keep me from going home. It makes me feel sad to think of Mollie, my family, and especially my father being captive to the Yankees," he said wiping the perspiration and rain from his forehead.

"I understand your feelings, James. I'd be resentful if some army of occupiers kept me from the ones I loved," William compassionately responded. "My McGregor clansmen were Highlanders and Covenanters who moved to outright political sedition in Scotland's Killing Time. The English under bloody Cumberland hunted and exiled my people to the point that we had to change our name to keep from being hung by the neck. So I understand your feelings of exile."

"I've heard that my father took the oath of allegiance to the Federals. It kind of bothers me to think he sold out to them. My uncle, Dr. Macgill, is sitting in a prison up north because he would not compromise his beliefs or swear a false oath. My father is judge of the Orphans Court. I'm sure he didn't want to acquiesce. His alternative was prison. My mother died March 14, and if he had gone to prison there would've been no one to take care of my brothers and sisters. On top of this he's unwilling to condone my move from medicine to soldiering. My home is now in my mind. I have faith in God that he will eventually see me safely through this war and allow me to go back home. This is my ardent hope, and that keeps me fighting," James said with a troubled look on his face.

"Vittles boys, for breakfast we's havin' parched corn, mule without salt, and no coffee! Same as yesterday," Creole sarcastically said as he slunk by the fly.

"James, I'll certainly keep you in my prayers. You can count on me to be a friend," William said as he stood and moved toward their mess table. He patted James on the shoulder. "I'm sorry about the loss of your mother. I'd think that it'd take some time to heal your soul."

James had had the six guns along the York River manned all night. No one knew if the Federal gun boats and troop transports might try and slip by them. They were ready if the Federals tried to instigate an attack farther inland. He felt something in the air, and he figured today would be his indoctrination into horse artillery tactics. He had learned everything he could from Captain Pelham, a fine teacher. He sensed today was the day those lessons would go into practice on the Yankees.

Suddenly, he heard distant rumblings of artillery to the west. The sounds of the guns had confirmed his suspicions. He quickly moved to his mess table, filling his stomach with corn and beef. The forlorn feelings he had shared with William soon were replaced by warm food in his gut.

"Eat hardy, men, no telling when our next meal will come. I heard the same artillery you did. I think we're not long for blockading the river. Lieutenants, I want harnesses and traces ready to go in a moment's notice by nine o'clock," Pelham announced to James and Lieutenant McGregor.

The tension in the air mounted. James could sense a change in Captain Pelham's demeanor. Sitting with him at their mess table was Bill Clem, Creole, Robert Mackall, and Henry Matthews.

"Means we're raring for a fight, I suspect," Henry said.

James favored them with his opinion, "This is going to be a dreadful war, boys. I shouldn't be surprised if it makes a Napoleonic thunder over the centuries—creates a mighty legend like Greece and Troy! I believe the keystone of the arch will be collected of three—the armies in the field, the women of the South, and our families back home. The struggle promises to be Homeric and memorable."

"Lieutenant, you always seem to have something right insightful to say, but you sure pick the dandiest times to say it," Robert observed while filling his plate with beef. "But we're right ready to follow you."

"After you finish here I want the team watered, traces and harnesses laid out and ready. The Yankees are on the move to Richmond, and we've got to stop them," James directed.

⌾⌾⌾

Pelham stroked the twelve-pound Howitzer muzzle as though it were a farmyard dog as he spoke to James and the other officers at around eleven o'clock.

"They'll be on us like a June bug on a duck as we move closer to the battlefield," Pelham said to his officers. "Keep vigilant for Yanks in the woods off the roads. We all know our orders; keep close together on the road. Lieutenant Breathed you take the front with the Blakeley."

He knew Pelham had received orders to relocate three cannon to Williamsburg and three to Fort Magruder. He had readied their cannon. He heard distant noises of artillery fire, which had become more intense as the morning hours whiled away.

"Yes, sir," James said with a proud salute.

He returned to the column and mounted Billy. Pelham gave the orders to march, and the column lurched into motion. After a few short miles away from the river, James saw crows come cawing from the tall pines to a sizable field of early wheat. Then he saw Pelham direct the six guns to the crop field as a Confederate cavalry regiment passed them by.

He heard a sudden burst of musketry: *Zzzzz-ip! Zzzzz-ip!* In the distance, he saw a flash of the stars and stripes through the woods, across the road. Blue uniforms in the woods, moving toward the artillery column, snapped them into action.

"Force the march!" Pelham shouted as he waved the teams onward.

James rode the muddy roads alongside the artillery; the streams swollen from the May rains. As they labored down the rough road, he smelled the fragrance of the air changing. First it was greening poplar and oak, next, pine forests and newly ploughed land, the scent disseminating from holly and dogwood trees blew in and out of his nostrils. They came off a side road that intersected with the Country Road between two Confederate redoubts.

They came up the Country Road, and each team of twenty-four hooves slugged through the pouring rain. His guns and caissons slid heavily into mud holes, the horses strained, but their harnesses and traces kept them fast. The drivers focused upon whip and voice to frantically move their deadly arsenals into battle. James swore at the men up and down each hill and dale, eager to motivate his lead, swing, and wheel drivers. They dragged on to the next mud hole, each seeming deeper than the last. His adjuration conveyed a clear urgency to the drivers. Finally, they reached the right side of Fort Magruder and the junction of the Telegraph Road.

James and Pelham were in the lead, fast approaching Stuart on the better road. They rode up to Stuart, and James could see the light of battle rage in Stuart's eyes.

"My Mamelukes have arrived on the field!" Stuart said to Pelham, with a pleased twinkle in his eye.

"Batteries—Halt! Sir, your orders; my horse artillery is on-line," Pelham reported. James halted Billy next to Pelham and Stuart.

Stuart issued orders to Pelham while gesticulating where he wanted a vigorous fire from the three guns laid down over General A. P. Hill's infantry in front and to the right of Fort Magruder.

The battery horses bent forward, tightening in their traces as the drivers yelled. James heard the rumbling wheels, jingling harnesses, and saw the mud churning under hoofs kicking it up, creating a wild scene of pandemonium. He could not see through the impenetrable cloud of rain and the amethyst haze of smoke from the brisk musket fire.

He ordered a halt as the men leaped to the ground from their steeds, the guns were planted, the limbers dropped, prop poles placed, the horses loosed and taken behind the fort. The men were clad only in trousers and shirts, their sleeves rolled up as if the pouring rain did not exist. The cannoneers scurried into their gun positions, and James believed his artillerists were raring for a fight as they stood awaiting orders from on high.

"Load!" he hollered. "Commence firing!"

All his gunners' movements were swift and rhythmic. At moments he could see them clearly, but then the riflemen's smoke swallowed them and they appeared ghostly in the windless air. He heard horses neighing to the rear; abatis of logs were before them.

The powder monkey handed the round to gunner number two, Bill Clem, who opened the rear of the gun and shoved it in. Gunner number one, Robert Mackall, stood at the ready. Gunner number three, Henry Matthews, thumbed the vent and sighted the cannon as Matthews adjusted the trail spike. The powder monkey got another round from the men at the limber; James stepped clear of the gun to see the effect of the shot.

"Ready!" James said as Matthews punctured the cartridge bag with the vent pick. Gunner number four, Creole, attached the lanyard to the friction primer and inserted the primer in the vent.

"Fire!" James commanded as Creole yanked the lanyard.

He heard a loud cannonade roar from his twelve-pound Blakeley breech loader. The fervent artillerists worked their piece and got off three rounds per minute. James saw Matthew's face pale, sulphur tainted, and his eyes troubled. Matthew took off his straw hat and wiped his forehead with a large red handkerchief as the cannon boomed.

"I want counter battery fire on those six Yankee guns to our front," James shouted as four more Federal cannon were rolled into place next to the six guns already there.

An oak, struck and split by solid shot, fell to his rear. He heard the sound of screeching artillery shells from the Federals' batteries and the enfilading rifles' minies penetrating the horse artillery line. It created chaos around them as the rain had become mixed with iron in a storm of shot and shell. Few of his soldiers were hit, though the gray trees did take a beating. The Federals were firing high, James thought.

Great and small branches were lopped off by fire around him, and in the dim light of the rain they tumbled down. He heard exploding shells tear twig from limb; they fell in a shower of slivers, chopped clean from the trunk. Limbs crashed from leafy level to leafy level until they crashed to the ground. Beneath them, James heard cries of warning, and, when necessary, his artillerists scampered out of the way. He saw younger trees being cut short at their bases, falling over to the terra firma, crushing the undergrowth, as above the sulphurous cloud of war wafted through the trees.

ఌౚౚ

Firing had continued for the better part of an hour when Pelham galloped over to James and relayed the orders from Stuart.

"Develop the enemy and enfilade their position down the Yorktown Road," Pelham firmly said to him, his outstretched arm pointing in the direction of the Yorktown Road.

"Yes, sir!" James replied. "Limber! Forward!"

His artillerists stopped firing and the teams were brought back from the rear and hitched to the cannon.

"Left oblique—March!"

James led the cannon from Telegraph Road at Fort Magruder to enfilade Yorktown Road. His artillerists' powder-grimed faces told the story of their efforts as they moved to the nexus of the battle. James again deployed his cannon on a knoll as his dog of war barked with vehemence and enfiladed the Yorktown Road with deadly effect.

The Federals' marching looked like toy soldiers to James. The rain fell on their flags, and the flags drooped around the baton. He saw horsemen galloping point to point along the Yorktown Road. In the interlude between the artillery thundering, James heard the tap of drums and bugles blowing. The moving soldiers were coming toward them, targets awaiting shrapnel and shot from his obliterating barking dog of war.

His artillerists sprung into action with redoubled effort, sponging, ramming, priming, aiming, and firing to great effect. He commanded the artillerists amidst frenzied shouting. Wild courage, much manliness, much gallantry, fervent dedication to him and the cause; the civilian artillerists made him proud.

"Keep the fire hot! Fire at will!" James hollered.

He watched a shell belched forward from the Blakeley strike the road just in front of the Federals. The shell ricocheted frightfully and tore a soldier's arm off. The blast covered all the Federals with a dull mantle of mud. Another shell followed, digging up the earth in the field, uprooting and ruining the early wheat. Then the elevating screw of his Blakeley gave way. James was able to continue to deploy the piece despite the broken screw. The sound was deafening, a complex tumult that echoed in his ears.

"Double canister! One hundred yards," James cried out.

James saw the Blakeley fire, and a pink mist exploded before the cannon. The line of Federal infantrymen evaporated, their body parts flying in all directions as they tried to move forward into the Blakeley's canister shots.

The cannonade was furious, relentless. When he paused to look at his pocket watch, he was surprised to see that the time was five o'clock. They ran out of ammunition and had to pull back past Fort Magruder to Williamsburg. His cool leadership had manifested itself on the battlefield. Like the Greek demigod Hercules sent out by Eurystheus, king of Mycenae, to conquer twelve tasks, James had accomplished his first horse artillery task. He thought there would be many more to come.

He rested by the broken Blakely. His men stood around him and talked of the tangle with a sense of pride in their first battle achievement as Stuart Horse Artillerists.

James's mind wandered from the pedantic conversations of his men. He thought that beside every marching soldier there also marches an invisible woman. Mollie must be doing her part on the home front. This brought a warm and comforting feeling to his heart, which put him at ease. He felt that, for the first time, he had equaled her deeds of espionage. Quickly, he wrestled his competitive spirit back, realizing his pride had gotten the better of him.

Everything was about his love for her, not the battle of his own pride, he thought.

17

The Invisible Hand of a Medicine Man

or

The Family Sacrificial Lamb

SUMMER OF 1850

A FEW DAYS AFTER the fight at Williamsburg, James had been tending to wounded Confederate soldiers. He sat alone late one night by the campfire. He reflected on how it was that he was called to practice medicine. He remembered one day in his youth when he and Willie sat on a flatbed wagon at the end of the plantation drive. He looked down the road to see his uncle, Dr. Macgill, driving a buggy pulled by a little brown mare that he recognized as Bella. James wiped the sweat from his brow and thought this was going to be more fun for a twelve-year-old boy than school could ever be. He was on summer break from the grammar school of the College of St. James.

"Good morning, James," Dr. Macgill said. "Good morning, Willie. James, are you ready to find out how a country doctor spends his time?"

"Yes, sir," James replied as he climbed into the buggy next to his uncle. They turned back toward the Sharpsburg Pike, "You don't have to wait, Willie. I'll be home by and by."

They headed the short distance toward the Toll House.

"Mornin', Doc. Hello, James," a towheaded boy said, greeting them as he sat on the Toll House fence. "You and Bella makin' your rounds I sees. What-ya got today to keep the doctor away?"

James watched his uncle motion for the tollgate to be swung open with his right hand as he tossed the boy a customary apple. Dr. Macgill held the reins of the two-seated buggy in his left hand and gently patted the reins on Bella's back as the tollgate swung out so they could pass. His uncle reached in his pocket and pulled out a coin, which he flipped to the boy for the toll.

James was excited, but worked hard at being serious. He admired his uncle who was a great storyteller, but who also liked to play practical jokes. He knew his uncle's homespun wit was popular on the political circuit, though he had a keen edge for any opponent. James, like most of the voters in Washington County, had heard many of his uncle's tales. He suspected he would hear a few more this day.

A few miles down the Sharpsburg Pike, James noticed a woman coming through her apple orchard, of which the county had many. She motioned to the doctor as if she had something important to share.

"Why, my sakes, Doctor. Where'd you get that child? He ain't one of your'n, be he?"

"No, he's my cousin. He belongs to Judge Breathed over at Bai-Yuka Plantation. He's going to learn how to practice medicine for a few weeks from the Blue Ridge to the Conococheague. Today we're bound for Sharpsburg. James, introduce yourself to Mrs. Greene."

"Howdy ma'am. I'm James Breathed. My daddy wants me to go for a preacher when I grow up, but I thought today I'd discover doctoring. My uncle is taking me out on his country rounds to teach me all about allopatics!"

"James, that's allopathic medicine I'm going to demonstrate for you."

They all laughed, and James whispered to Mrs. Greene, "Is it very far to town?"

"No, honey, 'taint no ways now. You've to pass over the 'Jordon River' first. And don't you mind the doctor. He ain't happy 'less he's foolin' somebody."

They rode on.

"James, the Jordon would be Antietam Creek. I'll explain shortly," his uncle said as he clucked to Bella to move forward and climb the long hill of Nicodemus Heights.

From the top, they could see directly beyond the sluggish yellow waters of the Antietam. Cornfields covered the slopes and bottom land with small woods interspersed.

"I certainly love this view of the cornfields and the Antietam Creek. There's something so peaceful here, it 'bout near gives me chills," James said as he studied the groves of hickory and the scampering gray and fox squirrels.

"Indeed, it's peaceful. Your home being only ten miles from this place, you should have Willie bring you out here more often. I'm sure your father would allow you to come here with him when he visits his tenant farms along the pike."

Many varieties of birds were fluttering in fields and trees as they passed by, and James was especially fond of birds and their ways. He knew the jaybird's screech, and their dictatorial calls, feathered like soldiers in their blue and white frock coats. He heard a catbird singing in a pine as they passed under; while off in another woods he heard the persistent tapping that only the pileated woodpecker made.

Farther down the road over a cornfield he spied a few great vultures, which, because of the extreme height at which they flew, made them appear to be blue feathered. The ill-favored scavengers brought an uneasy tension to his now peaceful soulfulness. The great birds flew over Antietam Creek waiting for something to die. Two more vultures appeared, soaring securely on the high air currents with no more motion than a cloud, eying the cornfield for carrion.

His uncle suddenly whistled *Bob White*. The call brought James out of his dark reverie. The partridges, answering from a stubble field, showed where they hid. His quick ears enabled him to point them out with a gleeful smile on his face.

"Lad, where were you just now? I think I lost you in the clouds. What was up there that had you in such a trance?"

"I saw something in the sky; there were four blue-clad vultures. You couldn't see them from your side of the buggy, 'lessin' you looked straight up. I bet my rifle isn't able to shoot far enough to kill them things."

"I'll grant you they're ugly, James. I wouldn't go killing them without a mighty good reason. God made them to do his dirty work. You've a vivid imagination, lad. That woman we met back at the orchard was a Dunker. Since you're setting up to be a preacher, let me tell you about the Dunkers and their beliefs," his uncle said as James intently listened, eager to learn. "The Dunkers have a yearly baptism in the Antietam. The creek becomes their River Jordon, and Funkstown, back up the road, is their Jerusalem. Have you studied John the Baptist and the River Jordon in School yet?" his uncle asked as the buggy wheels rolled loudly over the macadamized pike.

"I know the story from the Gospels. I understand the Dunkers must get their name from dunking the whole person under the water. I'm pretty good at Bible; I know how to make sense of the stories in it," he proudly said.

"Actually, James, they dunk each person three times when baptizing them. Another thing, they don't call themselves Dunkers. They call themselves the Schwarzenau Brethren. They don't believe in fighting or fancy churches. I talked with farmer Mummas who lives just east of here. He's already set aside the land for their church on this very pike. He told me it won't even have a steeple or any type of ornament."

Since James didn't seem very interested in Dunker theology, his uncle asked, "James, what do you plan to do with your life?"

"I want to be a doctor like you, a healer of men, or a surgeon maybe. Besides, I don't know what my father really does anyhow."

"Lad, he's a provost at the college and the judge of the Orphan's Court. He uses his legal training to settle estates in Maryland. You know that, James," his uncle pointedly said.

"I suppose he's an important person, but that kind of work doesn't mean anything to me. I want to do something with my life that stops suffering in people's lives!" he retorted as he looked admiringly at his uncle with a gleam in his eye.

"James, you're a smart boy! You can do whatever you'd like to do with your life. If you desire your life to have meaning, I should think you'd consider medicine over ministry. If you chose ministry you might become the 'family sacrificial lamb' and that does not fit your personality."

James was quiet for a time while he thought how the sacrificial lamb concept tied in with him and his family.

"I love God and want to do right by him. Plus, if'n I preach about God he'll love me even more," James blissfully said, believing that he might be justified by works as opposed to grace. "How does that make me a sacrificial lamb?"

"Sometimes a man wants his son to become a minister for reasons he can never quite get clear in his mind. Some folks think that having a minister of God in the family somehow makes it a godly family." His uncle paused, and then continued, "But unless you're called by God, and you can sacrifice your life to his work, you may never be compensated for your efforts. You may have to forsake yourself as far as a wife, and maybe never even have children. Would you want that for your life, James? Many Episcopal ministers are 'great thinkers,' but they struggle financially in most cases. Would you want to give your life to the ministry because your father wanted you to? Or would you rather do the will of God if he wanted you to do something else?"

James thought about what his uncle had said.

Then his uncle added, "God gave you the gift of the awareness of life. All in all, I'd like to see you become a doctor."

"Father thinks I'd make a good priest, but warned it's a demanding profession. My cousins from Poolesville, John and Richard Williams, are staying with us while they go to St. James Grammar school. John isn't very strong. He's always talking about God. The ministry is all he thinks about. Richard is younger and stronger. He's for reading all the time, and constantly asks my father about what lawyers and judges do."

"Sounds like Richard may not make a good minister. The law and religion seem to have little to do with each other as professions."

James pondered a while. "Well, I know my father has family money. So I don't have to worry about making money. But should I become dependent on my family to become a minister in the Episcopal Church? Most of my classmates who come from money, except Cousin John, don't seem to be serious about God at all."

"James, my advice is don't be dependent on your family's money. You should go out into the world and make your own way. I believe 'every tub stands on its own four legs and worships God.' Become a 'Great Man' like Thomas Carlyle wrote about in his works."

"You mean become a 'Great Man' on my own and not rely on my family? Stand on my own two legs as a doctor, but still worship God?"

"By all means, James, become a doctor; I feel certain you've the gift. You may even find a cure for some infection of the lungs, like pneumonia. Matriculate into the School of Medicine at the University of Maryland. I know all the faculty there. Dr. Nathan Rhino Smith is one of the most outstanding modern surgeons in the country."

"I'd love to study under a great doctor instead of a religion teacher, even one as good as Reverend Kerfoot," James concluded.

"Then, between us, let's consider the issue settled. Finish the college preparation and come intern with me for two years. I can find you living accommodations in Hagerstown. You can see your family when you wish at Bai-Yuka Plantation during your internship with me."

"Where's Mollie gonna be?" James said out of context. "Where'll she be learnin'?"

"James, your cousin Mollie is being educated at home by tutors. She'll remain in Hagerstown and finish her proper training as a Southern woman should."

"She's my favorite cousin. She sure is hard headed and has a real temper. Shucks, when she disagrees with something a fella says she comes right out and tells him. Do you think we can get along?"

He could sense his uncle was caught off guard. The subject was dropped, and James again looked around at the bird life.

Their buggy had moved briskly over the well-kept Sharpsburg Pike, until it turned on to a dirt road that they followed for three or four miles. The previous day's rain made the road muddy. James could hear the slow suck of the wheels in the mud, as they sank into some of the dirt road's deeper mud holes.

His uncle broke the silence, "Now I need to teach you some pharmacopoeia on your first day as an aspiring doctor."

They came to a stream. The dirt road ended at the water's edge, so they had to ford it. The doctor put his feet up on the dashboard while James put his feet under his bottom to keep them dry as the water rushed in and flooded the floorboard. Their horse struggled to pull the buggy forward across the deepest part of the stream's center currents. Once across the stream Dr. Macgill began to explain pharmacopoeia to him.

⁂

"I tell you, doctor, that last dose took hold right smart," Mrs. Jones said whose son, Billy, had come down with stomach problems.

James thought it was chilson fever, which the doctor had described on the buggy ride to the farmhouse.

"Well, I thought it would," his uncle said.

"Could it be chilson fever?" James asked.

"James, I last gave him bumpers of bicarbonate of soda mixed with Brown's Essence of Jamaica Ginger. It seems to have worked—didn't it Billy?" Dr. Macgill said as he rubbed Billy's scruffy hair. The smell of cooked bacon permeated James's nostrils.

The corral out back made James aware of where these smells disseminated from, even before they arrived in the house.

"James, I see a lot of children's diseases: sore throats, congestion of the lungs, as well as pneumonia. You've wrongly referred to pneumonia as 'chilson fever' or liver trouble. When you go to the School of Medicine, you're going to find a cure for pneumonia, aren't you, lad?"

"Yes, sir," James assuredly replied as he sat on the bed next to Billy, a red-headed, freckled boy of a young age. "You believe that I can, so I believe I can. You said I could do anything with my life, so finding a cure for a terrible disease is what I aim to do. I'll help a whole lot of people live better lives. Maybe even more so than I would in trying to help people as an Episcopal minister, I suspect," he enthusiastically said.

"Lad, I also give a lot of calomel in pills. It has better effects than come from powders. Gagging on the pills is an issue for a lot of my patients, so powders are also effective. My other pharmacopoeias I give in liquid form, which I replenish from a bottle I carry in my side pocket. Grab the bottle, James, and I'll mix up the bumpers of bicarbonate of soda and show you how I do this for Billy," his uncle directed, looking across the bedroom at him.

James walked over to the doctor's capacious apothecary side-pocket bag and pulled out the bottle of liquid he requested. He carefully studied the manner in which his uncle created the concoction.

"Billy, open wide, this will get you over your stomach problem, I promise," Dr. Macgill said as he pinched Billy's nose. Billy dropped his jaw open. "One-two-three and down the hatch it goes."

Dr. Macgill gave a little clap of approval as Billy shook his head violently and swallowed the medicine. His uncle again patted Billy on the top of his head and wished him all the best in recovery.

Mrs. Jones led James and his uncle downstairs to the kitchen. She compensated the doctor for his house call and offered James a half-rack of salted pork ribs for his involvement in his first healing excursion. James thanked Mrs. Jones and packed the cheesecloth wrapped ribs into the rear compartment of the buggy.

"I'll call on you next week when I come this direction and see how Billy is doing," Dr. Macgill called to Mrs. Jones as he waved good-bye. He and James drove away from the farm to the next house call.

Having called upon several farms in the course of the day, and the afternoon shadows beginning to lengthen, his uncle pointed Bella up the lane of the last farm they would visit this day.

☙◉❧

Dr. Macgill diagnosed a little boy named Adam with inflammatory rheumatism. His uncle humored Adam by having him cut long stripes of linen and steep them in a cold solution of bicarbonate of soda. They wrapped the limbs firmly, and Dr. Macgill gave the family directions to have the bandages changed frequently. Before departing the farmhouse, James watched his uncle walk over to the boy and rub his chin. His uncle drew out a bottle of julep from his apothecary and leaned down to the bed where the boy lay in pain.

"Which do you like best, Adam? Will it be scraped apple or currant jelly?" his uncle asked while setting a bottle of paregoric on the bed stand.

"I hate 'em both," the poor little mite cried.

This was James's department, that of scraping the apple. James spread the apple on a teaspoon, then he poured the powder on; after that there was a covering of more apple scrapings. He thought the weight would cause the powder to ooze out on the sides so that even an idiot would not have been deceived.

Adam would not open his mouth.

"Adam, my uncle has given me this medicine many times when I was sick. It's not so bad," James stated.

His uncle was quick to react to Adam's unwillingness, as he had a remedy. Dr. Macgill held Adam's nose, compressing the nostrils so that the boy's lips had to open to gasp for air. James nimbly slipped in the teaspoon, turned it upside down and then slowly removed it so as not to drop even a particle of this precious dose of medicine.

"The julep will stretch his muscles a bit. He doesn't need any more medicine. Keep those wet bandages on his legs. Now he's going to get well," his uncle announced with certain assurance to the boy's concerned mother.

James and the good doctor headed back toward the buggy after being compensated. As they headed back north on the Sharpsburg Pike, James felt that they had accomplished a fine days' work.

His uncle explained the usage of quinine in tea for women. He explained the same medicine was used for men in whiskey; the men seemed to take to the whiskey over the tea. He shared the art of bleeding for headaches, fevers, and for congestion of the lungs. He told him darkies were also bled for their ills and were generally diagnosed by the generic term of "misery."

"I lead a strenuous life, lad. Sometimes I ride twenty miles in the night to see to a patient on his deathbed. Yet, my faith in God always keeps me cheerful," his uncle said as they arrived at the high road on the Sharpsburg Pike at Nicodemus Heights.

"I see what you do as a good country doctor. I want to be like you when I get through the School of Medicine. You really think you can get me into the school if'n I study hard at the College of St. James?"

"I'm a graduate of the school's class of '23," Dr. Macgill stated. "No question. I'm still close to Dr. Smith. You work hard and study everything you can in relation to medicine. We'll work together as a team of proud medical people. We'll develop a family tradition of doctors. I think your cousin Charles Griffith is also going into medicine."

James, again, was staring at the blue-hued vultures that had now landed next to the cornfield below Nicodemus Heights. He observed the giant carnivores devouring a gray fox. The birds picked through the gray fur coat and dined on the red meat. He saw that the meat was torn from the carcass at the edge of the cornfield; it was a bloody mess as the vultures drew the fur coat from the body to get at the meat. He was mesmerized by the sight and asked his uncle to pull the buggy over to the side of the road.

"I hate those demons; they're tearing up that poor fox. Let me run down there and fight 'em off! I'll throw rocks at them to make 'em fly away and leave that fox alone.

The fox has done nothing wrong, but is being destroyed by those demons," James said as he pointed at the vultures.

"James, there's nothing you can do. It's a part of nature; the stronger creatures are feeding off the weaker ones. The fox was likely sick and the fitter vultures are now eating it to survive. This is nature's way, my lad."

"Someday I'll come back here and shoot those blue demons," James said in a low, even voice as his uncle prompted Bella with the reins and moved her along the road toward Bai-Yuka Plantation.

18

The Brilliant Exploit

JAMES HEARD A DISTANT train whistle coming from Kilby's Station, which was the station nearest Mrs. Mordecai's farm on the Richmond, Fredericksburg & Potomac Railway. He had cooked and prepared his three days' rations for a venture that was to leave at 2:00 am, whence he knew not, nor where bound, nor for what purpose. A great many of his comrades-in-arms suffered from measles, mumps, fevers, typhoid, and malarial pleurisy pneumonia. John Pelham had a bout with "yellow ganders" and had magnanimously recommended that James lead the Stuart Horse Artillery in the morning.

Two o'clock came too soon; he awoke feeling as if he had closed his eyes barely a moment ago. He heard the cry for "boots and saddles" ring out and thought that more than the summer heat had drained his energy. Wiping his eyes, he got to his feet and then lifted his artillerist jacket that he had used as a pillow. He ran his arms into the sleeves of his gray jacket with its lieutenant's insignia on the collar.

"All right, boys, time to get the teams saddled, harnessed, and hitched to the equipment. It's looking like scores of cavalrymen will be needin' our fire power if we run into Yankee cavalry. I don't know where we're headin' but I gotta feelin' it ain't going to be comfortable," he said as he started barking orders to Creole, Henry Matthews, Bill Clem, Robert Mackall and the fresh fish, Reverend Zimmerman.

He had come to admire Reverend Henry Zimmerman who was an easygoing and charming fellow, acquainted with everybody—a Presbyterian employee of the Lord, now employed to do the righteous work of an artillerist. He thought others were lean and not so well fed, but this fresh fish was as stout and strong as a bull. The reverend wore the gray uniform of an artillerist with the swath of red around the collar and the kepi. His magnificently fitting uniform was pristine with parallel rows of gleaming buttons precisely spaced. He hopped about and chirped with a Virginian's dialect like a tomtit; he was the soul of good humor and enjoyment, with an affable character.

"Sergeant Shaw, you see to it that traces and saddles are ready to move out double quick. I want no dilly dallying this morning. We're on an important mission, and I aim to find out what exactly it is just now. Understood?"

"Yes, sir. I'll see to zat directly," Emmett Shaw replied with a sharp salute as he turned on his heel.

Leaving the men, James went to locate General Stuart and found him at his headquarters tent. He discovered Stuart dressed in his double-breasted gray shell jacket, with rows of polished buttons laced with a braid, a tasseled yellow sash and a gray cape with scarlet lining. His buff-colored hat was looped on the right with a gold star and ornamented with a black floating ostrich plume. He brandished a sabre and a LeMat revolver. His thigh-high cavalry boots were freshly polished.

"Mornin', Lieutenant. I assume your two guns are being readied for the ride?" Stuart inquired, as Fitz Lee and Rooney Lee joined the circle of officers.

"Yes, sir! My artillerists are seeing to it as we speak," James answered as he pointed in the direction of the horse artillery camp.

"Gentlemen, I'll share with you the direct orders from General Lee himself if you'll gather around my table where I can read from the light."

James noticed that a lighted candle lantern hung from the tent pole near the entrance to his tent. The small table was to the left of one of the flaps and the lantern illuminated the handwritten orders from General Lee, which Stuart had placed on the table.

"To summarize the main points," Stuart said, "we are to '*Make a secret movement to the rear of the enemy . . . with a view of gaining intelligence of his operations, communications, and of driving in his foraging parties and securing such grain cattle.*'" Stuart then skipped to the end of the letter: "*Remember that one of the chief objects of your expedition is to gain intelligence for the guidance of future operations.*" The Federals have been fashioned by McClellan's skilled hand into as fine a fighting machine as any general need wish for his tool. This tool awaits us out there this day. However, from the Potomac to the Dan, from the Eastern shore to the Alleghenies, the flame of patriotism is burning high and clear in this Confederate army," Stuart pronounced as he looked to his officers. "Fitz, your First will be in the lead followed by Rooney's Ninth, and the Fourth will fall in with four companies each under your command. I want Will Martin's two hundred and fifty pickets to fall in behind the Fourth and, Lieutenant Breathed, you're in command of two guns. My prized horse artillery will be the rearguard. Is this understood?"

A harmony of officers' voices rang out, "Yes, sir."

Stuart produced a map of the area and roughly traced his intended route for the officers. As James looked on, he thought about how his artillerists might operate in such difficult terrain.

"Our objective is to secure intelligence. Cooperation in whatever might occur will be vital to the success of our mission. If there're no questions you're dismissed to mount up. Godspeed!"

As the officers walked away, James felt that much potential danger lay ahead. As commander of artillery for the first time behind enemy lines, his energy level was heightened. He knew he would have to keep his wits about him.

◌◌◌

"By piece—from the right—front into column!" James cried out. "Sergeants Shaw and Hoxton, follow the road to the left—March!"

James watched as his orders were fulfilled and the front gun moved out under Chief of Piece Shaw who was to the left of the lead driver, followed by the caisson fourteen yards behind it. Next came ten mounted artillerists in a column of twos. Lieutenant McGregor quickly followed the caisson with his rifled gun and the second caisson with the appropriate space interval behind, followed by another ten of his mounted artillerists.

James rode at the center of the column. Rain began to pelt down. He pulled his kepi tightly down on his head as protection. The twelve hundred cavalrymen ahead departed the Brock Turnpike and headed to Yellow Tavern. The road was churned into a muddy slush under the artillery equipment's lumbering wheels. The six-up teams of horses strained under the burden.

"Trot—March!" James said. The pace quickened to catch up with the cavalrymen, and mud flew from the wheels.

His guns glistened beneath coats of rain. The yelling men, the drivers loudly encouraging the horses, the horses pink-nostriled and wide-eyed, all came somehow, helter-skelter, down the long winding road. James pressed his artillerists, and when he saw the rear of the cavalry column, he commanded anew, "Walk—March!"

James rode beside Private Zimmerman in the column of mounted artillerists and started a conversation. "What denomination are you, Reverend? Where did you do your seminary training?"

"I'm a Southern Presbyterian. I got my bachelor of divinity at Union Seminary in Richmond, class of '50. I'm an Old School Presbyterian and do not believe the church should make laws to bind my conscience."

"I did my theological training at the College of St. James outside of Hagerstown. I've studied the *Institutes* at First Presbyterian Church in Baltimore, which I attended while I was in medical school. I'm a Calvinist at heart. I suspect we've got a few more things in common than simply the war," he said, reflecting back on his seminary training.

"The New School Presbyterians, whom we split from in '61, almost worship the Federal government. A Reverend Dr. Gardiner Spring, the pastor of the Brick Presbyterian Church in New York City, got his Gardiner Spring Resolution passed through our General Assembly. It, in fact, made loyalty and allegiance to the government a term of communion in the church.

"We Southerners couldn't tolerate it any longer. We broke from the Yankee-loving northern church. They're full of themselves. Them Northerners were the ones who had operated the slave trade and grown rich from doing it. Brown University was founded with a slave trader's money, but tell them that and they look at us Southerners like we're barbarians for having the slaves they brought over in the first place," George said, whom James now recognized as having a mind as astute as his own.

"I can see we're like minded on many subjects, Reverend," James said. "I'm trained as a doctor and here I am doing all this killin'. You're a man of peace and now joined up to do killin', too."

"Who's this Creole artillerist at the head of the column? George asked. "He's a little wild-eyed."

"He's a Cajun scalawag with the French pox, which I suspect makes him as crazy as anything else. He seems ta have the Virginia quickstep more than any man I've ever seen. He don't think like Eastern Christian folks. I never joke with or about people I don't like."

"Them Creoles is mostly Catholic. Most of them believe in juju and voodoo black magic just to hedge their bets. Creole don't seem quite right in the head," George said as they rode over a small tributary, the rain continuing to pelt their bodies.

"Reverend, been good to talk," James said. "Give you some advice. If we get into a fight today with Federal artillery, you can dodge a ball that is passing better standing, for you can tell where it is going when it is bouncing on the ground. Keep a clear eye and you'll have a lot better chance of staying alive. If they come a flying, stand fast and do your job, for only God's providence will determine your outcome."

"Said like a true Calvinist, Lieutenant. Godspeed!"

James led the artillerists on to the Mountain Road through Goodall's Tavern, and then along the South Anna River north, where they then encamped for the night at the Winston Farm near Taylorsville. They had come twenty miles at least, James figured.

◦◦◦

James was tired of the rain. Although he was not superstitious, James thought it was Friday the 13th when he saw scout Mosby ride into camp. James had ordered a noise-less camp with no bugles or pageantry for secrecy, because he thought stealth was of the utmost importance for the mission's success. The road was clear of Federals so he moved the artillerymen forward to Hanover Courthouse by early morning. There they discovered thirty Federal cavalrymen, and when Stuart learned of the presence of this enemy the news acted upon him like a blow of a sword. Observing a wild excitement in Stuart, James heard him cry out, "Bring up a squadron! Bring up the cavalry! I'm going to charge! Bring me a squadron!"

This was all James needed to hear.

"Form section—Left Oblique!" James ordered. "March—Guide right!"

"Form section—Left Oblique!" Shaw and Hoxton cried out as the Stuart Horse Artillery went into supportive action as the muddy melee began.

James observed the action from the road as he heard Stuart's next command shouted, "Form platoons! Draw sabre! Charge!"

An enthusiastic number of squadrons raced forward after the blue clad men. James's friend and fellow physician Captain William Latané had his sabre drawn and was leading the charge. James thought that Latané seemed to enjoy it with the zest of a foxhunter, as did the rest of the cavalrymen at the head of the 9th Squadron.

In an instant, James watched as his countrymen struck the enemy with a force like thunder. Suddenly, the Federal cavalry was joined by two whole companies. The fighting became hand-to-hand, and the woods became the scene of violent combat.

"Steady, men. We've no shot that would not kill as many of our own," James said while standing erect in his saddle and looking for an opportunity to let his dogs of war bark.

He saw hand-to-hand combat between Latané and a Federal officer who, with his pistol, felled Latané. James slumped back in his saddle as he witnessed Latané fall lifeless to the ground.

Still no shots could be fired by his artillerists, much to his frustration. The Federals reformed twice more and were routed each time by his Virginia cavalry comrades. He saw that Fitz Lee had gotten permission from Stuart to pursue the retreating Federals, and the gray cavaliers tore after them like so many bloodhounds after fear-stricken deer. The woods in front of him and his section of cannon finally cleared; his artillerists reformed to move out.

As he rode past the carnage next to his ten mounted artillerists, he believed the element of surprise was gone.

"Somebody's darling," Creole said as he looked down at Dr. Latané's dead body with five bullet holes in his torso and his uniform all bloodied and charred as a result of how close the killing shots were fired.

"Yeah, Creole, just think of how many lives he might have saved as a doctor," James said with a sneer of disrespect toward Creole as he rode by him.

"Better him than me," Creole said to him.

The stress of command turned his focus inward. Latané was the only Confederate who had died in action that day. A doctor like himself, Latané had died for the cause; but James had lost a true friend who was also a professional and a warrior. When would his predetermined end come? How many lives would that keep him from saving as a doctor? But here he was again in the saddle of destruction with his cannon. Did it all make sense, he pondered. He heard orders echo to move out south behind the column of cavalrymen.

James traveled a mile farther on Billy and then stood aside under the low pines while the horse artillery went by. The two guns overtook him in the dusk of the rain, in the long howl of the wind and the dash of the pelting drops. He thought, like the iron chariots of Plato, the horses were trotting, the gunners clinging to the caissons and limber boxes wherever they might place hand or foot; the mounted artillerists were spurring alongside.

"Lieutenant, I need to ride forward to speak with General Stuart," James said to McGregor with a salute. "Keep the men moving and I'll return shortly."

James rode up to Stuart who was communicating with Fitz Lee and Rooney Lee as the column of bedraggled horsemen passed by them. Amidst the drenching rain, Stuart was laughing and shouting his camp songs, with the rain descending in torrents from his heavy brown beard. James felt this was a slight bit odd. He joined the circle of horsemen for he knew nothing else to do. He needed some direction for his artillerists.

"Lieutenant, what say ye?" Stuart asked as he completed a verse and began to talk some sense. "Fitz here ran them Yankees like a coonhound and treed a bunch of 'em. Bully for you, Fitz."

"Sir, we couldn't get off a shot back there," James said. "Would've killed as many of ours as Yanks. The melee was too tangled in the woods for artillery."

"You done good, son. We need to discuss turnin' back our ridin' around the Yanks. What say ye, Fitz?"

"I feel like we got what we came fur, maybe time to head back?"

"I think we should go on and ride all the way around them Yanks," Rooney said. "If'n they don't know we're here now, they never will. Let 'em come out and fight us. Let's keep going south."

"Lieutenant, you got a mind in this?" Stuart probed.

"Let's keep 'em on the run. I say we head south and go right round 'em," James answered.

"To die game," Stuart said. "We head on to Old Church."

James turned from the men and rode back to the rearguard and rejoined his horse artillerists. They shortly came to Hopewell Church, and then headed toward Garlick's Landing with two squadrons to apply the torch to the Federal's supply depot. He saw overturned wagons strewn about the road, abandoned by the Federals as they now knew of the Confederate presence.

His artillerists were patient, famished, and piteous. Behind them the horses were heavily coated with mud from the myriad of mires they had driven through. Guns, wheels, and caissons were all plastered with mud. Not an inch of bright metal showed. His men were in no better shape, covered from head to foot with mud and mire, wet through as their clothes clung to their skin like cheesecloth to a salted ham hock. Their worn uniforms had been roughened by thorn and briar that hung over the road and tore at their flesh. The water poured off their bodies; it dripped from the unfurled flags, yet the Stuart Horse Artillery moved forward. Now behind enemy lines, they had new anxieties to motivate their actions.

James was now traveling with his old comrades of the 1st Virginia Cavalry.

"Captain Hammond, how's the war been treating you?" James asked.

"Well, Breathed, you seem to still be kickin' up mud I see. Looks like command is suiting you well. We might have a use for those guns when we get to Garlick's Landing."

"Thomas, Daniel—good to see you again. Cavalry suiting you well I see."

"Sure enough, James. We miss George, but we're getting along fine without him. You're moving up the ranks I see," Thomas replied, who had been bound for Harvard before the war.

"Pelham was too sick for this mission so they gave me command. Your family's doing well, I hope?"

"They be missin' us, but we be fightin' for 'em," Daniel said. "Just like you, James, as a Marylander, you understand."

"That's the worst of this foolishness. I wish they would stop it! I don't mind hard-tack, or fighting, or sleeping in the rain; what I do mind is never being able to go home! I wish old McClellan would go home and see his wife, and let me go home and see my family! We could then come back and blaze away at each other with some satisfaction!" James concluded.

Suddenly, both the rifled and the howitzer cannon became stuck in knee-deep mud. All the lashing of the teams and all the tugging and swearing of the gunners could not extricate them from the quagmire.

The cavalry halted. James had to think quickly if he was going to keep up.

"Beat the Dutch," he said to his friends. "We've been through the mill, but them guns aren't movin'."

"Breathed, looks like you going to have your work cut out for you today. We'll go on to do our torchin'. You catch up when you can," Captain Hammond said.

"Tarnation! We might have to turn back to the main column. Carry on, Captain."

With that, James jumped from Billy and looked at the two cannons stuck firmly in the mud up to the axles. He watched the two squadrons of the 1st move out in the rain. He called over Lieutenant McGregor. The cannon in section stood next to each other as his drivers hollered and lashed at the six-up team to move forward through the mud. But the guns would not budge. Finally after a great deal of energy was exerted by McGregor's drivers, his cannon came out of the mud.

The cannon, however, would still not move in the quagmire. Chief of Piece Sergeant Shaw came up to him.

"Herrgoot, Lieutenant," said Sergeant Shaw, who was of German stock. "Zat can't be done!"

James caught the sergeant glance at the ambulance which accompanied the expedition, with its treasured keg of liquor.

"Yust put zat barrel on zeir gun, Lieutenant, and tell ze men zey can only have it if zey will pull srough!"

"Lieutenant McGregor, what do you think of Sergeant Shaw's idea?" James asked with the face of a skeptic.

"It's worth a try," McGregor replied with a laugh, as he motioned for the keg to be placed on the gun.

"O Be Joyful is the reward for freeing this limber and cannon from the mud," James said to his artillerists.

James saw that his artillerists Private James Gray and Reverend Zimmerman were the first to dismount as they leapt into the knee-deep mud. They grabbed hold of the wheels and put their backs into pushing the wheels forward as the drivers lashed at the horses.

"I'd swim the Mississip at the Delta for bust head," Creole said as he leapt down from his horse to aid his comrades.

James stared at the cannon as it seemed to inch forward, the horses straining to pull the artillery piece out of the quagmire. With all ten men in the mud pushing, pulling and groaning like mules, the limber and cannon were coming out when, suddenly, he heard the limber pole give way with a loud snap. He thought the cannon had moved forward enough in the quagmire to unlimber it and free it.

"The devil," he shouted. "We've lost the limber."

Grabbing his kepi from his head, he beat it on his thigh and looking to the heavens, shook his hands and tightened his fists. He threw his kepi on the mud-soaked ground and stamped his feet in a childish rage as his men watched.

"Men, we'll never again lose a piece of artillery or equipment as long as I'm in command! Do you understand? Get this in your heads; I'll never tolerate this, nor will you ever allow this to happen again, understood?" James said defiantly as he looked down upon his artillerists who stood in the mud hole in shame.

"Yes, sir!" the artillerists echoed.

"Well, we got one gun and limber out and almost another. You're entitled to your O Be Joyful. Ten minutes before we move out, have at it."

❦

The return ride to Tunstall's Station was not a happy ride for James. He festered in his saddle the whole way and wondered how he was going to explain to Stuart that he had lost a piece of equipment. When they arrived at the station, the evidence of what had occurred hours before drowned out his despair. He looked around and saw cut telegraph lines. A place on the tracks looked like a tornado had hit it; timbers were strewn in every direction. He halted the horse artillery.

"What happened here?" he asked Stuart.

"The east bound train, heading to White House Landing, ran the barricaded gauntlet as our cavalrymen shot the engineer and wounded many Federal passengers. I assume by now the remaining passengers have informed McClellan of our cavalry's presence."

James saluted Stuart and realized the commander would not care about losing a piece of equipment; there were more important matters he had to consider. His artillerists rejoined the cavalry.

They moved out south to Talleysville, arriving later that night. Their chores came first, that of feeding and watering the tired horses. They had covered forty arduous miles; it was time for a short respite as night fell over the artillerists. James himself was exhausted.

At midnight, under a bright moon, James pushed on as Stuart pressed them forward in the direction of the Forge Bridge over the Chickahominy River. James and his artillerists followed behind Stuart. Riding in the depths of the woods, James heard the owls hooting and whip-poor-wills crying out; the stunted trees with their knotty branches and thorns reached out to seize the clothes of his weary troopers. Desolation reigned there. James unconsciously placed his hand on his pistol as he was riding along. He thought it important to be ready for any enemy in blue as the maze of forests, swamps, and sluggish streams and narrow, confusing roads could be hiding Federals. He kept his lynx-eye on all the fords of the Chickahominy River. Taking note of the fast-running high river that made the fords impassable, it was Stuart who he believed would have to find the route to safety on the other side of the river.

By dawn the weary artillerists and cavalrymen reached Forge Bridge near Sycamore Springs; rains had swollen the river. James watched Rooney Lee try to swim his horse across the river. But the water was too high, and Lee had to turn back. James believed feelings of anxiety were now on the muddy and begrimed faces of his artillerists. With a swollen river to their front and the Federals behind, he was expecting to be attacked any moment by Federal cavalry, maybe even infantry. He placed his two cannon a half mile from the ford with a squadron of the 1st Virginia Cavalry to guard in case of a Federal attack.

"Lieutenant McGregor, I want you to keep a keen eye out for the Federals. If they come at us, open fire with all you got. I'll give you command to have my men do the same," he ordered. "I'm going to find out how long General Stuart thinks it'll take us to get over the river."

"Yes, sir," McGregor replied.

He hastened Billy to the ford where the road to Providence Forge and Charles City Court House crossed the river.

"Sir, we've the rearguard covered," he reported to Stuart who looked rather anguished and alarmed as to the danger his troopers were in. "How long do you expect we'll have to hold?"

"We're working to tear down that barn and build on the old piers of the bridge. We should soon be swimming our horses, and your artillerists should be crossing by 1:00 pm."

"Very good, sir. We'll cover the rear until all our troopers are crossed," James said, saluting and turning Billy back in the direction of the guns.

Three hours later he and his artillerists crossed over the river. James ordered three men to stay behind to burn the bridge. He thought they were now thirty miles from Richmond, twenty of which would have to be crossed before reaching their lines.

"Boys, the whiskey is yours, share and enjoy. I feel we're home safe. We've ridden around McClellan and you deserve some O Be Joyful. Finish her off," James said as the artillerists drove into Buckland Plantation, the home of Colonel James Wilcox.

He watched as Creole sprang from his horse. He was the first artillerist to dismount and run for the keg. Creole filled his cup to the brim and swallowed it down in a gulp. Then he took another.

James had said farewell to Stuart, who was now on his way to Richmond with his coveted information. Stuart had told Fitz and James to ride on after five hours rest and the men had been supped.

His men's faces were haggard from want of sleep. To the men resting on the rain-soaked soil, the scalding coffee, corn bread, and bacon were the equal of any feast. James watched Creole get tight in no time. Soon he was asleep under a tree with low hanging branches.

James's artillerists were gathered. They were seeking the fresh fish's wisdom. James was close enough to hear their conversation, but he did not impart his wisdom upon the situation.

"Never thought we'd make it all the way around them Yankees," Bill Clem said. "I drove them horses hard, even harder after Lieutenant Breathed got us fired up after the broken limber pole."

"Ye done good, Bill. You served the cause good," Robert Mackall said. "We've never put a shot out. We could've if'n we'd had to."

"I never lost faith in the Lieutenant. Even when we was stuck in the mud. But he sure can get hot," Henry Matthews said.

"Look over yonder at Creole," Robert said. "He done passed out from gulping down the whiskey. He's a scalawag. Them Cajuns are a strange lot."

"Boys, I know I'm new to your fightin'. I've an idea if you like to prank the scalawag under the tree. I got something to fix 'em good," Zimmerman said.

"What would that be?" Henry asked.

"See them chickens over yonder?" Henry said. "Pull a head off one of them, squirt the blood in a cup and dip the whole head in the blood. Let me tell ya, I studied a little of the Cajun juju. Hang the head on a string over Creole asleep over there. When he awakes you'll see a Cajun jumpin' like you never seen before!"

"I'll do it! He brings us Jonah anyhow," Bill said. "Would be fun to see him jumpin'."

James watched Bill place the chicken head on a string over Creole's nose. When Creole awoke after his four-hour sleep he stared straight at the chicken head. He swore up and down and began shaking. After that he crossed his chest in the name of the Father, Son, and Holy Ghost. His face became a ghostly white color. His comrades were bent over in laughter.

"Devil, boys, my number's up! It won't be long now! I's a dead man!" Creole shouted.

James looked over to McGregor and grinned, thinking to himself it couldn't have happened to a better man, saying nothing of the black snake.

19

No Man Left Behind

JAMES LAY IN THE shade of a sycamore tree near the Sudley Church crossroads. He reflected simply that he had been here before, nothing was new under the sun; he knew he would do his duty as a matter of honor. The weather had been fine, but a bit dry. He was satisfied with the work accomplished by his men since General Lee and the Army of Northern Virginia had headed north, leaving General McClellan and his army cowering at Harrison's Landing. He believed McClellan was the best general the Confederacy had on their side! James laughed out loud at his own joke.

In fact, James had never felt better, reflecting that since Lee had taken command of his artillery forces two months ago, it had been victory after victory. Now, the blustering General Pope and his so-called Army of the Potomac had insulted Lee, his native state of Virginia, and made his revered Commander Lee angry. James chuckled, again, realizing that General Lee had sent General Jackson and General Stuart to destroy General Pope's base of supply, and that his horse artillery caissons were still carrying a lot of delicacies courtesy of Pope's commissary. At night he still dreamed about the flaming wreckage of trains and supplies burning furiously at Manassas Junction.

But it was now late August, and forced marches in summer heat had taken a toll on his men and their animals. He supposed that old Pope didn't know where Jackson was and did not know how to find out. Maybe Pope was waiting for McClellan to bring his army back to Washington. That would be smart, he believed, but Pope was not too smart. As soon as Pope found Jackson, the stubborn regimented soldier would attack just to show McClellan up.

James remembered the first battle that he was in between General Beauregard and General MacDowell, a full year ago. Now it was the afternoon of August 28th, as near as he could figure dates. He and his men settled into camp at the Sudley Church for a much-needed rest. James could hear the laughter of the men packed into the woods. He was still smiling over some banter he had had with Pelham.

Earlier in the day when Captain Pelham had ridden up, James had reported, "Ammunition has been issued as ordered. Caissons and limbers are all filled. I heard that General Stuart captured Pope's dress uniform and wants to form a cartel to exchange it for the plumed hat he lost to the Yankees."

"I've heard the same, Lieutenant," Pelham replied.

"Do you suppose the two men could just swap back their garments and we could all go home?" James said with a grin on his face.

"Maybe you should suggest it to General Stuart."

"Don't suspect Pope would go for it. Just an idea."

James saw the shadows in the churchyard begin to lengthen as afternoon wore into evening. Deeper in the woods, he heard an owl hoot solemnly and intermittently. He heard the rumble of artillery somewhere off to the west, which was ominous.

He walked back to his men who were polishing the "Springfield, Mass." that was also stamped "U.S." on the barrel of their newest gun.

"Lieutenant, nice to have this here rifled gun, compliments of General Pope," Private Mackall greeted him.

"The howitzers preformed good service, but now we have better guns. The best part of it is they're free and come with good ammunition!" James replied with a smile as he stroked the gun barrel like a pet dog.

Suddenly, the roar of cannon, much closer on the right, brought him back to reality. From the sound, it was clear that this was an artillery exchange. He and his men listened intently; musket fire was added. As the sounds of battle resolved themselves into one continuous roll, he knew this was more than a skirmish with passing Federal cavalry.

A courier galloped up to Captain Pelham and gave him a dispatch. Pelham read it to himself and then excitedly turned to James with the news.

"Lieutenant, I know it's almost dark, but General Jackson is deploying our three guns to his right flank about a mile and a half down the line. Quickly, harness your teams! I'll lead you to the front."

"Yes, sir," James said as he saluted Pelham, and then turned to his men and issued the necessary orders.

His artillerists' general response was a groan, but they moved.

Their trip along the lines in the dark woods was a nightmare. There were no campfires, no guides with shielded lanterns. James followed Pelham who set a rapid pace. He could barely see the outline of the rutted road as it threaded its way through the woods. The men cussed and swore in the darkness as the guns, limbers, and caissons bounced and rumbled through. James gritted his teeth and prayed he wouldn't hear the unmistakable sound of heavy wheels running over living flesh.

James assumed the road that had been running south, for as they turned westward and left the woods the light got better.

Pelham called back, "Breathed, when the road turns south again we must move off it through the fields on the right and go north of the next woods."

"Yes sir!" he replied. "Take the van! I'll stay at the turnoff to get the guns headed in the right direction."

James pulled up Billy and shouted orders to his men as they came up to guide right. He saw the first gun crew pass; the second gun crew was right behind them, but there was a gap between the limber and the caisson. He realized that the third gun was not there. He looked down the road and strained for sounds he knew so well. There were none. He now knew one gun was missing. For a minute anger gripped him, then anxiety. If the guns came up late and stayed on the Groveton Road, they would ride right into the Federal lines he thought; in a split second he decided to follow his two guns toward Pelham.

"We've lost a piece, sir," he gasped to Pelham as he dismounted in front of him.

"Damnation! We'll have to do with what we've got, Lieutenant," Pelham exclaimed. "This is Major Shumaker. We're under his orders."

James glanced toward the fight and saw a dense growing cloud of hot gray smoke and exploding shells and musketry mixed with urgent shouts of struggling men.

Pelham turned to Shumaker. "Don't these Yankee storekeepers know it's closing time? Why are we fighting in the dark?"

"Captain Pelham, these aren't Yankee storekeepers," Shumaker replied. "We've captured a Federal prisoner and we're facing Wisconsin and Indiana infantrymen."

"Damnation," Pelham replied. "No wonder."

"Take your guns and deploy them on that farm, close to the house. Enfilade those people; make it hot for 'em," Major Shumaker ordered as Pelham turned to James and said simply, "Follow me."

Turning to his artillerists, James shouted, "Section limber front. Follow my lead over the railroad cut. Forward! March!"

Pelham led James and his two guns through the deep twilight, illuminated only by the flash of battle. They picked their way slowly through the Confederate troops until they had worked their way around the western side of some farm buildings.

James turned the guns to face almost due east and witnessed something he had never seen before. There, on the opposite rise, stood two long rows of men firing at each other from less than one hundred yards apart. He saw the wounded fall where they stood; neither side advanced nor retreated. In the near darkness they just continued to load and fire. He realized that if Pelham had not moved them into almost a full enfilade position on the Federal lines, the guns could never have fired without killing as many friends as foes. The next instant the flash of the Federals' guns illumined his targets for a moment, and he was able to take aim.

"Two degrees elevation! Load canister! Fire!" James hollered. He did not have long to wait before observing the effect on the Federal lines.

The toughest Federal forces he had ever seen began to waver, but slowly. The Federal guns responded to his guns; a nearby rail fence draped with creeper was shattered as a Federal shell burst at its base, close to his gun. His artillerymen were sponging, ramming, priming, aiming, firing. His newly-acquired Federal three-inch rifled dog of war barked viciously.

Soon James realized it was time to move to a better location, "Limber up! Forward! March!" he cried out as the minie balls whistled all around his head.

They had not had a clear target for an hour. He stood rigidly and aimed by afterimages. Gradually the fire on both sides slackened as the Federals seemed to be moving south in the darkness.

Long after midnight he received orders to retire back behind the railroad cut with Shumaker's Battalion. Once his guns were properly parked, he posted a sentinel near the guns to report alarms and receive orders during the night. James pondered what might have happened to his third gun, and then he lay down in exhaustion to sleep near his men.

⋙⟐⟐⋘

James awoke the next morning after a troubled sleep. His artillerymen lay in the tall grasses on a stony ridge behind the railroad cut. He dreamt that death had reaped its toll all around the farm and barn where they had fought.

Blue and gray bodies lay strewn out on the ground much to his dismay, some missing heads, arms and legs, others with gapping flesh wounds where minies had shattered bones. He heard men groaning and crying for water, but he was helpless to attend to their medical needs. He looked over to see that the two-storied farmhouse had most of the windows shot out and hundreds of bullet holes riddled the lower exterior walls.

His waking from a dream proved that what he saw was from no dream. He was uncertain if he had slept or not. He wondered if his eyes burned from the smoke of battle or from lack of sleep, or from what they had seen. He had seen death, but the nightmare of last night was more than battle.

He realized that the armies had clashed for hours during the night, so close they could have thrown the bullets at each other, yet never advancing, never retreating, only loading and dying. His guns had broken the evil spell; only death could have stopped the killing. But how many of his friends fell in the darkness to his canister? The captured ammunition was good Federal ammunition, he mused, but what if it had been the poor product of the Confederacy, with short rounds? What if he had not been able to replace the smooth bores with the rifled cannon.

Realizing that unless the artillery fought beside or in front of the infantry, the danger to his friends would be as great as to the foe, he concluded. It was best to enfilade the enemy, for they had done exactly that last night.

He understood that Pelham had seen the field even in darkness and had placed them in the only location where artillery could affect the unearthly battle. It must have been by instinct that Pelham made decisions in such conditions, he thought. Did he himself have these instincts? He had at least learned he could aim at night by watching the afterimage of the cannon fire.

The morning disclosed that his aim had been true. Feeling elated in an instant; he suddenly realized that he had the instincts of a soldier. What had Walter Scott said about Claverhouse, Viscount of Dundee, who also had the instincts of a soldier, the cavalier who rode a coal-black stallion, raised at Glen Ogilvie and having had served under William of Orange, he mused? Something like, *Cool and collected in danger, fierce and ardent in pursuing success, careless of death himself, and ruthless in inflicting it on others.*

James reflected that Jackson was so, but his strength was of faith. Stuart was as Claverhouse, and yet he was not. Claverhouse was careless of chivalry and honor, but Stuart was always the glass of courtesy. Something about these last thoughts troubled him, but he had no time to reflect further.

Suddenly, he heard Pelham alert his artillerists to the approaching Federals from the south. James ordered the second day's rations quickly consumed and the horses fed, watered, and harnessed. His four guns were reassembled and deployed with the rest of Shumaker's batteries to engage and drive off the Federal threat. He and Pelham, on horseback, watched together as Federals approached. The enemy was still too far away to engage to advantage.

"Breathed," Pelham said, "Do my eyes deceive me or are those people sending only two regiments to try and take the whole of our artillery? This has got to be a diversion, ignorance, or gross stupidity."

"Based on what we've seen of Pope, I suspect the latter," James replied.

His artillery scarcely had to fire a shell, since the Confederate infantry down by the railroad embankment broke up the attack before the sparse Federal line could get in musket range of his guns.

Pelham spoke, "That couldn't have been a serious attack. No doubt it was supposed to be a diversion, but the other attack is late. If the diversion is here, the attack will be at the other end of the line. Have the men stand down. Have them ready to move immediately if we hear any serious sounds of battle from the left. The Sudley Church flank is our most vulnerable."

James replied, "Yes, sir," as he thought of one word that described the measure of his commander. Instinct.

୧ଓଵ

James's morning passed slowly into afternoon. The Federal attacks were neither coordinated nor very heavy. He, Pelham, and the rest of the horse artillery waited for orders. Sometime in the early afternoon James heard sounds of battle from the distant left, which brought Pelham to his feet.

"That's it! Mount up fast. Back to the Sudley Church," Pelham exclaimed. "I want you to limber up and move this gun to the left flank of our line across Bull Run," the captain said as he pointed toward the location he desired.

"Yes, sir," James replied with a salute. "Limber the gun! We're moving out!" he shouted to his artillerists as he sat his horse and looked toward the new location through his field glasses.

He watched Creole, Mackall, Zimmerman, and Clem handle the gun as the drivers, riding the six-up team, came from the rear pulling the limber.

"We're going to a hotter place on the field. Bet we're going to catch hell," Clem said to Zimmerman. James listened in on their rhetoric.

"Have faith. You ain't gonna die until the good Lord wills it. If I told you once I told you a hundred times, have faith," Zimmerman replied.

"Amen!" Clem responded.

His drivers wheeled in order to hook up to the gun; the horse holders passed the other artillerists their horses.

"March!" James ordered.

His band of dust-covered brothers rode at lightning speed behind Jackson's line to the north of Bull Run. Something in Pelham's voice set the men to work faster than usual; the guns of the horse artillery headed east with a purpose.

Shortly after they reached the Sudley Road, General Stuart galloped toward them, his horse well lathered. He drew up beside Pelham and James and said, "Glad to see you, Captain. You'll advance your guns with all speed to the support of the endangered left of the army. The Yankees are moving around our left flank. It looks like a couple of brigades, but it may be a full corps. If they get around Sudley Ford and past the mill, they may get in our rear. Jackson has already sent the trains to Aldie. Find a secure place to flank those people and keep them bottled up before they can get over the streams. It looks like they don't have much of a plan," he paused for a moment gesturing to the north. "Oh, one more thing. The Sudley Road is too hot. You'll have to go around the woods."

"Do I report to someone over there?" Pelham asked.

"Yes, but I don't know who. Use your judgment," Stuart responded as he rode off.

They raced their guns around thick woods and over fords to get on location east of Bull Run and well beyond Jackson's left flank. Six sweating and straining, pink-nostrilled and fiery-eyed horses pulled their guns.

James saw their newly arriving infantry forming behind the railroad cut to slow the Federals. Fighting had commenced. He rode to a good piece of ground and stopped.

Pelham pulled up beside him and said, "Lieutenant, place your guns here! Those are Patrick's men to our front. Our guns will be in support of them until I give you further orders. Understood?"

"Yes, sir," James said as he reined Billy back to bring up the guns.

He surveyed the ground. The railroad bank would cover the infantry, but his guns would have no cover. He deliberated that the Federals would have to advance across open ground to get to both the infantry and his guns. He spied woods to the south to hide his guns from the Yankees, but it was on the wrong side of Bull Run! There did not seem to be any Federal artillery close, but long-range artillery could be a problem, he believed. It wasn't perfect but unless the Federals sent most of a corps they would have a hard time turning their flank.

James did not have to wait very long before his guns were needed. The Federals started to advance what looked like a brigade, maybe two, James thought. They were moving toward the railroad embankment.

Pelham ordered shell and canister within James's audible range. His guns' effectiveness was immediate and deadly. Through his field glasses James observed that the Federal advance had stopped. They sought shelter behind the only thing available, a rail fence. He saw that, after a few minutes of Confederate infantry and artillery fire, the Federals began to withdraw.

As soon as Pelham saw the enemy break he called out, "Double your rate of fire!"

James and his men responded, but not without cost as a twelve-pounder shell burst over his gun with a horrendous noise. Three of his horses were hit by the shrapnel, and crumpled to the ground; the lead driver lost both legs, the swing driver was hit in the hip, and the wheel driver suffered an arm injury.

"Remove those wounded men from the field," James ordered as artillerists pulled them from the wreckage by cutting the traces to free the unwounded horses.

Hearing a caisson explode with a frightful brilliance and a reverberating sound, James observed that a piece of shrapnel that had hit Sergeant Hoxton in the arm was creating a bloody mess of his upper extremity.

"Private Matthews, help the sergeant to the rear. Private Zimmerman, take his place on the gun," James commanded.

Another screaming shell dug into the earth and exploded, showering his men and their beasts with mud and debris. Bravado kicked into his soul as he unflinchingly looked over the sights of the loaded gun and observed its line and range. His brave artillerists, pale and sanguine, served their guns and threw well-directed shells against the Federal artillery that had moved onto an opposite knoll.

"Fire!" James hollered as his guns hurled round messengers of death toward their Federal counterparts.

James viewed the effect of the impact of the shells through his field glasses, satisfied to see disabled guns, panicked horses, and Federal artillerists on the ground.

To the right he noticed the batteries of A. P. Hill's division begin to suffer dreadfully; the horses were terrified with the pandemonium of battle. He saw them jerk their heads back, as they neighed wildly—some escaped their holders and galloping aimlessly across the field.

James witnessed shells arriving in a stream, carrying death as they struck flesh or ploughed into the terra firma. The deafening sounds of battle surrounded James and his men. He construed that when the shells burst in the air it was like the ancient Greek gods were angry above, sending crackling thunder bolts toward earth.

To his horror the blue sky was gone. The battle's magnetic energy pulled together thousands of men before him; hundreds of guns and horses ballistically pranced to and fro as the Federal forces tried to breach Jackson's flank. He saw a multitude of the Confederate brigades dashing against them, hurling them back like great ocean waves upon the shoreline.

Blinded by the battle smoke, first heavily settling, and then drifting off like clouds blown by a capricious wind, James was confused as the battlefield appeared and disappeared in flashes, visible and then obscure.

In the woods, at the base of the hill behind him, there arose a clamor and the bellowing thunder of Armageddon. He turned and saw a fresh brigade of Confederate infantry. The sweat-soaked men rushed by his guns like a gray wave into the chaos of the battle.

Not believing their audacity as they stepped through the burning broomsedge where many a dead and wounded soldier lay, James was further infuriated as he struggled to identify the aster and goldenrod, ironweed and sumac, dying as soon as, he believed, his infantry comrades would be—dying in battle. The brush was burning as his comrades rushed through it, it all created a panoramic image of hades in his mind.

Up and down Jackson's line his fellow artillerists' fire boomed like titanic kettle-drums, whittling away the Federal infantry. He could not believe that still the Federals plugged the gaps with fresh men and continued to advance; the fight was approaching its critical moment he thought.

Pelham returned at a gallop and reined up in front of James. "I've been unable to locate General Stuart for some time now. But General Jackson has told me to act as the occasion might require," Pelham said to him as he sat his horse next to him.

"Sergeant Shaw, report," Pelham shouted. "I want you to find General Hill and advise him of our disposition and need for reinforcements. Return with his orders. My compliments to the general."

His artillerists reached deeper and deeper into caisson and limber chests. They cast anxious glances rearward toward the ordnance wagons that were growing ever more empty of powder and projectiles. James, too, became concerned as he knew the ordnance train was running low. He heard the neighing of the horses to the rear and thought that as long as the ordnance train held out his boys would do their duties.

"Private Zimmerman, ride to the rear on the caisson and reload the chest. Report back to me with what remains of our ammunition supply. Load shell! Five hundred yards, two-inch fuse," James commanded as the number-five gunner handed Private Clem the shell and Private Mackall rammed it home.

James saw Creole prick and prime the cannon. Matthews nodded off Private Creole as he pulled his thumb from the vent. Private Matthews straightened the lanyard and looked back to him as he sat Billy with his one arm up in the air and the other hand holding his field glasses to his eyes.

"Fire!" James commanded as his arm sliced in a downward motion.

His gun's carriage swayed back as the blue smoke exploded from the muzzle, sending its projectile toward the oncoming infantry in blue.

His artillerymen grabbed hold of the wheels, rolled the piece back into position and reloaded it. James mused that the gun was like a hungry dragon, always in need of the black powder and projectile; it was a ravenous fire breather eager to belch its flames. He observed an enemy incoming shell that hit the ground and dug a trench under the right wheel of the gun; it didn't explode.

"Remove that shell. Reload!" he cried as Private Zimmerman, the man of faith, believed it was truly a dud shell and obeyed his orders.

⟳

The Federals had now closed to a distance of two hundred yards, fast approaching his gunners. They came on, five men deep at the double-quick.

"Load! Double canister!" he ordered as he waited patiently as his men laboriously but skillfully did their jobs—heedless of the approaching danger.

"Fire!" James commanded.

His artillerists' blast dropped twenty men to the ground as the angry piece shot hundreds of iron flesh-piercing balls amongst the enemy lines. He watched through his field glasses as the Federals moved the last hundred yards across the field, still at a double-quick pace.

When they were within forty yards of the gun, he heard a Federal colonel cry out, "Halt! Aim! Fire!"

The Federal volley seemed to create a breeze, which James felt. It had an effect upon the leaves of the trees; the vegetation rustled. A sprinkling of small boughs and twigs, cut in an instant, fell upon James's shoulder and then onto the ground.

He thought the colonel, whom he saw charging his position, had the air of a Roman consul: round, strong, with a bullet head bared to the breeze. His close-cropped black hair, short black beard, beaked nose, bold eyes, and red cheeks intuitively made him realize that he was a determined fighter.

The artillerists whom he was so proud of had gotten off a quick volley when suddenly a regiment of Confederate infantry emerged from the woods behind him. His gun was now more of an expensive prize than ever, he surmised, for the Federal regiment would have to fight hand-to-hand to get it.

"Forward, boys, after the gun!" he heard the Federal colonel cry out. "The gun shall be ours before this battle ends! I want it as a memento for this day!"

James heard the command while he sat his horse like a figure out of an old European master canvas.

The Confederate infantry, with fixed bayonets, swarmed past his lone gun like enraged hornets looking to sting and kill whatever was before them. The fight turned into a vicious melee as James watched his gun with one eye and kept the other fixed on the melee to his front. His artillerists were going back to the limber chests pulling out classical Roman Gladius artillery swords to defend themselves. Others went into the melee with their artillery implements turned into weapons.

The melee came closer and closer to his gun. He steadily sat his horse, his left hand gripping the reins tightly as he pulled his revolver. The entangled men of blue and gray pushed and shoved each other; bayonets struck torsos and men fell to the ground in anguish before him. The dust swirled in every direction, making it hard for him to see anything clearly.

The crackling sound of muskets firing pierced his ears as more men from both sides joined in the fight. His lone gun, prized by the Federal colonel was now protected only by him, as it stood unmanned.

"You shall have it over my dead body!" James screamed as he stared at the Federal colonel who came out of the dust storm like a ghost.

James pointed his revolver and fired point blank range at the colonel. At least two bullets slammed into his torso, and he fell to the ground. He watched the colonel crawl to the base of the gun leaving a trail of blood behind him in the dirt. He grasped the right wheel of the gun.

"I've you now, you devil!" the dying colonel cried.

"Yes, Colonel, but the gun is still mine," James said as the brave soldier took his last breath.

When James looked up the Federal forces were pulling back. The Federal reinforcements that had been seen earlier off to the right were moving farther right, screened by the woods from his guns. It was time to move back, to resupply, and get attention for his wounded.

"Limber to the rear, men; it's time to call it a day," James ordered to his exhausted artillerists. "If we get any closer to the heat, we're going to lose limber and caisson chests."

Suddenly, a shell screeched in toward the muzzle of the cannon where Private Creole stood. James stared in shock as the shell exploded in Creole's abdomen, completely tearing his body in two. His head and the upper part of his torso shot like a man out of a mortar into the air and fell twenty feet in front of the gun. The bottom half of his legs and torso were blown back into the cannon. Blood and entrails splattered his stunned comrades.

"Pick up his body and put half on the limber and his other half on the caisson. No man left behind!" James proclaimed calmly as if referring to some nameless cadaver back in his medical school lab.

"March! Forward! Guide right!" James ordered while working to avoid the heat of the creeping flames that had been set by Federal counter-battery fire.

"Right Wheel! Trot! March!" James commanded.

At the moment he gave his order, the top half of Creole's body tumbled off the limber chest. He realized that the shells were not coming as quickly, but they continued nonetheless as he and his men tried to exit the battlefield.

"Halt! Private Zimmerman and Matthews, retrieve the body!" James ordered. The two men dismounted their horses and retrieved the torso.

"Forward! March!" James boomed. They finally exited the battlefield to safety; Creole would be missed by them all.

20

Special Order #191

SEPTEMBER 13TH, 1862

THE DAY BEFORE MOLLIE had witnessed the Confederate cavalry skirmishing in the streets and fighting their way out of town on West Patrick Street. Out her window this morning she saw the early morning streets bustled with excitement. She came downstairs to the dining room of Lieutenant Colonel Charles Trail, a loyal Federal, and his wife Ariana, her childhood friend. When Mollie entered the dining room Charles immediately arose and a maid pulled her chair out so that she could sit with her host and hostess. Mollie looked as aristocratic as the setting. They sat at the breakfast table in the Trail mansion at 106 Church Street in Frederick City.

"Good morning, Mollie," Ariana said.

Mollie wore a subdued-green day dress; her parted black hair was drawn into a bun. She wore a brooch at the collar, which was pink; it was decorated with a raised white female cameo.

She thought Charles was a straightforward type of man. She knew he was dedicated to improving his six already-prosperous farms near Frederick County; he had been appointed Lieutenant Colonel of the 1st Regiment of the Potomac Home Brigade, in charge of volunteer recruitment. His moustache, full goatee, and thick head of black hair were all perfectly groomed. He was dressed in a finely tailored three-piece suit; his overcoat was laid on a side chair, a cravat was tied under his collar, and his gold pocket watch chain hung from his vest pocket. He pulled it out to determine the hour.

"We should have our breakfast if we're going to make it out to David Best's farmhouse before the entire Army of the Potomac descends upon our city. I've been told they're coming into town on the Georgetown Pike," Charles said as he signaled the maid for breakfast.

Ariana sat to the right of her husband and Mollie was seated on his left. A servant poured the coffee from an elaborate silver coffee piece, part of a complete matching silver set decorating the table, with candlesticks, creamer, sugar bowl, and flatware. Mollie looked at the fine blue and white Canton china ware, which was richly decorated with traditional hand-painted river scenes and other views of domestic life in China.

Ariana was accustomed to the finer things in life. Her father, Colonel John McElfresh, had married the daughter of Francis Mantz, the wealthiest citizen of Frederick County. Mollie recalled that the colonel and her father had been elected members of the state reform convention. Her father was the convention chairman, and the two politically powerful Marylanders had forged a strong friendship during their time of service to the state.

She had waited until the end of her stay with the Trails to bring up her agenda in relation to her imprisoned father. "I didn't want to impose on our friendship, Ariana, but I do want to discuss my father's imprisonment before I've to leave today," Mollie said as she looked across the table with sad eyes. "You and Charles know my father well. He's a man of character. Because of his moral convictions, he has been unable to take the 'Ironclad Oath' while being imprisoned at Fort Warren. The climate of Boston has greatly impaired his health. He has rendered his medical services to his fellow prisoners and the Federal guards alike. He even has Federal testimonials to his impartial conduct. Surely those in control of his imprisonment can see he does not pose any threat to the country."

"I've been to Fort McHenry to see to the needs of the imprisoned Confederates there. I understand what your father's compassion has done for the spirits of those imprisoned with him," Ariana said.

"Your father is a fine Marylander who has served his state in the past. Why don't you feel your father can take this oath unconditionally?" Charles asked.

"I've a few of his letters here. I'd like to share some of what he writes to me. This is one point to which he cannot swear, *'that I will at any and all times hereafter, and under all circumstances, yield a hearty and willing support to the Constitution of the United States and to the Government thereof.'* He says in his letter, *'How can I, a moral man, swear to support anything a government might do in the future, not knowing what crimes that government might commit?'* A tear came to her eye as she read. "He also wrote that he struggled with this line, *'that I will give no aid, comfort, or assistance to the enemies of the Government!'* He has written here that this violates his Hippocratic oath."

"Mollie, my dear, I can feel how this troubles your heart," Ariana said as she took Charles's hand, which was resting on the tablecloth. "Charles, will you see to Dr. Macgill and find out what might be done to obtain his release from Fort Warren? Mollie, set your mind at ease over this matter. Once Charles has explained your father's position to the authorities, I feel certain the weight of his opinion will have your father freed."

"Mollie, my dear, I've know your father a great number of years. He's a man whose honor is above question. I also know many of the senior officials among the president's advisors. I'll plead his case and see what can be done to win his release. Your father is not a threat to this government," Charles said. "In fact, his continued confinement distresses many of the best men of Maryland, without whose support Lincoln will find this state hard to control. Rather it's in the interest of the Union that he be freed and returned as soon as possible."

Mollie relaxed, for she could perceive that, as Charles enlarged upon the issue, he was already beginning to formulate his argument by which her father's ordeal would soon be ended.

Breakfast ended pleasantly; Charles had her bags brought from her room and packed onto her carriage. The Trails' carriage was also brought to the front gate. The two carriages proceeded through the hustle and bustle of Frederick City toward the Georgetown Pike. Their objective was South Hermitage Farm, to check with Charles's tenant, David Best, to determine the condition of his crops. Charles also wanted to make certain that the advancing Federal army was aware that the farm was owned by a loyal Union supporter.

Mollie noticed that the morning dew was still glistening on the wheat fields as they arrived at the toll house on the Georgetown Pike where Charles paid the toll for the two carriages. As they moved out from the toll house, Mollie noticed some commotion ahead along the Pike on a secondary road, off to the left. Charles had his carriage pull off to the side of the pike so that he could speak with the soldiers. Alfred did the same. Mollie dismounted from her carriage and followed Charles to the kibitzing soldiers.

"Good morning. I'm Lieutenant Colonel Charles Trail with the Potomac Home Brigade. What is all the commotion here?"

"Sir, Private Mitchell has found an envelope. In it is an official looking order with some cigars. He found it under a locust tree in this wheat field," a soldier replied.

"This is my wheat field. Let me see the orders," Charles said as she moved a little closer to him.

"Yes, sir," the soldier of the 27th Indiana Regiment replied as he handed Charles the order. Charles read the orders just loud enough so that Mollie could hear the names of all Lee's chief lieutenants. An official looking signature was affixed to the bottom of the order. She also noticed it was called "Special Order 191," and she pondered what this might mean.

"Sergeant, I order you to deliver this missive to your superior officer as quickly as possible. Soon there'll be a whole corps coming up this road to Frederick City. I should think General McClellan would very much like to know the information written in this order. Carry on," Charles commanded.

They returned to their carriages. Alfred, at her directions, moved her carriage down the Georgetown Pike and away from the excited Federal soldiers. She immediately realized that General McClellan would soon know the location of every unit in the Army of Northern Virginia. Her carriage then followed Charles and Ariana's to the farm of David Best, located a little farther south.

Charles helped Ariana down from their carriage and then graciously came over to Mollie's carriage and helped her to the ground. She glanced at the two-story farm house with its red tin roof. There was a wooden, tin-roofed barn behind the main house and a small well house in the front yard; the main line of the Baltimore & Ohio Railroad ran to the left of the house.

Alfred stayed near the carriage as she followed her friends into the house to have a cup of tea before saying good-bye. She remained a short time in the parlor of David's home, being polite, but really wanting to leave in order to get her intelligence forwarded into the right hands. After the tea, she kissed both of her Unionist friends on the cheek and bade them good-bye.

Turning to Charles she said, "I've got to get back to my mother in Hagerstown. It looks like I'll have to leave now to avoid being caught between two armies, if it's not already too late. Thank you for your many kindnesses and for any help you can give my father in coming home to my family. What's the best way I can go to avoid a clash of arms?"

Charles replied, "I'd go south to Buckeystown, then turn west to Jefferson. You may be able to get back to the National Pike at Middletown. But be careful."

"We've relatives in Jefferson. If I can't get through, I'll at least have a safe place to stay," she replied.

Mollie exited the house and Charles showed her to the carriage. In the back of her mind she was thinking not of her friendship with the prominent couple but of the back roads which she and Alfred must take. They would have to cross the Catoctin and South Mountain ranges in order to get home to Hagerstown.

"Alfred, make haste for we've a long trip before us," she instructed. She smiled deceitfully and waved to her friends, the Trails, who were standing in Mr. Best's front yard.

∽◌৪৩◌৵

Her carriage emerged back onto the Georgetown Pike and headed north toward Frederick City. They turned left onto a road that led them over to the Buckeystown Road. They moved like the wind but paused for a moment at the intersection; the two horses were now pink-nostrilled and breathing heavily.

"Which-away, Miss Mollie?" Alfred asked.

"Turn south. I think this is the road to Buckeystown."

When they arrived in Buckeystown, they discovered a Federal presence. A stern looking Federal officer with bars of his rank on his collar stopped them at the town center and held the horses' bridles.

"Where're you going, missy?" the officer asked. "There're Federal troops clogging the roads and we don't need civilians adding to the confusion. I order you and your darky to head back east to Frederick, if you know what is good for you."

The five-shot Colt patent revolver helped her to feel comfortable. Its presence had given her a feeling of security in past situations. She placed her hands back in her lap as would any proper Southern woman.

"I need to get home to Hagerstown before the hostilities break out. My mother's very ill, I must see to her," she responded to the officer.

"You're a little late. Fighting has already started. We're right on the Rebels' heels to the west of here. I'm going to turn your horses and see you on your way east, understood?"

She knew time was running short; Alfred whipped the two-up team. They headed east on the Manor Woods Road, as they were told to do by the officer. Within a few miles they arrived at a grist mill on the Monocacy River. She smelled the burning wood fumes in the air. Water was pouring over the wheel, which powered the mill. The first level was built with old stone, and red brick comprised the second level. Smoke poured from a chimney at the far end of the building.

"May I help you, miss?" the owner asked as he emerged from the building.

"Yes, we've been turned back from Buckeystown. We need to get around the town and head west on the Manor Woods Road. My mother is very ill in Hagerstown. Can you help us do this without running us into any more blasted Federals?"

"A Southern man myself—I'd be happy to oblige you," the proprietor said.

He gave her directions of back roads, which he assured her would be clear of Federals.

The Monocacy flowed so beautifully to the rear of the grist mill, she thought. It was a wonderful time to see its pristine clear waters tumbling and flowing over the smooth rocks. Such a beautiful river she thought, in the midst of so much turmoil.

They raced on. After traversing the back roads, they found themselves once again on the Manor Woods Road.

Suddenly, before them stood two armed Federal pickets, muskets ready at their sides.

She leaned over to Alfred, a strong and muscular man, and stated with an urgency in her voice, "This time we're going through at all costs! Get ready to kick and run," she said. As they approached the Federals she reached for her Colt.

"Stop," the picket said as he tried to grab the bridle of the horse closest to him.

Mollie pulled her revolver from under the carriage seat and pointed it at the Federal. Before he could react, she fired the revolver. The bullet pierced the soldier's right shoulder. His musket tumbled to the ground. As he stumbled backward Alfred kicked the other soldier to the ground, then lashed the reins on the backs of the two horses. The carriage took off like a shot. Dust flew behind them as they raced away, obscuring the soldiers' aims. The soldier Alfred had kicked stood up, took aim, and fired at them. The wounded soldier pulled his Colt .44 caliber revolver and feebly fired a few rounds.

Mollie recovered while they raced through the open farmland. She could not help but observe the magnificent barns sturdily built of stone. The barns she observed had a second floor made of wood, which overhung the ground level. She was puzzled by how these details of the barns fascinated her in light of what she had just done. She thought she was being blissful, trying to ignore her reality.

The warm breeze blew back around the bun of her hair as Alfred cantered the team. She saw that the golden wheat was ready for harvest, and the smell of sweet corn filled her nostrils.

The horses were tiring and were fully lathered by the time they came to a road. They traveled on this road for less than a mile before they arrived at the intersection of the Jefferson Pike.

"Alfred, turn right!"

They came to a steep grade, which she remembered was a pass to the Catoctin Range of mountains.

Guns firing to her right echoed, probably from Federal and Confederate cavalry, but she was uncertain.

"Alfred, we must hurry if we're going to get past the fighting and over to Turner's Gap at South Mountain. I must get my information to General Lee," she exclaimed with a deepening concern.

They came to the Point of Rocks Road. The carriage was now dusty and one of the wheels squeaked. They turned left onto the Harper's Ferry Road for a short distance, then they arrived in Jefferson.

"Alfred, my father named this town when he lived here many years ago. Back in 1832, the city was incorporated with the help of Father and William Cost Johnson. A lot of Macgills came from here. I'm sure they'll help us. We need fresh horses. These two are worn to the bone."

"Miss Mollie, I's see these to a livery. You see's whose you can talk with that's yourn kin-fowk."

She remembered her uncle Dr. Thomas John Macgill who lived on the Harper's Ferry Road near the town crossroads. She recollected he lived next to a feed store with a livery out back; she hoped he had horses.

She found Uncle TJ standing on his porch, looking toward the sound of the firing in the pass. She alighted from the carriage and threw her arms around her uncle. She quickly explained her mission. She also informed him of having shot a Federal picket in order to make her escape.

"Child, you've had a hard day. Tell your coachman to bring the carriage around back of my house to the livery. I'll get you some fresh horses," her uncle hastened to respond to her.

She watched Alfred and her uncle set to work changing out the horses. She waited on them, nervously pacing the livery floor. Suddenly, she heard a bugle call and the thunder of galloping horses.

"Mollie, you stay here and hide yourself while Alfred finishes harnessing the horses. Alfred, cover Mollie's bags with that canvas tarp. I'll go see who they are."

She rushed up a ladder into the loft and hid herself behind some hay. She was still able to see Alfred at work covering her baggage. She began to sneeze uncontrollably due to the dust in the hay.

"Miss Mollie, keep quiet if'n you's to save yourself from what might'in be Yankees," Alfred said.

"I'm trying, Alfred!"

It wasn't long before her uncle returned with four Federal cavalrymen accompanying him. She ducked back farther behind the hay and listened to the conversation.

"We're looking for a young woman and her coachman. She shot a Federal picket on the Manor Woods Road," the officer in blue gruffly stated. "Who does this darky belong to? Why is he harnessing the horses, doctor?"

"He's mine. I'm getting ready to head out and aid your wounded. I asked him to harness a new team of horses. I had lathered up the first team getting back to town with a sick patient just before you arrived," Dr. Macgill calmly replied.

"Very well, doctor. We're the First New York Cavalry. We're going to take South Mountain in the morning. We'll be on the lookout for this young woman. Good day to you, sir," the officer said as he exited the livery.

Mollie realized the cavalrymen had searched all of Jefferson and were now on their way out of town.

Once their fresh horses were in harness they continued north five miles on Middletown Road toward Middletown. From a distance she saw smoke billowing above Middletown. She heard cannon firing and realized that the Federals had gotten to the town. She thought she would be unable to pass through, but then she noticed Confederate cavalrymen on the road ahead. They sat their horses—with carbines at the ready.

"I'm Miss Mollie Macgill, officer. Move aside, for I've extremely important military information I must get to General Lee, wherever he is on the other side of South Mountain."

"How do I know I can trust you, miss?" the officer inquired, a captain whose faded cavalry jacket was dusty from long field service.

"Do you know my beloved Lieutenant James Breathed of the Stuart Horse Artillery? I know he must be in the vicinity! Take me to him! He'll vouch for me," she offered with an expectant look on her face.

"His is a name I know for gallantry. Follow me, Miss Macgill. I'll escort you to where I think he is."

They followed the captain westward over Catoctin Creek in order to avoid the battle currently raging in Middletown.

When they came to Old Sharpsburg Road the officer informed her, "I think the lieutenant is up this road at Fox's Gap. If not, I'll take you along the Bolivar Road, which runs into the National Pike just below Turner's Gap."

The shade from the trees had covered the landscape by the time they had driven west on the Old Sharpsburg Road toward Bolivar Road and Turner's Gap. Peering over her shoulder, she saw the beautiful Middletown Valley at dusk, which lay behind her like a diversified and illuminated map. Its quiet calm, wooded hills, pleasant fields, and hamlets stretched behind her. Before the sun set above South Mountain, she heard the sounds of booming Federal cannon rolling across the Catoctin Range. She believed the Federal vanguard was advancing; the next day's Sabbath would not be pleasant in this part of Pleasant Valley.

They turned onto the National Pike and headed up the dirt road, which was steep at places. She observed that the jagged rock ledges and outcroppings shot up in places like a valley of the shadow of death. They passed by in the dark. She began to say the twenty-third Psalm.

When they arrived in front of the Mountain House at Turner's Gap, she guessed it would have to be after 10 o'clock. The arduous adventure had come to an end for her. She was exhausted to the point of almost being delirious, but was more elated than she could ever remember having been.

The captain looked to her and said, "Miss Macgill, I'll inform General D. H. Hill you're here awaiting an audience with him. I'm sure he'll see you when he's finished addressing his officers for the morning's battle."

"Thank you, thank you," she said as she climbed down from the carriage. She looked at the two stories of gray stone that comprised the inn which sat back only a little ways from the National Road.

She waited some time before a number of officers came out of the inn's front cupola entrance. She spied James. He saw her, too.

"Why, Mollie, you're the last person I'd ever expected to see here," he exclaimed as he stared at her in disbelief. "General Hill, allow me the pleasure of introducing you to Miss Mollie Macgill of Hagerstown, daughter of my esteemed medical mentor, Dr. Charles Macgill."

General Hill took her hand and kissed it. "It's my pleasure to meet you, Miss Macgill."

"General, I've traveled all day from outside of Frederick City, through picket lines; I was even forced to use my revolver on a Federal picket who would not let us pass."

She garnered all the officers' stern attention.

James listened attentively to her. His look betrayed gentler feelings. General Hill, staring in awe, began to ask her about her perilous trip; she cut him off. "General, some soldiers found a copy of an order numbered 191. I know not what it signified. But this order is now in the hands of General McClellan since this morning."

She noticed General Hill's face went gray. "You're sure?"

"I saw the order with my own eyes! I saw your name along with Generals Jackson, Longstreet, McLaws, Anderson, Walker, and Stuart. From what I could make out, your forces are going to be on both sides of the Potomac, some attacking Harper's Ferry and some headed towards Hagerstown. McClellan knows this."

"Summon a courier at once," General Hill ordered. "I'll need to get this information to General Lee immediately. The outcome of our fortunes weighs in the balance. If our courier has to ride all night, he must deliver this information to General Lee's headquarters."

"I'm glad I could be of service," Mollie offered as she collapsed into James's arms.

"Lieutenant Breathed, see to Miss Macgill's needs. I'm sure you're famished, young lady," the General said as he clasped her hand in gratitude.

He supported her as they made their way to the secluded rear of the Inn to get some food. He ducked to go under the low door beam as he took hold of her hand.

"James, you look splendid in your artillery uniform," she said as the two sat at a small wooden table awaiting dinner. She felt the rustic wooden interior of the Inn being warmed by the fireplaces at both ends.

"Mollie, you risked your life to do what you did. You're indeed brave. You never cease to amaze me."

"James, I'm no more gallant or noble than you, or any other of the brave young men who risk all for their country. What you and your men do on the battlefield is decidedly more important than what I did today."

He reached across the table and held both of her hands. He pulled her close enough to kiss her on the lips. A warm feeling of strength and comfort emerged from his kiss.

"Mollie, to our many bonds of affection, your bravery adds a band of steel. I've thought of you on so many long and cold nights. When will this war pass so that our two souls can be together?"

"I don't know James."

A steward placed a bowl of warm beef stew before her. He dropped her hands so that she could enjoy her food. The aroma of lightly spiced stew filled her nostrils and she began to eat.

"Do you know what is going to take place here in the morning? The entire Federal Army of the Potomac will be coming up South Mountain in force. I'll do my best, a mile or so from here at Fox's Gap, to stop them."

"I've only done what I clearly saw as my duty. In the morning it'll be your turn to do yours. We're of one mind and accord in this war—as horrible as it is."

"I must see you and Alfred off to Boonsboro on the other side of the Gap," he concluded as she finished her food and the hour grew late.

They walked hand-in-hand out of the Inn into the darkness and back to the carriage. He helped her into the carriage and kissed her good-bye. Just before the carriage moved away, he quickly asked, "Any news of your father?"

"None," she said as she looked back and blew a kiss to him.

Then it hit her, she thought if she was ever identified as the woman who shot her way through the pickets, what chance would she ever have of seeing her father again? The reality of what she had done struck her with full force and it was only by exerting her will to the utmost that she could keep from fainting.

Two troopers were assigned to escort her carriage back down the road toward Hagerstown and she carried a pass signed by General Hill.

After the carriage was safely away, James mounted Billy and returned to his artillerymen feeling reinvigorated and inspired to face the Federal enemy in the morning.

CHAPTER 21

Here I Stand

HE WAS AWAKENED AT the early dawn by the day's sounds of musketry. He thought there was insufficient light to enable his artillerists to open with their cacophony of cannon fire. The light of the dawn illumined the fog in the ravine before him which hung low to the ground.

He wiped the sleep from his eyes as he stood on Nicodemus Ridge. He had enjoyed a deep slumber under a caisson which was situated a quarter of a mile from the Dunkard Church. In his boyhood days, he had passed by this ridge countless times while en route to Sharpsburg. He recollected one such passing accompanied by his mentor Dr. Macgill. They had observed blue hued vultures ravaging a grey fox in the Millers' cornfield on the opposite side of the Hagerstown Pike, into which he now stared directly.

He knew the village of Sharpsburg, a little over a mile down the Pike, was located on a succession of ridges, marked by the gently-flowing Antietam Creek to the east and the Potomac River snaking to the southwest. He could see before him clumps of mature woods with little undergrowth, the cornfield and orchards that were scattered with limestone outcroppings.

"Nothing can be more solemn than the time of silence waiting for the summons to battle," he said to Private Henry Matthews as he looked through his field glasses to see massed blue infantry to the northeast marching down the Hagerstown Pike.

Privates Bill Clem, Robert Mackall, and Henry Zimmerman stood in close proximity to him all dressed in their West Point steel gray uniforms.

"They're getting ready! There they come! Let's give it to them!" Private Henry Matthews excitedly cried out.

"We'll let them come," he responded. "They're a little out of range. Captain Pelham will give the order. You know my boyhood home is less than ten miles from this very spot."

"Must make you want to fight all the harder, I reckon," Henry said.

"If we break this day my family may well be in danger. I'm gonna fight hard, for their sake."

After a few moments, he heard Pelham shout, "Fire!"

His command opened the battle from the Confederate left flank; Poague's field pieces and his horse artillery section, with the other horse artillery guns, opened fire with thirteen pieces. Their sulphurous clouds belched forth from the cannon into the Federals marching south on the Hagerstown Pike. Their firing tore into many bluecoats as the Federal infantry approached a large cornfield. The Federals quickly formed lines of battle, as James's artillerymen rained shell and shot down on them.

"Increase elevation five degrees, two-second fuse, shell, two thousand yards!" James cried out to his gunners.

Private Mackall received the shell and placed it into the muzzle and Private Clem rammed it home.

"Now we've got the range on them," Mackall said as he stepped back from the muzzle, leaned rearward, and covered his ears.

"Prick and prime!" Sergeant Shaw hollered out.

James sat on Billy and observed the enemy forces through his field glasses. Private Zimmerman nodded off Private Matthews as he tightened the lanyard.

"Fire!" James hollered. "Reload!"

Their position was immediately bombarded with shells from the myriad Federal cannon. The incoming shells flew in at a fast and fretful cadence. The smoke hung thick and James could barely make out the lightning flashes that erupted from the Federal guns counter-battery fire. The earsplitting voice of war hammered away deeply and reverberated through his body.

A shell dug into the earth in front of his section and exploded. A heavy rain of dark earth splattered his uniform. It pattered against his guns and showered his artillerists. For a moment the air was a thick twilight. Shattered limestone sparkled and fell back to the ground.

"Whew! The earth's taking a hand! Anybody hurt? Load . . ." James commanded.

James could see other Confederate shells hitting stacks of grain. The exploding projectiles set ablaze the harvested grains; livestock hit by stray bullets lay kicking and dying on the battlefield. The smoke that arose above the cornfield drifted toward his position.

He thought the Southern Cross had come to the aid of conquered Maryland and the iron legions of the North. He thought he must break the rod of the blackamoor's god and free his brothers and sisters of Maryland from the oppressor. Their slavish chains of subjugation had to be freed from the tyrant's fetters. He thought, *we've crossed the Rubicon to fight this day!* Maryland was in his mind. She was a "weeping maiden," bound and fettered, seeking relief.

"Keep the fire steady, boys, we've got the range now!" James hollered as he rode Billy behind the guns, cheering his artillerists.

General Early's brigade hunkered down in the ravine over which his guns fired into the cornfield. Hell itself seemed to have broken loose in all its terrors, he thought. After a few hours of continuous firing, James paused to stare incredulously at the devastation of dead men and horses in the cornfield to his front; the Mumma Farm house was ablaze and black smoke billowed from it.

"Lieutenant Breathed, our ammunition is low!" Captain Pelham shouted to him. "How long can we hold in this position and sustain their counter-battery fire?"

"Sir, I believe it's time to reposition our guns," James replied as the counter-battery shells were whirling overhead, some exploding and raining down shrapnel on his artillerists.

"Limber up," Pelham commanded as he reined his horse to the south. "Follow me."

"Form section," James commanded as the artillerists prepared the two pieces to move.

They loaded their implements, and the horse holders appeared from the rear of the ridge.

Private Moses Febrey suddenly appeared before James's eyes, careening up from the south with a full ammunition wagon. Febrey pulled up behind the caissons of James's section of guns.

"Private Febrey, your timing couldn't have been better," James said with a be-grimed sooty smile on his face.

"Sir, there's more where this came from," the slender soldier said as he dropped the reins and helped unload the ammunition.

"Clem, Matthews, Mackall, and Zimmerman get this ammunition unloaded and into our caissons and limbers."

His artillerist ran over from their pieces, stepping over dead and wounded comrades, to follow his orders.

"We're given'm hell, sir!" Clem shouted. Sweat poured off Clem's brow and black soot was smeared all over his face and arms.

"That we are, Private," James responded. "I suspect we're just getting started. It's going to be a long day! We've got lots more killing to do! We're going to be doing it as Marylanders on our home soil!"

"That we are, Lieutenant! Marylanders have come to free the 'weeping maiden.'"

His artillerists worked quickly to transfer the rounds even as the cracking and thundering of impacting counter-battery fire encumbered their efforts. James's other artillerists had moved their cannon and limbers to the wagon to be replenished with ammunition. Once the ordered tasks were completed, the horse artillery was ready to move out.

"Left—Oblique!"James hollered to the drivers. "March—Guide Right."

At a gallop from out of the smoke coming from Nicodemus Ridge, James rolled his section of guns. Leaping and thundering he raced Billy down a ravine and up to a little knoll to the north of Hauser's Ridge. His horses, pink-nostrilled with blood shot eyes, pulled the hot tubes of death after him. The horse teams strained up the knoll. At the top of the knoll, with iron clanging and traces taut, they stopped at the place James had marked for the guns: a cornfield to their front.

At once James commanded, "Limber—Front."

His gunners sprang from their horses into action. No sooner did they settle into their new positions than the woods crawled with blue clad men coming toward them, firing their muskets, their bayonets gleaming from the reflection of the sun.

James triumphantly moved to the rear of his guns and shouted, "I'm a Marylander, boys! I came home to my weeping maiden. My home is not ten miles from this battlefield. I intend to carry her where she belongs—to the Southern Confederacy! Are you with me boys!"

"Yaai, Yai . . . Yaai, Yaai Yai . . . Yaai!" his boys cried out with the Rebel Yell.

At times, the artillery fire was so fierce and violent that one continual roar of thunder echoed and rolled across the sky. The musketry fire was equally severe and raged as furiously. Its dreadful, deathly crash vied with the deafening roar of the rumbling artillery. However, no man quailed under the fiery vortex of battle. Every man and officer stood fast, suffering and dying for their dearly loved liberty for which they fought. God had willed this liberty to them as sons of the Southland.

General Stuart had busily positioned some field pieces next to James's section of guns. Stuart stopped to confer with General Early and James.

"The Yanks are pushing across the Hagerstown Pike into the woods, General. I don't want Lieutenant Breathed's guns and my 'pet horse artillery' to get flanked. General, do you think you could assault the western flank of the intruding forces?" Stuart asked as the minies whizzed by them.

Suddenly, the courier who sat his horse next to them took a minie with a thud to his chest and pitched from his horse. Another minie or two hit Stuart's horse. The horse's front legs collapsed, throwing Stuart over its head to the terra firma.

"Sir, are you hit?" James yelled as he leapt from Billy to help Stuart from the ground.

"I'm good. The Yanks couldn't hit the broad side of a barn," Stuart responded as he brushed off the dirt from both his light blue trouser legs and well-polished top boots. He picked up his broad brimmed black hat, looped up on one side, with two glossy ostrich plumes of the same shade.

"General, now's the time for that assault; it seems they're getting closer to our position," Stuart exclaimed.

"Yes, sir. I'll commence the attack at once," General Early replied. "I'll coordinate my attack with Generals Jackson, McLaws, and Walker."

James remounted Billy and returned to the command of his section. His artillerists were firing at an anxious rate, since they, too, could see the coming of the new Federal assault. Tops of trees were being shattered by their fire, and the heavy limbs and branches fell to the ground crushing Federal soldiers underneath. James witnessed the pandemonium and broke out in hilarious laughter, although he was rather unsure of why he was laughing.

James saw that the Federal corps was emerging from the woods. His guns were there to push them back into it. The Federals broke in the woods when a withering fire came at them from three sides. Bluecoats streamed out of the woods in disorder like weasels caught in the henhouse by an angry farmer with a shotgun. His cannon shook the firmament, and the Federals quickly pulled back from the entanglement.

Shortly after this Federal attack in the woods had been repulsed, James saw Stuart, Jackson, and Pelham speak to each other at the rear of his section of guns.

He heard the conversation and agreed with their conclusions.

"God has been very kind to us today," Jackson said. They had been fighting over four hours.

"Sir, we may be able to do more damage from higher ground. I recommend we move to the top of Hauser Ridge over yonder," Pelham said as he pointed over to the ridge a few hundred yards farther south.

"Yes," Stuart said. "I agree with Captain Pelham, General Jackson. We should move to higher ground. I don't know if they'll try to come at us through those woods again after what we did to them after their last attack, but higher ground would be advantageous."

"General Stuart, you know best what your horse artillery can do and where they can best do it from," Jackson responded as he removed his kepi and wiped his brow. "So be it, gentlemen."

"Limber up," Pelham cried out as he pointed to the Hauser Ridge. "We're moving to higher ground."

⌘

James thought that the fog of war had materialized hours before General Lee and General Jackson conferred in relation to an audacious turning movement of the Federal right flank. He was unsure of what to make of Stuart's plan, under Jackson's orders, to rally the twenty-six hundred cavalrymen and the thirteen hundred infantry on the Cox Farm, which was adjacent the River Road, to attempt this bold tactical movement. James was the commander of two of the nine horse artillery guns that were a part of the Stuart cadre.

James, Jackson's officers, Stuart, and Pelham had gathered at the base of an old hickory tree.

"Have you a good climber in your command?" General Jackson asked of Colonel Matt Ransom of the 35th North Carolina Infantry.

As if on cue, Private William Hood leaped forward. James watched this thin, bearded soldier take off his shoes and, like a squirrel, shimmy up the old hickory tree.

"How many troops are over there?" Jackson asked the private.

"Oceans of them!" he said. Minies were so continuously singing that he ceased to heed them whizzing around his head.

"Count the flags, seh," Jackson said.

"One, two, five, eight," Hood replied as Jackson repeated each number.

"Thirty-seven, thirty-eight, thirty-nine," Jackson said. "That'll do. Come down, seh. We'll further consider smiting the Amalekites and driving McClellan into the Potomac."

"Can we out flank such numbers?" Stuart asked.

"Don't know unless we try," Jackson replied. "Order your men into formation!"

They moved out toward the hamlet of New Industry and the Potomac River. They arrived at New Industry, where Pelham was sent east on a road that connected with the Hagerstown Pike.

"Lieutenant Breathed, deploy your guns on that eminence parallel to the pike," Pelham ordered, near a deployment nine hundred yards from a large Federal artillery massing of guns on a ridge.

Pelham shouted, "Fire!"

Within fifteen minutes Pelham ordered James to pull back. James and his artillerymen retired to their former position.

"Do you think we really had a chance to flank them?" James asked Pelham as they retreated back to Nicodemus Ridge.

"Oh, we must stir them up a little and then slip away," Pelham responded.

"The men are in wild spirits! I am too, sir! If we're going to fight to the finish, I'm in," James said to Pelham.

"Stuart is a wise tactician; he retreats in order to fight another hour. I fear our losses would've been substantial if we had tried to flank the Yankees' right."

James led his men back to Nicodemus Ridge where he could see the lines of fallen dead soldiers massed two and three deep in the cornfield.

The remainder of the day he spent firing his counter-battery fire at the same Federal artillery massed on the ridge.

⁕⁙⁕

As the sun began to set behind their position on Nicodemus Ridge, James and Pelham determined it was time to take a look at their handiwork. They rode out to the woods and saw that the blood-soaked ground was strewn with human wreckage. The conflagration had beaten the soldiers, blue and gray, like wheat beneath a hail storm. The Federals had fallen in rows as they had marched. Upon the ground lay men with their eyes gone, their jaws shot through. One soldier's jaw still moved up and down, seemingly to the tune of a death requiem. James bent over this unconscious Federal soldier, gave him a drink from his canteen and closed his shattered jaw.

"I struggle to comprehend what we've done this day. But, as a doctor, I still feel compelled to aid the wounded, us or them," he said.

"I understand, Lieutenant. You've a higher calling than I. I admire your compassion for our enemy."

Federals, with their arms and legs mangled, with their thighs pierced by minies and bowels spilled out onto the ground, were too numerous to count. Soldiers who had gone into the woods as whole men now lay withering with a hand or foot gone. He heard men crying out for water, for God and Mother; soldiers shook in the chills of death's grip. In the hot, half-clouded sunset, flies swarmed and lighted on the eyes and entrails of dead horses; these scourges of the aftermath of battle crawled inquisitively under forage caps that covered dead men's faces, with no interest in the rifles at the soldiers' sides.

They returned to the Confederate line and concluded that the two armies, exhausted and hungry, had confronted each other like two gladiators waiting for a signal to strike again. However, they both knew there would be no more fighting this day and likely not the next.

His artillerists threw themselves upon the warm earth and slept with the resolve of the dead. Wondering what all the carnage of this day had produced, James surveyed the battlefield with his field glasses. Then in the back of his mind he began to sound words of a tune that brought some sanity to the insanity, a song that he and his men had sung as they had crossed the Potomac River into Maryland weeks earlier:

> The despot's heel is on thy shore,
> Maryland!
> His torch is at thy temple door,
> Maryland!
> Avenge the patriotic gore
> That flecked the streets of Baltimore,
> And be the battle queen of yore,
> Maryland! My Maryland! . . .
> Come! 'tis the red dawn of the day,
> Maryland!
> Come with thy panoplied array,
> Maryland!
> With Ringgold's spirit for the fray,
> With Watson's blood at Monterey,
> With fearless Lowe and dashing May,
> Maryland! My Maryland!

22

The Angel of the Confederacy

MOLLIE HELPED HER BROTHER, Dr. Charles Griffith Macgill, pack the landau with medical supplies and hundreds of bandages. The two were headed south out of Hagerstown the second day after the battle. They had heard through the headlines of the *Hagerstown Torch*, and from the comments of local eyewitness citizens, that the waters of the Antietam Creek had been stained crimson under the Rohrback stone bridge the day of the battle. Dead Federal soldiers' bodies had bled as they floated down the Antietam Creek into the Potomac River. Many bloated bodies drifted for miles down the river.

Her brother had borrowed their father's Major General's Maryland Militia blue uniform and secured it with his father's green medical sash at the waist. Mollie was to act as his nurse assistant so that they could avoid any suspicion of being considered Southern sympathizers and possibly subject themselves to Federal arrest. She had secured a medical pass to aid the wounded Confederate soldiers from the U.S. Sanitary Commission the day before they departed Hagerstown.

"Sir, I'll need to see your pass if you plan to travel onto the battlefield from this point," a Federal soldier said at the crossroads of the Hagerstown Pike and the country road that lead to Bakersville.

"Nurse, show this soldier our pass," Charles Griffith responded.

Mollie pulled the U.S. Sanitary Commission pass from her bosom and presented it to Charles Griffith who then showed it to the Federal soldier.

"You're clear to move out, doctor."

Her brother reined the two up team to turn left at the Hutsell Farm toward Smoketown. Outside of Smoketown they came to a road and doubled back, then headed south again. In the outlying farms, which had been the battlefields, they saw tidy, fruitful tracts of land in complete desolation. Fences had been torn down, fields of grain and corn flattened, livestock driven off, prim orchards stripped bare, and beehives smashed on the ground. They saw smoke billowing south of them. The acrid smell of rancid human and horse flesh baking in the sun, the smell permeating the air. Everywhere a sea of broken men heaved across the battlefield.

They approached the lane to Samuel Poffenberger's farm. Samuel owned ninety acres of good farm land at St. James, and he was a good friend of both the Breathed and Macgill families. Samuel was a little older than Mollie and had married Catherine the year before. Charles Griffith reined the carriage to the front of the gray stone two-story home that featured two chimneys, one at each end of the house, resting on arches. The home had a large veranda and front yard, now all matted with straw, a covering of blankets, and wounded Confederate and Federal soldiers.

They exited the carriage. Charles hitched the horses to a rail, and they walked a distance from their landau toward the front door of the home.

"Water . . . for God's sake, give me a drop of water," a Federal soldier pleaded while looking into Mollie's eyes and reaching his arms toward her. She observed that his badly wounded leg was bandaged with corn leaves. The blood seeped from under the leaves, staining his blue uniform.

"I'll return when I can, soldier," Mollie compassionately said. She reached for a hand and, squeezing it firmly, listened to his piteous begging for water.

Mollie left him, and she and Charles weaved through the wounded soldiers and met Samuel on the veranda.

"Charles Griffith and Mollie, you're a welcome sight. We've so many wounded here we're overrun. They bring more by the hour as they find them alive in Mr. Miller's cornfield. I hear tell not a stalk of corn remains standing," Samuel said. He was a tall, slender man and wore bib overalls and smoked a corncob pipe.

"We've brought a great many bandages, quinine, and other medical supplies for the aid of the wounded," Mollie said.

"The Ladies Union Relief Association from Hagerstown is aiding soldiers all over the battlefield. Are they here?" Charles Griffith asked.

"We don't want to get caught for our sympathies," Mollie said as she looked at the other women who were aiding the wounded.

"No, I've not heard that organization mentioned here." Samuel answered. "But, there is a Miss Clara Barton in the house who has also brought supplies. I think she is a New Englander by the way she speaks. Would you like to meet her?"

"That'd be fine; we'll work with her," Charles Griffith said as they all walked into the house.

Mollie smelled death in the air of the house. She saw furniture had been cleared from the parlor and the kitchen. The downstairs had been turned into an operating facility. The doors had been taken off their hinges within the house and were mounted on empty flour barrels to make two operating tables. The exhausted regimental surgeons were covered from head to foot with the blood of the sufferers, discoloring their white aprons. The regimental surgeons looked tired, but the tables continued to be washed down with water after each operation. Mollie felt a sudden hint of nausea as she watched limbs being thrown out the kitchen window to land in an ever-growing pile.

Samuel hailed Nurse Barton. "Allow me to introduce you to Dr. Charles Griffith Macgill and his nurse Mollie. They've brought medical supplies and bandages as you did," Samuel said. While he spoke, Catherine walked into the parlor, came over to Mollie, and gave her an exhausted hug. Mollie and Catherine spoke quietly to each other while Nurse Barton and Charles Griffith conferred.

"Doctor, what regiment are you with?" Nurse Barton asked.

"The Twenty-fourth Maryland Militia," Charles replied.

"Fractured arms and legs need tending to. Can you and your nurse get to work right away? We've lined up the greenstick fractures in the yard. Do you have a supply of splints?"

"Yes, Nurse Barton. I brought a number of splints from the Hagerstown Hospital and from my practice. We'll go to work right away," Charles Griffith said.

Charles Griffith and Mollie returned to the carriage to retrieve the splints and bandages.

"What did you think of Nurse Barton?" Mollie asked.

"Seems nice enough, but a true Yankee."

"Think she'll turn us in, or did she believe your uniform story."

"Well, as long as we work with both our soldiers and theirs we should be fine."

"Catherine told me it was the Stuart Horse Artillery that did a fair amount of damage in the Miller's cornfield. I suspect I'm seeing James's work firsthand in this war."

"We'll have to see what we can do to reconcile his account, but first to the Confederate wounded."

She thought that it might be difficult for her to work on the Federal soldiers. She was not sure why this thought came to her. Charles Griffith had an oath that compelled him to labor despite the color of the uniform, but she had not taken such an oath.

She walked to the stream behind the house and filled a bucket with muddy water as Charles Griffith, now wearing an apron, unloaded bandages and splints from the carriage and delivered them to the location in the yard where Nurse Barton had lined up the wounded soldiers. Mollie walked with her bucket of water to the soldier she had spoken with earlier. She knelt by him and ladled some water from the bucket.

"Here you are soldier."

"Thankya miss. My leg hurts somethin' awful bad. I think the minie went clean through. Couldya get me some that laudanum?"

"I'll see what I can do for you. Drink first; I'll get you a new dressing for that leg."

"The horrid smell of my rotten limb is nearly as bad as the whole we've had to contend with in the battle," the soldier said when she returned with some clean bandages to dress the wound. "Doya think they'll cut her off?"

"I can have Dr. Macgill look at it; he can tell you what he thinks. Remain still, I'll fetch him over."

"Doc, this quinine keeps me parched for water, sleepy, and foolish," the solider said as Charles Griffith approached. "Ya got anything stronger for the pain? Think they goin' ta take her off?"

"Soldier, let me look under these corn leaves and do some probing around," Charles Griffith replied as he opened his surgeon's medical instrument bag. "What's your name soldier?"

"I'm Private Peters, but everyone calls me Dead-eye. I was sharp shooting for the regiment. It looks like some Johnny Reb got me good."

"Drink this," Mollie said as she gave him some laudanum.

"The whiskey smells mighty good 'bout now."

"Bite this stick and lay back, Dead-eye." Charles said. "Mollie, hold his hands while I do some probing."

"Aaaawwweee," Dead-eye hollered as he bit the stick and took the pain.

"It'll have to come off. I'm sorry, Dead-eye. There's nothing we can do but cut off the limb," Charles Griffith said as he completed the probing. "Mollie, get this man one of our Petit's screw tourniquets and apply it. It will save his life while he awaits the surgeons saw."

Mollie and Charles Griffith spent the rest of the day working on soldiers, both blue and gray, setting fractures and splinting limbs. Nurse Barton frequently checked on them as they did their work. Mollie heard the terrible agonizing screams continuing to come from inside the house. They spent the night at the home of the Poffenbergers.

❧❧❧

The next morning they departed in search of Captain David Smith's farm. They had been told it was one of the largest Confederate hospital locations outside of Sharpsburg, and on the road to Shepherdstown, Virginia.

They drove the landau carriage back to the Smoketown Road and then continued south through woods that she saw, to her horror, had seen some horrendous fighting. They saw many medical corpsmen hauling away the wounded. They were appalled by what they witnessed as scavengers robbed the living and the dead of anything worth stealing. The burial details were hard at work, placing the Federal dead in individual graves with wooden markers at their heads.

They turned back onto the Hagerstown Pike after passing by the Millers' cornfield. She saw one soldier along the Hagerstown Pike who had fallen with his head downhill in a pool of blood, which had run from his body and collected in a ditch. Flies swarmed. The soldier's face was black, eyes open and staring seemingly right at her. His tongue protruded and his whole body was swollen. The coat of his uniform was pulled from his chest and abdomen area. All around the soldier were similar loathsome and mangled objects of death. She asked Charles Griffith to pull to the side of the pike, and then she vomited over the side of the carriage. She pulled a handkerchief up over her nose to keep from vomiting again.

As they traveled, Mollie saw that hogs were rooting among the dead, adding to the grotesqueness of the rotting carnage. The task of burning hundreds of dead horses decomposing under the September sun had begun by Federal soldiers left in details to clean up the battlefield. The stench was sickening. The Hagerstown Pike was so full of wagons and men on foot that they could barely pass by.

They saw caissons, overturned and smoldering, surrounded by debris of dead horses and soldiers strewn all over the battlefield. Overturned wagons, muskets, cards, Bibles, and haversacks littered the ground. Dead men were in neat rows visible from the road. She thought she saw that, hidden under thickets, other dead soldiers were turning black and bloated while awaiting burial. She saw amputated limbs piled up outside the makeshift hospitals as they passed south on the Hagerstown Pike. Incessant buzzing flies tormented the living and fed off the dead.

The two worked to govern their emotions as they passed by the Dunkard Church where piles of limbs, several feet high, slumped outside the church window. They saw the appalling sight of bloodied men on porches and lawns, the Mumma Farm house and barn burned to the ground. They continued south on the pike and eventually arrived in Sharpsburg.

She noticed that many families had flocked to Sharpsburg in order to reclaim bodies, enclose them in coffins, and escort them home via wagon or train. The town had become a focus of wonder and horror, and was crowded with civilians and tourists alike attracted by the hope of experiencing the sublimity of a battlefield, she thought. Relatives in search of kin were among entrepreneurial coffin makers and embalmers who had located their tents between buildings on the narrow Main Street. She saw civilians gawking at the embalmers and the rows of coffins awaiting freshly embalmed bodies.

She read one of the newly erected signs on Main Street for embalming or "disinfections" as it was known in Hagerstown. The tent had a sign set up over it which she read:

> Lewis Ernde, Furnishing Undertaker, Hagerstown, MD.
> Bodies taken from Antietam Battlefield and delivered to Cars or Express Office
> at short notice and low rates.
> Residence East Antietam Street, near Female Seminary.

They moved through town toward the Captain David Smith farm. She had learned that Captain Smith, a cabinet maker, had a one hundred thirty-five acre farm at Antietam Station. He had offered his house and farm as a hospital to the Confederates. The severely wounded soldiers were left behind because there was no way to transport them.

There was so much blood dripping out the back of the wagons and spilling on the dirt roads that, eventually, the mud became red as the wagon wheels ploughed through the country roads and streets of the town. When they arrived at the farm, they discovered straw on the ground with blankets on top, just as they had seen at Samuel's home. Men laid around in various states of dress and undress, the wounded waiting in rows in the captain's farmyard. It was as if the sea had washed the wounded up, and the tide had laid them out in rows as it receded. Many parts of the Confederate uniforms were cut away. Charles Griffin drove the carriage onto the farm and parked it near the farmhouse.

Hospital attendants walked among the make-shift outdoor beds, giving cool water or bathing a brow. Many knelt to hold the hand of a soldier.

"Charles, we must discover what we can do for our men who suffer so. I also want to find out if James is among the wounded here," Mollie said with a sad face as she looked into the farm yard.

"Mollie, you mustn't worry yourself about James. I'm sure he's fine and is amongst the living, departed back into Virginia with General Lee's army. You did what you could do when you got the 191 orders to General Lee. Now you must rely on the providence of God."

"Yes, brother. Let us continue our work here. I'll discover what the providence of God has done with my James."

They exited the carriage and went to work unloading the rest of the supplies they had saved for their Confederate wounded. They entered the house of the captain and were not surprised to find that tables and doors were being used as examining and operating tables.

Mollie observed the surgeons perform amputations, their aprons drenched in blood. The hour was late; their trip from Samuel's had taken most the day. When they left the house to view the carnage in the barn, they discovered lanterns and candles stuck in the ends of weapons, which provided illumination for the work of the doctors. It was evident they had days of work ahead of them, and so the two settled into the task before them.

⁂

Mollie and Reverend John Augustus met a few days later. They were attempting to determine which of the wounded should be lined up for the surgeons and which should be left alone, and which to assign to the dismal parades of ambulance wagons already making their way to better facilities at Hagerstown and Frederick.

John had been sent by Charles Baker with financial aid to help the wounded Confederates, and he had run into Mollie and Charles Griffith at Captain David Smith's farm.

Mollie wondered why the burial of the Confederate dead did not begin until four days after the battle had ended. Now the burials at the farm were numbering in the hundreds. Soldiers were dying in great numbers, despite their efforts to save Confederate lives.

Mollie and John were at the bedside of a Confederate soldier. She held his hand while John prayed.

"Our Father, who art in Heaven, hallowed be thy name . . ." John prayed. "Tell us your name, soldier."

"I'm Private Vanderhault. I've been a good soldier, but I fear God and his coming to take my soul."

"Son, I want you to know what it means to die a 'good death.' He that would die well must always look for death, every day knocking at the gates of the grave; and then the gates of the grave shall never prevail upon him to do him mischief," read John. "You fought hard for our country and our cause, my son. I'm not concerned for or about your spiritual condition for I feel you shall peacefully accept God's will, even when it brings death to you. Your acceptance is an important sign of your spiritual condition. Know that Christian prudence is a great security against the fear of death. For if we be afraid of death, it is but reasonable to use all spiritual arts to take off the apprehension of the evil. Therefore we ought to remove our fear, because fear gives to death wings, spurs, and darts," John read from Taylor's work *The Rule and Exercises of Holy Dying*.

"Yes, you'll meet in the green field's of Eden," Mollie told the dying Confederate soldier. "Let me read you Reverend John Sweet's '*What Is Death?*'"

She proceeded to read this piece to the dying soldier. It seemed to bring peace to his soul.

He responded to her saying, "Mother, I die happy. I see the angels coming with bright garlands for my brow." The dying soldier sighed as he breathed his last breath.

John closed his eyelids. He said another prayer, passing the Confederate soldier's soul to God.

"I think he died a good death don't you, John Augustus?" Mollie asked as she pulled the blanket over his face.

"Death is to be welcomed, not to be dreaded; it need not challenge God's fundamental goodness. Christ died for us, that, whether we wake or sleep, we might live together with him. Now we must minister to the others, who're so many, also at death's door."

Mollie spent the rest of this day alongside the Sanitarians, agents of comfort amid the misery borne from the battlefield. She dispensed soup, light biscuits, tarts, bread and butter, and milk to the Confederate wounded. She dressed numerous stumps of amputees. She helped the Catholic Daughters of Charity and the Special Relief Services' women distribute extra clothing, procure special foods, and pass out reading material.

She administered, at the end of every night, whiskey, sugar, and water—a toddy— to the men that was much appreciated for the alleviation of pain. The soldiers began to see Mollie as an angel of the Confederacy. She only knew to do what she could for her country and the cause. Her brother also continued at Captain David Smith's farm, working to exhaustion, for he gave himself no rest in view of the overwhelming suffering of humanity.

Mollie thought that maybe she was not such an angel after all. If it had not been for her getting the 191 order to General Lee, she thought, maybe this battle would not have happened in the first place. When she closed her eyes at the end of another long day of ministering to the wounded, a feeling of remorse and guilt overwhelmed her. She tried to sleep, but could not.

23

Wisdom of Thine Elders

Fall 1845

A month after the battle outside of Sharpsburg James was pondering all the fights he had been through to date. He did not know where all his fighting spirit had come from. He recalled a pleasant time with his grandparents in Berkeley Springs. He had been excited about the grand opening of Colonel Strother's partially completed Pavilion Hotel. His neighbor, Edward Colston, had an oval horse racetrack, located just outside of Berkeley Springs, and Strother had coordinated the opening of the Pavilion Hotel with the fall races at the race track.

His grandparents, Isaac and Kitty Breathed, had traveled from their farm outside of Hancock, Maryland. Their bay, a prize-winning thoroughbred named Harrod, was to be entered into the featured race of the day. They had spent the night with their son John W. and his family at their Fruit Hill Manor.

They all traveled down the Cornelius Road from the manor, accompanied by three special little people. His grandmother Kitty held his three-year-old sister, Priscilla, in her lap. James, being a rumbustious seven-year-old, sat in the back of their buggy with his five-year-old sister, Jane. The mountain air was filled with the odors of fall, and the leaves had begun to turn the hills into a pageant of beautiful colors.

While working in his mercantile store on Fairfax Street, James's father stayed behind; he was busy overseeing the shuttling of tourists on his Dandy Jack Stage Line from Berkeley Springs to the Hancock Depot of the B&O Railroad. His mother, Ann Macgill Breathed, remained at the manor to tend to his one-year-old brother, Isaac, named for his grandfather.

"Fine day for racin', Master James," Isaac said as he reined the buggy, carefully keeping Harrod at a safe distance behind the horse's lead strap.

"Sure is, Grandpa! I'm so excited to see Harrod run. I know he'll whip all the other ponies good." James joyfully replied.

"Me, too," Priscilla said, who, at her age, was just beginning to get vocal and learn to express herself.

As his grandfather drove to the race track, Jane poked James in the ribs. "Whadja do that for?" squealed James.

"Because you was there," Jane said. "And I felt I needed to poke ya."

"Children, settle yourselves! I know you're excited to see Harrod race. We'll be at the track shortly," Kitty scolded.

His grandfather Isaac was a seventy-four-year-old country gentleman with white hair and sideburns. His neatly tied cravat gave him an air that set him apart from other, more rough hewn, country folk. His frock coat was cut in at the waist with tails that came down to his knees. Under the coat he wore a vest on which his gold pocket watch chain was draped from a button hole. His black topper was decorated with a gray silken band.

His grandmother Kitty had beautiful sparkling hazel eyes that sat enshrined beneath graceful brown eyebrows, sufficiently marking her as a woman of loftier character. She wore a bonnet tied with a pink ribbon under her chin and a day dress of a floral pink rose pattern.

His grandmother was a Lyles from a family as prominent as the Breatheds'. Her father, Dr. Richard Lyles, was a surgeon with the Maryland Militia in the Revolutionary War. His grandmother often recalled to James many stories she had heard as a child about that war.

As they reached Wilkes Street his grandfather reined his team to the left, toward the race track and parallel with the Warm Springs Ridge. He guided the buggy north up the street until he found his way to Edward Colston's home, where people had already gathered.

James had always admired the one-story house with its raised veranda decorated with four small ornately carved pillars. The veranda overlooked Colston's Bottom, the area encompassing the oval race track. Warm Springs Run flowed between the house and the race track.

"Afternoon, Isaac, Kitty. Brought your grandchildren to see Harrod race today, I see," William Harmison greeted. He was one of the trustees of Berkeley Springs.

Isaac halted the buggy in front of the veranda in order to converse with some of the other trustees, Phillip Pendelton and Colonel John Strother, who both had walked over to say hello.

"How are you, Isaac?" Phillip said as he shook Isaac's hand and tipped his hat to Kitty.

"That fine animal of yours is going to give ours a run for the money, I suspect," Colonel Strother rather matter-of-factly stated.

"I've been working him every day to get him ready for this race. He's in fine condition. We'll see what he can do," Issac replied, grinning.

"I hope you, the Mrs., and the grandkids will come over to the hotel after the race. I've arranged for some fine eats, music, and desserts including seven kinds of cakes, ice cream, frozen custard, and pound cakes."

"We plan to attend. Thank you kindly," Isaac graciously said as he patted the reins on the backs of the team to move toward the bridge over the Warm Springs Run.

After they had crossed the bridge, James saw that the colonel's many guests had flocked to the oval track, and the attendees were dressed in their Sunday best. The women had packed buggies with fine picnic foods to be enjoyed alongside the rails. They rode by him with black parasols to shade themselves from the early October sun.

James was able to see the oval. The inside rail was painted white, and a tall tower structure stood halfway down the track. He assumed this tower to be the starting post. Recently arrived pleasure-seekers had already parked their luxurious carriages inside the rail and had begun to spread their picnics on the lush green infield grasses. He began to feel the excitement as hundreds of people, all dressed in fancy clothes, crowded onto the track infield.

"Look over yonder, I see Buck waiting for us. He's waving his hands," James excitedly said as he pointed to where the other horse owners had gathered next to the post.

His grandfather's stable boy, Buck, was a local Hancock farm lad who had been working with his grandfather to train Harrod. He could ride him like the wind and would be Harrod's jockey for the race. Isaac drove over to Buck and set the brake on the buggy.

"How're you, son? You ready to ride and win the trophy?" Isaac asked as he shook Buck's hand.

"Yes, sir. Let me get 'im brushed and saddled. We don't have too much time before they want to post 'em."

"I'll help ya," James said as he enthusiastically leaped from the buggy.

As the men prepared Harrod, Kitty watched, holding Priscilla in her arms while holding Jane's hand. Isaac held the lead strap while the others worked together to get Harrod ready to race.

"Get'm brushed good, boys. It'll make him go that much faster if he feels real handsome," Isaac said as he patted Harrod on his mane.

James watched Buck place the English racing saddle on a specially cut saddle blanket and then tighten the girth strap. He then bridled him and led him to Warm Springs Run for a little water.

"To your post!" James heard the cry ring out from the tower.

James helped Buck mount Harrod and trot him into position at the post. They all moved to the infield in their buggy and found a spot at the final turn at the head of the home stretch.

James came up to the rail, followed by Isaac, Kitty, Jane, and Priscilla. He saw the horses nervously throw their heads as they moved into position behind the starting line. A black stallion reared and kicked its front hooves wildly in the air; when the horse settled, his trainer brought him to the line.

Bang!

The starter gun had fired, and James watched the horses take off!

Harrod got off to a great start; he could see Buck hitting Harrod on the rump with a switch as the horses came around the first turn. The mud from the track shot off hooves and kicked up in the air as the pack of twelve horses came to the second turn. Harrod seemed to be running well, James thought. As the pack of horses began to stretch out, Harrod maintained second place along the back straightaway. Then on the third turn Harrod came snorting around for the lead. As Buck booted and switched him, the horse finally made his closing move. Harrod, all lathered up, increased his lead to a full length ahead of the other horses.

As he thundered by James, standing at the rail, he hollered, "Go, Harrod, go!"

He saw Harrod thunder by the post in first place. James ran from his grandparents, past the finish line, to find Buck and Harrod. He jumped up and hugged Harrod around his neck with an uncontrollable exuberance. He so loved horses, especially fast-running horses like Harrod that matched his competitive demeanor.

The onlookers gathered around Harrod and enclosed him within their circle. Colonel Strother broke through the crowd bearing a horseshoe-shaped wreath of flowers, which he placed on Harrod's neck.

"Ladies and gentlemen, today's winner, Harrod, is owned by Isaac and Kitty Breathed of Hancock!" Colonel Strother proclaimed to the crowd as he shook hands with Isaac. Isaac graciously took the trophy awarded him. "Now won't you all join me for the grand opening of the Pavilion Hotel in town?"

❧❦❧

"Isaac, that's a mighty fine horse," Mr. Harmison offered. "I suspect there won't be any horse swapping for that fine steed."

"No, sir. He's a keeper. Buck here's a mighty fine jockey. Couldn't have done it without you, boy," Isaac said as he patted the lad on the back.

They gathered on the front porch of the hotel. The hotel faced north toward Warm Springs, to which James often walked to in order to get the bubbling pure water for his family. James heard the mountain music being played, which he thought added to the festivities of the grand opening. Fine foods were being served by the servants who wore white gloves. Silver serving trays featured goblets filled with apple toddies. It had been a plentiful apple harvest; James had helped some of the locals make the cider from crushed apples, which was then fermented into apple toddy.

"Ma hats off to ye, sir," Robert Ferguson Bridges said with a thick Scottish brogue. "I sawn ye at the vegetable mart in Hancock at an ootby. Lat me innin masel and ma son. I'm Robert Ferguson Bridges and this be ma son, Robert. Ma faimlie and I live i' the old Donavan Haddin on Main Street i' Hancock. I teel eighty acres ootby of Hancock. But, I'm i' tender health."

"Pleasure to make your acquaintance, sir. This's my wife, Kitty, and my three grandchildren James, Jane, and little Priscilla," Isaac said as he shook Robert Ferguson's hand and then the younger Robert's. "How old are you, son?"

"Fifteen," Robert responded. "I'm lairnin' for the Presbyterian ministry. Ma pa is lairnin' me the Scriptures and all the doctrine fae the old country back in Fife County, Scotland."

Robert Ferguson wore a neatly tied cravat, a black vest, and a frock coat cut in at the waist with tails down his back. He was a dapper looking Scotsman and walked with a cane. He had a stern mouth with austere eyes, which cast a piercing but radiant glance. He had somewhat of a pug nose, and his hands had been made leathery from the hard labor in his farm fields. His polished leather shoes led James to believe that Robert Ferguson was an honorable man who kept his Sunday best ready for events like this one.

"We're Episcopalian," James announced as he sidled over to talk with the younger Robert.

"My pa was ordained a ruling eller in the Hancock Presbyterian Kirk on August the second," Robert countered. "Presbyterians were founded by John Knox o'er i' Scotland i' the ear' seventeenth century. Pa is gang to lairn some of oor doctrine to the local parish people around here who've recently formed a Presbyterian Kirk i' Hancock."

James thought that Robert was a quick-witted boy, tall and slender for his age with distinguished facial features. His forehead sloped to bushy eyebrows that set prominently over deeply receding eye sockets. His hawk-bill-shaped nose also set him apart in appearance from other boys. Robert was dressed in a neatly pressed white shirt that he had buttoned up to the top around his neck; his pants and his vest were of a dark blue color.

"Young man, what book are you holding?" Kitty asked the younger Robert as she joined in the conversation.

"This is ma Bible, the King James version," Robert replied. "I's recently confirmed a Presbyterian. The kirk parishioners over in Hancock gave me the Bible."

James watched Colonel Strother, with an apple toddy in his hand, join the circle of the Breatheds and the Bridges.

"Isaac, would you care for a toddy?" Colonel Strother asked. To Robert Ferguson he said, "And you sir, are welcome to one as well."

"Thanks, but I daurnae on a maitero of ma religious fegs. I'm a seacht Calvinist Presbyterian. I take ma fegs doctrines very scaurly. I don't drink, gamble, or dance for this is of the devil, and I don't labor on the Sawbath Day. I believe my Savior forbids such ill-trickit of sin," Robert Ferguson said to Colonel Strother. "But I'm enjoying yer music and would inbring a tassie of straight cider. The fiddling reckons ma of my home in Fife County, lallan which I left in 1816 to come to America."

"Well, sir, far be it from me to interfere with a man's religious convictions. Darky, bring this man a cup of cider and his boy, too," Colonel Strother said. "I suspect a fine Virginia cigar would also be out of the question?"

"Might be for Mr. Bridges, but it's not for me," Isaac said as he reached forward to take a cigar from the hand of the colonel.

"Did ya see Harrod fly like the wind, Colonel!"

"I sure did, James. He whipped my horse as well!"

His little sister Priscilla, cradled in his mother's arms, reached out her hand and touched Robert's hair, as her grandmother stood next to the boy in the circle of conversation.

"Pretty little girl, Mrs. Breathed. How old is she?" Robert asked as he reached up and held Priscilla's little hand.

"She's three, Robert."

"Well, I think it's time for the ribbon cutting ceremony," The Ccolonel said. "The Breatheds and the Bridges, I hope will join us?"

"We'll stay for the cuttin', but we'll be going back to Fruit Hill Manor shortly thereafter," Isaac replied.

"We'll do the sae," Robert Ferguson said as they walked to the front door of the hotel.

⚬⚬⚬

The clear blue October sky and the warm sun, which was beginning to set behind the stately Fruit Hill Manor, enticed James and his grandparents to the front porch. This two-story manor home was one of the finest in Berkeley Springs. It sat up above the town, fronted by a sprawling cleared field. Isaac and Kitty loved to sit in the rockers with their grandchildren as the sun set behind the manor; they told stories of how things used to be in the old days.

The family's darkies lived next door in a smaller home, making it amenable to the catering of their every need. James saw his father, John, come into the drive. He had closed the mercantile store and was returning home to his family. James talked with his grandparents while they watched John Breathed approach.

"James, did you know that your grandma's father was a surgeon with the Maryland Militia in the Revolutionary War?" Isaac asked while rocking.

James, who sat at his grandfather's feet, had yet to learn this bit of family history. "No. What was his name? I've never heard grandma tell of him."

"My father's name was Dr. Richard Lyles," Kitty said. "He told me many a story when I was a little girl of what it was like to be a surgeon following the Continental army."

"Tell me one, Grandma."

"I remember his telling me about the Battle of Cowpens. There was a particularly bad British cavalry officer there named Banastre Tarlton. He was a mercenary who fought for himself and for what he thought he could get from the British if the Continental army was defeated."

"What's a Mercenary?"

"A mercenary is a soldier who fights for pay alone. He does not really care about the cause for which he fights," Isaac said. "The British employed a large number of Hessians to fight in the Revolutionary War. Although Tarlton was British, he was really only fighting for land which he thought the government would give him if the British won the war."

"If'n I ever have to fight a war, I'll fight for a cause not the money," James emphatically announced. "Why else would one fight and risk gettin' killed?"

"Fighting to protect your home against an invading force is worth fighting for, James," Isaac said. "Never submit to a foreign power which is invading your homeland. The British invaded the colonies during the Revolutionary War. We finally threw them off our lands. Then we threw out all the Tories who were sympathetic to their invasion."

"If'n any foreign power tries to take Fruit Hill Manor, I'll get a gun from Pa's store and shoot all their soldiers dead," James exclaimed as he balled his fist and showed it to Isaac.

"Good boy!" Kitty said. "Your great grandfather, Dr. Lyles, would be proud of you for never submitting to a foreign power. He did not submit either."

"Now go and wash up your hands, for supper is almost ready. You did a fine job today readying Harrod for the race. You may've been what helped him win today!" Isaac suggested as he patted James on the head.

24

Wilfred of Ivanhoe

The Celtic Ways

October 8th through 12th, 1862

The Bower, the home of the Dandridges, east of Darksville, Virginia, was where General Stuart and his artillerists encamped in late September and early October. The elegant and charming three-story manor, with its seven-column front porch that wrapped around the right side of the decidedly Southern home on maintained grounds, provided ample room for his men. James thought the home elegant as he sat to be entertained by some of Stuart's staff.

In particular, James enjoyed Major Heros von Borcke's "Doctor and Patient" skit in the parlor of the home. James also enjoyed the music of Major John Pelham, singing tenor, while Heros von Borcke sang baritone. Stuart sang bass, John Esten Cooke, Captain W. W. "Billy" Blackford, Lieutenant Channing Price, and "Honeybun" Hullihen also shared their musical harmonies. The 2nd Virginia Cavalry provided not only fighting men but two excellent musicians: Sam Sweeney on the banjo and his brother, Bob, on the fiddle. To round out the musical montage was "Mulatto Bob" on the bones. It was marvelous entertainment to his ears.

James had sat in on a war council earlier there. Stuart had received orders from General Lee to head north on an expedition with 1,800 troopers to seize horses; property subject to legal capture; and functionaries, such as magistrates, postmasters, and sheriffs as hostages to be exchanged for Confederates whom the Federals held imprisoned in the north. A railroad bridge over the Conococheague Creek outside Chambersburg, Pennsylvania, was a specific target for their destructive arm of the expedition.

After moving out from Darksville the next day at 2:00 pm, James and the others met up with the brigades of General "Rooney" Lee and General "Grumble" Jones on his way to meet up with General Wade Hampton's brigade on the Winchester-Martinsburg Turnpike. Their plan was to head north to Hedgesville, which was a short distance from the Potomac River. Major Pelham accompanied two of Captain Hart's guns in the middle of the column, and two of James's guns were located at the rear of Stuart's column.

"Here we go again, riding into the fool McClellan's forces and territory, right under his nose, just like the last time," Private Zimmerman observed to James while he watched the mud from the drizzling rains roll off the artillery equipment's wheels.

James's twenty cannoneers in the section rode behind the four teams of cannon, limbers, and caissons. He observed that the rolling, hilly terrain was covered with trees, their leaves barely beginning to change to the amber, red, and orange colors of the fall season. The aromas of fall percolated through his nostrils. He could also smell lathered harnesses of leather, sweaty horseflesh, and perspiration emanating from the body odor of his men.

"No telling what we'll encounter in Maryland. Seems we would've had more support from the locals' enlisting when we were outside of Sharpsburg in September. Private, I can assure you once we get above the Mason-Dixon Line into Pennsylvania, the locals won't be hospitable," James replied.

James's artillerists and their equipment rambled north on the turnpike and then veered off on another road, which then took them to Hedgesville. The town was no more than a crossroads; but it was far enough back from Federal pickets on the Potomac River so that they could remain hidden from their adversaries. They set up camp.

"Captains Breathed and Hart, keep your fires at a minimum tonight. We don't want to be spotted by the Federals," Major Pelham ordered as he turned toward the low tones of the music coming from the camp of Stuart's staff, who were bivouacked in close proximity to General Stuart.

"Yes, sir," the two captains responded as they turned to their men.

His artillerists tended to the needs of the horses, then broke out their rations and sat around the small fires.

Private Zimmerman and Sergeant Shaw were sitting on either side of James. Henry was quiet for a moment, then said, "I recall you're a well-read man of the classics. Are you familiar with Sir Walter Scott?"

"Of course!" James exclaimed. "A marvelous writer; especially when it comes to chivalric knights of old. He's a gifted poet as well. I principally admire his *Ivanhoe*, which I'm rereading now."

"I'm rather biased to his narrative poems. A verse from *Marmion* has always reminded me of you. Would you like to hear it?" Henry asked leaning forward to look at James.

"I certainly would."

Henry spouted eloquently as if he were back in a Presbyterian pulpit:

His square-turn'd joints, and strength of limb,
Show'd him no carpet Knight so trim,
But in close fight a champion grim,
In camps a lender sage.

"Reverend, words spoken like a true and experienced prelate. I'm flattered. Maybe you can help me understand some of the dog-eared pages in the novel that I have questions about. A learned prelate such as yourself might know the answers to them," James responded as Lieutenant Emmett Shaw, well educated in the German old country, leaned forward to listen to the conversation.

"I understood what Sir Walter Scott was trying to say in relation to the oppressed Saxons who wanted to be free from the yoke of the Normans in King Richard the First's England. They believed they could at least elevate themselves into national independence. I think this was the literary point that Scott was trying to accomplish with the novel. But, I didn't understand a passage which I'll read to you when I get the novel from my satchel," James said. He stood, retrieved the novel, and then returned to the campfire circle. He found his place in the book and read:

"And swine is good Saxon," said the Jester; "but how call you the sow when she
is flayed, and drawn, and quartered, and hung up by the heels, like a traitor?"
"Pork;" answered the Swineherd.
"I am very glad every fool knows that too," said Wamba, "and pork, I think,
is good Norman-French; and so when the brute lives, and is in the charge of a
Saxon slave, she goes by her Saxon Name; but becomes a Norman, and is called
pork, when she is carried to the castle hall to Feast among the nobles. What dost
thou think of this, Gurth, ha?"

"Well, Captain, I think the French refer to pig meat as pork and the Germanic-English people refer to it as swine. I think what Scott was saying here was that the mixing of the words pork and swine produces a better language. The analogy points to the message in his novel, which was about the mixing of the Normans and the Saxons making for a better people in England," Henry said.

"I've read ze novel, too," Emmett said. "And I see zat ze mixing of enemies blood of ze Normans and ze Anglo-Saxons was what Scott was trying to say. He was meaning zat ze *mixing of language and ze commune interests is a good ding. But, zer is one ethnic group which feels ze pride of triumpf, while ze azser groaned under all ze consequences of defeat.*"

"Yes, I remember reading those exact words or very close to them in this novel," James said while turning to Henry who was eager to speak.

"My mother's people are from Coleraine," Henry said, "a city in the Ulster Plantation area of Northern Ireland. They were Scots-Irish Presbyterians who moved there after the 1745 Scottish uprising, and then came to America shortly after that conflict.

My father's side of the family emigrated from Prussia, near a little village named Hettenleidelheim. They were southern Germanic people; they fit right in with the Scots-Irish people in the Appalachian area where they settled.

"My mother's side of the family hated the English because her ancestors were denigrated by them in the old country. I would agree with Scott in that the Norman-Cavaliers in the South and the Anglo-Saxon Puritans in the North should find a way to get along in order to forge one strong Union in America. However, my Scots-Irish people were ground to dust and made to *groan under all the consequences of defeat* just as Emmett quoted Scott. New Englanders are no different than old Englanders overseas. I believe the Yankees aim to do the same thing to my people again. That's why I'm fighting here today!"

"My Scottish people are from north of Carlisle, England, on the border of Scotland," James said. "My great grandfather was born in 1717 and immigrated to the Hagerstown area. He married in 1740 as soon as he arrived in Maryland. He spoke with a Gaelic dialect and was part of the Great Migration, when so many Scottish people came to America," he said with a sense of pride in relation to his roots.

"I was, at first, a nationalist before ze war broke out," Emmett said. "But, much like William Gilmore Simms was a Unionist, he zen 1855, realized ze Puritanishe-Bostonion-'Frogpondians' were all Transcendentalisten out of Henry David Shoreau's school of twisted sinking. Harvard was full of zem. Zey sought light came from within, zer John Wintrop's and Cotton Mater's mission of 'a city on a hill' was to zem a manifest destiny to rule over all ze azser peoples that did not believe like zem.

"My mazser was from the Protestanten Ulster Plantation area of Ireland. My German fazser was a Lutheraner from Mainz, not far from where your family was from, Henry. I, too, soon realized zat ze Yankees had violent prejudices against my Irish-Southern roots. If I had chosen to submit to zem like ze Saxons in Scott's *Ivanhoe* had to submit to ze Normans, I would razser be dead. So I'm fighting for my liberty, like my ancestors in Norzern Ireland fought for zeir freedom from ze English, who saw zem as subhuman herdsmen."

"Southerners are to the Yankees as the Scots are to the English. They simply want us wiped out, as the English did in the old country," Zimmerman said.

Dogs should not worry dogs where wolves and foxes are to be found in abundance, James said, quoting Scott from the text before him that he read by the fire's light. "I suspect we've wolves and foxes to confront in the morning. I've one last poem to read before I retire. I'm a little uncertain of its meaning but here it is:

> *Norman saw on English oak,*
> *On English neck a Norman yoke;*
> *Norman spoon in English dish,*
> *And England ruled as Normans wish;*
> *Blythe world to England never will be more,*
> *Till England's rid of all the four.*

"Sounds to me like the biblical verses which refer to selling your soul to gain the world," Zimmerman offered, kicking an ember back into the fire circle. "More Yankees I can send to *hell* with our tubes full of hot iron the better. We'll not be part of their manifest destiny nor their puritanical mission of 'a city on a hill.'"

"Amen," Emmett exclaimed. "We'll not be part of zeir empire building."

"Goodnight, scholars," James said as he turned away from the campfire to get some rest.

⁂

Early the next morning, at a staging ground called Liverpool, James was at attention with his artillerymen as Major Pelham inspected the pieces. They were a mile from McCoy's Ford and the dense fog limited visibility to no more than thirty yards.

"Check your tack, men!" Major Pelham cried out while looking up and down at his artillerymen, ready to move out. "Forward—March!" rang out the command.

"Forward—March!" James repeated to his sergeants, Hoxton and Shaw.

James spurred Billy forward, once again at the rear of the column, with Captain Hart's section in support of General Wade Hampton's brigade. James and his men were to cross the Potomac first. He came to the banks of the river, splashed Billy into the water, and rode out to the middle of the river.

"Keep them horses tight in the traces!" James commanded as water splashed around the ammunition boxes. "Not too fast! Keep our powder dry!"

He saw his guns safely across the Potomac. Reflective of home, now that he was on Maryland soil, he struck up another conversation with Private Zimmerman.

"Why do you think Cedric the Saxon would not drink to the health of his own son, Wilfred of Ivanhoe?"

"I suspect it was because Ivanhoe was not obedient to the manners and customs of his father."

"Does a willful son have the right to adventure out on his own, to forge his own life even if it's contrary to his father's wishes?" James asked.

"That's certainly what Ivanhoe did," Zimmerman replied. "Does that present an issue to you personally, Captain?"

"Well, I'm a bit at odds with my father because I made a change in my career from a doctor into a military man. Scott notes that in *Alfred's day that would have been termed disobedience and a crime severely punishable.* I'm only doing what I believe is honorable and heartfelt in relation to fighting the war."

"This is something that you should not question," Zimmerman said. "You've placed your calling to country ahead of your calling to save life as a doctor and your father's design for your life."

"To be totally honest, Reverend, my mentor in the medical field is my uncle. He's now imprisoned because he refuses to take the Yankee oath. He sits in Fort Warren as a political prisoner due to his honor. My father has taken the oath; he sold out to the Yankees in my mind."

"Seems that bothers you more than leaving the medical profession to fight. Am I correct?"

"Well, I suspect I might never get my father's blessing *since he refuses to pledge to my health*, as Scott noted Cedric refused to do to Ivanhoe's health. But, I juxtapose my uncle's imprisonment and my father submitting. I don't know what to make of it."

"You'll figure it out," Zimmerman said. "For now, let us go get some Yankee horses!"

⋘ೞ⋙

Lieutenant Benjamin Stephen White, James's cousin from Poolesville, Maryland, was guiding General Stuart at the head of the column on the Mummert Road heading into Pennsylvania. Their expedition had missed confronting five thousand Federal soldiers marching to Hancock, Maryland, when the Federals had earlier crossed the National Pike at the home of W. C. Cline.

The expedition reached the Pennsylvania line midmorning. Stuart rode to the head of each brigade to read his orders: *We are now in enemy country. Hold yourselves ready for attack or defense and behave with no other thought than victory. If any man cannot abide cheerfully by the order and the spirit of these instructions, he'll be returned to Virginia with guard of honor.*

"Well, I guess that implies that if you've a point of conscientious objection to invading the United States, now is your time to tuck tail and move out," James said to Major Pelham.

"President Lincoln called up seventy-five thousand troops to invade our country and suppress our liberties and rights to form an independent nation. I bet not one of our artillerists of the Stuart Horse Artillery will leave for we're now in fighting mode," Pelham replied.

"Let's get north. Plenty of good Norman and Belgian horse flesh up there to pull our artillery equipment. Time to acquire it for our use, wouldn't you say, Major?" James asked.

"By all means, Captain. Forward—March!"

The cloudy overcast day produced a rain that suppressed James's spirit. He knew the Confederate troopers had been dispatched to acquire horses from unsuspecting farmers. He had overheard Stuart give them orders to assure the farmers, with receipts, that they could submit to Jefferson Davis in Richmond in return for Confederate script.

He and his artillerymen rode toward the town of Mercersburg and soon arrived in the town square. He saw that the square had four intersecting streets, flanked by late Federal and Greek Revival buildings built with detailed brick and gray stone. The Old Mansion House Hotel on one corner was built of gray stone and featured a two-storied porch in front. Colonel Murphy's Hotel was the sight of an 1856 political address by soon-to-be President James Buchanan, James recalled from his history studies as he surveyed the square. The William McKinstry's Tavern, also built of gray stone, sat on the northeast corner of the square. Shannon's Hardware store was built like the Tavern, and it was located on the southeast corner of the square. The General Mercantile store of J. N. Brewer was across the square.

"Captain Breathed, I want your two guns placed in the middle of the square," General Stuart ordered. The rain came down in torrents.

James sat Billy, the rain dripping from his red kepi onto his oilcloth rain gear, while he studied Main Street through his field glasses.

"Yes, sir!"

"Captain Hart, take your section and secure the perimeter of the town," General Stuart ordered. "No citizens in or out of the town, and silence those church bells!"

"Yes, suh!" Captain Hart saluted. He urged his horse forward, along with his guidon bearer, out of the square.

"Generals Hampton, Lee, and Jones, instruct your men to search for the magistrates of the town counsel and any other officials they can find and bring them to me at the Steigers's house where Major Pelham has established a headquarters for me. Your troopers are to purchase what they need from the local merchants. If they'll not accept our script, then they're at liberty to acquire what they need by any means necessary, understood? It's suppertime. Move out!"

"I usta wrestle black bears with my Bowie knife back in South Carolina," General Hampton said. "Are my troopers at liberty to use their Bowie knives?"

"Yes, General. Whatever means necessary," General Stuart responded with a grin on his face.

The gathering of officers broke up. James reined Billy toward his guns in the square.

"Boys, keep a look out for anything that seems threatening. Fire and ask questions later," James said as he peered down at his artillerymen. "Should be plenty of pickings in these stores. Let the troopers have first go around, and then we'll get what is left over."

He watched Colonel M. C. Butler's 2nd South Carolina troopers of General Hampton's brigade dash into J. N. Brewer's store. They helped themselves to hundreds of pairs of shoes and boots. He later found out Mr. Brewer refused to take their Confederate script.

"Captain Breathed, you're welcome to send a few of your artillerymen in before we clean him out," Colonel Butler said to him.

"I'll send a few at a time. My men could use some new boots."

The soldiers' two and a half hours of military occupation resulted in the arrest of one home guardsman, who thought he could stand up single handedly to the Confederates; the arrest of eight magistrates; the securing of an important map of the surrounding farms; and the acquisition of six hundred pairs of boots and shoes. James ordered the limbering of his two guns, and his section took up the march at the rear of the column, heading east on the Old Mercersburg Road toward Bridgeport.

He looked ahead of the column and noticed a civilian man in a wagon conversing with a few of his comrades. The round-faced man had a properly shaven face, only having a small loop of a thin beard from sideburn to sideburn. He finally pulled his wagon parallel to James on the side of the road.

James inquired of the man, "Suppose you let us have those horses?"

"Oh, no! I can't do that. I need these horses for my business."

James drew his pistol, pointing it at the man to show his resolve.

"Oh! You can't scare a butcher with firearms like that. We see too much blood in our business for that."

"You'd best fall in with that wagon and those horses or you're going to see some more blood right now," James said. "What's your name?"

"George Steiger, I'm the butcher in Mercersburg."

"Well, George, I believe General Stuart just supped at your home. Thanks for the Yankee hospitality. Now fall in line with your wagon and horses."

"Very well. Seems I've no choice in the matter."

The column moved through Bridgeport and St. Thomas and then on to Chambersburg. When they arrived there later in the evening, James placed his two guns on a hill outside of Chambersburg. The position held a commanding view of the town. He watched twenty-five troopers ride away into the town with a white flag of truce. He discovered later that the citizens knew of their imminent arrival due to harried reports coming from Mercersburg and the telegraph communications. Before General Stuart could have the telegraph lines destroyed, word had gotten out to the Governor of Pennsylvania that the area was under assault from the Confederates.

After the town surrendered, James positioned his cannon within the town square. He had an old battle flag tied to the spoke. His guns presented an ominous threat to the citizens. The bank was sequestered for greenbacks, but the money had already been moved, due to the knowledge of the Confederates' movements. His artillerymen had found straw hats, which were typically worn by the local farmers. They wore them to keep the rain from their countenances.

"Breathed, where'd your men come up with those straw hats?" General Stuart asked while passing by the cannon on the square.

"The locals gave them to us," he responded on behalf of his artillerymen.

"You look like a bunch of farmers. Nice look, but a little odd for military men," General Stuart smiled.

"Thanks, General."

James remained virulently on guard around his guns that night. He did not know if the citizens could be trusted or if the Federals were aware of their presence.

The next morning his column, led by Lieutenant White, marched on the road leading to Gettysburg. Before departing Chambersburg, Rooney Lee's brigade set fire to the Cumberland Valley Railroad Depot House and machine shops, which were loaded with ammunition. James heard a tremendous explosion to his rear.

Their expedition reached Cashtown and then turned south on the Ortanna Road through Fairfield on the road to Emmitsburg, Maryland. James knew the troopers had continued to gather horses in Pennsylvania.

He learned of the capture of a Federal courier near Woodsboro, Maryland, who was bearing dispatches to the scouting party of Rush's Lancers. The intelligence had informed General Stuart that the Federal cavalry under General Pleasanton's command had eight hundred troopers five miles to their west. The word had been passed down his column that they could expect Federals ahead.

He also learned from this intelligence that Pleasanton did not know where the Confederate forces were located.

James's column rode all night. Many of the men fell in and out of sleep in the saddle, though they roused twelve miles from Hyattstown, yet still a desperate distance from the Potomac River crossing. The danger of Federal forces was on all sides of their expedition. James rode on assuming the "gods of war" would procure his safety.

James's cousin, Lieutenant White, continued to lead the columned expedition that advised General Stuart.

Suddenly, before James's eyes, Federal General Pleasanton's expected cavalrymen appeared.

Major Pelham exclaimed, "Captain Breathed, deploy your guns on that knoll. I want fire on those Federal cavalrymen!"

James's men broke off from the column and deployed the guns. His artillerymen began to fire when, unexpectedly, they experienced counter-battery fire. The rapidity, simultaneous firing and accuracy of the Federal guns prompted James to quickly pull his field glasses and take a closer look at the Federal adversary. His artillerymen continued to blast away at the Federal cavalry, but he, for the first time in the war, was shocked to have a worthy foe firing at him.

"Boys, keep up the good work; we're having effect. Private Clem, move the trail two feet to the right. I want fire into those woods where I see Federal guns!" James exclaimed pointing in the direction of the bursts of smoke. "They're dropping shells in our pockets! I want those guns silenced!"

The Federal cavalry charged across the open field, but James seemed unaware of their movements. He wanted to annihilate the guns in the woods. The melee that broke out between the Confederate cavalry and the Federal cavalry was intense, but James did not interfere with it. He wanted those mysterious guns.

"Captain Breathed, I want one gun to stay here and break up their cavalry. You're to move forward with the other gun to protect our crossing on the Potomac," Major Pelham commanded.

"Limber up, boys, we're moving out one gun. Sergeant Shaw, get a move on," James responded, waving his hand in the air.

Lieutenant White maneuvered the column forward through dense woods on a road that had not been used in a long time. The road came out between the mouth of the Monocacy and Poolesville. From there they moved toward the river, and James followed with one cannon. There were hundreds of Federal infantry at the ford. In the other direction he spied Federal cavalry. The artillerymen whipped the beasts that moved the equipment; their lives were dependent upon it.

When the gun arrived, James was at a fevered battle pitch, as he knew that the success of the entire expedition was now in his hands.

"Deploy here, boys," James commanded as he had the men set the cannon on the C&O Canal towpath. "I want fire on those approaching infantry."

James began to work the cannon in a radius of 180 degrees. In one direction he ordered the firing at infantry; in the other at the cavalry.

"Turn the cannon, Private Zimmerman! Lay your hands on and put your backs into it! Private Mackall, do your part and get that cannon moved. The cavalry is coming in the other direction!" James exclaimed as he pointed up the towpath.

The work of James and his men warded off the enemy as the Confederate column crossed the ford in the river and made their way from Maryland back into Virginia. He observed troopers, bringing two to three horses, splash across the Potomac. He became an artesian who had mastered his brush, which was a weapon of death that neither the Federal infantry nor the cavalry could overcome. He enabled his comrades to escape near entrapment in Maryland by his working his one cannon ferociously, firing to his left and then to his right. Finally, much to his relief, the other three guns had splashed across the Potomac.

When all of his comrades had recrossed the Potomac under pursuit from the Federals, hundreds of horses in tow, James commanded the limbering of his gun. He and his artillerymen recrossed the Potomac as a hail of bullets chased them across the water. The other three guns fired from the banks on the Virginia side to protect the hair-raising crossing.

Safely on Virginia soil, James gasped for breath and looked for cover. When the Federals realized their pursuit was futile, their firing stopped.

Later in the day, he encountered a Federal trooper taken prisoner.

"Sir, who are you with?" James asked.

"The 6th Pennsylvania. Rush's Lancers, sir."

"Who is commanding that horse artillery which I've fought this day?"

"That is Alexander C. M. Pennington, West Point's finest, Second U.S., Battery M," replied the prisoner with a sense of pride.

"How do I know this name?" James pondered with a quizzical look on his face.

"He's a New Jersey man, if that helps."

"I'll think on it. Thanks."

25

Unconditional Release from an American Bastille

&

An Old Baltimore Friend

HAVING RECEIVED WORD OF her father's release from prison, Mollie had come to meet him in Baltimore. She and Alfred departed from the home of Mr. and Mrs. Thomas C. Jenkins, Esquire, at 180 North Calvert Street at 5:30 am. At the terminal of the Philadelphia Wilmington & Baltimore line of the President Street Station she awaited the arrival of her father's train. She assumed the long trip from Boston would have exhausted her father, already weakened by fourteen months in an American bastille. She thought her father had probably traveled from the prison at Fort Warren to a hotel in Boston, and then by train to New York City. Changing trains in New Jersey he would have taken the Camden & Amboy line to Philadelphia. Late that night he would have taken the Philadelphia Wilmington & Baltimore Railroad for a morning arrival in Baltimore City.

Alfred waited in the family's landau, which was parked outside the station. She stepped down from the carriage and entered the station. She was thankful this day of November 28, 1862, had finally arrived. Her father's tribulation was now coming to a conclusion. The beautiful old station offered a comfortable reception hall at the city terminus, and she sought the warmth of its confines. She looked around at the six-columned exterior hall. Its two stories inside were plainly decorated. Benches for those coming and going were placed throughout the station.

She pondered who might have been instrumental in the release of her father. She recalled pleading with Charles and Ariana Trail in Frederick City, but she had no way of knowing if Charles had done anything to secure her father's liberation.

Mr. Jenkins was a longtime family friend of her father's, going all the way back to their service on the 1832 General Committee for Reform of the Constitution of Maryland. The Jenkins family had immigrated to Maryland in 1660 and certainly, Mollie thought, they had amassed some influence in Maryland and Washington City. As well, Mr. Jenkins was a powerful businessman. He served on numerous boards of directors including the Baltimore & Ohio Railroad Company, the Baltimore & Susquehanna Railroad Company, the Parkersburg and the Central Ohio Railroad Company, and the Merchants and Miners Transportation Company. He had served as the vice president of the Baltimore Board of Trade and was currently a director of the Mechanics Bank and the Savings Bank of Baltimore.

A train whistle blew, announcing the arrival of the train. Startled out of her thoughts, her heart rhythm quickened; she began pacing the small reception hall. She heard the screech of metal-on-metal of a locomotive. Amid the detraining passengers, she strained to catch a glimpse of him.

Suddenly, she saw her father as he entered the reception room from the train platform. He looked pale and much thinner than she had ever seen him. He had on the suit he was wearing the day he was taken from their home in Hagerstown; as robust and stout a man as he used to be, he now barely filled it out.

"Father, I'm so thankful to see you safe and alive! We've missed you so much!"

"My beloved daughter, you look splendid and as vibrant as I've been imagining you'd look," her father replied as he embraced her with a hug. He placed a kiss on top of her head.

"Come, Father, I've made arrangements for our stay here in Baltimore with your old friend Thomas Jenkins."

"Well, my dear, as you might imagine, I've no bags. The Federals were rather inhospitable in relation to the prisoners retaining belongings."

"Alfred awaits us in the landau outside the station. Let us carry on to Mr. Jenkins's home."

They exited the station hand in hand.

"Hello, Alfred! Good to see you, my friend."

"Marse Macgill, good ta seesa ya. Welcome home!"

Alfred opened the door for them. He then drove north on President Street, turned left onto Pratt Street, and took a right turn on Calvert Street.

En route, Dr. Macgill turned to Mollie and said, "If I had to raise my fingers to the brim of my hat in a gesture of gratitude to those Yankees, I'd rather have stayed in jail until I died!"

"Father, I do so understand your sentiments! There is so much I've to tell you that I couldn't share with you in our correspondence."

"We best be guarded about our conversation in the presence of Thomas."

"Yes, Father. Did you know that his son John Carrell Jenkins left his Maryland Guard Battalion to join General Lee's army in the 21st Virginia Regiment 'Maryland Guard' Company B? He subsequently died of typhoid in West Virginia. To top that, his other son, Captain George Carrell Jenkins, is on the staff of Confederate General Lunsford Lomax as a quartermaster."

"This war is certainly confusing to Marylanders, breaking apart families, father against sons in this case," Dr. Macgill said. Nevertheless, we don't know where Thomas stands on his loyalties to the Union."

⋅⊙⊙⊙⋅

Alfred guided the landau to the carriage block at 180 North Calvert Street. A household servant exited from the front door to greet them. The Irish servant opened the carriage door and helped Mollie from the carriage first and then assisted her feeble and tired father.

They stepped into the entry hall of the home where there was a hand-painted canvas floor cover that replicated ceramic tiles. Two alcoves in front of them held tall hand-painted statues of Greek origin. The gasolier hung down in the center of the entry hall and featured a circle of six finely etched glass globes.

"Charles, my old friend, how good it is to see you," Thomas welcomed them as he reached out his hand to shake her father's. "Do come in. You must be weary from your travels all the way from Boston."

"It's been a long journey indeed."

Mollie observed Thomas's dress, a white collared shirt that had pointed edges below his chin. His white curly hair distinguished him as a man of stature. His prominent nose, thick eyebrows, and heavyset face set off his sharply tied black bowtie. He wore a dark blue vest and a frock coat. She had heard her father talk about his contemporary; the two had spent many long hours together, prior to the war, working on political issues of the state of Maryland.

"I've prepared a room for you to rest after breakfast. Won't you and Mollie join me for a meal before you recline to recapture your strength from travel?" Thomas asked her father.

She saw his wife, Louisa Carrell, descend the stairs, gracefully guided by the finely carved wooden banister.

"Hello, Louisa. You look wonderful!" Charles exclaimed. "I see you're taking fine care of yourself."

"Charles, it's good to see you," Louisa responded as she extended her hand, which her father gently kissed as a gesture of respect.

They walked into the next room to the left of the entry hall. Mollie marveled at the fourteen-foot tall ceilings and the lavishly draperied windows. A tall, ornately carved gold-rimmed mirror hung above a fireplace. The dining table in the middle of the room was set with fine china, and a discriminatingly carved Georgian English oak server with a marble top was placed opposite the mirror on the other side of the room. Over the dining table was a gasolier that illumined the room.

Her father helped Mollie with her chair as Thomas assisted Louisa. Mollie thought Louisa was a very pretty woman in her lovely silk paisley dress. Louisa's pale facial features indicated that she did not spend much time outdoors.

After a fine meal, Charles got some rest before they reconvened in the library for cigars and conversation prior to supper. As the cigars were offered by the Irish servant, Mollie knew the general conversation would ultimately turn to politics.

ↄ◌ⓔ◌৲

"Father, share with us your experience of imprisonment. I know it had to be far worse than you were able to let on in our correspondence," Mollie said. She settled into a patterned upholstered rocking chair close to the carved marble fireplace; the fireplace mantel had another gold-trimmed mirror. Set upon it at each end were vases filled with peacock feathers.

"Well, after a five-day stay at Fort McHenry here in Baltimore," Charles said, "we were taken to Fortress Hamilton in New York Harbor. It wasn't long before we were moved to Fortress Lafayette, which consisted of ten casemates on each tier of the fortress. Four were assigned to the political prisoners. The darkies were still removing dirt and rubbish when we got there. The front rooms were twenty-four by fourteen feet, each lighted by two small loop holes in the outer wall. Those casemates were dark and damp with only a fireplace, which did little to keep us warm. The routine to which we were subjected seemed to have the deliberate purpose of adding insults to our stay. When servants brought in the meals, a sergeant stood guard. The sergeant would sometimes set the meals outside for a few hours before serving them to us. The knives and forks were counted by him after each meal. Lieutenant Wood, who commanded the fortress, was no gentlemen and cruel of heart. He caused us to be subjected to indignities that were needless."

"Charles, I'm so sorry that you were exposed to such terrible treatment. To my knowledge you had done nothing to deserve imprisonment in the first place," Thomas said as he puffed his cigar and blew the smoke up over his head.

"My political prisoner friends—Chief of Police George Kane, Mayor George Brown, Charles Howard, and his son Frank Key, and many of the Maryland legislators—were resolute that Mr. Lincoln could not treat fine upstanding citizens of Maryland with such contempt," Dr. Macgill said.

"I sympathize with you, Charles," Louisa responded. She sat next to Mollie in another rocking chair.

"In President Thomas Jefferson's 1801 first inaugural address, he clearly stated the importance for all citizens having the freedom of person, under the protection of habeas corpus and trial by impartially selected juries. Mr. Lincoln denied myself and all of the Maryland political prisoners this right," Charles indignantly said.

"You most certainly were denied this right guaranteed by our state and federal constitutions. Didn't you even provide medical aid to Federal soldiers when General Patterson was first occupying Maryland early in the war?" Thomas asked.

"Yes, I did. I informed them of this when they came to take me away. It fell on deaf ears."

"Father, what happened next?" Mollie asked, eager to hear more of her father's travails.

"Many letters were written to the powers that be in Washington City. Including letters to Honorable Simon Cameron, Secretary of War; Commander-in-Chief Lieutenant General Winfield Scott; Honorable William H. Seward, Secretary of State; and President Lincoln himself. These letters described our deplorable living conditions and treatment. I signed the letter to the president in which I noted that there was a contagious cutaneous disease spreading, which would result in a serious general disorder if our situation remained unimproved. Early in October we only heard back that our petition had been forwarded through Colonel Townsend. No reply was ever received from Washington."

"Your petition was ignored?" Louisa said with a ghastly look on her face.

"Yes, ignored. We were given one hour in the morning and one at night to walk on a patch of ground within the fort. Many of our personal letters were returned to us because they contained facts the government did not desire should be known, or reflected on the government itself. We were locked up every night from dusk until sunrise, and lights had to be put out at half past nine o'clock. One political prisoner had an acute attack of pneumonia and lay for ten days in a damp dark gun battery with thirty other prisoners. I obtained permission to take him some little luxuries. I found him lying on the floor upon two blankets in a high fever without even a pillow under his head. I finally got him removed to a hospital on Staten Island."

"Father, you're so courageous to have risked your own life for the life of your fellow prisoners," Mollie said.

"Mollie, my Hippocratic oath requires me to do so. Late in October we were moved from Fortress Layette to Fortress Columbus on Governor's Island. We boarded the steamboat State of Maine with over one thousand other men, many were soldiers who had been taken prisoner at Fort Hatteras. There was a plot that brewed to overthrow the crew and go to Halifax. I talked them out of it, for we didn't have enough coal to make the journey and the vessel was not seaworthy. We stayed on board for two days before arriving at Fort Warren on the evening of October 31st. They fed us rancid blubber, crackers, and water. We were treated with as little consideration as cattle."

"Charles, you've certainly been through an ordeal," Thomas said continuing to puff his cigar as he grew more intent on the story.

Charles continued his tale. "We finally arrived on the forty-three acre island of which the granite fort enclosed five or six acres. I was placed in a lower casemate, without windows, with my cellmates Dr. Jeffreys of Norfolk, Dr. Lindsay, Dr. Page, Thomas W. Hall of Baltimore, and a few others. Colonel Dimick offered me a better room. I declined as I didn't want to incommode some poor sickly fellow. I sought permission from the colonel to administer medicine. They supplied the medicines to affect the most dangerous cases. Here, Thomas, take a look at this letter signed by eighty of the prisoners I tended to," Charles said. He stood and handed Thomas the letter, which he read aloud:

Fort Warren, Mass.
July 31, 1862

To Charles Macgill, M.D. of Hagerstown, Md., now a Prisoner of State at Fort Warren:

Your fellow-prisoners, confined with you for many months in this Bastille, have been too often indebted to your professional skill for relief from painful and, in many cases, most dangerous illness; and in their social intercourse with you have found so much to admire that they cannot, now on the eve of departure for their beloved country, part without returning thanks and giving expression to their grateful acknowledgements of your disinterested conduct. Hoping that you may be speedily restored to the quiet pleasures of your happy name.

We are your friends,

"You're to be commended Charles for your tender care of your comrades in prison," Louisa said.

"Yes, Father, I'm so proud of you for standing your ground for liberty on the basis of your convictions," Mollie said. She stood and walked over to Thomas, who gave her the letter, which she then returned to her father with a hug.

"In my ninth month," Charles said, "Judge Pierpont and General Dix came to see me. They offered me my release if I'd sign the oath. I told them I'd neither degrade myself in my own estimation nor disgrace my record in the eyes of my people by taking that oath. General Dix responded to me that 'There is nothing against you, Doctor, it's true. But you've been arrested and are now held by the government and, as this has engendered some hard feelings, perhaps we must still hold you.' He also told me that John Schleigh the postmaster, John Cook the blacksmith, and Robinson the shoemaker of Hagerstown were the men who accused me."

"Father, those common men aren't worth trusting, and everyone knows that Mr. Schleigh was put there as a political favor by Mr. Lincoln," Mollie said. A fit of rage came over her face and her cheeks turned red.

"Daughter, calm yourself. One never knows who your real friends are in a time of war. Thomas, here's my copy of a letter which I finally used to get out of my imprisonment," Charles said. He walked across the library and handed the letter to Thomas who then read it aloud:

Parole of Dr. Charles Macgill
Fort Warren Mass.
Sep 2d 1862

Sir,

I am a prisoner at this place, where I have been since the beginning of Nov. last, having been arrested on the 1st day of October last, in Hagerstown, Maryland, where I had resided, in the practice of my profession, for many years. The cause assigned for my arrest has never been communicated to me. Having been unable to procure a release to return to my home & duties. I, at one time, sought to be exchanged so that I might pass into the Confederate lines. The Government of the U. S. & that of the C. S. however, have since adopted the humane act of treating surgeons, even when taken in battle, as non-combatants, & discharging them without conditions, so that exchange has ceased to be applicable to them any longer. I am still willing to go South, if I am not permitted to resume my practice at home, & it seems to me to be as much the interest of the U. S. as of opposing authorities, that no obstruction would be assumed to the entrance of competent surgeons into the Southern territory. I understand from the actions of the two governments already referred to that it concedes any professional functions to be those of mere humanity and entitled as such to all protection & encouragement. The large number of wounded U. S. prisoners whom the fortunes of the war are constantly throwing into the hands of the Confederacy must give ample force to this consideration, at the present time—restricted as the Medical assistances & services of the Southern army are well known to be—by the fidelity with which I am capable of discharging my professional duties, without respect to persons. My services rendered within your knowledge, when I was in charge of Gen Patterson's body guard at the Hospital in Hagerstown, will give your every assurance.

I take hand therefore to propose to the government through you, that upon being released from custody, I will give my parole to repair at once to the Southern lines & dedicate myself exclusively to professional labor.

I will thank you to give this application the proper direction, with your endorsement, if you approve it, & shall be pleased to have your acknowledgement as in receipt.

Very Respectfully
Your Obd Serv
Chas Macgill M.D.
Surgeon Gen'l Hammond
U.S.A.
Washington D. C.

"Charles, you were wise to conceive of such a letter," Thomas said.

"A refusal to acquiesce in the proceedings by which the government had out-raged the people of Maryland was the only mode of resisting arbitrary power that was left to us. We had no hesitation in adhering to our course. I deemed it to be my destined duty to defend, to the last, every privilege and right to which, as an American citizen, I was born. Each of us political prisoners determined at the outset to resist to the uttermost the dictatorship of Abraham Lincoln and, having done so, each of us had the satisfaction of feeling, as he left Fort Warren, that he had faithfully, and not unsuccessfully, discharged a grave public duty," Charles responded.

"Charles, we're both from Old Line Maryland families. You know my loyalties to this state. This war has torn my family apart with the death of John and George serving the Confederacy. Things are changing, and our old ways and the old families are no longer all who are in power. There're newcomers like Horace Abbott with his rolling mill and Ross Winans, the powerful industrializer and railroad inventor, who now also have power and influence in this nation and state. They care nothing about the old ways which you and I know so well," Thomas said.

"Thomas, Mr. Lincoln's disregard for the rule of law and the centralization of power isn't what the founding fathers had in mind when they wrote the Declaration of Independence and the Constitution. The centralization of the railroads as the United States Military Railroad that is now in existence as a result of the Railways and Tele-graph Act allow Mr. Lincoln to seize and operate any railroad or telegraph company's property or equipment if required for war use. I feel this sets a bad precedence for American capitalism—centralization. I suspect it'll happen to the medical corps next if it has not already, then banking and financial institutions. They gave us so few news-papers in prison it was hard to know what was going on outside."

"Charles, it's the way the country is moving. I don't believe it can be stopped. I'm on board with it and suggest you consider how you might move in this direction as well."

"Gentlemen, shall we move to the supper table?" Louisa asked as she felt the energy in the room was rising.

"Charles, three of my Merchant and Miners Line steamboat ships are now troop transports. The *Joseph Whitney* I sold outright in August of 1861, *S. R. Spaulding* and *Benjamin Deford* are now under a lease contract with the Federal army. Nothing wrong with government control as long as they pay private enterprise for it," Thomas said as he patted Charles on the back while they walked into the dining room.

"Still don't like what Mr. Lincoln is doing with his centralization policies to win the war. It is too dangerous for the future—no telling what kind of out-of-control spending it could lead to," Charles responded as he helped Mollie into a chair at the table.

They stayed one more day with the Jenkins before travelling to Hagerstown. There was much lively conversation between the two old friends, despite the fact they had clearly grown apart on their views of the war and the two nations.

On the trip home over the National Turnpike to Hagerstown, Mollie shared with her father her spying exploits that had begun at the Cary home in Baltimore City with her cousin Corporal Lige White. She shared her experience of meeting Winslow Homer, the *Harper's Weekly* illustrator, on the Williams's farm and how this led to passing information to Lige, which went directly to General Evans. She explained to her father that the outcome of the Battle of Ball's Bluff was a result of her espionage.

She reminded him of his old friend Colonel Jacob Hollingsworth and her ride behind enemy lines, passing from one courier to another, until she met up with James at Oatlands Plantation. She could not keep from telling him of the romantic kiss in George Carter's garden that James so unexpectedly gave her.

The letter from John Augustus to Charles Baker had opened the door for her to discover what General McClellan was doing with all the ships he was requisitioning for the government. She explained how she got this information to Christian Emmerich's shop where Charles Langley got the intelligence to Lige's couriers who went directly to General Johnston, who then thwarted McClellan's Peninsula Campaign.

She shared with her father her experience with Charles and Ariana Trail on the way to David Best's farm outside of Frederick City. She told of running into Federals in Buckeystown, finding her way around the city only to be faced with shooting a picket to pass by. She explained that she was almost captured by Federal cavalry in Dr. Thomas John Macgill's barn. Arriving at Mountain House she imparted the vitally important intelligence of the 191 orders to General D. H. Hill.

Finally, with a sense of regret she told him of her work as a nurse after the horrific battle outside of Sharpsburg. She tried to hold back her tears because she in some way felt like her getting the 191 orders to General Lee made her responsible for the bloodshed of the battle.

"My dearest, you certainly have been a busy woman while I've been sitting in prison."

Alfred drove them west toward their home.

"Father, I told James I'd do my part, and I have!"

26

Autographs & Horse Artillery Fightin'

Battle near Kelly's Ford, Virginia

MARCH 17TH, 1863

JAMES SAT ON A rail of the Orange and Alexandria Railroad track behind the abandoned house of Mr. Barber, the president of the line, only a few miles north of Brandy Station, Virginia. He and his battery's artillerymen were camped all around the house. All were trying to keep warm as the temperature hovered just above freezing.

He pulled his gray great coattails over his legs that were stretched out before him. There had been scant activity over the winter since the battle at Fredericksburg in mid-December, and he found himself bored from the monotony of routine camp life. He was not alone. He thought John Pelham was off visiting one of the attractive young women in Orange Court House to relieve his boredom. James, meanwhile, stayed behind with the horses and his artillerymen. Yes, rank indeed had its privileges. James had learned that Stuart was attending to a court martial in Culpeper, and Fitz Lee and his brigade of troopers were also there.

James was in a particularly thoughtful mood as he reflected back over the winter months. Knowing he had done his part at the Battle of Fredericksburg, where he had fired over Pelham's forward guns, made him feel good. He had not gotten any real credit for his part in the resounding Confederate victory, not that he was looking for any. He had brought two guns on the Stuart-engineered Dumfries Raid later that month, but it did not amount to much in capture of equipment or men. The Hartwood Church raid led by Fitz Lee should have stirred the Federals into reprisal, but here they sat—no action.

His teeth chattered despite the sun beaming on him. He looked around at the muddy conditions. The five inches of snow that had recently fallen, then melted, had turned the roads into quagmires. It had been an exceptionally cold and hard winter. He was growing tired of gathering forage, keeping his mounts fresh, and awaiting battle.

James wondered how Mollie was getting along now that Dr. Macgill was home from Fort Warren. Would she resume her spying for the South, or had she done her share for the cause? Her mother was sickly and maybe she had resigned herself to taking care of her. He was most assuredly ready for spring campaigns and an expeditious end to the war.

He stood from the rail, crossed over the second rail, and entered the woods on the other side. His boots sloshed in the snow-melted, saturated ground as he scoured the forest floor for a stick that he could whittle. After finding a nice one he recrossed the rails. As he walked back into camp he heard a train whistle, far off in the distance. He withdrew his pocket knife and whittled at the stick as he walked.

"Private Mackall, you havin' a pleasant day in this cold?" James asked as he threw a splinter from the stick with the blade of his knife.

"Doing the best I can ta stay warm, Captain."

"Horses been watered recently?"

"We've just returned from takin' care of it, sir."

"Good. I 'spect I'll be in the house if I'm needed."

"They's awaitin' you there, Captain."

James turned from the private and squished in his boots through the mud to the Barber House. He entered and found it to be cozily warmed by the fires in the fireplaces at each end of the parlor. He walked over to the fire to warm his hands and was greeted by Private Matthews.

"We've been expecting you, Captain. Come see what the boys have put on the wall! Make ya real proud of your artillerymen."

Curious now, James followed the private into another room. Before his eyes he beheld a magnificent scroll of names on the wall, drawn in charcoal. There were sixteen names written within what looked like an ancient scroll, curled at the top and bottom. On the bottom of the curled end of the scroll was the word *Marylanders*. Above the scroll was a fancy pennant drawing. He admired the artistry of the work, and then read aloud the text he saw there:

Stuart Horse Artillery, Breathed Battery's—Rifle Gun—On Picket March 16th 1863.

"Fine piece of art, gentlemen, but you boys got too much time on your hands. I suspect you're as bored as I, so I can't blame you for fillin' time with art making! At least someone will know we were here in the future," James said as he looked around at all the other graffiti on the walls left by other soldiers.

"Captain, I done a special piece of art for you," Matthews announced. "Come yonder and take a look."

Private Matthews walked with him over to an image of a man with a goatee drawn on the wall.

"My spittin' image if I do say so myself!" James exclaimed. "Henry, you must think somethin' of me to put me on these walls. I'm truly honored by your artistic merit. I suspect I best be signin' the wall myself, just to verify that I was here and approve of your art."

His artillerists had gathered in the house and they broke into a round of applause, which made him blush.

Henry Zimmerman hollered out, "Three cheers for our commander! Hip, Hip Hurrah!—Hip, Hip, Hurrah!—Hip, Hip, Hurrah!" The artillerists yelled out as a train thundered by the house, shaking it, while blowing its whistle.

Matthews handed a sharpened piece of charcoal to James as he was walking over to the wall to sign it. *Jas Breathed, Captain Commanding,* he wrote.

James turned to his men and said, "I'm honored. Now it's getting dark, and we need to start our supper messes. I'll be around to each mess tonight. We'll see who honors me the most by which mess stirs up the best grub for me to taste. Let's get to it and enjoy ourselves tonight; we never know when the infernal Yankees will come a-knocking at our door. Oh—thanks for the tribute and the art."

⋘⊙⋙

The next morning James was up early, for he didn't sleep well in the freezing temperature. He rubbed his hands over his great coat trying to warm up his arms; the fires from the night before had almost gone out. There had been gaiety and celebration in the night over the dedication of the art on the walls, evidenced by a few empty moonshine jars he picked up and threw into the woods on the other side of the tracks.

When he looked up, he was totally caught off guard to see Generals Stuart and Fitz Lee, with Major Pelham and Captain Gilmor, all riding into the camp. Their lathered horses were reined to a halt where he stood.

"Captain Breathed, you're to move your battery as quickly as you can raise your men and harness your teams. I've received reliable intelligence that the Yankee cavalry commander General Averell has moved from Morrisville to the vicinity of Kelly's Ford. He aims to make his way to Culpeper. Seems his commander, General George Stoneman, has had enough of our 'raids' into their territory on the other side of the Rappahannock," Stuart empathetically stated. "General Lee and I will be on this side of the ford if they are able to get by the forty pickets we already have at the ford. Position your battery at old man Brannin's farm. You'll have plenty of targets, for Averell has a division under his command."

"Yes, sir. Sound the reveille, private," James responded as he looked over to a soldier with a bugle in his hand.

"I know Averell well, Captain. He was my roommate at West Point, and he'll be cautious. Your artillery will be vitally important in the outcome of this engagement," Lee said.

"Captain, I'll ride ahead and find the best roads to get you to the Brannin farm," Pelham offered.

"Very good, Major," James replied as he saluted Pelham with respect.

The four officers rode off quickly, followed by the five Virginia cavalry regiments of the brigade. James hollered out commands throughout the camp. Adrenaline was now pumping through his veins. It wasn't long before the horses were harnessed and placed into their four-up teams; caisson teams and ammunition wagons were also readied for the battlefield. He saddled Billy and rode through the camp making his men ready for battle.

Chiefs of pieces, Sergeants Emmett Shaw and William Hoxton, were busy seeing to their sections as he rode up to them.

"Sergeants, make sure your limbers and caissons are filled, going to be a long day stoppin' the Yanks from gettin' to Culpeper," James commanded.

"Zat se trus, Captain, zer must be plenty of firin' today to halt off a division from komming here!" Sergeant Shaw replied.

"I've seen to it personally, Captain," Sergeant Hoxton replied.

"Get 'em ready to move out," James said to the two sergeants.

"Boots and saddles! Poles up! Prepare to move out!" the sergeants ordered, and their command raced throughout the camp.

James rode to the head of where he wanted the column to form in the road. "By piece—from the right—front into column!" James commanded as he pulled his gauntlets on his hands. "March!"

His four sets of cannon with limbers and caissons formed into a column; the groups of ten mounted artillerists fell in beside the guns, with the ammunition wagons to the rear of the column. His artillerists moved out across the Orange and Alexandria Railroad tracks to march to the Brannin farm.

"Trot Out—March!" James commanded. The column stretched a good distance behind him, the horses and equipment splashing mud from the country roads. The teams of horses pulled and strained. Hot air blew from their nostrils, producing steam as it hit the frigid spring Virginia clime. The column moved expeditiously toward the farm.

As the column trotted into Brannin's farmyard, James saw an old man sitting on the front porch of the two story farmhouse with its red tin roof and a tin roof extending over the front porch. The old man was smoking a corncob pipe. James gave a wave of his hand to the Virginian who, in reply, swung his hands open before his legs as if to say, *My home is your home, have at them Federals.*

"Form line advancing—right oblique—walk! March! Guide right!" James commanded. The four guns formed a straight line to fire into the Federal cavalry division, which had formed behind a stone wall less than a half mile to their front.

The commands were repeated by the sergeants, and they formed their sections ready for battle. The tension was thick, for the noise of carbine and revolver fire filled the air before them.

In the far distance James could see a red brick mill that stood six stories high at the ford. To his immediate front his Confederate cavalry comrades were firing at the stone wall behind which the Federals had dismounted. When the artillerymen were in place at their guns, James dismounted Billy and stood ready to command the battery.

When the rifled guns were in position and loaded he gave the command, "Battery—Fire!" All four guns unloaded their missiles of death into the Federal cavalry line along the stone wall.

But the Confederate cavalry was not able to hold after numerous assaults on the stone wall; after his artillerists had gotten off a number of rounds his comrades raced away from the stone wall on the road that led to Kelly's Ford. The two regiments to his front were breaking as the Federal cavalry began to remount behind the stone wall to give open battle in the fields.

"Limber!" James commanded as he himself remounted Billy in order to move to a new position farther back.

Privates Clem, Mackall, Matthews, and Zimmerman picked up the trail of their gun and turned it to the limber hook as the four-up team had been positioned to accept the gun.

"Private Matthews! Move quickly! We've to get the hell out of here! Those Yankees are bearing down on us fast!" James hollered at him and the team of artillerists.

"Yes, Captain! Doin' fast we can!" Matthews responded. Sweat poured from his face; the temperatures had risen.

"On the right onto line!" James commanded.

"Section!—Right Wheel!" Sergeants Shaw and Hoxton commanded as they turned the battery to the rear.

"March—Guide right!" James commanded as his battery rapidly moved out across old man Brannin's farm field, back toward the road.

"Section into column!" James commanded, as he pointed his sabre to mark the spot where he wanted the column to hit the road. "March!"

His column hit the dirt road like a shot and thundered up the Kelly's Ford Road away from the fight and the noise of the carbine fire. Riding in front of the column James came to the Newby Road and ordered one cannon into position there. The rest of the column followed his lead along the road. He strategically placed the other three guns on the high ground off to the left of the Newby Road. The final cannon he positioned not far from the Providence Church at the intersection of the Carolina Road and the Newby Road. The vantage point of the open battlefield before him was excellent.

◈

A battle royal opened from the second gun position. He rode back and forth between the guns, giving encouragement and cheer to the artillerists.

"Captain, don't let your fire cease. Drive them from their position," Pelham commanded as they met up at the cannon closest to the Providence Church on the ridge.

"Yes, sir, Major!" James shouted. "We're givin' 'em hot shell and their Schenkl shells are doing nothing to our positions. They must've gotten wet as they crossed over the ford."

Pelham rode off toward Colonel Owen's 3rd Virginia Cavalry on the left flank of the Confederate line. James had been observing the 3rd charging and reforming around the house. His guns were firing relentlessly into the Federal cavalry ranks in that vicinity.

"Private Zimmerman, you're makin' me proud! Private Clem, keep up the good work," James shouted as he looked through his field glasses to see the effect his shots were having on the Federal positions.

"Sir, there they go charging again into the Yanks in front of the house!" Private Mackall said.

"Shell, one thousand eight hundred yards, three second fuse, load!" James commanded. "Fire!"

"Got 'em good that time Captain!"

"Cease firing! That one was too close to our boys!" James replied, surveying the landscape with his field glasses.

James viewed Fitz Lee and Stuart through his field glasses. With their sabres they cut and slashed at the Federal cavalrymen at the center of the open fields. They charged and reformed into the Federal troopers repeatedly throughout the afternoon hours.

During a lull on the battlefield, James looked at his watch and discovered the time to be around three o'clock. Only minutes passed before the two great cavalry forces again clashed sabres and fired revolvers, each side trying to drive the other from the field of honor. Then came a redoubled charge, and in response James moved down to his gun at the Newby House.

"Captain, we've 'bout driven them Yanks from their guns. If'n we had some more troopers we'd overrun them guns. Some o' them troopers gone run into the woods and is a hidin' on us. Hard to get 'em in the woods, seh," the gunner said. Black powder soot covered his face and hands.

"Keep a steady counter-battery fire on their artillery. Sergeant Shaw, how're you holding on ammunition?" James asked.

"Zat wagen do hinge is still half full, have enough left sir, I sink zey are kaput slowly, zeir artillery isn't reaching us, poor targeting I guess," Shaw responded as he pointed to the ammunition wagon to the rear.

James spied through his field glasses to see the woods that the private had indicated. He saw the Federal troopers heading to the woods of tall oaks on their left flank. They had good cover from his artillery fire. He spied the Federal horse artillery open fire in the middle of the plains before him.

"Concentrate your fire, Sergeant, on their horse artillery! I want it knocked out before dark! It's getting late in the day! Am I clear, Sergeant?"

"Yes, Captain, will do."

James galloped the ridge, back toward the Providence Church to check on the other guns before riding to the gun at the end of the ridge close to the church. He arrived in time to see the assistant on the staff of Fitz Lee, Lieutenant Minnigerode, with a body draped over the back of his horse. James spurred Billy with all speed, galloping to the caisson behind the gun where there was a crowd around the horse.

"Captain, they've killed poor Pelham!" the lieutenant exclaimed.

James dismounted Billy and ran to the body of his commander. He saw the blood dripping from the back of Pelham's skull. Upon discovering that Pelham yet lived, James immediately became the doctor of old. Dr. William Murray, the battery's surgeon, was also on hand. The two of them took Pelham's unconscious body from the horse.

"What can we do?" the lieutenant inquired.

"Stretch him out on his side," James ordered. Dr. Murray nodded his head and concurred.

"Bring some lint and gauze wraps so we can stop the bleeding," Dr. Murray shouted out.

"Rest of you men back to your posts," James commanded as he tended to his comrade.

The doctors applied gauze bandages and stopped the bleeding. They helped get Pelham back onto the horse and ordered the lieutenant to find an ambulance as quickly as possible to get Pelham back to Culpeper.

James returned his attention to the action on the battlefield. Through his field glasses, he witnessed the Federal cavalry retreating back toward the house. The fight was coming to an end. It was not long before the Federals disappeared from the field. All that remained were dead and wounded men, dead and dying horses. The battle of Kelly's Ford had come to an end, but, James hoped, the life of his beloved commander had not also come to an end.

⁓⊙⊙⊙⁓

James knocked on the door of Judge Henry Shackelford's red brick two-story home on Main Street in Culpeper late that night. He and Daniel Shanks had ridden from their camp to see to their commander's condition. The door opened slowly and the judge stood before them.

"I'm Captain Breathed and this's Lieutenant Shanks of the Stuart Horse Artillery. May we come in?" James sheepishly asked.

"You're welcome. The major is upstairs being seen to by Dr. Herndon and two other doctors. Captain Gilmor's also with them."

James and Daniel walked up the stairs into the room where the major lay comfortably in a twin bed. The room was well furnished and the four poster canopied bed was a fitting resting place for his commander, James thought. He immediately noticed Judge Shackelford's daughter, Bessie, sitting on the corner of the bed and pressed against the backboard. Her left leg was crossed under her right, which supported her and extended to the floor. With a pillow in her lap she cradled the major's head. He noticed her beautiful blue eyes, the depths of which were streaming with tears onto the corner of the pillow. Her delicate strength of nose, chin, and mouth were sullen as she could not stop the flow of tears.

"The doctors say he is dying. I'll never forget him; I couldn't help but be drawn to him. He always had the answers to my questions before I even asked them. He knew my mind better than I knew it myself," Bessie said as she stroked Pelham's forehead. "If there was ever a joke to be played, one had to be a jump ahead to get it played before John could get it over on ya."

"Miss, we know how you feel. He has been our faithful friend and commander so long we'll be lost without him," James responded. He wiped his sleeve across his nose and eyes, drying his own tears.

"We used to dance till all hours of the morning. He was so strong and masculine; but you wouldn'ta known it unless you danced with him," Bessie sobbed.

Captain Gilmor came over to James and patted his shoulder trying to console him. Lieutenant Shanks came to the other side of James and did the same.

"Miss, I been fightin' with him since the beginning of the Stuart Horse Artillery back by November of '61. We been through a lot together; he's like a brother to me."

"T'was shrapnel that hit him. We removed it, but he hasn't regained consciousness," Dr. Herndon reported as he showed it to James.

"Good God! It coulda been from one of my shells toward the end of the fight! Hard tellin'; it was such a melee of horses blue and gray on the field today," James sobbed.

The bedroom door opened and there stood General Stuart. He entered and knelt at the side of the bed and held Pelham's hand.

"No, my son! Not you my faithful comrade!" Stuart blubbered. He removed his plumed hat, and the tears flowed from his beard to the bed quilt.

Suddenly, the room went silent as Pelham gasped for his final breath. Dr. Herndon looked to his watch and declared him passed at a little after 12:00 am.

27

Fur-a-Flying

SEPTEMBER 21ST, 1853

As MOLLIE SAT ON the front steps of her home, the cool April breeze jaunted her memory back to a day in her youth. She recalled the pleasant cool air of September as she had walked down the stairs of her Hagerstown home on South Potomac Street. Alfred held open the door of the small black carriage as she stepped on the oval mounting pad and found her place inside the enclosed two seater. She pulled the skirt of her plain dark green dress up into the carriage. He closed the door behind her. Her mother waved good-bye as Alfred climbed onto the driver's seat, picked up the reins, and gently patted them on the back of the mare.

"Miss Mollie, yous ready for your first day of schooling," Alfred asked, speaking through the glass pane window behind the driver's seat.

"Yes, Alfred. I'm looking forward to the opening of Hagerstown Female Seminary today. The Lutherans have done a fine work to build such an institution here in town."

Alfred drove her to the seminary, located on the eastern extremity of Antietam Street. As they approached, she looked out the window at the four-story brick building with its Romanesque style. Steps led up to a four-columned front portico. The roof featured an ornate cupula. Her new school, which sat on a hill overlooking the town, offered a delightful view of the valley and mountains. She saw that the rear of the building, laid out in proper English fashion, was set for a game of croquet.

She was excited to meet Reverend C. C. Baughan, the principal who orchestrated the study of one ancient and one modern language, a complete knowledge of English grammar, composition, penmanship, mental and written arithmetic, geography, history of United States, and Biblical recitations, together with some degree of musical culture. Bachelor degrees in both classical arts and music were offered, and she had chosen classical studies. The seven faculty members developed gentleness of manner, sweetness of character, and gracefulness of bearing in the young ladies, all of which attributes the feisty fifteen-year-old Mollie needed in order to develop her Southern womanhood.

Her carriage ascended the front hill of the seminary, approached to the foot of the columned portico, and then stopped.

"Here ya be, Miss Mollie. We seesya after your schoolin'," Alfred said as he opened the carriage door.

She stepped down from the carriage. "Don't be late, Alfred."

"Yes, Miss Mollie, I'll be waitin' fer ya."

She climbed the front steps, a proud new student with an apple for her teacher, her lunch, a paper tablet, and pencils. The curls of her black hair hung down onto her forehead, and the rest of her hair was done neatly into a bun on top of her head. Her pretty, fair Scottish skin gave her a radiant beauty that boys often doted upon. Her finely manicured fingernails and wrist bracelets gave her an air of being a sophisticated young lady. She entered the front door and was met by a faculty member.

"And who might we have here?" Miss Johanna Troutwein, the teacher of Italian, music, painting, and drawing asked.

"I'm Miss Mollie Macgill from Hagerstown. I'll be studying the classics. Will you be my teacher?"

"Yes, Miss Macgill; I teach Italian. I believe you're in my first class. Please follow me; I'll get you situated," Miss Troutwein responded. She was fashionably dressed, wearing a subdued plaid dress with a white lacy collar.

Mollie followed Miss Troutwein through a maze of halls on the first floor, finally arriving at the teacher's classroom. They entered the classroom together, and she found her way to a desk with a wooden chair.

Mollie looked toward the head of the classroom. On the blackboard Miss Troutwein had written *Good Morning Class.* A United States flag, with thirty-one stars on it, was attached to a pole on the right of the blackboard. Miss Troutwein's desk had fresh flowers in a glass vase that was filled halfway with water. There were many other young girls sitting in rows of desks behind Mollie, and to her right and left.

Mollie looked over to the young girl to her left, "Hello, I'm Mollie Macgill."

"Hello, I'm Annie Artz. I'm boarding here. I'm from Illinois," Annie said. She was smartly dressed and had a peculiar accent that Mollie had not heard before.

"I don't know much about Illinois. Where're you from in Illinois?" she inquired.

"The North Shore, outside of Chicago."

Mollie then turned to her right, suddenly recognizing an acquaintance. "Hello, Olivia McKee. Seems we're not only neighbors, but classmates."

"Yes," Olivia curtly answered.

Reverend Baughan entered the classroom and the jubilant smile on Mollie's face disappeared instantly. A stern look was set on his face. "Good morning, ladies. I'm your principal. I wanted to welcome you to Hagerstown Female Seminary. I'm a Lutheran minister, and we'll be teaching great thought from Martin Luther, our denominational founder. He was an ingenious man who gave rise to the Protestant Reformation in Germany. If you don't know of his works, I'd recommend you study them, for they're seminal works to faith in this American nation. His Ninety-Five Theses of 1517 taught that salvation was a free gift of grace through faith in Jesus Christ. He translated the Bible into German, which made the Scriptures more accessible to the common man. This eventually led to the King James Version of the Bible, which we study today."

He exited the classroom, leaving Miss Troutwein in control of her students. She instructed them to take out their tablets of paper for some work on penmanship. "Please write on the top of your tablets where you are from and something about your family which you'd like to share with the class."

After time had passed, Miss Troutwein asked the students to present their works. "Miss Macgill, please share."

"I'm Miss Mollie Macgill from here in Hagerstown. My Scottish people hailed from James Macgill, Esquire of Edinburgh, in 1545. His descendant the Reverend James Macgill was sent, in 1730, to the vestry of Queen Caroline Parish in Anne Arundel County, Maryland, by Lord Bishop of London through the Church of England. King George the Second was the ruler of England at the time. My family has lived here in Maryland ever since King George. We're now Episcopalians at St. John's Episcopal Church of Hagerstown."

"Very good, Miss Macgill. Who else wishes to share their writings?"

"I will," Olivia called out. "My people just got off the boat from Scotland a generation ago, and we came to Hagerstown. I don't know nothin' about my past, but we're good people. All I know is that we came to America to get a start, so my Pa told me. I plan to learn to read and write real good while I'm in school here."

After several others shared, Miss Troutwein introduced Quackenbos' First Lessons in Composition. "Please take another sheet of paper and work on this assignment, which I'll write on the board. Take your time; there's no hurry to get it done," Miss Troutwein said as she wrote the assignment on the blackboard.

After Mollie and the other students had had adequate time to finish the assignment, Miss Troutwein called the class to attention.

"Please turn in your exercises before you depart for recess. Croquet is awaiting you out behind the building."

Mollie and the other girls handed in their work and headed to the rear of the building. She and Annie walked together out the back door. Together, they approached the croquet playing grounds. They each picked up a mallet and walked over to the hoop at the starting point of the game; Olivia came up behind them and intended to join them. They each laid down their balls and, in turn, batted them forward on the course of hoops.

"So, Mollie, I heard that your brother Charles Griffith is going to be a doctor," Olivia initiated.

"Yes, he wants to practice someday like my father. I'd think he'll make a good doctor," Mollie replied as she batted the ball to the next wicket.

When they came to the first hoop, Olivia batted Mollie's ball out of play, which raised her ire. On her next turn, Annie went forward to the next hoop and then batted Olivia's ball out of her way.

Mollie's competitive spirit came alive in the game. She hit Olivia's ball, and then she stepped on her ball and smacked Olivia out of play.

"You think you're so smart. I know your mother is a gossip and your brother, Charles, isn't smart enough to get into medical school. Maybe only if your father helps him!" Olivia shouted with an evil face directed at Mollie.

"You brat! I'll bash your head in with this mallet if you ever say such a thing about my brother and mother again," Mollie exclaimed as she approached Olivia. She held with her mallet over her shoulder, ready to swing.

"Try it, you sissie. I'll rip your curls out of your head!" Olivia countered.

"You best run now or I'll . . ."

Miss Troutwein came running from the back steps of the building in the nick of time to keep Mollie from taking a swing at Olivia.

"Mollie Macgill, put down that mallet right now!" Miss Troutwein exclaimed. "You're to go straight to the principal's office now, young lady!"

Mollie dropped the mallet and followed Miss Troutwein to Reverend Baughan's office. When they arrived Mollie was made to sit down and wait while Miss Troutwein explained to the principal what she had witnessed on the croquet grounds.

"Miss Macgill, please enter my office," Reverend Baughan said. "Have a seat here. Can you explain your unladylike behavior, which Miss Troutwein shared with me?"

"Yes, sir, I most certainly can. No one will ever get away with insulting my brother and mother. If they do, I'll do what I just almost did to that immigrant, Olivia—take their head off with a mallet!" she agitatedly responded. "I'm a lady, but my people are from a close-knit clan in Scotland. We fight for each other, and that's how I was raised, to defend my people."

"Well, Missie, you're from a very respectable family here in Hagerstown. I'd not want to expel you on the first day of school. But if I ever have trouble with you again, don't think I won't do it. Now you go on to your next class and behave yourself. Stay clear of people who aren't in your class of citizens here at this school. You're a proper lady. I want you to act like it. And learn to control your temper in the future, understood?'

"Yes, sir," Mollie responded with much relief.

"I'll write a note to your parents and send it home with you. You're to deliver it to your father when you get home."

"Very, well."

Alfred arrived in the afternoon to pick her up. He helped her into the carriage. Miss Troutwein was there to see her off.

"Mollie, you make sure you give this note to your father when you get home," Miss Troutwein said with a disappointed look on her face.

"Yes, ma'am; I'll see to it," Mollie responded as she stepped into the carriage with a bit of shame in her soul.

On the carriage ride home, she thought about what her father and mother might say about her behavior on the first day of school. But in her heart, she knew she had defended her family's honor. Whatever punishment her parents might divvy out, she resolved to take it with a sense of pride.

The carriage pulled in front of the house on South Potomac Street. Alfred opened the carriage door for her. She entered the house and immediately went to her father and mother.

"This note is for you, Daddy," she sheepishly said as she handed the envelope to her father. "I did nothing wrong."

Her father read the note, and then handed it over to her mother to read. They both looked perplexed after reading it.

"Mollie, how could you disgrace the family after only one day of school?" her father asked.

"Daughter, you've done what none of your siblings have done. You've brought shame to your family. Can you explain yourself?" her mother demanded.

"Well, that immigrant, Olivia McKee, insulted you, Mother, and Charles Griffith, too. All I did was stand up for you both. I'd not allow her to belittle you. How can you fault me for being in defense of my own family members?" Mollie shot back with a perplexed look on her face.

"Daughter, we understand your love of your mother and brother, but disgracing us at the new school is difficult for us to understand," her father said. "There're other ways that fine families like ours deal with the likes of the McKees."

"Daddy, you've taught me to be proud of our Scottish heritage. We're a noble people. When a peasant immigrant insulted our family, I simply reacted in defense of our heritage. How can that be wrong?"

"My daughter, I suspect you're right. You did the right thing; we were not there. We trust that you reacted valiantly on behalf of our heritage. For that you should be exalted. But in the future learn to control your temper. We'll teach you other ways of dealing with the likes of the McKees."

"Yes, Mollie; I've often thought you were too prideful. But, I do understand your pride."

"Thank you, Mother. I'll learn to control my temper," she replied as her family prepared for supper.

28

Chancellorsville—An Incredible Gamble

MAY 1ST THROUGH 3RD, 1863

DURING APRIL, THE SPRING burst forth in Virginia. The Virginia landscape reminded James of his home state of Maryland, with its lush greenery and pink and ivory blossoming dogwoods. The Stuart Horse Artillery was now commanded by Major Frank Beckham. The men were slow to accept Beckham, due in part to the devotion to their lost comrade and chieftain, Major John Pelham. But, also, his men did not understand how James had been passed over for leadership.

"Load, shell, two thousand yards, three second fuse!" James commanded. His two guns were deployed in an open field on a farm off the Brook Road that ran north to the Orange Turnpike.

Late that afternoon, his men were clearing the road for Brigadier General Ambrose R. Wright's Georgian infantrymen to pass by. This fight did not last long before all the Confederates were in the clear and safe.

"Limber-up boys, time to move down the road!" James cried out. Privates Zimmerman, Clem, Mackall, and Matthews responded to their officer's clarion call.

His limbered guns moved south on the Brook Road, and then turned left onto the Furnace Road at a steady clip. They reached Catherine's Furnace late in the day and prepared to bivouac for the night.

The stone furnace smokestack sat in the center of the compound. It was attached to the engine house, which was surrounded by the casting house to the rear of it, a blacksmith house to its front, the bridge house to the back, and the coal house behind it. James had learned that the furnace was owned by Charles C. Wellford, a wealthy dry-goods merchant, whose substantial home was a short distance up the narrow dirt road before the railroad cut to the south.

Late at night, after his artillerymen had gotten word of the morning's planned attack, General Stuart and John Esten Cooke rode onto the grounds at Catherine's Furnace. Cooke came over and shook James's hand.

"Breathed, are you well?" Cooke asked. He was a well-known novelist. James had read his works and admired him for his literary achievements.

"John, well as can be expected, considering the Army of the Potomac is encamped only a few miles away."

"Breathed are you ready for a fight?" General Stuart asked.

"Well, General," James said in a low tone, his horse between Cooke's and General Stuart's, "I understand I'm to keep only a few yards behind the line of sharpshooters as they advance. If I see an opening, I'm going ahead."

"Good. I know you'll do what you say, Breathed. Get everything ready," General Stuart ordered.

"A message, General, in reference to the movement in the morning. Your cavalry will move in front and on the right flank," Cooke said, giving the paper message to General Stuart. He slid his gauntlets on his hands and picked up his reins.

"Good!" Stuart exclaimed. "That's exactly what I designed doing. My force is small, but it'll do the work."

James and Cooke exchanged salutes with General Stuart. They returned to their respective camps.

On the eve of what promised to be a great battle, the moon was high and bright. The mood of his soldiers had many elements as the time slipped into the cold and damp night around Catherine's Furnace. He believed the element of fear was in the mind of many. The more faithful among them envisioned Christ in the Garden of Gethsemane as he held his cup of fear up to his maker. The fear was hidden amongst his men. Like frigid, cold waters, it dripped onto the brow of a man. James felt the anxiety grow steadily as the hour approached dawn.

᪣᪣᪣

The next morning, James's column moved out early in the dewy dawn. His and Captain McGregor's batteries were at the head of the column with General Fitzhugh Lee's 1st Virginia Cavalry troopers. James observed General Jackson talking with two men. One looked like a local boy and the other was dressed as a hunter in deer-skin clothes. Behind James was Brigadier General Robert E. Rodes, sitting on his horse in front of his lead division of infantrymen. The line of infantrymen stretched so far to his rear that, when James peered back over his shoulder, he could not see the end of the column.

Ahead of him, in the light shadow, a wild turkey crossed the trail, coming out from the primeval forest of thick pines and hemlocks. James believed that soon there would be more frightened creatures fleeing from the woods in all directions, including men dressed in blue uniforms. The impassable second growth woods off the trail frustrated James because there were lateral vines that could reach out to trap the unwary and entangle his guns. An odor from dwarf pine and oak perforated his nostrils.

The forest floor was compacted with leaves that had fallen from mighty trees; sweet gum mixed with purple Judas-tree leaves. Rotting logs had multicolored fungi growing on them; the dogwood trees here in Virginia, he noted, had just passed out of blossom.

Bill Clem rode proudly on his sixteen-hands steed next to James. James realized that the route General Jackson had chosen was so narrow that only one cannon could pass at a time on the trail behind the 1st Virginia troopers.

Bill leaned over toward him and said, "Old Jack is going around the bull's horn; unless the bull keeps his tail twitching quickly the old veteran warrior will have a grip on it before the sun sets."

"You've a good point, Private. We need to catch them Yankees where they're not expecting us. I suspect Generals Jackson and Lee know best. We're the dice they're gambling with," James replied as he gave a pat to Private Clem on the shoulder, reassuring him.

James crossed Poplar Run Ford, a very small tributary.

"I sees them! T'wasn't nothing but a fox squirrel. Reckon't won't do to shoot him? Squirrel stew would be good vittles right about now," Private Clem said, now riding beside other men.

"Don't you dar!" Robert Mackall responded. "There ain't to be no firing out of this pine clump exceptin upon the enemy. Remembers, we've strict orders from General Jackson to be quiet."

"Boys, keep it quiet," James hissed as if he was a school teacher scolding his students.

His artillerists plodded along behind the 1st Virginia Cavalry, following some circuitous route.

Once his artillerists had arrived at the crest of a ridge on the Orange Turnpike, Major Beckham rode up to James and said, "Captain, position your first two guns on the turnpike in the front of General Rodes's line of infantrymen. Then I want them followed by another one of your cannon and one of McGregor's guns. In support, I want Captain Moorman. Understood?"

"Yes, sir," James responded, and then rode off to position his artillerymen for the attack.

Upon fulfilling his orders, he saw the robust Prussian Major von Borcke ride up to Generals Jackson, Rodes, Colston, A. P. Hill, Stuart, and their staffs who had gathered around a gigantic oak tree.

After they had talked, Jackson pulled out his pocket watch and then wrote a note. General Rodes returned to his position on the turnpike. Rodes approached James who was mounted on Billy while he viewed the Federal position through his field glasses.

"How long will it take to get all your divisions into place?" James asked.

"Not long, Captain. Will those boys stand?" Brigadier General Rodes asked of James as they patiently waited to move out.

"Stand?" James growled. "Damn straight, sir. When those boys leave their guns you'll not have a man left in your division. I'm going to take them in with your skirmish line and show you damn Tar Heels how to fight!"

James reined Billy away from General Rodes and went to the head of his section of guns. He saluted Private Matthews, the lead wheel driver of one of his two guns that sat abreast on the turnpike. Then James saluted 1st Lieutenant Johnston who was in command of his first section of guns. He pointed to the azure sky where a few white clouds were floating over the Federals.

"Boys, I know there're two Federal guns planted on the turnpike ready to fire upon our approach. We'll have abatis and other obstacles to move around, but keep driving forward!"

After delivering his talk to the front section of guns, he rode back to 2nd Lieutenant Shanks. The next two guns were under Captain McGregor's command. He saluted Captain McGregor and Lieutenant Shanks. He repeated his observations to the officers and his artillerymen.

The ground before his beloved brothers in arms was undulating with small hills and dense woodlands. It would not be an easy attack, James mused; but with such a mighty force and the element of surprise, the Federals would not stand much of a chance. The hour was growing late. He pulled his pocket watch from his vest pocket to see the time was 5:15 pm.

James then rode to the front of the first two guns to confer with Major Beckham.

"Captain, you keep the front section moving forward; find positions for them to fire from. When the infantry has passed by your position, I'll limber and send forward the rear section. We'll leapfrog our way right into Hooker's vest pocket. Clear, sir?" Beckham asked.

"Yes, sir!" James exclaimed with an exuberance he had not felt in his life.

Moments later the bugle sounded and the mile and a half battle line of infantrymen stepped off. The Rebel Yell reverberated. "Yaaaih! Yaaiih! Yaaaaih!"

"Forward—March!" James shouted. His hands were shaking inside of his gauntlets.

James's section of horse artillery drove in a thunderous beat in front of Rodes's line of infantrymen. When they had moved out, far in front of the infantrymen, his drivers shouting, his horses' pink-nostrilled, wide-eyed, and lathered in the heat, James halted the advance and his gunners jumped down into action.

His pieces fired their deadly iron projectiles filled with death, dealing consequences wherever they landed amid the Federal ranks.

Using his whip James helped to drive the horses forward. Then he moved out in front to find the next position for the leapfrogging guns. He heard Major Beckham directing the rear leapfrogging of the guns, moving them at a gallop to stay ahead of the infantrymen as the line swept relentlessly forward.

James listened to the roar of battle as it filled the air on both sides of the Orange Turnpike. He discerned that officers could not be heard. He saw that chaos ruled as the battle line moved forward. He viewed regiments getting tangled and the Confederate line at the right flank of the attack come to a halt. So loud were the cracks of sound, so steady the repetitive noise, that orders coming from his encouraging officers were not heard. The hurricane sound of shot and shell engulfed the turnpike.

He looked around at the soldiers in blue. They seemed to have lost control as they threw away everything in order to lighten their load. There were piles of knapsacks along the road. Blankets by the hundreds were strewn beside them. Relentlessly, he guided his section forward. He discovered that the Federals had abandoned their rifles. He came across two batteries of Federal artillery, standing alone, and not a man in sight. Horses stampeded up the turnpike and through the woods; cook fires were blazing under cooking pots suspended by rude camp cranes.

Soon, the Federals started to rally. They formed lines of battle before James's guns. It was then that James heard the *zipp! zziipp! zzzip!* of minies passing by his ears as thick as locusts in Egypt. His men incessantly continued firing, and the bass of his guns answered the sneering treble of the minies.

"Load—shell—eight hundred yards—two second fuse—Fire!" James exclaimed as he rode Billy alongside the gunners.

He stopped long enough to view the impact of each shell. Each shot seemed to take out ten or twelve men as the shell exploded.

"Excellent work, men! Limber—front! Move out!" James shouted, his adrenaline driving him forward.

James could think of nothing more glorious than the fact that he had helped mutilate the Army of the Potomac. He again peered through his field glasses and found a new position he wished to occupy.

His artillerymen had rotated the gun, hooked it to the limber, and were awaiting orders to move out.

"Men—Right oblique!" James ordered. Private Matthews brought the reins down on the backs of the lead horses. "I want to be on that knoll in front of those pines to the right."

James rode past the bodies of ten Federals that lay heaped together from an artillery shell explosion. The limbs of the soldiers had been torn from their torsos and shrapnel had mutilated their bodies. He knew it was his handiwork, and he tipped his hat sardonically to the dead foes.

The sun's rays had begun to fall slantingly between the oaks' trunks. The afterburn that shot from his section's cannon mouths flew like golden arrows.

"Captain Breathed, we must keep moving forward. How're you fixed for ammunition?" Major Beckham asked, riding alongside James as the section moved to its newly anointed location beyond the pines.

"We're holding out," he responded.

"Excellent," Major Beckham said. He turned his horse and headed back to the rear section of guns.

James glanced at his pocket piece and noted the hour approached 8:00 pm. Suddenly, a counter-battery shell struck his friend, William Evans, in the gut and blew him asunder. James's section had experienced no loss of life, but Captain McGregor's section did not fare as well.

Major Beckham found James and said to him, "I'm satisfied that no good will be accomplished by replying to thirty or more guns, so have your men cease firing."

James's horse artillery had moved with unyielding enthusiasm and alacrity, for they had virtually annihilated the entire corps as they were caught at rest.

"Young man, I congratulate you and the brave men under you," General Jackson announced to Major Beckham after the fighting had died down for the night. James sat his horse next to the major.

"Captain McGregor's section lost many men, killed and wounded. But, Captain Breathed's section came through nearly untouched," Beckham reported.

"Captain Breathed, I'm also indebted to you for your valiant conduct on this field of honor," General Jackson said.

A burst of gunfire startled them all.

"What was that?" Major Beckham asked James. "I gave orders for a cease fire! Captain, I want those guns silenced; ride to them and give them my orders."

James rode off from the presence of General Jackson and Major Beckham to discover what the firing was all about. He found that Colonel Crutchfield of Jackson's artillery had opened fire with Captain Moorman's two Napoleons and one rifled Parrot gun. Moorman's guns did not have the range; they were firing from a distance of 1,200 yards at Chancellorsville Heights and Fairview.

"Captain Moorman, Major Beckham has ordered your guns to cease firing," James said to Captain Moorman.

"Yes, sir," Captain Moorman replied.

Suddenly, hell broke loose as counter-battery fire came storming into the area. Artillerists and soldiers hit the ground to avoid shrapnel flying in all directions. The attack did not last long so James remounted Billy and rode away when it was safe to do so.

James reported back to Major Beckham in relation to Captain Moorman's initiative to fire under his own orders. He then rode back to his men on the battlefield and ordered the removal of Private Evans's mangled body. It was wrapped in a blanket and sent back to the location where the attack had begun.

"Privates Mackall and Clem—grave digging duty. Privates Matthews, Zimmerman, and the rest of you artillerymen, replenish the limbers and caissons so we're ready for battle in the morning," James ordered.

That night his men gathered around the shallow grave dug under a grove of pine trees. They paid tearful tribute to their fallen comrade.

"Reverend Zimmerman, could you say a few heavenly words?" James asked of the private.

"Certainly, let us bow our heads. Lord, God, in the presence of his comrades-in-arms and his own brother Benton Evans, we commend Private William Evans's soul to you from whom he has come . . ."

At the conclusion of the graveside service and the planting of a simple wooden marker at the head of the gravesite, Major Beckham called forth his officers.

"Gentlemen, we've accomplished a heroic deed today. I don't know where in Greek mythology such a sweeping defeat of an enemy is reported, certainly there's some reference to it. We wiped out an entire corps of the enemy and our artillery was at the head of the attack. For this you should each be proud of your men's achievements on this battlefield. Now gather all the men; I'd like a word with them."

James's officers went out and called up their men. They gathered in the darkness of the night.

"Men, the principal difference between the man in the ranks and the officer in the Stuart Horse Artillery at such times as this is the level to which the individual's attitude and actions influence and have impact on the lives of others," Major Beckham said. "The cowardly soldier who dares not face death but chooses to drop out of harm's way, may not influence the course of the battle. But the captain, who is valiant in moral and physical courage, bears the responsibility of the lives of his fellow artillerymen who depend on him and are sworn to obey his orders."

James removed his kepi and scratched his forehead; he gazed over at the major.

"We're gallant for the day, and for this every man in this horse artillery unit should be proud. We ran the Eleventh Corps all the way into Hooker's open arms!" said Major Beckham.

The cheer went up. "Hurrah for the Stuart Horse Artillery!"

"You men deserve food and rest, for you've not had any in two days. I'll speak with General Stuart in regard to the morning plan of battle. You should know that both Generals Jackson and A. P. Hill have been wounded. General Stuart is now in command of General Jackson's corps. You're dismissed. Captain Moorman, may I have a word with you?" Major Beckham reported.

"What happened to General Jackson," James asked.

"No one knows exactly how either one of the generals were wounded, but it is an obvious loss for the Confederacy," Major Beckham responded with a dire look on his face.

"I think we should have a moment of silence for the generals and all the wounded men who are in need of the saving graces of our Lord at this time," the pious James suggested.

The soldiers all bowed their heads and after a time of silence each man departed to bivouac for the night.

29

Fading Light

Battle near Brandy Station, Virginia

Evening of June 9th, 1863

James's body exuded strength, and his intense blue eyes expressed terror to his enemies, but even his powerful physique was exhausted after tenaciously fighting all day. The discipline of the medical profession served James well as an artillerist. Every time he saw the aftermath of a battle, he was weakened and unnerved by the appalling carnage. He beheld the flesh of ravaged bodies of both man and beast that lay dead or in agony. He heard a cacophony of human suffering arise from the field before him, a requiem of dying, as some moaned and others cried out from their pain. He could feel the pain of the dead and dying. He was thankful to be counted among the living.

It was approaching dusk and the setting sun offered little respite from the summer heat. His artillerymen fell asleep where they had last fought. He saw one private who had been engaged in the day's battle acting as if the battle was still on. The gunner, Private Mackall, could not pull himself out of the action. He worked with rigid mechanical motions as he moved rounds from their ammunition caisson to the limber chest as if there were more firing to be expected.

Walking over to Private Mackall, James asked, "How'd you fare, Private?"

These few comforting words seemed to rouse the soldier from his trance. Reaching out his hand, James touched Private Mackall on the shoulder.

"I'm still in the land of the living, sir. I reckon you could say I fared well. Captain, your next order. We're quickly running out of light."

"I think the Yankees have had enough for this day. They'll not return. We gave more than we received. I think that's all the Yanks can take for one day."

As the private stood down, James's thoughts turned to what an impossible challenge it was going to be to clean up the carnage. Because the Yankees had left the field, it would be the Confederate army's responsibility to clear the wounded and dead. The battle had been a surprise to Stuart, his artillerists, and the Confederate cavalry; no hospitals had been established prior to the battle. James decided to rally the men in order to try and save life he had, for hours, been trying to extinguish.

"Men, form up; I've a few words!" James hollered.

They gathered around him at the cannon, covered with grime from the smoke and dirt of the battlefield, their faces and hands almost black, their uniforms torn from bullets that were near misses.

"Artillerymen, you did a fine job here today; I'm proud of each and every one of you," he told them. "You should be well assured that I've taken note of those of you who conducted yourselves beyond the call of duty. It was a tough fight, and we stuck to our guns."

James stepped over a dead Confederate cavalryman lying on the battlefield, moved closer to one of the artillery pieces, and placed his hand on the warm barrel.

"The enemy will not return this day; our scouts have seen them recross the Rappahannock. Those Yankee sumbitches will not be back tonight!" James stated with his head bowed low. "See to the needs of those who were not as fortunate on the field of honor; tend to each one's wounds. Those able to handle stretchers are to work with soldiers strewn before them as was their usual procedure. Wounded horses on the ground are to be shot, wounded Yankees watered from canteens. Confederates are to be moved to the St. James Church for medical treatment. There's not much time to tarry for there's only a little light left."

Feeling a hand tap his shoulder, James turned to see assistant surgeon Dr. Maxwell Alexander. The surgeon had walked out of the church, located only a short distance from where James had been talking to the men. "Captain, will you please follow me to the church? I personally need you in surgery. You'll find we already have our hands full with the wounded. Your country now needs your medical calling."

James dismissed his men, who then broke up into details to begin the process of clean up. "How many regimental surgeons do we have here today?" James asked Dr. Alexander.

"Not many, that's why I've come for you."

Leading Billy by the reins, James followed Dr. Alexander who weaved around the dead bodies on the battlefield. St. James Church was a small white-washed clapboard structure with a graveyard out back. A few graves were already piled with amputated arms and legs. Local dogs and hogs had found their way to the pile. An orderly, arriving with a new bucket of arms, shouted to shoo them away. The animals returned as soon as the orderly left.

The front doors of the church had been taken down and were now serving as operating tables that rested across the pews. The wounded patients had been filled with brandy and were then moved to St. James Church to amputate legs and arms. The scene was ghastly, James thought, now commonplace battle after battle, and he had become accustomed to it.

It was the fortunate soldiers who had made it to the St. James Church, for many wounded soldiers were still out on the battlefield. Here James knew the surgeons would determine if a life had any possibility of being saved. Once a man's life or death issues were resolved by doctors, he was either helped or was left in a comfortable place to ascend into the heavens.

Lanterns gave off a dim yellow light inside the church, the glow bright enough to reflect off the blood that covered the floor. James saw the orderlies administere laudanum to help the wounded with their pain. Enough of this alcohol and opium mixture would knock a man out, and a little more would kill the man. Brandy was also liberally administered to the soldiers crying out in pain. The butcher shop smell, which had filled James's nostrils from the battlefield, grew and intensified in the church; it was enough to make him sick on the spot, but he controlled himself.

Dr. Alexander motioned James to the front of the church, where an apron stained crimson with blood was given to him. James already had blood on his hands from the battlefield, which he couldn't remove before he went to the makeshift operating table. He simply wiped his hands on the apron.

"I see your reputation as a warrior has not impaired your proclivities of doctoring," Dr. Alexander said, observing James while they worked.

James began to prepare himself for surgery by readying the saws and utensils. He used creek water to wipe clean the blood-stained instruments.

James responded, "Thank you, Doctor, your proficiency with the blade is well known. We've much work."

A soldier in a filthy gray uniform was placed upon the table door before James. One of Major C. E. Flourney's 6th Virginia troopers. He had been struck by a minie ball in the thigh. The hole was an inch across, which allowed James to dig his finger into the gaping leg wound. The leg lay at an unnatural angle. James straightened the leg and looked around for the orderlies.

"The femur is completely shattered," he said. "This leg will have to come off."

Alexander examined the three-inch hole that came out the back of the leg. Placing three fingers into the hole, he reported to him that he felt splinters of the bone. He watched Alexander probe.

"If this leg doesn't come off there'll be certain gangrene," James said.

"I agree," Alexander responded.

The wide-eyed trooper screamed in pain. Sweat poured off his forehead.

"Don't take it, please!" the soldier begged them.

The soldier had lain on the battlefield for hours and his wound had become crusty with blood and dirt. When James loosened the tourniquet the wound bled anew. Over the wound a thick scab had formed, thanks to the Lambert field tourniquet. James cut away the scab with a scalpel. The massive amount of blood loss had induced delirium, and the trooper's panic-stricken cries filled the church. The weakened patient required three orderlies to hold him.

"Chloroform, now!" James ordered.

An orderly came quickly and poured some of the liquid onto a cloth. James took the cloth from the orderly and positioned it over the nose of the restrained trooper. Picking up a pair of scissors, James cut away the raggedy gray uniform, now stained red with blood.

"The chloroform has taken effect," Alexander said.

James picked up the scalpel and cut the bloody skin around the entire leg in a circular pattern so that the muscle could be worked with next. The trooper lay still on the table throughout, a clear indication that the chloroform and brandy had settled the man into an unconscious state. But James knew that at any time the trooper might stir, and so he ordered the three orderlies to continue to hold the soldier firm. James cut on the leg. Lice crawled from under the trooper's pant leg. Alexander brought the second blade into use and cut the muscle from around the bone.

James cut back one inch of the muscle in order to get good closure. Alexander grasped the femoral artery with the forceps and pulled it out. Quickly, he tied it with a suture; the bleeding stopped. An orderly handed James a saw to cut through the bone and round off the end above the knee so as to form a smooth surface behind the dangling and twitching muscles. Once the bone was cut through, James sewed the ends of the muscles together over the bone. Next, he pulled the skin over the bone and sewed the flesh to form a stump.

James applied a styptic iron perchlorate solution to the wound in an effort to cut down the residual bleeding, and then dressed the stump with lint scraped from blankets; bandages were then applied over the lint. The tourniquet was released and the doctors found that only a small oozing of blood flowed from the wound. As the man came out from under the chloroform James ordered more laudanum and brandy to ease the man's pain.

James took a moment to wash his hands in the bucket of creek water before he instructed the orderlies to remove the screaming trooper to the rear lawn of the church. This trooper was one of the lucky ones; for he had been treated before he bled to death. This brave trooper had made a monumental sacrifice for the cause and would be going home.

Walking to the door of the church, James looked out at the sea of wounded men. An orderly walked over and offered James a flask of brandy. He turned up the flask and deeply drank.

He then pointed to a wounded trooper before him on the church grounds. "Next."

The orderlies responded quickly to his cue.

James was exhausted, but he knew this life-saving work would energize him to carry on all night long. Many of the dying cried out to him, but his experienced eye would determine who should be given another chance at life. He wiped the sweat from his forehead and dried his hands on the apron. The orderlies had the next patient on the stretcher. They moved the patient past James as he stood in the doorway.

"Ready the saw, orderly. Give 'im plenty of chloroform; he'll need it."

"Thank ya, Doc. Do what you can. I trust ya, Captain," the friend and fellow Stuart Horse artillerist responded.

⊱⊰

At dawn, James walked away from St. James Church, overtired and bleary-eyed. Because of his labors the pile of arms and legs had grown, but lives had been saved. The smell of the burning wood from the camp fires around the church reminded him of the smoke that came from a train engine, thick and dense. It was strange to remember that he had fought, mysteriously, because of a train ride east and a chance encounter with a flamboyant United States Army lieutenant, with whom he had shared a covert life-altering conversation.

30

Accidental Fire & Feint

Aldie, Virginia

JUNE 17TH, 1863

TRAVELING EAST ON THE Little River Turnpike, the Breathed battery moved stealthily in the direction of Dover, Virginia. The unmacadamized turnpike featured specially cut stone to permit traffic even in the wet season. As they came up to Little River, James's sensibilities told him that the oppressive heat would need to be combated with a water break. By haystacks and waving corn, by dense green woods and whispering creeks, under blue sky and to the song of birds, through an agrarian land of prosperity, he and the 1st Stuart Horse Artillery battery had moved into Loudoun Valley. The Loudoun Valley separated Lee's army behind the Blue Ridge Mountains and Hooker's army behind the Bull Run Mountains, a scant fifteen miles away.

James ordered the battery to halt and water all the horses. He had the bugler sound the call for a water break to which they were eager to respond. By the hoof prints already stamped into the ground, he could see that the dispatched troopers of Colonel Rosser's 5th Virginia Cavalry pickets had earlier watered at the same place. His mount, Billy, was also in need of water. He dismounted and led him to the source of the small tributary.

"Hot today, Private Matthews. We don't know what lies ahead, expect trouble," James said as he removed his kepi, filled it with water, and flung it back over his head. The water splashing over his shoulders refreshed him.

"Captain, the Breathed battery was born ready for brawling with Yankees!" Matthews responded with a broad smile.

The break was long enough to get the battery horses watered, and he then felt it was time to move out. He knew the squadrons of the 1st, 2nd, 3rd, 4th, and 5th Virginia Cavalry also needed to water. For him a sense of endless repetition was growing in this war. The repetition of battle sounded monotonous notes. A hot wind blew by his ear. The constant care for his men and horses at times felt to him as if he were in a tunnel with no light at the end. He yearned for Maryland and Bai-Yuka, but there was no going home until the war was decided one way or the other. His persistent desire to be with Mollie, to love her, also had been thwarted by this infernal war. He wondered about the different course his life could have taken if he had simply stayed in Washington County and practiced medicine.

He remounted Billy and had the bugler sound the call to move out. They reached Dover. He looked down the turnpike and suddenly saw a trooper galloping toward their location, dust spewing in all directions.

"Captain Breathed, I've orders from Colonel Rosser. He has located a lion's share of Yankee cavalry. You're to deploy your guns on high ground in an eastern direction up the Little River Turnpike. I'll relay this same information to Colonel Wickham and Colonel Munford," the courier exclaimed as he gasped for breath.

"Yes, sir. Give my regards to Colonel Rosser and his pickets."

A surge of adrenaline came from deep within his belly—that familiar charge that inspired him into a gallant mode. Any calm within was expelled from his soul, and he became blind to anything but getting his guns into action. He gripped his reins and turned Billy back toward his artillerymen. They knew the look on their commander's face meant danger lay ahead; it was all too familiar to them.

"Battery!—Left oblique!—March!" James ordered. The cannoneers moved off the turnpike and maneuvered the cannon to a position in an apple orchard on a farm at the crest of a ridge.

It was not long before the cannon bursts shrieked and whistled. The orchard grew dense with sulphurous smoke. From the ridge ahead the Federal horse artillery answered, but it was a far lesser storm than his guns had let fly. His more powerful hurricane, launched from the crest of the ridge, could sadly also reach out and touch Confederate troopers.

While the Federal counter-battery cannon fire shook the terra firma all around him, he hollered out commands. The Federal shells extended so near that he could see them. Like winged birds of prey, they flew so close that their oncoming features became a recurring nightmare. Sponging, ramming, priming, aiming, firing was their only response to the incoming projectiles.

"Captain, a great force of cavalry! Pleasanton, I reckon, or Satan himself—ahead on the turnpike," the distinguished white-haired Colonel Munford shouted to James. "I'm deploying Captain Reuben Boston east on the turnpike for reconnaissance. Mind your fire!"

"Yes, sir," James replied.

"You've got two squadrons dismounted, placed on your left, on the other side of the turnpike near you," Colonel Munford reported to him as they both looked up the turnpike to see Captain Boston's troopers cantering forward with carbines at the ready, pointed skyward.

James fired his guns, and on occasion he saw through his field glasses a gray trooper go down into the dust on the turnpike and a riderless horse come galloping to the rear. He was unsure of the progress of the engagement, but he didn't like to see so many horses from Boston's troopers coming back riderless.

A 5th Virginia trooper excitedly rode up. "Captain Breathed, you're to cease firing! Your ammunition is faulty and is exploding over our own troopers. Captain Boston has been captured, along with most of his troopers by the 2nd New York and the 6th Ohio Cavalry regiments. I escaped, but they are coming this way with a full head of valiant bravado."

"Cease firing! Cease firing!" James ordered his artillerymen.

Now, he could not help but feel a great deal of remorse. This feeling he had experienced before in the Shackelfords' home in Culpeper, for he thought the shrapnel from his guns had been responsible for the death of his beloved commander, John Pelham.

Despite all the courage he could muster to remain stoic, James pulled Billy's reins back after the guns fell silent. Lieutenants Johnston and Shanks looked at him. James saw the sad looks on their faces, which reflected their instant comprehension of his remorseful facial expression. His emotions had betrayed him.

He gathered Sergeants Shaw and Hoxton and the two lieutenants to give them the news. "Gentlemen, our ammunition has been exploding prematurely and we've taken out some of our own troopers. Captain Boston and his cavalrymen have been captured, and the Yankee cavalry is getting up the courage to come at us again. Lieutenant Johnston, continue to stay back in reserve. I'll need to converse with Colonel Munford. I'll be back shortly."

He rode Billy to the back of the apple orchard where he found Colonel Munford and Colonel Wickham in conversation. "Colonels, my artillerymen have been firing faulty ammunition and a number of Captain Boston's troopers have gone down due to our accidental fire. Your orders?" James asked.

"Captain, you're not at fault. Don't blame yourself for something you didn't have control over. They'll be coming again up the turnpike and we'll need your guns to hit them as they ride into us. I've ordered the Second, Third, and Fifth to charge over the Adams' farm. They have cover behind haystacks and there is a ditch in which they can take cover. But your guns can hit them before their blue-bellied troopers get to cover," Colonel Munford ordered.

"Yes, sir. I'll return to my guns directly and be ready for their charge," James responded.

His melancholy feelings subsided after getting positive reinforcements from the colonels. As a firstborn, he always had taken his responsibilities in life very seriously. He reasoned this might have been why he felt so poorly about the accidental fire incident that had taken out some of Captain Boston's troopers. The lull in the fight made it evident to him that the Federals were repositioning their cavalry for an all-out offensive charge. He arrived back to the three guns. Although the remorse was just below the surface, he knew he had a man's job to do this day.

Before the muzzles of his three guns were amassed a great number of Federals prepared to charge. "Fire!—Reload!" James hollered. Through the smoke he saw the foe poised on the rolling farmland. The counter-battery fire, back on the hillside, fired a shell that split a railed fence into kindling wood upon impact. Shells began raining and bursting above. His sheltered battery horses had at first been behind the ridge and were undisturbed, but one was now wounded and then another, as the whistling shells flew overhead.

Then the recurring nightmare became a reality. A direct hit from counter-battery fire tore an arm from gunner Hebb Greenwell. Greenwell's right shoulder and arm were no more and blood spurted from where his arm and shoulder had been moments earlier. He fell to the ground and his body was removed to the rear by his fellow gunners. Artilleryman Thomas Parker, stooping over a limber chest, was struck between the shoulders, crushing flesh and bone. Instantly he was transformed into a bloody pulp. James felt at a visceral level further despair, for the men he saw killed were working for him while manning his guns.

The maelstrom became violently evident to him as Colonel Munford's cavalrymen charged before his guns. He could see the mighty wave of blue troopers leap over the ditch and come up a slope into a field of haystacks. The rough and broken ground where the engagement took place made it difficult for both sides to stay mounted for long. The blue and gray clashed amidst the haystacks, and the Federals dismounted and drew carbines, all witnessed by James through his field glasses. The critical question now was how his guns could be effective without hitting his own comrades in gray.

He decided to concentrate his fire power on the Federal counter-battery position and take out the guns on the opposite ridge.

"Sergeants Shaw and Hoxton, front and center!" James ordered. "I want your maximum effort on that ridge. Let the cavalry fight it out to our front. Understood?"

"Yes, sir, Captain!"

James witnessed the final charge across the field. The Federal cavalry was forced back by the gray sabres. It was a beautiful sight to behold, yet experience told him that the battle was not yet over for the day.

"Captain Breathed, I need one cannon on the Snickersville Turnpike. Now that we've got them on the run, they'll likely try and flank us on our left. Take care of it," Colonel Munford said as he saluted him.

"Yes, sir!" James replied.

"Lieutenant Johnston, report!" James said as he looked to the rear to spot him.

"Sir!"

"Take one gun behind the ridge on the Cobb House Road to the Snickersville Turnpike. Find an advantageous position for the gun. You'll have the troopers of the Second and the Third in support. Colonel Munford fears the Yankees will try and out flank us up the other turnpike. I'll stay here for a time and continue counter-battery fire. I'll be over shortly."

⤷⊙⊚⊙⤶

The engagement had all but ended on the right flank by the time James rode Billy on the Cobb House Road toward Lieutenant Johnston's position. His proclivity was to move cautiously on the lone gun while he traveled along the interior line. The remorse of the accidental fire incident traveled with him as he cantered Billy toward where the fighting seemed to still be heavy. Neither could he rid his mind of the sight of his two men being killed earlier by the counter-battery fire.

He arrived behind the gun, riding Billy through the sorghum planted to the rear of the gun emplacement. He tied Billy to a branch of a low hanging tree limb and walked toward the gun emplacement as the piece unloaded a bucket-full of double canister. He looked out to see vines growing over stone walls. The vines concealed the walls, which made them appear to be hedgerows. The nature of the macadamized, sunken road made for a perfect killing field. Bodies dissembled in every manner were heaped in piles, mixed with horseflesh, and barricaded the turnpike.

His worn boots, covered in dust, dug into the loose earth as he walked. He saw the moving blue cloth and the smell of sweat-drenched bodies, of burnt black powder, of shredded leather, of horses' and humans' spilt blood. It all hit him. He staggered. Suddenly, his vision darkened in the oppressive heat. A wave of nausea took his breath from him and left him white-faced and weak. He stepped behind a large oak tree, not having been seen by the busy gunners, and violently vomited. There was nothing but empty emotion that came up from the depths of his inner bowels, for he had not eaten all day.

When he regained his composure, he knew his sickness came not from the carnage before him, but instead from war itself. He was appalled by the needless deaths that those Federals had suffered simply because some fool officer thought the turnpike needed to be taken. He now, in his heart, questioned the reasons for the carnage. He had never seen such a mass of human and animal destruction piled in one place. The pointlessness of the slaughter horrified him. Lieutenant Johnston had simply followed orders given to him, and the Federal troopers had followed theirs by riding up the turnpike to their deaths. It was all senseless.

He came out from behind the tree and immediately hit the ground with all the other artillerymen to escape a blast of iron shrapnel that passed overhead. This scrape raised his ire, and his Celtic passions overwhelmed him.

He walked up to Lieutenant Johnston. "It's all this infernal tactics and West Point tomfoolery! Dammit fire! And flush the game!" James said as a stream of canister tore the blue troopers further asunder. He had a reckoning at that moment in which he realized that his artillery tactics would no longer be by the book.

"Captain, it seems the First Massachusetts can't get enough iron today. They've come around that curve between the white house and the stone wall on the right two times already. We can see the sharpshooters' bullets creating flying dust from the blue jackets as the bullets strike the Yankees dead and add them to the pile of carnage. Then we fire with canister. When they're not charging suicidally up the turnpike, we take a few shots at the counter battery on the ridge down below," Lieutenant Johnston explained to him. Sweat rolled down his face.

"You're doing your duty, sir. Your country can ask no more from you, neither can I," James responded. "Here they come again! Load!—Double canister!" James cried out impulsively, taking over for Lieutenant Johnston.

In an instantaneous line of flame—trees, men, grasses, shrubs—were shredded by a rake of canister shot gone forth. Patches of clothing, twigs, and body parts flew; the ground was littered with bodies from the cannon fire's fatal path. The position behind the stone wall where Lieutenant Johnston had placed the lone gun was impenetrable, James thought. He had trained the lieutenant well.

James looked to his left and saw the dismounted Virginia cavalry regiments unloading their carbines into what was left of the standing Federal cavalry. The Federals tried to fire back, but he could see that this charge would be their last. James figured their commanders could not suffer much more needless death this afternoon.

The third assault indeed was the last of the day, and the order from General Stuart was to fall back to Rector's Crossroads that night. As he sat Billy, gazing at the carnage, Colonel Munford rode up and said to him, "I don't hesitate to say I've never seen as many Yankees killed in the same space of ground in any fight I've ever seen."

James thought to himself that he had. The scene before them was in a recurring nightmare that had begun to plague his sleep. There would be no escape from himself. Admitting to his dark reality, he recognized that he had become a killing machine for a cause that was becoming more confusing with each engagement. It was not the confusion that a simple mind could be plagued with; a mind like his suffered from much internal conflict, which he didn't dare share with another soul.

"Sir, we've done our duty honorably as soldiers this day. The Yankees still don't know where the Army of Northern Virginia is. Now we must look ahead and rejoin them," James said as he rode next to Colonel Munford. His battery trailed behind as they moved back to Rector's Crossroads.

"I'm with you, Captain Breathed. Your courage and display of honor today was most inspiring to me and my men. Godspeed, Captain."

"Good evening, sir," James replied as Colonel Munford spurred his horse toward his command.

James looked over his right shoulder as Colonel Munford rode ahead, and there he saw his friends from the 1st Virginia Cavalry.

"Evening, James," Thomas House said.

"How ya been keeping yourself, James," Daniel Cushwa said.

"Boys, not seen you and the First for a while. Glad you had a piece of the Yankees today," James said; the light from the moon was all that was now allowing them to see each other.

"We wanted to thank you, Captain. Your guns saved our hides today. Daniel and I rode with you some time back, but we never thought your guns would help us in a scrap with the Yankee cavalry like they did today," Thomas said as they moved toward Rector's Crossroads.

"Just doing what I can for the cause, boys. Glad my guns got you through the day safe and alive."

"They did that, Captain. Hope you'll come around to the camp tonight," Daniel said.

"I'll see if I can make it."

"Evening, Captain," Daniel and Thomas said simultaneously.

"Evening, Privates."

31

Preparation for the Fallout of the Coming Fury

Late June 1863

MOLLIE WAS THE EMBODIMENT of southern charm as she placed a serving tray, crowded with glasses of fresh-squeezed lemonade, on the low table. The five men and one woman who sat on the front porch of the Breathed home admired Mollie as much as the refreshments she served. Mollie, her father, and her brother, Dr. Charles Griffith Macgill, had been invited to Bai-Yuka to meet Dr. John Cullen, the medical director of Longstreet's corps. Mollie had attended the wedding of Judge Breathed to his second wife, who was the sister of Dr. Cullen. Ortelia Cullen Breathed was now with child, and Mollie believed Ortelia would make both a good mother in her own right and surrogate mother for James, whose mother had died in '62. Dr. Cullen had come for a visit, for both personal and professional reasons, as he was explaining to the group gathered on the porch.

Mollie knew that Dr. Cullen had a great deal of secret military intelligence, which he might discretely share. The austere-looking doctor, with long white bushy side-burns that came all the way around the side of his cheeks, needed something from the people assembled. But what the doctor needed she knew not. His gray three-piece colonel's uniform gave the impression he was well healed, and he must certainly have been esteemed to garner an appointment to such a high level position in the Army of Northern Virginia.

"Ortelia, you seem content here at Bai-Yuka. You've got quite a responsibility keeping up with all the judge's children. Now, another child on the way; congratulations to you both. Judge, I often hear reports of James's gallantry with the horse artillery. He has become a fine warrior for our cause," Dr. Cullen reported on this warm summer afternoon. "Perhaps, after all this is over, we can welcome him into the Medical College of Virginia, where he can resume his profession."

"John, the judge and I are content here at Bai-Yuka," Ortelia replied with a concerned look on her face. "Now that Isaac and Francis have gone off to fight like their older brother, James, we're even more anxious about what the army is up to next."

"Davidge and Barlow are riding with the First Maryland Cavalry, and the family keeps them in our prayers. I even hear tell of my son, young James, wanting to get into the fight. He has always been a hard one to control, so his mother and I keep a close watch on him," Dr. Macgill said.

Mollie recalled other pleasant times when, as a young girl, she visited the cousins at Bai-Yuka. Where were those halcyon days? She recalled summer picnics with the Breatheds and the constant teasing she gave James. Today, all she knew was worry for him and his safety as he fought the Yankees. The charmed Southern life of plantation picnics, Negroes serving them, the bonds of community and family were now all being threatened by Yankees who she wished would simply leave her and their way of life alone.

But this was no longer to be, she thought, for Mr. Lincoln had declared the slaves free in the Confederate States of America. Although the proclamation did not require the judge to set Willie, Sarah, and their family free in "Loyal Maryland," he had done so. They had subsequently moved on to Baltimore in search of work and had not been heard from since they left Bai-Yuka. Alfred and the Macgill family servants had also been set free. However, they had chosen to remain with the family as paid servants.

Judge Breathed's words broke her reveries. "This war has plagued the Whites, Williams, Macgills, Bridges, and Breatheds, and God knows how many other of our old Maryland families. We have all suffered for a cause that affects this state, but in which we are left without a voice. We should thank the Almighty, every day, that his providence has protected our families from more severe losses or even deaths on the battlefields of this war. Now that Priscilla is with child, we extend our prayers to Robert Bridges' home in Hancock, asking for his providence to be with my beloved daughter. Shall we have a word of prayer and would you lead us, Dr. Cullen?" the judge asked.

"Certainly, let us join our hearts in prayer," Dr. Cullen said. *Almighty God, in these troubled times of war, we ask that your providential hand be with these five families, as they each give of their manpower and resources to help bring thy will to this broken land. It is through our simple faith that we know great miracles and great battles can be won. As David slew Goliath with a stone thrown from a sling, we pray that the stone the Confederacy is about to throw may defeat our enemy in the coming days. Enable us to prepare ourselves for thy will. Amen.*

"Doctor, you've revealed through prayer the reason for your professional visit. Would you like to share with us how we're to be a part of your plan?" Mollie inquired.

"Yes, Mollie. You're astute. I've brought a map of Hagerstown to share my plan if you all would gather closer around this table," Dr. Cullen replied. He spread a large street map on the table, placing lemonade glasses on the corners. "General Lee knows Virginia cannot continue to sustain the Army of Northern Virginia. As long as the

North controls the sea, we cannot stay on the defensive without giving up all of Virginia north of the Rappahannock. Consequently, he is taking the war north to attack the capital of Pennsylvania. Hagerstown sits astride a vitally important supply line. If the army is to remain in the North and we eventually turn east toward Philadelphia, Baltimore, or Washington City, we could defeat the Yankees on their own soil."

"If General Hooker moves the Army of the Potomac quickly, General Lee may not make it that far," the judge proclaimed.

Dr. Cullen confidently replied, "The destiny of these two great armies isn't our concern; it's in the Almighty's hands. We must inform the citizens of Hagerstown, that on behalf of their humanitarian hearts, they must help us prepare hospitals for the wounded coming back, regardless of the outcome of what lies ahead in the next few days or weeks. I've marked on the map the Franklin Hotel, the Washington House, the Lyceum Hall, and the Hagerstown Female Seminary. All of these locations would work well for hospital sites."

"I'll volunteer as chief surgeon to head the hospitals in Hagerstown," Dr. Macgill said.

"I'll go north with the army," Charles Griffith offered. "I think I can be of more assistance to the wounded in the field."

"Charles Griffith, I heard the Stonewall Brigade was looking for a chief surgeon. You might find them and inquire," Dr. Cullen responded.

"I'll pack my medical bag and leave tonight," nodded Charles Griffith.

Mollie's mind began to churn with ideas, "I believe it's not too late to get an article into the *Torch Light* newspaper tonight. It comes out day after tomorrow. I'll write the article requesting spare beds, bandages, and any medical supplies to be delivered to the sites you've indicated. I will oversee setting up the Hagerstown Female Seminary to receive wounded. I graduated from the seminary and know every inch of the building. We can remove the doors and place them on the desks for operating tables. I'm sure the people of Hagerstown will respond just as they did after Sharpsburg."

"Excellent! We've got the beginnings of a plan. I knew I could count on all of you to serve our soldiers," Dr. Cullen said. He looked over his shoulder to see a white collared Episcopal priest walking toward the porch.

"Good afternoon, Reverend Kerfoot," the judge said, rising quickly to meet the newly arrived visitor and giving Dr. Cullen time to casually fold the map. "To what do we owe your always welcome visit this beautiful day? May I introduce you to Dr. Cullen, medical director of General Longstreet's corps?"

"Well, I just thought I'd stop by and say hello to the various good neighbors of the College of St. James. You're the first stop of the day. I brought you and the Missus a loaf of fresh baked bread. I hope I'm not interrupting. The colonel looks to be on important business."

The reverend stepped onto the porch and pulled up a wicker chair to join the circle of friends. Dr. Cullen explained to him about setting up hospitals over the course of the next few days. Mollie knew the reverend's Unionist position as the headmaster of the College of St. James, but she also knew he was not political at heart and that he would respond to the humanitarian calling. Then the tide of the conversation turned to Maryland, secession, and the war.

Judge Breathed spoke. "Dr. Cullen, I've introduced Reverend Kerfoot. He is the headmaster, and a professor, of the College of St. James, just over there to the east. But you should know that Dr. Kerfoot does not favor the breaking up of the Union. Like many Maryland men, he has a partisan view of this war."

Dr. Cullen looked closely at Dr. Kerfoot and then spoke. "Dr. Kerfoot, it goes without saying that you are an intelligent man, and though you favor not our cause, the fact that you are standing on this porch attests to your open mind."

"As a headmaster of a college for young men from both North and South, I must keep my mind open," replied Dr. Kerfoot with a slight smile. "But if you mean that I do not espouse a radical cause to justify this war, you are correct. This war seems to me to be the result of misguided or hypocritical politicians of both sides, who used their wiles to rush to war against the will of the people, at least in the beginning."

Dr. Cullen replied, "Surely a man has the right to prevent the invasion of his home. At the beginning, I thought secession rash, but once Mr. Lincoln called for an army to use against his own countrymen, my loyalty to Virginia left me no choice but to defend her."

"Your loyalty to your state does you honor," replied Dr. Kerfoot. Then, as his smile faded, he continued, "But my case is different. I'm a naturalized citizen. Thus the solemn oath I took was to the United States of America, not a particular state. I take my oaths very seriously, being sworn in the presence of God." Then, turning toward Dr. Macgill, Kerfoot added, "I think Dr. Macgill will understand my seriousness in regard to oaths, for I know of no man to whom the taking of an oath was more serious. His previous position in relation to oaths bears full testimony."

Dr. Macgill sat silent for a moment before replying, "I wonder, Dr. Kerfoot, if you would've taken the oath forced on me? Namely, to swear in advance that I would support any action of the United States in the future, no matter how barbarous. And as this war goes on, I find the barbarity of the Federal forces, witness General Pope, as fully justifying my reticence. Yes, oaths before God, whether taken or abjured, are a severe test of conscience."

Dr. Kerfoot replied, "Indeed. And I do hold that no oath to an earthly power should bind a man against his conscience. Revolution may become a duty, but only in case of wrongs so extreme as to absolve allegiance, and make resistance a duty to God. I cannot concur with the views and convictions of those who think that result is now reached. But I trust and revere those men who, in good conscience, view their oaths as conditional, those conditions broken, and their allegiance now due to their states. And, so trusting, I sit among you in friendship."

Judge Breathed spoke up. "Dr. Kerfoot is, as you can see, a man of honorable convictions, who allows those with other honorable convictions freedom of conscience. He has even planned his course if Maryland secedes, haven't you Doctor?"

"Yes," replied Dr. Kerfoot. "I'm a man of God and no politician. If, as I fervently hope and trust will not be the case, Maryland were to secede, I'm prepared to live in submission to the civil authorities. Even Bishop Whittingham, who is a more determined Unionist than I, has agreed to immediately remove the Prayer for the President of the United States from the liturgy in the event of Maryland's secession."

Dr. Cullen spoke again, "I think your liturgy is safe, Dr. Kerfoot. We had hoped that our invasion a year ago would encourage the people of Maryland to throw off the Federal yoke and join us. We've no such illusions now. I think, even if we're victorious at arms and we obtain a just peace, Maryland will not join us. What think you, Judge?"

"As to after the war, with the South independent, I could not say," the judge replied. "But during this war, it's not in Maryland's interest to secede. There is too much Union sentiment in the north and west of the state. The Mason-Dixon Line is indefensible. Nor do I think the North will cease this war leaving the mouths of the Chesapeake Bay and the Mississippi River in the control of another nation. With the control of our own ports, we would have free trade with Europe and this would cripple Northern trade. Before the war, unjustly high tariffs on the South gave favorable control of commerce to the North."

Dr. Macgill added, "Nor would Maryland care much about losing her slaves. The judge and I've already freed ours. In fact, both the North and South should've looked to Maryland for the solution to the problem of slavery. Maryland has more free Negroes than any other state. We've about as many free Negroes as slaves, with the momentum moving farther toward wage labor each year. But, face it, gentleman, this is not about slavery; it is about race. If the slaves were white, as they once were as indentured slaves, do you think slavery would not have been abolished long ago?"

Dr. Cullen answered, "The radical abolitionists never gave us the chance. They would promote servile war in our homes, with the Nat Turners and John Browns committing unthinkable atrocities. No, they demanded immediate emancipation, with no true thought for the emancipated, but only their own political gain. What do you think will happen to those poor emancipated Negroes suddenly turned loose in a ruined economy?"

"If Mr. Lincoln is to be believed," responded Judge Breathed, "they will all be sent back to Africa. Has that rail-splitter learned nothing from our efforts to do just that since the end of the slave trade? The Negroes do not want to go!"

Dr. Macgill quickly added, "Maryland even established a colony in Africa for freed slaves, but it did not thrive. We gave that colony freedom. Why, Dr. Kerfoot, I think it was one of your own students that drew up their constitution."

To this Dr. Kerfoot nodded sadly, then added, "And when the power was turned over to the manumitted slaves, they passed a law instituting slavery. Your point is well taken, Doctor. Colonization will not work and President Lincoln is misled if he believes it will."

"And so the war goes on," said Dr. Macgill. "For my part, and I think I speak for most of Maryland, I believe the Confederate states should not be held against their will, even if Maryland chooses to remain in the Union. But for believing that, I'm thrown into prison, without charges. All I wished to do was practice my profession, as I've always done, impartial to the politics of the patient."

"Just as I would bring such spiritual encouragement as I can summon to all, regardless of allegiance, as I did on South Mountain and at Antietam Creek," said Dr. Kerfoot. "But because I'm known as a Union man, my wish is granted and yours denied, Dr. Macgill, because you are perceived otherwise."

Dr. Cullen responded, "The war goes on, but perhaps not for much longer. If we can defeat the Army of the Potomac and cut off Washington, we may gain our independence yet."

Dr. Kerfoot shook his head slowly, "I'm no more a military man than I'm a political man, but I know the North. They'll not accept defeat, and they've the manpower, resources, and resolve to keep fighting. The Confederacy has the resolve, but little else to win."

"Whatever the outcome of events, we've our duties, each according to his conscience," Dr. Macgill said.

"Amen," Dr. Kerfoot responded.

The conversation lapsed, and Mollie felt a general sadness come over her while listening to the conversation. Then, for a reason she could not name, she began to cry. Softly at first, but upon feeling more intense emotions coming on, she excused herself and went inside. She passed the mirror in the parlor, glanced at her image, and felt a sudden chill. She realized that she had been in the presence of four eminent men. She thought they all were intelligent, all were men of the highest character, all had acted honorably, but all were powerless to stop this insane war. A deepening twilight had suddenly seemed to darken apace, and her heart was heavy with foreboding. Her eyes fell on a small ambrotype of James framed on a side table. Her heart was overcome, and her tears uncontrollable.

⌀◉⌀

A few days had passed since the conversation on the porch when Mollie and Dr. Macgill found themselves standing at the entrance to Hagerstown Female Seminary. Dr. Cullen and Charles Griffith had departed to align themselves with the Army of Northern Virginia on its way north. The news of these events had spread by word of mouth and her article in the *Torch Light*. The citizens of Hagerstown were approaching with wagons filled with bedding, bandages, and medical supplies. The first to arrive was Dr. Wroe.

"Good morning, Dr. Wroe. I suspected a native Virginian such as yourself would respond to our call," Dr. Macgill said as he walked over to Dr. John Wroe's wagon, which was filled with medical supplies. The men shook hands.

Mollie admired Doctor Wroe. His sideburns and white hair were known to all the people in the area. He was an honorable man and a faithful servant to the Hagerstown community. He had been taking care of soldiers in private homes who were sick with typhoid, debilitus, diarrhea, and other diseases.

She and her father had arrived early and had paid some local boys to begin the process of removing some of the desks and chairs from the classrooms to the basement.

"Keep up the work, boys! I'm expecting many beds this afternoon to fill the rooms. Billy, you show Dr. Wroe to one of the rooms you've emptied," Dr. Macgill said as he looked toward the strong boy.

Mollie lent a hand to the doctor and helped him unload the supplies into one of her old classrooms. She looked off from the high eminence of the seminary to see more wagons coming from Hagerstown. By the time they had completed this task, more Hagerstownians were beginning to arrive, their wagons full of other supplies and beds.

The afternoon heat wore her down, but she persevered, knowing that her actions where somehow going to help save lives, and maybe even James's life for all she knew.

In one of the many wagons coming up the drive, she saw one of her least favorite Hagerstownian couples, Catherine and George Bowman. The couple owned a successful confectionary and bakery business on West Washington Street in town. Catherine's sister Maggie Greenawalt was with them. Maggie had at one time pointed a finger at her accusing her of stealing a cookie from her sister's store. Maggie had become an evil witch to her ever since that day. The short, round-faced, black-haired woman had gone so far as to rather obnoxiously declare her allegiance to the Union, claiming that all Southerners were vile Simon Legrees.

"Afternoon, Miss Mollie. Are you and your father trying to defend the Republic by supplying this hospital? I suspect your father must've learned not to dabble with the Republic after his time in our American prisons," Maggie said with a smart look on her face.

"Miss Greenawalt, with all due respect as my elder, we're here for humanitarian reasons. Our motives are indifferent to the color of a wounded man's uniform," Mollie retorted. She then turned to see her father walking over to the old Conestoga wagon.

Dr. Macgill walked up. "Good day to you, Miss Greenawalt, and to you, Mr. and Mrs. Bowman. Thank you for responding to our call for humanitarian aid. What did you bring with you in the wagon?" Dr. Macgill asked.

"We've got two beds, and we'll offer baked breads for patients. Is there anything else you would ask of us, Dr. Macgill?" George replied as he pulled his long gray beard and adjusted his round eye glasses on his nose.

"We could use your observatory on the roof of the bakery. With a good telescope or pair of field glasses you may well be able to spot troops coming from the North before we can. Let me know the moment you see anything," Dr. Macgill responded.

"We can do that. I'm on the roof almost every night looking at the stars anyhow."

"Great! Mollie, call the boys to get these beds."

∾⊙⊙∾

At the end of a long day, Alfred drove Mollie and her father back to their home on South Potomac Street. They were exhausted, but she was convinced they had done the best they could to prepare the seminary for whatever resulted from Lee's army moving north. After dinner she and the doctor sat to talk with her mother and siblings.

"Mary Ragan, the Yankees have left me with few options. If Lee succeeds in the North and Maryland secedes, I think I'll return to my practice here in Hagerstown. However, if we suffer a defeat, I'll have no other choice but to retreat with the army as it moves back into Virginia. We'll tend to the wounded at the seminary, Mollie as one of my nurses, but then we'll have to go south to Richmond," Dr. Macgill explained, not knowing how his wife would respond.

"Father, I'll go with you," Mollie said. "Everyone in town believes our sympathies are with the South, and many say I've been overly active for the Confederate cause. I'll do no more than endanger the family if I stay behind. Alice and the others can take care of mother. What are your feelings?" she asked her mother, whose health had not been improving, and, in fact was getting worse.

Mollie saw that her suggestion disturbed her mother. Mary Ragan stirred in her rocker and began to rock more vehemently. She knew this behavior from many years of observing her mother. Mollie didn't want to distress her mother, but it could not be helped in this time of war. She felt close to her and was her mother's spitting image. All of Mary Ragan's refinements had been passed down to her through her prosperous Hagerstown family, and Mollie embodied these refinements, but with a twist of stormy ire to them.

"My child, you must follow your heart. If you think you can be of assistance to your father if he goes to Richmond, if that indeed is what happens, then you must go with him. Here in Hagerstown we'll all be under the constant prying eyes of the Yankees," Mary Ragan thoughtfully responded.

"Well then, the matter is concluded. We'll stay if we can, go south if we must," Dr. Macgill had the final word on the subject.

"Let's get some rest," Mary Ragan said, and with that they went to their beds, exhausted.

32

Gettysburg

The Arduous Journey Home & Trouble in the Streets

JAMES HAD SPENT A good part of the day using his cannon to strike terror into the hearts of the local citizens. Parts of the town were burning.

"Fire three more shells into Carlisle Barracks," General Fitzhugh Lee ordered to James.

"Yes, sir, General. Being that it's a few hours past midnight, it'll be hard to see the damage," James responded with all due respect to his commanding officer.

"Yes, Captain Breathed, but it'll let them know we're still here. I studied at the Carlisle Barracks and the people were kind to me. Sorry 'Old Baldy Smith' didn't give up the town as we had asked of him. Limber and then move out to Papertown so we can catch up with the wagon train going south to Gettysburg."

"Need more ammunition before we hit that battlefield," James responded. "General Stuart's had us on the move for eight days in Yankee territory with little rest or food."

"You're doing your duty, officer. That's all that matters in the face of more battle ahead. It is now Meade we face and the entire Army of the Potomac in the morning," General Lee said as he turned his horse and rode off into the night.

"Fire!" James hollered, and plumes of smoke made large circles of smoke into the moonlit night.

"Limber—front!"

James had done as he was ordered. He thought it seemed a waste of ammunition when the big fight would come in the morning and it would be needed, but who was he to judge the wisdom of his superior officer? After a short five mile drive, he and his men were reunited with the cavalry in Papertown. They got a few hours of sleep and some food before they were off to Halltown in order to fill their limbers and caissons.

However, when his battery and McGregor's section of guns arrived at the appointed location to reload ammunition, there were no ammunition wagons in sight.

"Private Matthews, have the limbers and caissons open and inspect all the equipment and tack. Make sure we're ready to load quickly as soon as the wagons arrive," James ordered.

"See to it right away, sir," the private responded.

"And send the ordinance officer to me right away."

A spindly, youthful lieutenant ordinance officer soon walked over to talk with James. "Yes, sir."

James could feel his blood pressure rising as the ordinance officer saluted him.

"How am I to get into this battle if I've no ammunition to fight with? Damn it, man!"

James paced before the ordinance officer, kicking the grasses and mud with his cavalry boots. He took his gauntlets from his belt and slapped them on his hand. Uphill and down vale, James let loose with a string of cuss words. So intense was he that the ordinance officer stood back a few steps. James's face turned scarlet red and his eyes stared intensely into the eyes of the ordinance officer.

"The ordinance wagons were to be here by now. I can't explain to you why they're not, sir," the ordinance officer responded as his hands began to shake.

The afternoon sun, in the cloudless sky, beat down upon them as they looked for the ordinance wagons that had still not arrived. Then, an incredible sound, nothing like James had ever heard before, reverberated in his ears. It was the sound of myriad cannon.

The firing continued for over an hour when, finally, the ordinance wagons arrived. General Fitz Lee had left instructions for James to march out the York Turnpike, into the rear of the Army of the Potomac, between the Hanover Road and the Baltimore Turnpike, once his battery was resupplied with ammunition.

"Privates Mackall, Zimmerman, Clem, and Matthews, get those limbers and caissons loaded, we've got fighting to do!" James hollered. The men came from under the shade trees and got to work.

His artillerymen responded in an equally excited manner. The forty artillerymen all pitched in and soon the limbers and caissons were loaded. James mounted Billy and gave orders for the battery to follow. James and Captain McGregor, with his 2nd Stuart Horse Artillery section of guns, raced off to join the rest of the cavalry.

They arrived at the far left of the line of Confederate artillery late in the afternoon. To his front he could see a barn with a stone base wrapping into the rear open door. He saw there had been a great deal of fighting around this barn, and it was evident that sharpshooters from both sides had been waging a fierce battle.

"Right—Oblique—Front into line—March!" James commanded. He positioned the four three-inch rifled guns of his battery along the line of the other Confederate guns, which strung out for a good distance.

James pulled out his field glasses. He viewed the center of the smoke-clouded field which, at the moment, was in an ordnance-shrouded melee of blue and gray cavalrymen fighting it out with sabres and pistols. He saw tremendous dust clouds and glistening sabre reflections as the hot sun beat down upon the fight. He thought there was no way he could fire without hitting some of his own troopers. He looked around the open farmland, which was crossed by stone and wood fences, and dotted with trees. At his back, on a slit ridge, he noticed a grove of trees. He had the artillerymen move the four-up teams and the horse holders there for protection.

Finally, he saw the Federals break and retreat back to their line of cover.

"Fire!—Reload shell—one thousand eight hundred yards—five second fuses," James ordered his gunners.

It was not long before he saw the Federal artillery answer his multiple shots with counter-battery fire that was deadly accurate. In fact, the cadence and accuracy was so familiar to him that he began to ruminate where he had experienced it before. Then it came to him like a bolt of lightning. It was in the fight before crossing the Potomac River after the Mercersburg raid. He could not make out the enemy artillery, due to all the chaos and smoke, but he thought it might be his worthy adversary, Lieutenant Alexander C. M. Pennington and his artillerymen.

"Let's give those Yankee guns hell the rest of the day," James exclaimed, breaking out of a trancelike mode of thought.

"Captain, keep up your firing—steady now—the Yankees are now retreating off the center of the field. General Hampton is down with a sabre wound to the head. But, I'm sure there're more charges left to come!" Major Beckham ordered as they sat their horses behind the guns.

James and his artillerymen fought the rest of the day, and at last dark took the fight out of both sides. The artillerymen fell exhausted by their guns, but they had held the field.

◆◆◆

James groggily arose from a sleepless night. Rain had soaked the left arm of his uniform. He ironically noted that it was the Fourth of July. What a way to remember independence from the British, he thought, with nothing but wounded and dying soldiers littering the battlefield before him.

"Captain, we're to be on the Cashtown Road as the rearguard for the army's retreat back to Virginia. Get your men awake, guns limbered, and we'll move out," Major Beckham ordered James. The major then turned on his horse to search out General Stuart.

James thought the driving rain would make the trip back to Virginia even more difficult. When he arrived at the rear of the army he saw wagons in rows as far as his eyes could see. The wagons to his front contained wounded soldiers, their blood dripping out to the ground below. The soldiers wailed cries of agony. He thought he had not done much to help them in the battle, but now he was in a position to help them in their painful retreat. They were his comrades in arms, and he knew the mood of the army had changed dramatically.

He looked over his shoulder to see a lone rider coming toward him.

"Lige White, good to see you, cousin," James said to the commander of the 35th Virginia Cavalry Battalion, which was now also a part of the rearguard.

"James, how did you fare the last few days?"

"Move out!" James hollered to the artillerymen. "I lost a few good men," he then said to Lige. "I hear tell the casualties are in the tens of thousands. This has been a dreadful fight, Lige."

"My Comanche's Battalion was scouting along Rocky Creek. On the third we were moving up toward York Turnpike with General 'Extra Billy' Smith's brigade in support. On the right of General Stuart's line, I noticed a Yankee cavalry regiment wheeling, and we attacked them. Stuart appreciated our efforts," Lige then explained to his cousin his exploits over the past three days.

James and Lige conversed while they plodded along muddy roads that had become mid-calf deep in places. All the wagon wheels and horses had created a flowing slurry. The next day, the rain pelted them as they made their way through the Catoctin Mountain range. James and his men were on constant alert, looking for Federal cavalry attacks from any and all directions.

James was relieved when the rain finally let up the following day. By mid-afternoon he and his artillerymen were pressing up the Hagerstown-Williamsport Turnpike. Finally, he was close enough to Bai-Yuka that he might try and go home for a brief visit.

Mollie was at her home mid-morning on South Potomac Street. She climbed out the third story window onto the balcony over the front entrance to the home and peered past the St. John's Lutheran Church to see that the Confederate cavalrymen had barricaded the narrow street with turned over wagons and barrels. Confederate troopers were riding up and down the street preparing for something exciting, but what it was she could only imagine. George Bowman had come by to talk with her father earlier in the morning to inform him that he had seen troop movements coming toward Hagerstown.

"Missy, you had better get off that balcony," a trooper in gray cried out as he rode by. "There's Yankee cavalry on the other side of the barricade and plenty of them."

She quickly climbed back in the window and there was her father looking at her with a stern face.

"Mollie, what did I tell you about exposing yourself to the street like that?"

"Father, I simply wanted to see what was happening on the other side of the street barricade."

"The Yankees know we're here; they've been uninvited guests before, so take this rifle and sit yourself behind the wall so you can peer out the window. We'll not have them in our house again. If we're to defend ourselves we'll do so. I need to get to the hospital, for I'm sure there will be need for my medical calling after this fight in the streets."

She took the rifle from him. She well knew how to use it. She loaded it with powder, rammed a minie ball down the barrel, and capped the gun. Then she pulled up a chair to the side of the window and sat down to wait. She looked around her room and her eyes settled on her four-poster, ornately carved wooden bed. The pink patchwork quilt had three china dolls at the pillows, each about two feet long, outfitted in pretty dresses. She had grown up with these dolls and, other than her family, she was closest to them. She confided her deepest and darkest secrets in the three inanimate girls. She rested the rifle against the wall and thought she would defend the girls to the death and would shoot any Yankee who tried to take her dear childhood friends.

Time passed slowly as she looked over to her bedstand and saw the clock's small hand on the two. Suddenly, she heard a burst of gun fire in the direction of the barricade and, not long after, a lot of Confederate troopers carrying a guidon with the number nine on it came charging down South Potomac Street toward the barricade. Immediately thereafter she saw gray troopers in full retreat being chased by Federal cavalry toward the square. Then came a loud bugle call; she saw a gray trooper carrying a guidon with the number ten on it slam into the blue and the gray troopers. She witnessed a great deal of confusion in the moments when she dared peer through the one open window shutter. She thought it must have been hard to see who to shoot or stab in the midst of so much smoke and rearing horses. The deadly melee was being waged in hand-to-hand combat, with the sabres gyrating, waving, parrying, and thrusting in all directions.

She felt as if she was, for the first time, actually in the battle itself. When she peered around the wall, through the open window, the glass shattered in the closed window and crashed to the floor. She was so startled that she pulled her head back to see dust coming down from the ceiling. Now she had been shot at. Whether it was intentional or not, it got her ire up. She looked toward the square and saw a large number of Confederate troopers charging the Federals who were coming from the direction of West Washington Street. She saw their sabres drawn as they crashed into the Federals, cutting and swinging the steel weapons. Soon the bloody weapons were returned to their scabbards and revolvers finished many of the Federals off. The action caused the Federals to pull back in front of her house toward the barricade.

The street settled for a while. She was able to catch her breath. She realized that she was sweating profusely. She heard cannon fire coming from the Female Seminary and she suddenly thought about her father. He had not told her which hospital he was going to. She heard a tremendous explosion and saw a plume of smoke go up in the air east of town. While she was looking at the plume out her window she saw twenty or so blue dismounted troopers stealthily making their way up South Potomac Street. They made it as far as the square when she barely could make out the command, which was hollered out loudly a half block away, "Now boys, give it to them!"

Then she saw the blue troopers working their way back, facing up South Potomac Street. When they got perpendicular to her house she eased her rifle out the window.

She spied a blue trooper with three yellow strips of a sergeant on his arm. She pulled back the hammer, aimed, and fired. *Boom!*

She quickly set the butt of the gun on the floor, pulled the ramrod, poured the powder, placed another minie ball at the muzzle, and rammed it home. She stood up behind the wall and looked for another target. The troopers were gone, but one of them lay across the street in a pool of blood, face up so that she could see that the bullet had struck him in his chest. She had shot and killed many deer, and she knew a killing shot when she saw it.

She stared at the man in disbelief, when suddenly there was another charge of mounted Federal troopers that went by her window. She saw these troopers push past the square, but they were then met by Confederate infantry who caused them to disperse back and onto the side streets off of North Potomac Street. After she observed this action, she returned her attention the soldier she had shot. He was not there. Evidently, someone had dragged away the body of the soldier.

∽⣿∾

A few days later, Dr. Macgill and Mollie were at the Female Seminary tending to the wounded. She was wrapping a bandage around a wound of a Federal soldier when Mr. W. W. Jacobs, a local citizen of Hagerstown with Union sympathies, entered the classroom-turned-medical ward.

"People tell me you're quite a markswoman with a rifle. I know you were in your home three days ago when the battle took place in the streets," Mr. Jacobs said as he adjusted his topper hat.

"Yes, I was at home when all that unpleasantness took place. I was with my family who were threatened by those dastardly Yankees fighting in front of our home," she said as she continued to wrap the wound.

"Well, not far from your home I pulled a mortally wounded Sergeant Brown of the Eighteenth Pennsylvania Cavalry off the street into a nearby house. Did you happen to get word that he was thought to have been shot from a window?" Mr. Jacobs asked.

"No, I didn't get word. But I heard there were Hagerstownians taking part in the battle on behalf of both sides. Were you engaged?" she retorted.

"Well, I've business to attend to. Have a good day, Miss Macgill."

"And you the same, Mr. Jacobs."

Mollie waited until she had finished wrapping the wound before she went to find her father. She frantically searched each room of the seminary until she found him tending to a wounded Confederate.

"Father, when do we leave for Williamsport?" Mollie asked with a concerned look on her face.

"We're loading all those able to travel today and moving out tonight. Why?"

"Seems to me the Yankees will be coming after our army and we need to get all the wounded loaded in ambulances and moved to Williamsport as soon as possible."

"I promise you, now that Charles Griffith is back with us, we'll move out tonight."

"Good," Mollie replied.

Mollie, Charles Griffith, and her father, with the help of many Hagerstownians, loaded the wounded Confederates that night. She said good-bye to her mother, and then Alfred drove the three of them to Williamsport in the landau carriage. They stayed in Williamsport behind the defensive line that stretched from Hagerstown to Downsville for four more days due to the flooded river. While there she searched for James, but discovered he was out with General Stuart defending the line against an attack from the Army of the Potomac, which was now present in force. Finally, the Potomac River subsided and the night of the fourth day in Williamsport she, Charles Griffith, her father, and the Army of Northern Virginia slipped across the river and moved onto Martinsburg.

In Martinsburg she accompanied her father on a visit to a local citizen's home. "Dr. Macgill, who's this fine-looking young woman you have with you?" General Lee asked as he sat in a rocker on the back porch.

"General, I've the pleasure of introducing you to my daughter, Miss Mollie Macgill. She has been a very busy lady in relation to helping our cause. You may remember her as the lady who, last year, delivered to you the information in regard to the number 191 Order," Dr. Macgill responded, as he presented Mollie's hand to General Lee.

"Very fine to finally meet you, Miss Macgill. I've heard so much about your espionage exploits to date."

"General, I humbly do what I can for my country, but it is nothing in comparison to what your great army has done and will continue to do," she responded as she looked at his gray beard. She was in awe to be in the presence of the general.

"General, I've come to you seeking a pass that would allow my son, Mollie, and me to go from here to Richmond to seek commissions from President Davis to serve in the Medical Corps. We can no longer live peacefully and unmolested by the Yankees in Hagerstown. We wish to start anew and work for the cause in a new home in Richmond. As soon as I get settled, I'll find a way to get the rest of my family to the city."

"I understand, Doctor. In this last campaign the army suffered tremendous losses. Yours and your son's medical service would be greatly appreciated in Richmond. I feel this war is still a long way from over," General Lee said as he turned and wrote out a note. "This should do," he said, and then read the note aloud:

14th July 1863

Dr. Charles Macgill Sr., Dr. Charles Griffith Macgill, and Miss Mollie Macgill have permission to visit the camps of this Army. Pickets and guards will allow them to pass within the lines.

R E Lee
Gen.

"Thank you, General," Dr. Macgill said. "And Godspeed to you and the army."

"Travel well, Doctor, and a pleasure to meet you, Miss Macgill."

ᘒᘓᘔ

A few weeks later, Alfred drove the landau carriage to the front of 316 East Franklin Street in Richmond City. Mollie, Charles Griffith, and their father needed to go to the Executive Mansion on Clay Street. Alfred jumped from the driver's seat of the carriage and opened the door for the three Macgills.

"Top of the morning to you, Alfred," Dr. Macgill said. "Please drive us to the president's home."

"Yessa, Doctor," Alfred responded. He closed the door after all three had climbed into the carriage.

Mollie held her skirt down as the carriage bumped over the cobblestone roads toward the mansion. When finally they all arrived, Alfred once again leaped from the driver's seat to open the carriage door.

"Here ya be, Doctor."

"Thank you, Alfred. We shouldn't be long."

Mollie looked in awe at the Executive Mansion. Before her was the building that served as the headquarters of the most important man in the Confederacy. The guards at the door inquired as to who they were and, once they gave their names, the front doors were opened for them. She stepped first into the entry hall and before her stood two Greek goddesses in alcoves, Comedy and Tragedy, with a double door between the statues. They all were guided through the double doors by a female servant to the central parlor. Mollie noticed something about the servant's eyes that were peculiar, but was unsure what it was that bothered her.

Once seated, Mollie looked around the room. She noticed a white marble fireplace with fresh-cut flowers in vases on the mantels. The wallpaper was a patterned burgundy red, and she thought it made the room rather warm. She noticed the large mirror over the fireplace, which was rimmed with finely carved gold-painted wood. The six-globed gasolier hung to the center of the room. They were all seated toward the fireplace, and she thought the president and Varina Davis certainly had fine tastes.

The president and Varina entered the room and the Macgills stood, "Welcome to the Macgills," President Davis said. He warmly shook the hands of the two doctors and kissed Mollie on the cheek.

Mollie studied his face after they all sat down together. She could not help but notice his high cheek bones, hawkish pointed nose, and tuft of chin whiskers sprinkled with some gray, but none in the hair atop his head. Her thoughts were that he was a neat man, as evidenced by the way he tied his cravat and how he wore his finely pressed three-piece suit. She looked at Mrs. Davis, also impeccably dressed, and noticed her beautiful cameo pin. Mrs. Davis had sad eyes and black hair that was parted down the middle. She thought Mrs. Davis was no beauty, but then neither was Mr. Davis a strikingly handsome man.

"Mr. President, we have suffered severe losses at Gettysburg, as you well know, and my son and I have come to request commissions to enlist in the medical corps of the Army of Northern Virginia," Dr. Macgill stated without hesitation.

"Doctors are in great need, now more than ever, with so many wounded after that horrific battle. I would be happy to commission you both."

"I served with the Stonewall Brigade at Gettysburg. I would like to retain my service with them," Dr. Charles Griffith said.

"Certainly, that can be arranged. And for you, Charles?"

"I suspect a general surgeon's commission shall be fine with me."

"And you, Miss Macgill, your exploits are now well known within my administration. I can only thank you for what you have done for our cause."

"I'm at your service, Mr. President," she said.

And then Mollie said to Mrs. Davis, "Mrs. Davis, who was that servant who showed us in? I noticed something about her eyes."

"Oh, pay no attention to Mary. She is a dim-witted and slightly crazy darky I've taken in full-time. She means nobody any harm."

"Mollie, what have I told you about such impoliteness?" her father scolded. "She has always been a curious person when it comes to meeting new people. Please forgive her, Varina."

"No harm in asking," responded Mrs. Davis.

The president wrote out the commissions from his desk upstairs, and they all saw the room from which the war was being run. Mary was in the room with them dusting while the commissions were being drafted. Mollie could not keep her eyes off her. They returned down stairs to the entry hall, and they exited the Executive Mansion.

"Good day to the Macgills," the president said and Mrs. Davis waved her hand. The Macgills climbed into the landau carriage.

"Godspeed to you both, and to the Confederacy," Dr. Macgill replied.

33

Your Men Would Go Anywhere for You

Near Orange Court House on the Willis Farm, James and his battery, along with the McGregor, Chew, and Moorman Stuart Horse Artillery batteries, settled into camp. He had impatiently awaited battle, and after a stalemate at Mine Run the armies of Generals Lee and Meade had come to no major engagement. He realized that days of waiting for the armies to strike at each other had created tension in the ranks of the Stuart Horse Artillery.

"Major Beckham, may I have a word with you," James asked as the artillerists were about the business of cleaning tack after their breakfasts.

"Captain," Major Beckham saluted.

"The men need to blow off some steam after so many days in readiness for battle. When I was at the School of Medicine I was on a club of nines. Nines was becoming popular in Baltimore, and I was the club's hurler. I know the rules to town ball or nines, which ever name one might wish to refer to the game."

"Yes, go on Captain."

"A couple of games this afternoon might be the very thing to boost the artillery-men's morale. We could have each battery pick a nine and I could explain to them the rules of the game. I'd get Private Matthews to make two balls. My battery could play McGregor's, and Chew's and Moorman's could square off in the open pastures of the farm. We could set out two diamonds with stakes for bases and have some fun this afternoon. The temperature is warm, and I think it would be good physical exercise for the men."

"The men are a bit fed up with the repetitive artillery drilling. This might augment the esprit de corps for each battery. I think this's a splendid idea Captain Breathed. Get your private to work on the equipment. Instruct other artillerymen to get the diamonds set, one in each of the open pastures over there," Major Beckham said as he pointed to the open pastures.

James looked around the Willis Farm, which was a cattle farm with flat fields that were suitable for the setting up of the diamonds. He thought there would be plenty of room on the first and third base lines for the rest of the artillerymen to watch their comrades play the game.

"Private Matthews, front and center," James hollered as the men moved about their business in the 1st Stuart Horse Artillery camp.

"Yes, sir."

"Private, go and retrieve for me two walnuts and two woolen socks and report back."

"Yes, sir. We going to be makin' our uniforms butternut color today?"

"No, just report back."

"Private Mackall, front and center," James hollered again.

"Yes, sir!"

"Private, I need two hickory limbs, three feet long and four inches thick. Report back to me when you have secured them."

"Yes, sir; anything for the cause, sir!"

"Privates Clem and Zimmerman, front and center," James exclaimed.

"Yes, sir! More drillin' this mornin'" Private Clem said with a somber look on his face, always the pessimist.

Private Zimmerman walked up behind the two in conversation, "Yes, sir!" the private answered.

"Men we're going to be playing a little town ball this afternoon. Mano versus mano, battery versus battery. Ever heard of it?"

"Yes, sir; I think the Yankees play a good bit of a game called nines," Private Zimmerman responded. "Sounds like a better way to spend the day than drillin' and cleanin' tack."

"You two are going to set out the diamonds in those two pastures over there. You'll each need five stakes for the hurler's position and the bases. Look here at this diagram I'm going to draw you," James said. He found a stick to draw with in the dirt under their feet. He flattened the dry dirt and drew a diamond. He then pointed his stick to the center for the hurler's position.

"At the home stake of the diamond you step off ninety feet to the first stake, ninety to the second, and so on all the way around the diamond until you get back to the home stake. Place the hurler's stake sixty feet from the home stake, directly in front of it. Take a maul with you to pound the stakes into the ground real secure. Any questions?"

"No, sir! We'll get her done just like you say," Private Clem replied. They both saluted him and moved on their way.

When James rose from his knee, he dusted off the dirt, and found that Private Matthews was standing at his side with the two walnuts and two woolen socks in his hand.

"Good man. Now let me show you how to make a pellet. Give me your pocket knife, Henry."

"Yes, sir."

James cut the neck of the sock thread and pulled on it to unravel it. Once he had it started he took a walnut from the private and handed him the sock. Before he started the pellet-making process he pulled down on his long goatee as if he was going to make a thoughtful decision in relation to the process. He tied the wool thread around the walnut tightly and started to wind the thread around the nut in all directions. The hull of the walnut was soon covered with thread and the pellet grew in size. He worked on the pellet until he got it to a size that he thought would work.

"Now, Henry, here is what I want you to make. I need one more like this. Then I want you to find some soft leather, maybe from some gauntlets, cut them into quarters and stitch it tightly around the pellet. Make sure there are no rough edges and make sure it's all secure. Then make another one. Clear, Private?"

"Yes, sir! You know your men would do anything or go anywhere for you. But, what do these pellets have to do with whipping the Yankees?"

"You'll understand this afternoon. We've got a pleasant day for December, clear skies. I've proposed to Major Beckham some recreation."

"Yes, sir," Henry said as he walked away from James with his orders.

"Ah, Private Mackall, I see you've returned with our hickory."

"Yes, sir," Private Mackall said. "What's your next order?"

"Find a good sharp pocket knife and another man to work with you. I want these hickory limbs whittled into bats, three and a half to four inches at the top and two inches at the bottom with a knob at the end. Make sure the bottom end is smoothed so that when you grip it you'll not get splintered. Understood?"

"Yes, sir," Mackall said. "When do you need them?"

"I want them by three o'clock this afternoon."

⁂

James heard Major Beckham's assembly bugle sound in between the two diamonds. Each home stake had been set back to back, about twenty-five yards away from each other. The four batteries had picked nines, and the thirty-six players gathered around him. James sat his horse Billy. He was above the players so that he could give the rules to all four batteries at once. The rest of the myriad of artillerymen settled in along the first and third base stakes of the two diamonds to watch their batteries slug it out.

"Gentlemen, a man you may have heard of, or may not have heard of, by the name of Henry Chadwick worked to establish organized town ball teams in Richmond beginning in 1848. While I was at the School of Medicine in Baltimore, I played on a nine and learned the game. I'm now going to give you the rules," he said. He turned in all directions to project his voice.

He had thought earlier he would not call the rules by their real name, which was the Massachusetts Game, for obvious reasons. These men hated anything New England, and they had fought to prove it. Instead, he plotted to give the game's origins to Richmond.

"Three outs retire the side, and we'll play nine innings or until dark. The nine with the most aces at the end of the innings wins the match. Foul pellets are those that land outside the line of the first and third base stakes of the diamond. Fly rule is in effect and pellets caught on one bounce are an out. Plugged runners that are burned with the pellet are 'dead,' so throw like you fire artillery and you'll have a 'dead' Yankee!"

"Hurrah, hurrah, for dead Yankees," went up the cheer from the artillerymen.

"Major Beckham and Captain Chew will be umpires. If batters refuse to swing at good balls they'll call strikes. Hurlers have to deliver the pellet with both feet on the ground. First Stuart Horse Artillery battery in red shirts will play Second Stuart Horse Artillery in white shirts. Captain Chew's battery in red shirts will play Captain Moorman's battery in white shirts. Play ball!"

James dismounted Billy and the nines went to their respective fields. McGregor's artillerymen were gathered along the third base line; and his men stood along the first baseline. James walked out from the crowd of his men and took the hurler's position.

"The First Stuart Horse Artillery starting lineup, gentlemen!" James said gleefully.

"First base, Private Mackall; second base, Private Clem; shortstop, Lieutenant Johnston, third base, Lieutenant Shanks."

His team walked out, tipping their kepis to the McGregor side of the diamond amidst applause from the 1st Stuart men.

"Left field, Private Zimmerman; center field—all the way from the Fatherland of Prussia! Sergeant Emmett Shaw; right field, Sergeant Hoxton; and catcher, Private Matthews." James smiled as he removed his kepi and saluted his players who had played on his team during this war, and had prevailed on the more deadly fields of death and destruction.

"Batter up," Major Beckham sounded off from behind Private Matthews who had taken his place at the home stake.

Captain McGregor walked confidently out of the third base crowd of artillerymen with the hickory bat in his hand. McGregor bent over and picked up some dirt, flushing the terra firma through his hands, and then spit on his hands as if to show his Scottish dander and ire was in fighting mode.

James stood poised on the hurler's stake and steadied himself for the first hurl of the match. He wound up and threw the first pitch right by the captain's astonished eyes. Private Matthews caught the pellet and threw it back.

"Come on Breathed, can't you do better than that," the captain tauntingly said as he swung the bat.

James tossed another, and this time the captain took a full swing and walloped the pellet into left field. Private Zimmerman ran full speed for the pellet and positioned himself under it for a perfect catch.

"You're dead, Captain!" Major Beckham shouted. "One out! Next batter for Second Stuart!"

The first baseman, Lieutenant William Elston, a South Carolinian by birth, walked out from the ranks. He was a friend of James, and they had already been through a few rough battles. The lieutenant flexed his muscular arms and picked up the bat left by McGregor around home plate.

"Batter up!" Major Beckham shouted.

James looked down the alley and threw a pitch that the lieutenant smacked on the ground to the shortstop Johnston. Johnston fielded the pellet and burned it to Elston. The pellet hit him right in the leg and he reached down and grabbed his leg in pain.

"Damn-nation!" Elston shouted as the 1st Stuart men broke out in cheers and laughter, jumping up and down on the first base side of the line.

"Batter's dead!" Major Beckham declared as Elston limped back to the third base side of the field.

"Next batter for Second Stuart!" Major Beckham hollered out.

The second baseman, Lieutenant Charlie Ford, proudly stepped out from the jeering and snickering ranks of the McGregor line.

"Batter up," Major Beckham cried out. The warm sun shone on the happy faces of the artillerymen who had not had such fun in a very long time.

"Bring it on Breathed! You'll not get one by me!" the lieutenant taunted.

James stood facing home. He placed his thumbs under his suspenders up against his red shirt. His masculine black hairs curled out the "V" in his shirt neck. He wound up and threw a fast one right by the lieutenant.

"Bet you can't do that again!" the lieutenant scoffed.

"Make sure of it! Here it comes!" James retorted.

The lieutenant knocked the pellet deep into right field and on one bounce Sergeant Hoxton acrobatically fielded the pellet.

As the runner rounded the first stake Major Beckham hollered out, "Your dead! Change sides!"

Ford beat his kepi on his leg and walked over to the second base stake. McGregor walked out to the hurler's stake and began to announce his lineup.

"For the Second Stuart battery we have Lieutenant Elston, first base; Lieutenant Ford, second base, Private French Campbell, shortstop; and Sergeant Chichester, third base."

A cheer from the third baseline went up as the infielders took their positions on the diamond. James noticed that some ladies from Orange Court House had congregated, and they were now settling into the crowds on all sides. This of course increased the intensity of the game, for now there were women at stake for the winning team to gloat over.

Not to be outdone by James, McGregor then shouted, "All the way from Italy—Private Paoli in left field, Private Irvine in center field, Private Coon in right field, and our catcher Private Shreve!"

"Play ball!" Major Beckham shouted as Captain McGregor rubbed the pellet with his two hands and clinched it tightly.

"Come on; let's see what you got, McGregor!" James snarled at the captain.

"Breathed, you can't hit my hurling!" McGregor responded.

The captain's hurl came fast right over the middle, and James swung with all he had. The pellet went flying out into left field and Private Paoli ran to get under it. Paoli stepped in a cow pie and his feet came out from under him. He landed on his back in the cow pie. Both sides broke out in laughter as the pellet fell to the ground a few feet from where he tumbled.

James ran to first base stake, tagged it, and rounded toward second. He saw Paoli stand up, grab the pellet and throw it to Sergeant Chichester who stood at the third base stake. James slowed, tagged the second stake with his foot, and stopped.

"Next batter!" Major Beckham cried out.

Private Clem emerged from the sideline, spit on his hands, and picked up the bat. He then firmly squared himself at the plate.

"Play ball!" Major Beckham ordered.

James was thinking he wanted to steal third base; as soon as McGregor let the pellet fly, James ran for it and slid on his belly, safely touching the stake.

Catcher Private Shreve caught the pellet, "Hey! You can't do that!"

"Part of the rules, did I forget to tell about base stealing?" James said with a grin on his face.

"You most certainly did," Captain McGregor hollered out in disgust.

"Well, now you know you can steal bases!" James responded.

"Breathed knows the rules. Play ball!" Major Beckham growled out.

❧❦❧

The game was played until darkness caused them to stop play. The amusements had much lifted the spirits of the men. His artillerymen hashed out the exciting plays and recounted them late into the night around the campfire. James laughed with them as they retold the story of the pellet landing in the cow pie, of Private Zimmerman and Sergeant Shaw running into each other while trying to catch a fly pellet, and of the pellet hit so hard by Private Mackall that it exploded.

34

Misery and Scarcity

CHRISTMAS 1863

MOLLIE, HER OLDER SISTER Ellen, younger sister Elizabeth, and Dr. Macgill departed from their home on Franklin Street to make the short five block trip to St. Paul's Episcopal Church in the landau carriage. Mollie believed that, on this Christmas Day, Christ was with her and her family in Richmond, those still in Hagerstown, and her three brothers in the 1st Maryland Cavalry.

Alfred brought the carriage to a halt in front of the church, and he quickly sprang down from his driver's perch. He was dressed warmly as the temperature was below freezing and the winds blustery. He opened the carriage door for them. Mollie was the first out of the carriage.

"Merry Christmas," Alfred said gleefully.

"Merry Christmas, Alfred," Mollie replied. She looked skyward at the church cupola that towered against the blue sky. She thought it on par with the Capitol building, which was across the street from the church. The impressive, tall Romanesque columns that stood before the entrance to the church made her feel blessed on this most holy of days.

She was in her fine burgundy silk dress, which she always wore to Christmas Day service. Her shawl covered her shoulders and her fur muff had kept her hands warm on the carriage ride to the church. Her father and sisters were also dressed accordingly.

When she entered the church she could smell the fragrant cedar branches that hung from the two upper balconies that ran perpendicular to the downstairs pews. The circular motif in the ceiling puzzled her, for she had never asked after the identity of the figure painted in the middle of it.

The Macgill family was warmly greeted by their fellow Richmond Episcopal parishioners. They were escorted to their pew; Mollie sat next to her father and her two sisters sat on her left toward the aisle.

Mollie leaned over to her father and whispered, "There's President Davis and Mrs. Davis up ahead of us a few pews. I wonder if Dr. Minnigerode will speak of the war today?"

"We'll soon discover, won't we, my dearest?"

The service commenced, prayers were said from the liturgy, Christmas carols were sung, and then came the reading of Scripture. She observed the austere, thin-faced rector with curly hair parted to the right come forth to the pulpit in his flowing robes and a red stole around his neck. She saw that all heads in the congregation turned to look at him as he placed his round-rimmed reading glasses on his nose and fastened them behind his ears. He opened the Bible. After he read the Scripture lessons with a slight German accent, the congregation responded, "The word of the Lord."

She listened intently to the homily, for the reader spoke in a commanding voice that projected to the rear of the sanctuary: *Over two and a half weary years of war have wrung this question of peace from the agonized heart of our bleeding country. Oh! That we could have peace this night as we celebrate the birth of the Christ child who came to bring a message of peace to mankind. The statesman exclaims peace, as he ponders the problems that demand solutions at his hands. Peace, sighs the soldier, as he wraps his blanket around himself and lies down to a restless sleep upon the open field. Peace! mourns the widow, as she reads the fatal news of her heroic husband and sons who have fallen on some bloody field and bitterly thinks of the darkened future in store for herself and her orphaned children who remain at home. The prayer of the land is for peace. You may hear it in the sanctuary, at the fireside, around the family dinner table, in silent chamber, on the tented field. When will it come? . . .*

Near the conclusion of the service Mollie and the family took the Eucharist at the rail at the front of the sanctuary. She walked back to the pew in a somber mood, for she knew that soldiers all over the North and the South would not be celebrating Christ's birth with a church service. Instead they would be in some dirty log cabin or on picket duty, and likely many would go hungry this most blessed of all days. She thought of James and said a private prayer for him when she sat down.

The Benediction was given to conclude the service. They greeted Mrs. Davis and the president, the most powerful man in the Confederacy, as the couple walked down the aisle to the narthex. The Macgill family exited the building and reentered the carriage that Alfred had waiting not far from the front of the church. The church bells rang as the hour tolled twelve o'clock noon.

⚬ↄ◑ᴑↄ

Mollie discovered when they arrived home that Miss O'Shaunsay had been busy in the kitchen preparing the Christmas Day feast. Miss O'Shaunsay, who had come down with the other two sisters from Hagerstown, now gave motherly direction to all three of them in the preparation of the feast. Although this meal would not be as bountiful as years' past due to scarcities of many foods and resources, Miss O'Shaunsay none-theless labored on as best she knew how.

"Ellen, do you remember our Nuremberg angel with her stretched out hands, holding a wreath in either hand, stern faced, and wings ready to take flight?" Mollie asked as she kneaded the pie crust dough.

"I certainly do," Ellen replied. "We always placed her atop the fir tree after we had it all decorated. I hope mother, Alice, and little Frank do not forget her this year. That angel has been around as long as I can remember."

"Do you fear for your husband, Major Swan?" she asked.

"I pray for him daily. This past June he was trying to raise a battalion of Maryland cavalry in Hagerstown, but that didn't work out. I hope he is at some place safe, and warm, on this Christmas Day. I miss his being here with us."

"Yes, I hope the same for James and all his horse artillerymen."

"Let's not speak of the war this holy day. Instead, let us give thanks for father, our new home here in Richmond, and the birth of the Christ child."

"Agreed."

"Elizabeth, please help Miss O'Shaunsay baste the turkey, while Mollie and I work on cutting the sauerkraut," Ellen requested as Dr. Macgill entered the kitchen.

"Ladies, you all are laboring so hard, I've brought you some eggnog. This should be just the thing to brighten your spirits around here on Christmas. Miss O'Shaunsay, how long until you need me to bring the turkey into the dining room?"

"Oh, Doctor, a few more minutes."

"Mollie," Dr. Macgill said, "I thought you and whoever else would like to go could come with me this afternoon to get seconds bread at Thomas McNiven's bakery over on North 8th Street, and then bring it to the Chimborazo Confederate Hospital. I figure our boys need some cheer on this day, too. I could also practice some medicine while we deliver the bread."

Soon after Dr. Macgill departed the kitchen, Alfred was summoned to serve the meal. Miss O'Shaunsay stayed in the kitchen to prepare the courses. Mollie had deco-rated the parlor and the dining room with pine, balsam, holly, and ivy. The presents were wrapped neatly and placed around the sides of the fireplace. There was no tree this year due to the scarcity of them. The smells of the cooked turkey, sauerkraut, and the evergreens wafted through the room and she was strongly reminded of Christmas days past in Hagerstown.

They all sat at the dining table. Dr. Macgill blessed the food and cut the tender meat from the breast of the turkey. Mollie was served first by Alfred, who then made his way around the table, serving the two other sisters and Dr. Macgill.

"I've seen the newest *Harper's Weekly* magazine. Thomas Nast has depicted Santa Claus in a patriotic Federal costume visiting and distributing gifts. I think the Yankees should have portrayed Mr. Lincoln as Scrooge from Mr. Dickens's *A Christmas Carol*," Elizabeth blurted out. "I hope all the spirits of the dead Confederate soldiers visit Mr.

Lincoln today, for he is truly Scrooge. And for that matter Santa should be wearing a gray uniform, not a blue one!"

"My child, you may think what you like of Mr. Lincoln, but I've witnessed an abundance of bribery, black market dealings, hoarding commodities, people in high office getting around rationing, and bureaucratic red tape in our own Confederate government, and people to make me question our side of the war as well," Dr. Macgill responded to his daughter.

"Elizabeth, you should be thankful for not having to be exposed to all the terrible things father is speaking of on this Christmas Day. We've been through a lot together as a family, but no matter what happens we'll always have each other. You should be thankful for family today. Remember what Dr. Minnigerode said this morning in his homily about our soldiers on the battlefields and peace, which is what we all must pray for now. Our own brothers, Barlow, Pat, and James, are among those on the battlefields of this war," Mollie responded to her sister sharply.

"Girls, let me tell you about the days when the Christmas season went on for seven days of constant parties, from plantation to plantation. When I was a young lad, my father and mother took us around to plantations in Harford County, north of Baltimore. Some plantations would have fox hunts, which I so much enjoyed, and others would have parties that went all night long. They served sack posset and syllabub which, as I recall, were rather strong spirits. The horse country north of Baltimore had wide open fields. I raced on my horse like the wind after the hounds on the scent of foxes," Dr. Macgill reported to his daughters.

"Sounds like a good time was had by all, Father," Ellen said.

"Yes, and later in my adolescent years, I can remember Christmas parties at Stoney Castle in Poolesville with your cousins, the Whites. They had a magnificent upstairs ballroom where we danced the night away. Maryland was a wonderful Southern community of good people. Now we're divided as a state and a people."

"Well, I've a Taffy Party to attend in the morning," Mollie said. "But it doesn't seem to be as joyful an event as you describe, Father. Shall we finish our meal and open the presents by the fireplace?"

"Yes, indeed," Elizabeth responded, eager to get to her bounty of gifts.

Mollie and her sisters were excused from the dining table as Alfred began to clear the table. They all four pulled up chairs in front of the fireplace and Mollie was the first to hand a present to her father. He opened the small oblong box and there was an ink pen of the finest quality.

"Why thank you, Mollie," Dr. Macgill said and stood to hug her.

They all exchanged presents that they had bought for each other and opened others that were given to them. Mollie especially enjoyed giving a present to Alfred, for she thought it had been more than once that he had saved her from perilous dangers over the war years.

Ellen was giving a gift to Miss O'Shaunsay when they all heard the tingle of the doorbell. Dr. Macgill went to the door and shortly called for them all to come to him. There, outside the door, stood a throng of warmly dressed carolers. They began to sing "Deck the Halls," followed by "O Come, All Ye Faithful," and concluded with "God Rest Ye Merry Gentlemen."

"Thank you, and have a Merry Christmas Day, yourselves!" Mollie and the family shouted out from the doorway as the carolers moved on to the next house.

❧◎❧

Alfred drove Mollie and Dr. Macgill to Mr. McNiven's bakery to get the bread. When Alfred turned off Broad onto 8th Street, Mollie saw that a bread wagon was backed up to the bakery. There was a darky loading loaves into the rear of the square wagon, which was pulled by a single horse.

"Alfred, back the landau next to that bread wagon," Dr. Macgill said out the window.

"Yessa, Doctor."

When the carriage was parked, Dr. Macgill exited and went inside to inquire about getting the seconds bread. Mollie stepped out of the landau and walked to the loading dock, which was about four feet tall. She peered across the dock and saw two people talking. She could see Thomas McNiven conversing with a darky woman. She wanted to say hello, but instinct told her to listen instead. She could not make out the whole exchange, but she understood the conversation to be about Confederate troop movements. The darky was reporting to Mr. McNiven. Then Mollie saw Mr. McNiven give the darky woman a piece of paper, which she read aloud with perfect English. Mollie pulled her head back from peering around the bread wagon at the moment the darky finished reading the paper.

Dr. Macgill came out from the bakery door with an armful of French bread wrapped in paper.

"This is all they've to give today," Dr. Macgill said with a remorseful look on his face. "Climb back in, Mollie. We'll be off to the hospital."

"Yes, Father."

When they were both back in the carriage, Alfred pulled out to the right, in front of the bread wagon. Mollie kept her eyes glued out the window, making sure that the curtain covered her face. Suddenly, the darky turned and walked toward their landau. She was amazed to see those same eyes she saw at the Executive Mansion. She now had identified the darky to be Mary, the servant in the house of Mrs. Davis and the president himself. Alfred drove southeast out Broad Street to Chimborazo Hospital.

"Father, you know who I just saw? Mary, the dim-witted darky from the Executive Mansion. She was talking to Mr. McNevin and reading a paper. I knew there was something suspicious about that darky the first time I saw her, the day we visited with President and Mrs. Davis."

"I thought Varina said she was dim-witted and couldn't read or write."

"On top of that," Mollie said, "I heard them talking about our troops' movements; looks like there's a rat in the woodpile."

"We'll have to make a stop by the Executive Mansion after we visit our soldiers at the hospital. I'm sure President Davis would like to know what you heard and saw today."

They went on to minister to the sick and bring cheer to the soldiers lying infirmed in the many wooden barracks, which created almost a small city upon a hill outside of Richmond City proper. They entered the first barracks they came to, and a sergeant approached them.

"State your business here, sir," he said curtly.

"I'm Dr. Macgill, and have my commission papers here from President Davis as a general surgeon. This is my daughter, Miss Mollie, and we've come to do what we can for our boys and bring some cheer."

"Yes, Doctor. We're thankful to have you both today. The men are rather down, as you might surmise. Anything you can do would be wonderful."

"Sergeant, do you have any men in this barracks from Captain James Breathed's Stuart Horse Artillery battery?" Mollie asked.

"Why, yes. Private John Dorsey who enlisted in Richmond, but is a Marylander, is a few beds up the main aisle on the left."

"Father, I'm going to chat with him first. I'll meet you back here."

Dr. Macgill agreed. He picked up his black medical bag and was off to clean abscesses and do any other simple surgical procedures he could in conjunction with the regular staff of the hospital. Mollie smelled putrid odors as she walked up the middle aisle and passed rows of beds. She suspected it was probably from gangrene.

"Hello, I'm Miss Mollie Macgill. I understand you were with Captain Breathed," she said as she pulled up a chair to be closer to Private Dorsey.

"Yes, Miss Macgill. I was with his battery until I took this leg wound on October fourteenth near Warrenton. Bullet went clean through, and I've been here ever since."

"It has been two and a half months since you've seen James. How was he doing when you saw him then?"

"He was fine. May I call you Miss Mollie?"

"Yes, of course."

"Miss Mollie, I've never known a more capable soldier to handle a horse artillery battery than Captain Breathed. I assume you've more than a passing interest in him."

"Why, yes. I'm in love with him, and he with me. But, this war has gotten between us and made our relationship difficult."

"I once fought beside him close to Sharpsburg, Maryland, for an entire day. He seemed to be impervious to shell or bullet as he commanded his guns firing into that bloody cornfield. Another time, just before crossing the Potomac back into Virginia, I watched from the banks on the Virginia side as he fired right and then left on the C & O Canal. It was as if he was Moses parting the Red Sea for the Confederate cavalry to pass to safety while being chased by the pharaoh of Egypt."

"I saw that cornfield a short while after the battle ended," she remembered. "I was sickened by what I saw."

"I certainly understand your feelings. We didn't often see the result of our deadly work. I also saw him command the battery and, seemingly, solely drive the Yankee cavalry from the field when we fought them at Kelly's Ford. He rode up and down the field and directed the fire of the guns with such effectiveness as I'd never seen before. But Chancellorsville and Captain Breathed's leading the thousands of men as they marched right into Howard's XI Corps, was his highest and finest fighting to date."

"I know so little of what he does. It is good to hear firsthand from a soldier who has fought alongside him. Are you related to Dr. Dorsey of Hagerstown?"

"Yes, he's a great uncle of mine and a very good doctor."

She looked up after an hour or so of conversation with the private and there stood her father. She thought if her father only knew what she had just learned, he would be as proud of James as she was.

"Son, can we change that leg wound bandage for you before we leave?" Dr. Macgill asked.

"Yes, Doctor, that would be mighty kind of you, thanks. I've enjoyed talking to Miss Mollie. Her beau is quite the artillerist, and it has been my honor to serve with him."

⟡⟡⟡

Alfred pulled the carriage up in front of the Executive Mansion. The guards immediately approached the carriage.

"State your business," the guard said to Dr. Macgill.

"I'm Dr. Charles Macgill, and I wish to speak with Secretary Colonel Harrison."

"I'll report to him you're here; remain in the carriage."

It was not long before Mollie and her father were let into the house to speak with the secretary. Henry, a house servant, showed them to a waiting place in the central parlor. They were sitting, patiently waiting, when the colonel walked through the doors.

"Colonel Harrison, we've got vitally important information that the president needs to hear tonight. Could you request an audience with him?" Dr. Macgill said.

"Yes, sir, I'll speak with him immediately."

Mollie and her father remained in the parlor, located to the left of the entrance hall, and waited. She was nervous, for she knew her information was important. She thought if it were not for the prominence of her father they would not have been able to even approach the president of the Confederacy at such a late hour on Christmas Day.

"Charles, it's good to see you and Miss Mollie again. What can I do for you both?"

"Mr. President, it is not what you can do for us, it is what we need to tell you that is most concerning and why we are here," Dr. Macgill responded.

"Do tell," President Davis said.

"Sir," Mollie began, "today, my father and I were picking up seconds bread to bring to Chimborazo Hospital. I listened to a conversation between a darky and Mr.

McNiven while father was getting the bread. The darky spoke of our troop movements and was able to read, in perfect English, a paper that Mr. McNiven gave to her."

"Yes, go on Miss Mollie."

"Well, when we pulled away from the dock, I saw those eyes, those eyes I didn't trust from the moment which I saw them here. It was Mary, the dim-witted slave that Mrs. Davis said to ignore. She is gathering information from within your home and passing it to Mr. McNiven," Mollie exclaimed while rising to her feet to make her point.

"I've known there was a leak in this house, but I knew not who it was. Thank you! Now we shall catch this viper at her own game. I shall plant false information on my desk. When she passes it on, the results will be known as a result of the Federals' response."

"Mr. President, I am grateful I could be of assistance once again. I'm your humble servant."

"Yes, I'll plant the information in the morning on my desk for her to read."

35

Rio Hill

JAMES AND THE STUART Horse Artillery had moved to a point on the Rivanna River. There, his men set about the task of building a winter camp beside a road that led from Madison Court House to Charlottesville, about eight miles from the town. The artillerymen built comfortable shelters, topped off with tents and stick chimneys. He shivered in the cold and detested the fact that he had to continually provide for his men and his horses. The war was wearing him out.

The monotony of camp life kept him eager for the action to fight a new battle, but he was not ready to engage the enemy again. The card playing, chicanery, joking, and storytelling were the only things his men had to keep sheer boredom at bay. The warmth of the campfire cheered his men's spirits. When his artillerymen were not cleaning tack or feeding their horses, they communed around the open cook fires. James had become the master of ceremony, a shaman of sorts, as he entertained the artillerymen with tales of combat from his earlier encounters with the Federals. He was a tried and true veteran and the men listened to his every sage word.

One morning, James was shivering against the cold as he watched a rough look-ing and heavily bearded Albemarle farmer enter the camp on a bay horse. The farmer dismounted and walked over to James.

"And what might the Stuart Horse Artillerymen do for you this fine morning?" James asked the farmer as he shook his hand.

"Sir, I'm accusing no one, but I've a good bit of forage that has done gone missing last night. Do you know who might have taken it?"

"I was here all last night with these fine men, who are defending your country. Our artillerymen are all gentlemen and would never take from your farm without asking first! I resent your even suggesting my men took it!" James whittled on a stick with his pocket knife as he spoke. During his reply to the farmer, he had observed Billy quietly nibbling on some of that fodder that had been sequestered the night before by his artillerymen. He knew the true origin of this fodder, but remained faithful to his men.

"Well, sir, I reckon I certainly support the cause and do not want to come off as being unpatriotic," the farmer said. "But I sure would like to know who is making off with my forage. I've got horses to feed, too!"

"You've my word, sir; to the best of my knowledge, I do not know who took your forage. And if'n I catch them, I'll let you know. Good day to you, sir."

"A good day to you as well."

After the farmer had ridden his horse away, Privates Matthews, Clem, Zimmerman, and Mackall approached James.

"Captain, I reckon you seemta always have our best interests at heart. Thanks for covering for us," Private Matthews said as he shook James's hand.

"Seems only fitting I look after the men who look after me, both on and off the battlefield," James replied.

"You knew all along it was us, right Captain," Private Clem said.

"We needed the forage more than he did. He can always find more. But our horses are getting thin. You boys did the right thing."

"Thanks for covering for us, Captain," Private Mackall said.

"Well, now that we have it, go and feed it."

"Yes, sir," Private Zimmerman said.

⌒⊙⌒

James was relaxing, singing songs, laughing, and enjoying the day of rest when, by noon, the camp began to prepare a meal. He looked up from the campfire to see his friend from the 1st Virginia Cavalry, Lieutenant Cunningham, galloping into camp. Cunningham was out of breath and his horse was lathered from the hard ride.

The lieutenant dismounted in front of James, saluted, and explained his sudden appearance. "There's a large body of enemy cavalry approaching!" Cunningham roared out. "I've seen the enemy. I've been closely observing Custer's troopers and their movements in their ride south from Madison Court House. They are coming right this way."

James quickly notified Captain Moorman, the senior commander in Major Beckham's absence, and the captain sent pickets forward to Rio Bridge over the Rivanna River.

"Sergeants Hoxton and Shaw, report," James said. The sudden peril made him king and commander. The pickets soon returned galloping back to camp confirming Cunningham's news.

Captain Moorman came scurrying over to him, "Captain Breathed, we'll not have time to move all sixteen guns to the hill to our rear. I'll redeploy twelve of them and you stay here as the front line of attack with four of them; understood, Captain?"

"Yes, sir!" James replied. As the sergeants reported in, James thought Captain Moorman was once again not going to cover his back.

"Lieutenant Cunningham says Custer has a brigade of cavalry with him and only a section of guns. We're to turn and deploy four guns north on the road to Madison Court House. We're the front line of resistance. Your orders clear?" James asked.

"Yes, sir!"

"I want some of the men to get long sticks and deploy behind those fallen logs in plain view. We must convince them, if they attack the camp, that we have infantry," he ordered.

James looked around to see that Captains Moorman, Chew, and McGregor were riding off with the guns they had limbered in a hurry. These guns were redeployed on a hill above the campground while Moorman sent out skirmishers armed with pistols. These men soon came flying back to camp with a large body of enemy cavalry in their rear. The Federal troopers were heading right for James and the heart of the battalion camp.

James had no more time to strategize; it was time for him to react. With a sabre in hand, he rushed to the guns, calling to his men to follow. He wheeled around the first gun he came to, trained the piece to bear upon the charging Federal cavalry, and drove home a charge. The Federals were now within fifty yards of the cannon and many of them were blown out of their saddles.

"Men, you've fought around these guns in many battles! Your first and only duty is to die by them. Will you do it?" James bellowed out.

A chorus of elated voices rang in support. His courage inspired the artillerymen to fire canister shots into the continuous oncoming Federal troopers. James fearlessly was everywhere behind the four cannon. He seemed impervious to the sporadic counter-battery fire of the Federal artillery that rained down upon the camp.

He and his men fought off the Federal troopers with ramrods, sponges, and whatever else they could find to defend themselves and their guns. The fierce hand-to-hand combat was terrifying to him, but he kept his cool in the midst of the melee. Eventually the bravado of the Federal troopers diminished, and they withdrew to a safe distance.

James thought they would come again. But he and his men would be ready, for their lives depended upon it. He viewed the enemy reforming not one hundred yards to his front. The Federals had set fire to the camp, and their winter quarter log cabins were now in flames. He saw horses running through the flames around the quarters and artillerymen trying to catch them up. Smoke wafted all around, and James knew the skirmish was not over.

The Federals suddenly made another charge into the camp. At the same moment an explosion from one of Captain Chew's caissons went up in a fireball that plumed in smoke. James was deafened for a moment as the reverberation of the explosion shook the ground. The blast seemed to explode in his ear drums. At that moment the three other batteries of guns on the rear hillside opened on Custer's troopers. A fusillade of shells shrieked overhead. The reopening of the Confederate guns caused the Federal troopers to withdraw from the camp.

Chaos reigned as his men tried to get control of the Federal assault. They swiped their sticks and sabres at the Federals. It was mayhem.

James roared out the command, "Mount!"

Twenty men followed his lead and grabbed sabres, clubs, and fence rails scavenged from around the campfires. James seized the moment and jumped up on one of the hastily saddled horses. His horse was shot by an errant Federal bullet. The beast staggered, sank from under him, and then rolled on him. He dragged himself from beneath the bleeding animal, rose to his feet, and rushed to a lead horse at one of the guns to the rear. He leaped upon its back and struck its rump with his sabre to force the animal to move.

"Charge!" James roared out.

At the forefront of his men, James led a headlong charge into the Federal cavalry that had repositioned just outside the camp. As he left the camp, enemy horsemen dashed toward him. The melee was tangled and confused. Blue and gray fought it out, neither gaining the upper hand. Men fell and horses ran wild through the camp.

With two of his gunners at his side in the midst of the melee, James pulled his revolver and opened fire upon the enemy horsemen. The line of Federals replied with a volley of carbine fire. Men went down. He realized that his gunners were all that stood between Custer's horsemen and his guns in the camp. He knew his gunners would have to stand on their own and defend the camp, with their only support coming from the rear as his fellow artillerists continued the frantic long-range firing.

Finally, as the skirmish ended, James made a rash decision to pursue the Federal cavalry. It made no difference to him how outnumbered he was. His ire was up, and this always had urged him forward.

Darkness had surrounded them on the move north. He finally arrived at Barboursville after a twelve-hour chase of Custer's brigade, taking prisoners as they went. When they got to the town, James and his men stopped to get a drink at the house of a citizen. The woman walked out of her house and reported to him that a great many Federal troopers had recently passed by her home.

"What's the matter?" the concerned citizen asked.

"We're chasing Custer and could use a drink of water," James said.

"Why you're none other than 'Old Jim Breathed' and your horse artillerymen, armed with fence rails," the citizen replied. "Your reputation precedes you, sir. You're more than welcome to my water."

The next day General Stuart reached the decimated camp. Freezing rains began to fall, prompting his artillerymen to proclaim that they wished the Yankees to be in the infernal regions. As the rain fell, it turned into sleet. Undeterred, the artillerymen set about the task of rebuilding their shacks and putting the camp back in order.

James returned to camp from Barboursville early that morning. He spied General Stuart surveying the artillerymen's camp. James dismounted the horse he had ridden hard. Both he and the animal were near exhaustion. James's first concern was for his men. He questioned a private who walked next to him as to casualties and then saluted General Stuart.

Stuart gathered the officers in the camp. He pulled off his gauntlets, rested his leg on a log, and placed the gauntlets on his knee. He gestured to the smoldering cabins that lay in ruin.

"I'm sensible of the distinguished gallantry which you have always displayed when you came in contact with the enemy. I can also assure you of my appreciation as your commanding general. I feel confident that Captain Breathed will soon be promoted for his fearlessness in saving the horse artillery from certain ruin."

"What should we do next?" James asked Stuart.

"You should labor to get your batteries in fighting trim as soon as possible. Your conduct in the recent attempt of the enemy here to seize your guns was in keeping with heroism, which has distinguished your career as a soldier," Stuart replied with a sigh. "I regret my necessary absence from my headquarters, which prevented me from seeing you on your recent visit."

"I was sorry that I missed you, too," James replied.

"Now I am expressing to you in person my congratulations upon your achievement, as well as my high appreciation of your gallantry."

General Stuart dismissed the officers. The general approached James and shook his hand. James, in his exhausted state, reckoned that the work and suffering he and his artillerymen had endured in this infernal war was but a prelude for the action to come.

36

The Next Man in the Link

Caught in the Spider's Web

MARCH 14TH THROUGH 15TH, 1864

THE HOUSE SERVANT WALKED with Mollie up the winding stair case toward the president's office. Mollie sat beside a round table next to President Davis's desk. She looked around the room and could not help but notice the huge map of the country that hung on the wall. A gasolier hung down in the center of the room, and a gas line came down from it to a lamp on the president's desk. The entire room was carpeted with a burgundy diamond-patterned weave. The door opened and Mollie stood.

"Miss Macgill, please stay seated," the president said as he approached her. He took her white-gloved hand and kissed it. "You look very pretty as always."

"Thank you, Mr. Davis," she said as she sat back down at the table. "Can you tell me anything of my beau James Breathed of the Stuart Horse Artillery?"

"The news is not good, so I've heard from General Stuart. They were encamped in winter quarters near Charlottesville when Federal cavalry under General Custer attacked their encampment. Custer's men destroyed the encampment, stole equipment, but Captain Breathed wasn't hurt. In fact, he and twenty of his men, armed with fence rails, chased Custer's men for twelve hours after the raid. You should be proud of the captain."

"Sounds like the James Breathed I know and love."

The president looked toward the map, sighed as his fingers pulled on the tuft of hair grown from his chin.

"I've called for you because I've an important task I need you to accomplish. Mind you, it could be dangerous. But knowing what you've already accomplished for this country, I'm sure you're up to the demands of the task."

She felt her stomach churn with anxiety, but she knew it was the motivational sort that had heightened her senses in her past adventures of espionage. She removed her white gloves and, with her right hand, patted her bun of hair on the back of her head, a nervous twitch she had.

"Sir, I'm always ready and able to serve my country, regardless of the danger."

"Good!" Davis said. He shifted in his place across the table from her. "Your intelligence on Mary was excellent. I planted on my desk false information after I spoke with you and your father on Christmas Day. The results of which did materialize through Federal reaction to the false intelligence. This confirmed for me that Mary was the inside leak that I had suspected was within the Executive Mansion. She has since disappeared without a trace. I feel betrayed and mystified by her sudden disappearance. Who knows what her real intentions were?"

"With all due respect, Mr. President, you may recall I questioned Mrs. Davis the day we first came to the Mansion in relation to who Mary was. Something about her eyes I didn't trust."

"Yes, I well recall your statement. Now I want to find the next man in the link of the Federal Richmond underground. With your help this can be accomplished. There is a trusted Union man who is a clerk in the Adjutant-General's Department at Richmond. We know about him, but he doesn't know we know this. He has access to information showing our regiments, brigades, divisions and corps, their movements, and where they're stationed. We monitor what information he sees."

"Sounds like you can do what you please with this Yankee traitor."

"Yes we can. We can use him to our advantage and here is how we can do it."

The president handed her a sealed envelope from his breast pocket.

"I trust you with this missive. The envelope and stationery are all the same as that found in this traitor's office at the Adjutant-General's Department. We've an expert man on copying handwriting who we used to create this missive."

"Now that Mary is gone, you've no way to get the information to Mr. McNiven without being exposed." Mollie responded.

"Correct. We've two newspaper boys at work around the Capitol building who are double agents. They're about fifteen in age, both with sandy blond hair with green eyes. Tomorrow afternoon at four o'clock sharp I want you to be in your landau carriage in front of the Capitol building, facing toward the Market District, on Capitol Street. You're to tie a white ribbon on the bridle of one of the horses before you depart your home. At this appointed time a newspaper boy will approach the carriage to sell you a paper. Let him into the carriage and then drive toward Mr. McNiven's bakery on 8th Street. It's better you don't know the newspaper boy's name."

She settled in her chair to move a little closer to the table as Mr. Davis spoke. She no longer noticed the room. Instead her eyes focused on the white tuft of hair on his chin. She hung on every word that came from his mouth as if her life depended upon it, which it could, as he had warned. She didn't see any inherent danger, so far described in the plan, but she expected it shortly.

"Are you afraid of any confusion at the Capitol building or maybe of the boy being spotted getting out of the carriage?" Mollie asked.

"In relation to the pick-up, no. There are many people around the Capitol building that time of day. But the drop-off must take place on Broad Street and 9th in front of the Broad Street Hotel so there is no chance of anyone in the underground spotting our boy getting out of your carriage. You're to switch letters with the boy on the ride to the drop-off. He'll give you the missive from the Adjutant-General's Department and you're to give him this envelope. Our missive has some correct intelligence and some false intelligence in relation to the spring campaign. Bring to me the boy's missive so we can see what other false intelligence is getting through to the Federal's high command."

"Sounds to me like that missive might be almost as important as the information I got to General Lee about the 191 Order in September of '62."

"Let's just say a lot of lives and the balance of the Confederate States of America may be determined by this missive getting into the hands of the Federal military high command. But your task is not over after you've let the newspaper boy out of the carriage. I want you to instruct your coachman to follow Mr. McNiven in his carriage to wherever he goes after the bakery closes. It'll be dark, more than likely, when McNiven leaves with the missive to deliver it to the next man in the link of the underground."

"Alfred has been a faithful servant, and he has gotten me in and out of some very dangerous situations throughout the course of this war. I know I can trust him to stay far enough behind Mr. McNiven's carriage so as to not be seen, but close enough not to lose him in the streets of Richmond."

"Excellent, Miss Macgill, your country is depending upon you. Now take the envelope and get Alfred to drive you home so you can get a good night of sleep and be ready for tomorrow afternoon."

"Sir, if I discover the next man in the link, what should I do?"

"Come see me again and we shall discuss it. Good day, Miss Macgill," the president said as he escorted her to the office door.

In the next room there were a number of officers waiting for an audience with the president. She felt quite honored to be so trusted and in the presence of other distinguished officers of the Confederacy. She went downstairs and, at the bottom, encountered Mrs. Davis.

"My dearest Mollie, you were certainly right about Mary. She has disappeared without a trace and my husband will not tell me why."

"I'm sure he must have his reasons," Mollie replied. "I hope you're doing well. Taking care of your five children must certainly be a full-time job, on top of being First Lady of the Confederacy."

"Yes, I do stay busy."

"Have a blessed day, Mrs. Davis; I need to be getting home. Lovely spring we're having."

"Good to see you again, Mollie. Godspeed."

Mollie politely curtsied to Mrs. Davis as a servant opened the door so she could exit the entry hall. Alfred stood ready at the door of the landau, helped her into the carriage, and closed the door. As the carriage pulled off, she looked out the back oval window of the carriage to see Mrs. Davis waving good-bye. She waved back as Alfred drove her home.

Upon arriving at 316 East Franklin Street she let herself out of the carriage, not even waiting for Alfred to open the door for her. She rushed inside to an empty house. She felt a little guilty for her next action. She thought of having a cup of tea, but she knew her real intentions were more devious than having a simple tea. The teapot came to a whistle, but instead of pouring herself a cup of tea she removed the envelope from her handbag. She carefully steamed open the envelope and pulled out the missive and read:

13th inst. March, 1864

Army of the Potomac
General Longstreet 1st Corps preparing to lead attack to capture Norfolk, Va., feint to be made on Williamsburg. General Ewell's 2nd Corps on Rapidan above Mine Run and General Hill's 3rd Corps west around Orange Court House, both at some distance from Chancellorsville and Wilderness. Stuart Horse Artillery encamped Charlottesville. General Stuart's Cavalry Corps west of Richmond. City of Richmond lightly garrisoned, prepare for Union attack on Capital City.

Babcock

Her hands, shakily and quickly, placed the missive back in the envelope while the adhesive was still sticky. She sealed the envelope back the way it had been when she received it. She felt naughty, but she figured if she was going to play such a vital role in the future of the Confederacy, she had a right to know what intelligence she was passing along to the Federals. Besides, she thought, what woman with her feminine wiles intact would not have wanted to know what was in the envelope?

⁂

The next morning Mollie was up early and, like a busy bee, she went straight into the work of cleaning the house. After breakfast with her two sisters and father, she went out to the back servant quarters to find Alfred.

When she found Alfred she said, "Alfred, I want the carriage ready to depart here at half past three and not a second later. I want this white ribbon tied to the bridle on the left side. We'll be making a trip to the Capitol building where I'll be meeting a young newspaper boy. He'll come with us to 9th and Broad, where you'll stop at the Broad Street Hotel on the corner to let him out. Then we'll move the carriage to 8th and Broad Street and wait for Mr. Thomas McNiven to leave after he closes the bakery for the day at six o'clock. You're to follow his carriage from a safe distance so he doesn't know he is being followed. It'll be dark, so you can't lose him. When he gets to where he stops his carriage, you must act quickly to conceal our carriage so I can use my opera glasses to see whom he is talking to," she said emphatically.

"Yessa, Miss Mollie, wheez can do this fo you. Sounds like trobles, so best brings your Colt revolver gun," Alfred responded.

"Yes, that is always a good idea; it has come in to usefulness in the past."

She returned to the house and after dinner she went back to her cleaning chores. Her two sisters and Miss O'Shaunsay helped get the house into immaculate condition. She showed no sign of anxiety to her sisters, but she felt the tension growing within as the hour neared. At half past three she told her sisters that Alfred was taking her to see some friends. She advised them that she was not sure when she would return, and so they should not count on her for supper.

Alfred was ready as she had requested, and they were off toward the Capitol on Franklin Street. When Alfred got to 9th Street he turned left and then made a right onto Capitol Street. He turned the carriage around so that it faced northwest toward the Market District. It wasn't long before there was a knock on the carriage door. She opened it.

"Yes, come in," she said to the newspaper boy who was dressed in bib overalls. His hands were dirty from the newspaper ink, and smudges blotched his face.

Alfred tapped the horses with the reins and they moved out. The boy sat across from her. He looked at her curiously.

"Do you have something for me, Miss?"

"Yes, and you've something for me, am I correct?"

"Yes, Miss, here is your envelope."

"And here is yours. We're to let you out at the Broad Street Hotel."

"Yes, Miss. Would you like a paper, for free!"

"Sure, I need to keep current on the news."

The carriage stopped. Up ahead, people were going in and out of the hotel. The boy opened the door, sprung out onto the cobblestone road, and quickly closed the door behind him. Alfred moved the carriage up another block so that Mollie could see the dock. A bakery wagon had just come back from its delivery and had backed into the dock. She saw on the other side of the wagon a horse and carriage, which she assumed to be Mr. McNiven's. She did see the newspaper boy go in and come out of the bakery office and then disappear into the crowded market. Now she simply had to wait. Fortunately for her, the weather was pleasant.

Alfred had climbed down from the driver's seat and removed the white ribbon from the bridle. She had not instructed him to do this, but it was the smart thing to do, for it brought attention to the carriage. She read the paper, concealing her face behind it, for Mr. McNiven certainly knew her face well. Two hours passed slowly, though the advancing darkness was to their advantage. She dropped the newspaper and peered through the side window. Mr. McNiven came out of the office next to the dock. She bent forward and tapped the glass behind the driver's seat. Alfred tapped back.

Mollie watched Mr. McNiven climb into his one horse buggy and pull up to 8th and Broad Street. He turned left onto Broad Street and made his way southeast. Alfred turned the carriage around and fell into pursuit. There were other horses and carriages on Broad Street, but the number of Richmonders who now owned horses had dwindled because the military had taken all the horse flesh they could get to fight the war. Mr. McNiven continued southeast on Broad Street past the Union Hill District into the Church Hill District.

When Mr. McNiven arrived at 23rd Street he turned, then turned again on to East Grace Street. She saw the turns and tapped on the glass again as her carriage rumbled up into the district. Alfred tapped back. She hoped he knew now was the time for real stealth. The buggy stopped in front of a large mansion on East Grace Street. At that moment Alfred turned the landau down a back alley behind some tall shrubs. The carriage was completely hidden from plain view of the mansion. But she was able to view out the back oval window, and with the aid of her opera glasses, see what was happening at the front door of the mansion. The entrance way was lit by gas lamps. She watched through the glasses as Mr. McNiven walked up the front entranceway and knocked on the door.

It was not long before a pretty lady came to the door. She was shocked to see Elizabeth Van Lew standing at the doorway. Mr. McNiven reached into his coat breast pocket and pulled out the envelope. He handed it to her, they hardly spoke a word, and he returned to his buggy. Mollie quickly tapped on the front glass of the carriage and Alfred was off in a split second through the alley.

As the carriage rumbled back into Richmond, Mollie thought about where she had met Elizabeth. It dawned on her that it was at the Taffy Pulling Party around Christmas time. She remembered that many aristocratic, society-type women attended this party. The Van Lews were among the gathered, for they were of this old-line ilk in Richmond.

Suddenly, Alfred knocked on the carriage window pane and exclaimed, "Miss Mollie, wheez got a darky following us on a horse!"

She picked up her opera glasses and looked out the back oval window to see a horseman following them in hot pursuit of the carriage. She now believed that the danger Mr. Davis had predicted was coming to be truthful.

"Drive on, Alfred, faster!" she exclaimed to him as this was all that she could think to say to him.

The dust flew from the wheels of the carriage as Alfred raced through the streets of Richmond back to 316 East Franklin Street. She felt nearly helpless. All she could do was look out the oval window with her glasses. She was sure of the rider's facial features as the carriage raced homeward. She memorized them as if her life depended upon doing so. When Alfred finally pulled the carriage to the rear of her home, the pursuing horseman disappeared into the darkness of the night.

It was when she felt safe again that she wondered how it could be that the next man in the link of the Richmond underground was actually a woman. Mr. Davis would be most interested in her discovery, she knew, but this news would have to wait until morning when her nerves had settled. And, she thought, *Who was the darky who chased them home?*

37

The Inferno of the Wilderness

MAY 5TH THROUGH 8TH, 1864

JAMES LOOKED TO HIS rear as he raced Billy along the Catharpin Road to find Dr. Almond's house. A long line of horse artillery trailed behind him, dust flying like a brown cloud. He thought they were running late. When he finally located the house, he sat Billy and directed Johnston, Shoemaker, and Thomson's batteries into the open fields around the house. He saw Major Chew, his recently promoted battalion commander, sitting his horse awaiting the arrival of the horse artillery. James rode over to Major Chew

"Major Breathed, secure the twelve guns in parade formation, and I'll be over to speak with them in short order."

"Yes, sir," James saluted. He spurred Billy into the dust created by the two hundred and sixteen horses that were needed to operate the three batteries of horse artillery. They were the vanguard, along with the cavalry, of the entire Army of Northern Virginia. There would be yeomen's work ahead to screen the Confederate army from the Federals.

James figured the temperature had to be approaching ninety as he pulled out his pocket watch. It was eleven o'clock. He noticed all around him the sumac, pine trees, and dense undergrowth that surrounded the open fields. He had fought here a year ago, so he and his artillerists knew the terrain. This field was not easy on men, horses, or equipment, all of which needed to maneuver nimbly in order to fire effectively.

He signaled for Captains Shoemaker, Thomson, and Johnston, and then spoke to them, "Forward into battery—left oblique into parade formation so that Major Chew can address the men."

James saluted his captains and reined Billy back toward Major Chew. Chew sported a thick moustache that matched his chestnut brown hair. James had fought with him from the time his Ashby battery was transferred over from General Jackson's

279

command to that of John Pelham. He guessed why General Stuart had promoted Chew to commander of the battalion and made James second in command. James felt it must have been in relation to Chew's Virginia Military Institute credentials. But that was no longer a concern for either of them, for they had talked it through as gentlemen.

James and Major Chew rode side-by-side to address the artillerists. Major Chew proclaimed, "Stuart Horse Artillerists and officers, today we face a determined foe who has returned to the Wilderness after being severely routed and turned back a year ago!" Huzzahs and cheers went up from the men in parade formation. "We'll once again turn them back above the Rapidan all the way to Washington City. East of us on the Catharpin Road is the vanguard cavalry of the Army of the Potomac, already engaged with our cavalrymen, I'm sure. I'll be leaving here with a section of Captain Thomson's guns to support our troopers. Major Breathed will remain here in command. Godspeed!"

James watched as Major Chew, Captain Thomson, and the section of guns with loaded ammunition caissons exited Dr. Almond's fields. Then James gave the command for the artillerists and their horses to stand at ease and fill canteens. The time passed slowly for him, and he seated himself on the front porch of Dr. Almond's house. Other officers joined him on the front porch, though the conversation was muted. James, left to his own thoughts, pondered many subjects ranging from special providence to Mollie. Out of nowhere, a courier came careening on his horse around the stone gate into Dr. Almond's fields. He rode directly to the house.

"Major Breathed, I've a dispatch for you from Major Chew."

James took the dispatch, opened it, and read:

2:00 P.M.
Northeast of Corbin's Bridge on Catharpin Road

Major Breathed,
Heavy cavalry fighting. Deploy Thomson section and Johnston Battery to our support, posthaste!
Very respectfully, your obedient servant,

R. P. Chew
Major, Artillery

James quickly gave the order to limber up the six guns. He led his men through the stone gate and rode east on the Catharpin Road. When he reached Richard's Shop he began to see the carnage from the day's cavalry battle. Troopers in blue and gray, and their horses, lay wounded and dying; sabres, carbines, and revolvers were scattered over the road and to the sides of it. The farther he lead his artillerists east, the more visceral evidence he saw—clear indication that there had been a very bloody contest along this road only hours before. The woods were on fire in places, and the stench of burning human and horse flesh filled his nostrils.

He galloped Billy across Corbin's Bridge over the Po River. He heard cries of wounded men along the path as the underbrush burned and engulfed the wounded. Then he heard the all too familiar sound of artillery fire. There was Captain Thomson and his guns on a knoll to the left of the road. He turned back to holler, "Left oblique—March!"

He reunited with Major Chew and brought his guns into the line of battle amidst thick pines. He conferred with the major as they sat their horses behind the guns.

"Major Breathed, we've at least two Federal guns to our left with a cavalry regiment. Farther to our front, on the Catharpin Road, there're two Federal cavalry regiments."

After James had the position of the Federals, he ordered Captain Johnston to open fire and knock out the Federal guns with case shot. The newly arrived section of Captain Thomson's guns went to work on the cavalry that was fighting on the Catharpin Road. A dense, asphyxiating pall of spent black powder hung low in the pines and, ironically, in the innocently blooming dogwoods. The haze made it very difficult for him to tell friend from foe as he tried to direct the eight cannonading guns.

It was not long before General Rosser and Captain Myers rode to the artillery and up to his side.

"General, we're doing what we can with the artillery to aid your fight," James reported to General Rosser who was out of breath.

James then remembered that the Virginian had been wounded at the fight at Kelly's Ford and recalled his valiant service at the Rummel Barn during the Gettysburg clash.

"Major, we can use all the help we can get; it has been a long and bloody day," General Rosser responded.

"General Rosser, I've a company of troopers on the other side of the Catharpin Road. What're your orders?" Captain Myers of White's Comanches asked.

"Let 'em out, Myers, let 'em out! Old White's in there, knocking them right and left."

"That sounds like my cousin, Lige White. He never did care much for Yankee cavalry!" James confessed to General Rosser as the general turned his horse and rode back toward the fight.

At that moment the Federals got off a well-directed case shot that exploded over Myers and James. The captain's horse reared and then bucked as the balls and shrapnel pieces rained down upon them. Nevertheless, James kept the guns hot at this position for a few more hours.

Just as James thought things were cooling off for the day, a fresh wave of Federal troopers charged west on the Catharpin Road. James and his men were now surrounded by suffocating sulfuric, blue-hued clouds of smoke as the cast iron canister balls shrieked out of the muzzles of the cannon toward the fresh troopers.

Colonel White rallied on the guns and braced himself for another charge.

"James, thanks for the support. It has made a difference in our driving back the Yankee cavalry," Colonel White commented as he wiped the black powder from his face with his gauntlet.

"Colonel, how can we fight those fellows with no ammunition? We'd as well have rocks as empty pistols," Captain Myers said to Colonel White.

"What are our sabres for?" Colonel White responded. He slapped his sabre on his horse's rear and inspired his troopers to follow him into a headlong charge east on the Catharpin Road.

James's artillerymen had driven off the Federal artillery. Now he focused on helping his cousin drive off the Federal cavalry. He began to change his tactics.

"Case shot, fifteen hundred yards—two second fuse—load!"

His artillerymen did as he commanded and elevated the screws so as to shoot over White's Comanches.

"Fire!" James cried out.

He took his field glasses from their case and spied the action of his cousin to his front. They were getting blasted by revolver fire.

"Reload!" James ordered. He knew his cousin really needed his help now.

"Wheels clear," Private Matthews shouted back to him.

"Fire!" James hollered. He had become ubiquitous and forgetful that he was no longer a captain, but a major.

The brilliant sunset ended the fighting for the day. The shadows that were cast amongst the thick tall pines made mortal combat impossible to continue in the killing fields. He and his artillerymen retired to the western bank of the Po River to bivouac for the night, far behind enemy lines. He ordered Captain Johnston to gather his worn-out and fought-out artillerymen so that he might address his old battery. He thought he needed to let them know that his new rank didn't mean he wasn't there for them as he had been since the formation of the battery.

After they had consumed their rations and gathered in the darkness with lanterns flickering, James spoke to them, as their friend and commander. "Gentlemen, today you fought well! I was once again proud of the way you handled your pieces. Privates James Ryan, Charles Wilson, and Edward O'Brien were wounded. I pray for their recovery. Private Ryan may lose a leg. I want to share with you from my studies of the classics of literature these thoughts from *Inferno*, best known as Dante's *Inferno*. *The eternal fire, which causes them to glow within, shows them red, as thou seest, in this low Hell.* Men, today we saw this low hell to which Dante refers.

"And further, I quote Dante in relation to this inferno which we all experienced today by this thought which I think best describes our adversary Lieutenant General U.S. Grant and the man behind him, father Abraham—the Rail Splitter, *Behold the savage beast with the pointed tail, that passes mountains, and breaks through walls and weapons; behold him that pollutes the whole world.* This Army of the Potomac pollutes our world of Southern culture, our lands, our way of life, and everything we hold dear in our lives! I implore us to fight like demons ourselves to stop the Yankees in this hell of a wilderness which burns from where the savage beast's pointed tail has set these woods on fire!"

"Major, we'll follow you into the fires of hell to slay the beast; we'll go anywhere you lead us!" private Matthews yelled out as the other men gave a rousing huzzah and the Rebel Yell went up.

"Boys," James replied, "I was just thinking as I've been talking with you here that I would rather command you old ragged rebels than be in command of Longstreet's Corps. We've been together many years now. I feel compelled to share with you some of my spiritual beliefs. I'm a Christian man. I believe in the Divine Creator who sent his only Son into this world. Because his Son rose from the tomb on Easter morning, we all have faith in the things hoped for, but not seen. We know we're living in a low hell as we fight here. Some of us may give the last full measure of devotion to our country. If you fight in fear of dying, you'll not fight with total gallantry. But, if you fight providentially, knowing that in faith there is a life after this life with the Divine Creator and his Son, then I believe you'll fight like Spartans at Thermopylae, to the very last man. The Spartans also fought an army of mercenaries who were invading their home lands, as the Yankees have invaded ours."

James looked around at the faces of the men gathered close to him, the lantern light flickering off their faces. They all heard the hooting owls and the haunting calls of whip-poor-wills as James spoke of Christ who himself was tested in his own wilderness trial by his adversary, Satan. James thought the beast of the Army of the Potomac was challenging him and every man in front of him, just as Satan challenged Christ to remain faithful to his Father the Creator.

"Gentlemen, this is a Holy War and a Crusade to rid the invading infidels from our soil," James said. "Their mystical religion has become that of saving the Union. Our cause is in line with that of the Creator. We must fight again to expel these infidels from our lands. General Grant will not relent, I fear, but we must persevere! Who is with me?"

"We're with you, Major," Private Zimmerman exclaimed as another round of huzzahs went up from the sooty-faced artillerists.

"Sleep well, gentlemen. We've got fightin' yet to do."

A day passed before James and his old battery were called back into early morning service.

"Major Breathed, I want you and Captain Johnston to report with your battery to General Fitz Lee on the Brock Road. He has barricaded both sides of the road overnight with logs. He expects heavy fighting along that road today," Major Chew ordered from his horse.

"Sir, we'll deploy immediately. After a day of rest the boys are ready for a brawl!"

James conferred with Captain Johnston and told him of their orders.

"Cannoneers! Prepare to mount!" Captain Johnston roared, riding back to his artillerists. "Mount!"

Again forgetting he was no longer the captain, James hollered out, "By piece—from the right—front into column—March!"

James trotted the column toward the Brock Road in search of General Fitzhugh Lee. When James came upon the 4th Virginia Cavalry "Black Hats," he heard one of them holler out, "Give way! Here comes Major Breathed of Stuart's Horse Artillery!"

James graciously removed his kepi and raised his right hand above his head as if he was Caesar himself passing by.

It was not long before they arrived at Todd's Tavern. He saw two bedraggled old wooden structures close to the intersection of the Catharpin and the Brock Roads. He rode a mile north on the Brock Road and discovered the general. The dense forest had given way to rolling farm lands.

"General Lee, where would you like us to deploy?" James asked as he saluted him.

"Major, we've two Yankee cavalry divisions to contend with today. You know your gunners better than I. Deploy for close range support of our three divisions. I've two lines of works built alongside the road. Wickham extends the line on the right; Lomax on the left."

"Sir, yes, sir! I'll deploy in close support!"

James could hardly keep from vomiting due to the stink of decomposing bodies and horses that littered the area from the two previous days of fighting. Men in uniform with their bloated bodies were strewn all about. The ball was about to begin, and he promenaded his guns to the dance floor.

His artillerists had been doing their deadly work when, at ten o'clock, James looked at his pocket watch to notice the time. Bullets had been whizzing by him and his men all morning, clearing the bark from the trees and dropping branches all around them. Then a courier arrived with a dispatch from General Lee ordering him to pull back south of Todd's Tavern to the Hart Farm. James retired his battery to the wide open acres of the farm.

"Gunners, prepare to open fire—Fire!" James roared out from his redeployed position, sending missiles of destruction into the Federal cavalry.

Counter-battery fire immediately fell into their ranks, wounding several of his men and horses.

"Major Breathed, General Wickham has fallen back into General Lomax's line. What can you do with your artillery to stop the Yankee advance?" General Lee asked of him.

"You shall soon see, General!"

With an hour of light left before sunset, James gathered his lieutenants. "Gentlemen, this is going to be a bold move, certainly not one described in the West Point

Artillery Manuals. We're going to limber front and charge through our cavalry line to within one hundred yards of the Yankee cavalry line of battle. Then we shall unlimber and let loose with double canister, driving them back to hell, from whence they came!" he told them confidently.

"Are you sure, Major?" Captain Johnston asked of him.

"Yes!"

When a sufficient amount of time had passed to prepare the artillerists for what was to happen next, Captain Johnston gave the order. "Form line advancing—left oblique—trot—March!"

James, at the lead, moved out in front of his gunners. When they arrived at the Confederate cavalry line of battle, it parted in four places to let them pass through. He heard one cavalryman say, "My God! Jim Breathed must be mad!"

James led his men to a most unpleasant position on the field. They quickly unlimbered and turned the muzzles, loaded canister, and opened fire. He saw dismounted Federals falling to the ground and others running for cover. Mounted men were tumbling to their deaths as their bloodied horses' flesh was torn from their bodies. The site was horrific even for him to watch, but the carnage of man and horses made him exuberant.

James looked around as the shadows of darkness lengthened their etchings upon the battlefield. He thought his gunners had possibly saved General Lee from the complete destruction of his cavalry. He and his artillerists retired from the field, and he reported to General Fitz Lee.

"Sir, your orders, sir?" James inquired.

"Major Breathed, I've never seen artillery charge cavalry in all my years of military service. Well done! We'll have to refortify our barricades along the Brock Road tonight for they'll be coming back this way in the morning. I'll need your men to help."

"You shall have them, sir. In the early hours of the morning, I propose placing my guns immediately on our line of battle to inflict great damage to the enemy."

"Major, we must hold long enough for Anderson's First Corps to position to our south as they're coming east on the Shady Grove Church Road. If we don't hold our first position, you're to fall back to the split of the Old Road and the New Road and find high ground at that farm on the left of the road. Place your battery there. I expect to see you along the Brock Road barricades early in the morning. Goodnight."

After a night of no rest and all work, James and his faithful artillerymen were in a supportive position to General Lee's dismounted cavalry division alongside the Brock Road. As they were located in dense dark woods, he would only be able to use the pieces in short range against charging Federal cavalry, mostly canister he surmised.

"Here they come boys!" James shouted along the line of battle. "Wait for it, wait for it! Fire!—Reload!"

James heard the first volley from the dismounted Confederate cavalrymen discharge. The thick hue of blue smoke from their carbines and his four cannon filled the opaque forest. Then he heard rapid firing from the Federal Spencer carbines. Kneeling gray cavalrymen dropped to the forest floor for protection from the seven shot carbines. He felt the advantage was clearly in the hands of the Federals. But his men did not quail under the withering fire. Instead, they continued to load and fire canister at will. He pulled his revolver and unloaded a few rounds into the fast approaching Federals, to no avail.

"Limber—front! Left oblique—March at a trot!" James ordered his artillerymen.

Before they were overrun by the blue cavalry, he had decided it was best to fall back to the second position. When they emerged from the dense woods onto the Brock Road, James had them at a canter. Alongside his artillery pieces were hundreds of troopers in gray racing their horses to the same second position. Bullets whizzed by all of their heads. When they reached the intersection of the Brock and Gordon roads, James led his men into a freshly plowed field. The mud hindered their speed, but the knoll he sighted to the left of the farm house required them to move through the field. He realized that there was no other route across the flat open terrain.

Arriving upon the knoll he commanded, "Unlimber—front—load case shot— one thousand yards!"

To his front all he could see were hundreds of cavalrymen forming squadrons on their guidons. The order to "dismount" rung out, and horse holders took three of their comrades' horses to the rear. An aggressive dismounted fight broke out between the blue and the gray cavalrymen as James's artillerists began lobbing case shot into the rear ranks of the Federal cavalry, knocking numerous men down at a shot.

James rode Billy behind the guns on the knoll, and then exclaimed, "Fire at will, boys; we're driving them Yankee cavalry boys back!"

He observed the Federal cavalrymen through his field glasses. They were beginning to pull back as General Lee's cavalrymen pressed forward. Thick battle smoke hung pall-like over the fields as the two cavalry divisions fought it out. Then he heard the blue cavalrymen's bugler call retreat, and the Federal forces withdrew from the field.

Suddenly, James saw why they withdrew. In the pine woods, one half mile away, Federal infantry came crashing out in a long line of battle. In grand array, the blue line of infantry swept over the field with flags unfurled, marching toward his position. The situation had now turned itself, for General Lee's small, much-reduced division was up against an entire corps of infantry. James could only guess that the Federal numbers were thousands of men strong.

"Keep up your fire, boys! I want those Yankee infantrymen shot down like fish in a barrel!"

"Yes, sir! Major, we're running low on long-range ordnance," Sergeant Hoxton responded.

"Don't worry! They'll be on us soon enough, and then we'll fire canister," James ordered.

He watched the blue wave of infantry approach steadily, backing off the dismounted gray cavalrymen. The blue line of battle, less than a quarter of a mile away, prompted General Lee to ride back to the knoll.

"Major, you're ordered to retire your guns," General Lee commanded.

"A few more rounds, sir! We've still got canister to fire!" James responded.

The minie balls were whizzing all around as he sat Billy.

Suddenly, the infantry began to break off. They seemed to be trying to out-flank him and enfilade his guns.

"Lieutenant Cosgrove, limber your section and prepare to retire the guns," James ordered.

At that moment a bullet grazed Private Matthews' head and knocked him senseless to the ground.

"Private Clem, get that man to the rear!" James exclaimed as he heard two loud thuds. He leaned forward to see blood streaming from Billy's front quarter. The horse tumbled to the ground, throwing James out of the saddle.

"Damnit, Captain! Those people have killed my horse! Get the first section off the field. We'll give them Yankees double canisters for killin' my horse!" James quipped.

"Fire!" Captain Johnston hollered.

James observed, at two hundred yards distance, dozens of infantrymen being shredded by the iron balls of canister.

"Captain, retire your third gun from the field," James ordered at the moment a minie ripped through the captain's shoulder. A flow of blood dribbled down his shoulder and stained his armpit. "Captain, stay on your horse and go with the gun. I'll tend to the last gun and keep them at bay until you're clear of the field."

James ordered the limbering of the fourth gun, and the four-horse team was brought up from the rear. At the moment the gun was limbered, the lead driver was hit and knocked from his horse. Then seconds later, the wheel driver's arm was shattered by a minie. James helped the wounded man to the ground.

"Take to the rear, men. I vowed to never let one of my guns fall into the enemy's hands! By God, I shall stand by my words!" James said to the two wounded men as the Federals were now within one hundred yards of the gun.

James jumped on the lead horse and began to drive the gun from the field when he heard familiar thuds. His horse dropped to the ground, rolling upon him as it did. He pulled his bowie knife, cut the traces off the horse, loosened himself, and mounted the second lead horse. As he reined the horse forward, he again heard the thuds of metal meeting horseflesh. Down went the other lead horse. When he peered over the dead animal's body, he saw the infantry within seventy-five yards of him.

He heard the cry go out from one of the approaching Federals, "Surrender that gun, you Rebel sumbitch!"

With mortal peril knocking at his door, he slunk to the rear of the second dead horse and cut the traces. Then with all the courage and stamina he could muster, he mounted one of the wheel horses and spurred it with all the life he had left in him. The horse cantered to the rear. As he moved out, he turned to the infantrymen, placed his thumb to his nose and wiggled his fingers in defiance.

He rode the wheel horse, pulling the gun down the Old Road to the Spindle farm. There he found cover behind Laurel Hill and Anderson's First Corps that had now arrived. The Confederate forces were firmly entrenched to meet the enemy infantry that he, moments earlier, had escaped from and delayed at the knoll.

James exhaustedly reflected back to his training in the classics and King Leonidas and the Spartans at Thermopylae. The Spartans had bought time for the Greek Navy to get into place in order to stop Xerxes's fleet of Persian ships filled with mercenaries. James felt utterly alone in this moment, his lone gun behind him.

James and his men had been grossly outnumbered, yet he had bought time for General Anderson to get his infantry into position in order to stop the beast from getting to Spotsylvania Court House. He wondered, *If he had fought to his death as a Spartan, and had his Thermopylian destiny fulfilled as he had once studied on the front porch of Bai-Yuka, would he have done for the cause a greater good that he so much desired to do?*

The question would haunt him. However, he felt assured the special providence of his Creator was with him this day. When he finally had rested a bit and his body had relaxed, he pulled out his watch to see it was only half past eight in the morning. It had been a most difficult day—and it had hardly begun.

38

Loyalty unto Death

May 10th through 11th, 1864

James and his battery were sent by General Stuart to stop the Federal cavalry from getting to Richmond. A day of rest after his stand at the Alsop House provided him with some respite, but it was not long lived. His friend Captain Johnston was wounded, so he encouraged Lieutenant Shanks, who replaced Johnston, to move the battery posthaste behind General Wickham's brigade of cavalrymen southeast from Spotsylvania Court House toward Richmond. James's tattered and exhausted artillerists were still intact as a unit and they drove the red-nostrilled four-up teams of horses pulling guns and caissons down roads behind the cavalry. The Confederate capital was now at stake.

His artillerymen and the cavalry first encountered General Phillip Sheridan's Federal cavalrymen at Mitchell's Store where Generals Fitz Lee, Williams Wickham, and Lunsford Lomax talked with General Stuart, but he did not engage his guns. Night was confused with day as he had marched through the darkness for hours, but there was more to come. He understood that the cavalry had to beat General Sheridan to the crossroads of Richmond, at all costs. Hence he hastened his men forward.

James arrived at the intersection of the Mountain Road and the Telegraph Road after two days on the move, the last of which was an all-night march. His 1st Stuart battery horses were jaded, and the collar harnesses had rubbed the horses' necks raw. General Stuart placed his battery on the right flank of General Wickham's brigade. Like an orchestra conductor, the general then placed his other six cannon on the crest of the hill, with Griffin's Baltimore Light Artillery at the center of the symphony in reserve on the Telegraph Road. Hart's South Carolina section was the bass drum to the left of Lomax's line along the Telegraph Road.

The Federal cavalry had arrived on the Mountain Road and was in position to the south, close to Yellow Tavern, an abandoned hostelry, on the Brook Turnpike only six miles from Richmond.

The ball once again opened mid-morning. James could see the Federal troops in the open fields not a half mile from his position.

"Load—case shot—thirteen hundred yards," James ordered from his new steed. Lieutenant Shanks repeated the order to his sergeants.

"Fire!" James commanded. Shortly thereafter, shells rained into the vast numbers of blue cavalrymen.

The counter-battery fire soon followed the initial firing from his guns. James pulled his field glasses from their case and viewed the situation before him as if he were Napoleon at Waterloo. Federal cavalry charges and Confederate counter charges raged all day and into the afternoon. When there was a lull in the fight, he rode from his position on the right flank of Wickham's line to the Telegraph Road.

The afternoon was upon him when he rode up to General Stuart on the Telegraph Road. The general told James that the Confederate cavalrymen who defended the road had been pushed north, but that they were already turning the Federals back. The general gave James a final order. "Breathed! Take command of all the mounted men in the road and hold it against whatever comes. If this road is lost, we're gone!"

James saluted the general whom he so greatly admired. Then James spurred his horse forward into the melee with no consideration as to who might follow him. He only thought to obey his general's orders. As a thunderstorm broke and torrents of rain began to fall, he headed south on the Telegraph Road directly into the maelstrom with mud shooting up from the hooves of his horse.

It was not far into his perilous journey that he ran headlong into a Federal cavalier dressed in a black velvet jacket, with a blue shirt and the jacket collar turned over the shirt collar. A brigadier's star was on each corner of the jacket. The slouch hat and a red scarf cravat marked the man as an important foe. James's ire was up, and he made a beeline for the red scarf. Seeing red himself, he crossed sabres with the Federal cavalier whose blond locks covered the back of his neck.

James exchanged a number of sabre slashes with the brigadier. He wheeled his horse about in order to slash at him again. The curly golden locks of the brigadier enraged him. He wanted nothing more than to cut them off with his sabre and severe his head from his body. The two officers fought to a draw, however, and James moved on to find his next adversary. His comrades fought alongside him as the torrents of rain fell. Cracks of thunder were confused with shots of cannon fire, but no one seemed to be concerned with anything other than the fight at hand.

He wheeled his horse again to see a Federal cavalryman to his front. The Federal fired and James took a glancing revolver shot to his side. He felt the shot with his gauntlet-covered hand and raised it to see blood. The wound only infuriated him. He charged after the Federal cavalier, drove his sabre through his chest, and then pulled the blade as the trooper fell to the ground.

James replaced his bloodied sabre in the scabbard and pulled his revolver. He spied a Federal officer and shot him dead. The officer tumbled out of the saddle as his horse reared and came down upon his back, smashing his face into the muddy road. Then from behind came an unexpected blow from a sabre. The blade gashed open the back of James's head. He fell from his horse unconscious.

When James regained consciousness he realized he was in the midst of the enemy's line. His comrades had fallen back, yet he was determined not to be captured. He spied a Federal officer nearby who sat on a magnificent black stallion. James pushed himself up from the muddy road, ran over to the officer, and grabbed his leg. He pulled the officer to the ground, mounted his stallion, and rode like the wind back toward his line on the Telegraph Road.

He heard voices from the Federals behind him yell out, "Kill! Kill him!"

Shots whizzed by his ears as he frantically spurred the stallion down the hill, waving over his head a sabre broken in the middle. When he came close to his line of cavaliers, he heard them shout, "Breathed! Breathed is not dead."

With blood gushing from his head and his side wound bleeding profusely, James responded, "Boys, I'm not dead yet!"

⊰✶⊱

After a short time had passed, James stood at the ready to man one of Captain William Griffin's Baltimore Light Artillery guns on the Telegraph Road. If he had been expecting a reprieve from the action, he soon understood he was wrong in his assumption. The blue-coated cavalrymen once again came charging at the guns. The battery was overrun, and he did all he could to hold them off with a ramrod in his hands. He knocked a number of the Federal cavalrymen to the ground, and then unloaded his revolver into them to keep them down.

Suddenly, he saw Captain Gus Dorsey of Company K, 1st Virginia Cavalry sweep the Federals back. As the Federals were moved back, he saw General Stuart gesticulating and yelling, "Bully for Company K!" At that moment a blue-clad dismounted cavalier, with revolver in hand, shot General Stuart in the abdomen. The bullet seemed to catch the general at the top of his breeches pocket. The general slumped over in pain, and he grabbed hold of the McClellan saddle to his front.

Captain Dorsey came to his aid while two other men kept the general stable in the saddle. It was not long before General Fitz Lee rode up next to the general and James.

"Go ahead, Fitz old fellow. I know you'll do what's right," General Stuart ordered as he saw some of his cavalrymen heading to the rear. "Go back! Go back! I'd rather die than be whipped."

James followed the general to the rear, up the Telegraph Road, and witnessed him being placed in an ambulance. Dr. Fontaine and the general's aide, Major Venerable and 2nd Lieutenant Aid-de-Camp Hullihen rode in the ambulance with the general and, alongside, three couriers.

As the ambulance made its way from the battlefield, James observed a large number of Federal cavalry forming for a charge on the ambulance. He quickly wiped the blood from the gash on his head, and then formed up a number of Confederate cavalrymen in order to protect his general.

"Charge," James cried out as the formed cavaliers met the Federal cavalrymen. Despite the blood dripping into his eyes, James fought valiantly to protect the general and the ambulance that was now racing off the field of battle. James rallied his men again as the Federal cavalrymen contested his demonstration. Napoleon had not fallen himself at Waterloo, but his army was defeated. James felt as if he were Napoleon, defeated on the battlefield, yet he had saved his general from the capture by the Federals.

After the general was safely away, James returned to his battery. As torrents of rain began to fall, he guided the battery over the Chickahominy River to safety for the night.

The night would be one of the loneliest nights of his entire career as a warrior. After a doctor stitched his head wound and wrapped it with a bandage, and then did what he could for the bullet wound to his side, James lay under a canvas and began to ponder.

He thought, *General Jackson was dead, General Longstreet had been wounded in the Wilderness, and now General Stuart was seriously wounded. How could the cause survive? The greatest generals were all gone. What was there left to fight for? Would he now try to inspire his men to fight as Spartans at Thermopylae, to the last man? What was left but his duty and his honor? For the cause was now dead as far as he could reconcile. What are we to do now that no more great generals survived to lead the Army of Northern Virginia, with the exception of General Robert E. Lee himself?*

James felt his head wound. He looked at his bloodied hand as the blood seeped through the bandage. Then he rolled to his side to feel where the bullet had entered and exited his body. His head and body were both in extreme pain. He took a swig of whiskey left for him by the doctor, but it did not seem to do much for his mental anguish. He could not drink enough to block out the psychological, emotional, and physical pain which he now lived with.

He realized that all he had left to fight for was his honor as a man.

39

Move Up Closer

They Have Got the Range, Boys

JUNE 10TH THROUGH 12TH, 1864

JAMES RODE TO THE front of his battery alongside Lieutenant Shanks. The fragrant smell of the lilacs and the gentle hum of bees buzzing the fragrant flowers reminded James of Bai-Yuka. Sweat streamed from beneath his kepi and made a grimy trench down his sideburns. The jingling accoutrements and the neighing of horses that strained to pull his cannon made conversation difficult.

The cavalry and four batteries of Stuart's Horse Artillery, now under James's good friend, General Wade Hampton's command, were making double-quick along the Virginia Central Railroad tracks in pursuit of the petulant General Sheridan's cavalry that had, a day earlier, moved out in a northwestern direction from Richmond.

"Major, he's a plumb beauty, that new black stallion you ride. Where did ya find him?" Lieutenant Shanks inquired.

"I got him from a Yankee officer. I pulled him from this stallion at Yellow Tavern. Good animals like this one have a terrible lot in this war, and the squabble is never theirs," he disconsolately responded as the cavalcade moved along the road.

He felt his side wound from Yellow Tavern, for it still bothered him. He pondered how it was that he had survived that battle with both a head wound and a revolver wound. Maybe the God of War or maybe his boyhood hero of the Mexican War, Samuel Ringgold, had protected him from above. After all, they were both horse artillerists.

He rode along and thought, *If there is a God of War or a God of any name who intervenes in the world, why would he be letting this terrible conflict go on and on? Where was God's merciful hand in all of the death and suffering as a result of this war? He knew both sides claimed God was on their side. Why then did God not intervene into this horrible war and bring it to an end?*

His plaintive thoughts led him to think of many of the founding fathers of the country, who were deists. He understood their theology bolstered the main point that "the Supreme Being" did not intervene into the world. This Being had simply created the world like a clockmaker and then set it ticking to its own ends. If deism was good enough for the likes of George Washington and James Madison, maybe it had some validity? What evidence did he have, after fighting the war for three and a half years, that God could or would use his supernatural revelation to intervene in this contest and do something about stopping it? He felt his faith had been shaken by his war experience. However Thomas Jefferson was a theist, which James understood to mean God was a personal creator and ruler of the world. James mused over the wrinkles that separated the deist and theist philosophies.

He and his men still had a long hard ride to get ahead of the Federal cavalry. He thought he had best save his energy and brain power for the fight which lay ahead.

When James awoke and realized where he had bivouacked for the night, not a half mile from Louisa Court House on the Virginia Central Railroad, he wanted to return to his sleep. Though it was still dark, that was not an option, for soon his two batteries would be needed in the fight.

"Lieutenant Shanks, see to getting the batteries harnessed and saddled up. I need to speak with General Lee," James ordered.

"Yes, sir, will take care of it right away," Lieutenant Shanks replied with a salute.

James walked to find General Fitzhugh Lee.

"General, what are your orders, sir?" James inquired.

"Major, your two batteries are to stay with me. We have made a plan of battle to meet General Hampton at Clayton's Store and there crush General Sheridan's cavalry. We're heavily outnumbered, but your fine artillerymen will even the odds," General Lee responded.

It was still dark when he made his way back to his artillery camp, but the men were prepared to deploy.

The morning's fight pushed the Confederates back to the railroad tracks. James had gotten word that General Hampton's wagon train had been captured by none other than the Federal showboat cavalier, General Custer. But James was determined to help reverse this series of events as he galloped onto the field with sections of Shoemaker's and Johnston's batteries. He observed the triumphant Wolverines at General Hampton's wagon train when, suddenly, General Lomax's 15th Virginia Cavalry slammed into them. They recaptured the wagon train and took Custer's headquarters wagon, four caissons, and other valuable spoils of war.

Custer's Federal Wolverine horsemen pushed forward, many and bold, as once again James was about to encounter his red-scarfed cavalry adversary. James brought his artillerymen up to the edge of the woods where he was prepared to engage. To his front he saw charge and counter-charge, forward surges and backward repulses. He saw carbine firing, sabring, war cries, loud neighing of horses, and hand-to-hand fighting. Blue and gray cavaliers' surges roared up and over the rises. Back and upward the mighty cavalries fought. His guns were now trained, but he could not fire, so indistinguishable were friend from foe.

Suddenly, he saw his opportunity. "Fire!" James roared out as he saw the red scarf cavalier riding like Tam O'Shanter and getting boxed in on three sides. Tearing the sultry air with shell after shell, he next took aim on another old adversary. He knew him simply by how the cannonading was commenced, its accuracy, and cadence of firing. It was Lieutenant Pennington's guns. He sat his black charger, removed his field glasses from their case to spy his old adversary, and checked his own accuracy. He saw galloping riderless horses across the battlefield, some wounded and neighing in pain.

"Move up closer; they have got the range, boys!" James commanded as Pennington's shells dropped all around them, splashing dirt onto their uniforms.

From his position behind the guns, he looked to his right as the artillerymen limbered to move forward. Suddenly, a shell burst. Lieutenant Hoxton was severely injured by the shrapnel.

"Private Matthews, help the lieutenant from the field," James ordered as the four guns moved closer to Pennington's battery.

The sanguinary fight went on for two more hours, for the two stubborn artillery adversary commanders would not relent. Late in the day, after the red scarf cavalier's troopers had been shot up very badly on two fronts, two other Federal cavalry divisions finally broke James loose from his position on the field.

Eventually, James and his men were pushed back to what he was told was the Wood's farm, where the attack had commenced from, next to the railroad tracks with the 7th Georgia Cavalrymen supporting his guns. As the day's conflict came to a close, he and his men fell back with General Lee on the Lastly Church Road.

⋘∘⋙

The evening was cool and a docile breeze blew. The campfires, up and down on either side of the road, burned with steady flames beneath the canopy of night. Men in a variety of butternut and gray uniforms lay strewn upon the ground like dusty walnuts dropped from tree limbs above. At the foot of the open fields, the batteries, wagon horses, and cavalry horses by the hundreds dined on the sweet grasses.

James waxed eloquently to Lieutenant Shanks and a few of his privates at the Lastly Church where his two batteries had settled in to bivouac for the night.

"Gentlemen, I've searched my biblical knowledge, thought through my classics, and I'm troubled to say I don't know if God or man is responsible for this hell of a war we're fighting. Thomas Paine once said, 'Ye that dare oppose, not only the tyranny, but the tyrant, stand forth!' I'm beginning to think it's not God, but a tyrant who is responsible for this war," he expounded as he leaned against a wheel of one of the guns of the batteries.

"Southern men know the tyrant to whom you refer can be none other than Lincoln," Private Matthews stated rather matter-of-factly as he rested his arms over the barrel of the gun.

"I've come to the conclusion that the 'Rail Splitter' has neither real religion nor belief in an afterlife as we all do. I think he has some sort of civil religion, a faith in laws, principles, causes and effects, or maybe even he has faith in natural religion. How could he continue to allow all the killing of Americans to go on, year after year, unless he had faith in what I have stated," James mused as he placed a blade of grass in his mouth.

Private Zimmerman spoke, recalling the thought of a fellow clergyman. "I knew Dr. John Brown, pastor of First Presbyterian Church of Springfield, Illinois, where Mrs. Lincoln was a member, but Lincoln was not. We corresponded prior to the war. He wrote me that in 1860, he knew the superintendent of Public Instruction, in Springfield. He told me this man, Newton Bateman, once was visited by Lincoln as he campaigned for president. Dr. Brown wrote to me that Lincoln was complaining to Bateman that the majority of local preachers did not support his candidacy. And that Lincoln said to Bateman, 'Mr. Bateman, I am not a Christian—God knows I would be one—but I have carefully read the Bible, and I do not so understand this book.' Lincoln went on to say, 'I know there is a God, and that he hates injustice and slavery. I see the storm coming, and I know that his hand is in it.' The most startling thing Lincoln said was that, 'If he has a place and work for me, and I think he has, I believe I am ready.'"

"Yes, but I thought the Yankees' war was about saving the Union, not doing away with slavery?" Private Mackall added to the conversation.

"I believe that Lincoln is like-minded with Maximilien Robespierre," James retorted. "The Frenchman reasoned that the Republic could only be saved by the virtue of its citizens and that terror was virtuous because it attempted to maintain the Republic."

"Reckon I don't know who the hell Robesparrie is," Private Clem remarked with a very confused look on his face.

"He was a leader in the French Revolution who tried to create a 'Republic of Virtue' through enabling enemies of the Revolution to be guillotined, without a trial, within twenty-four hours of their arrest. Like when Lincoln simply suspended the Writ of Habeas Corpus. And now, at the cost of hundreds of thousands of dead soldiers, he keeps fighting this war to save his molten golden calf of the Union," Private Zimmerman explained.

"What is crazy about Lincoln is that he has put his civil mystical religion of saving the Union before God, like the Israelites placed the golden calf before God, as though Lincoln is working out his salvation here on earth by becoming the savior of democracy and the Republic," James explained. "Lincoln's desire to have a strong centralized government, which Calhoun himself said would lead to a most corrupt and oppressive form of democratic government, is now taking over as we die trying to stop the 'Rail Splitter' from his agenda."

"I'm with you, Major; Lincoln is not 'Honest Abe.' He is simply working out his salvation here on earth by trying to kill us Southerners and get us and the slaves out of his way," private Mackall offered. "I heard he wanted to round up all the slaves in America and send them back to a colony on the continent of Africa."

"All we can do for our country is continue to put our lives on the line. General Robert E. Lee and President Jefferson Davis can ask no more from us. Gentlemen, it has been a long day of war. I need to retire. Sleep well," James said.

"Major, you're as grounded in theology as I am. I believe that all men are sinners, and we all have our golden calves to wrestle with. I would even go as far as to say the Confederacy has their golden calves," Private Zimmerman shared.

"This is true, Private-Reverend. I'll give your words some thought. God must be greater than choosing sides, but, I don't know why he lets this war drag on and on."

"Goodnight, Major," Private Zimmerman responded with a handshake.

⸎⸏⸎

The next morning James was in front of his artillerymen and the cavalry of General Fitz Lee's division as they redeployed from the Lastly Church on a circuitous route in order to outflank the rear of the Federal cavalry. James directed his artillerymen on the Charlottesville Road as it came out perpendicular to the Virginia Central Railroad tracks.

By mid-afternoon, James heard his general's command. "Squadrons! Right front into line! March!"

As General Lomax's brigade formed for the charge, James observed that the Federal cavalry was preparing to charge over the railway cut. His two sections of guns were surrounded by woods, and he was in a flanking position to the Federal cavalry.

The frantically hollering gray-clad cavaliers swept into battle triumphantly in a tremendous charge, and James's artillerymen stood at the ready at their posts. James watched them go forth, knee to knee, shouting, chanting; horse and man were one, unified war arrow shaft, aimed at the red of the enemy's blood. They went with an elevated, manly ecstasy, their bodies streaked with the foam that flew from their horses' mouths.

They galloped by James, carbines and revolvers at the ready, in a whirlwind of dust that raged like the cavaliers themselves. The infernal clangor, resounded with fury, called open the gates at the portal of hell as they rode toward the Federals in blue. The horses' stretched necks and manes seemed aglow with fire, and the frenzied cavaliers rode like the wind toward their foes.

James unleashed the full ferocity of his artillery pieces. Pandemonium exploded among the now-charging Federals. His new-found melancholy caused him to sit his stallion farther back than his aggressive temperament usually allowed. His wounds were not yet fully healed, he thought. This was only rationale he had for his timid behavior.

He endured this melancholy for a moment longer, and then spurred his stallion back into the fray of the artillery fight. He choreographed a leapfrogging of the guns as they fired double canister shot into the charging Federal cavalry.

Late in the afternoon, he ordered his guns to enfilade the dismounted Federal cavalry line. With the support of Colonel Munford's 2nd Virginia Cavalry, James was doing fine cannonading.

"Major, open fire on Custer's Yankees straight ahead. After you have softened them, my men will go in and finish them," Colonel Munford commanded.

"Yes, sir, General! Fire!" James ordered. He observed through his field glasses Custer's cavalrymen scattering like sheep in all directions.

After seven assaults, finally the blue wave broke for the last time. The fight at Trevilian Station was over at last.

James realized that, at the end of this second day of fighting, Federal brigade after brigade, van, main and rear, cavalry and horse artillery, ordnance trains, and teamster-driven wagon trains had all mysteriously disappeared back in the direction from which they had come, sorely whipped, and in search of the security of Grant's army.

He proudly stood next to the Stuart Horse Artillery flag, still flapping in the wind, which had been lovingly sown and bequeathed to the unit by the women of Charlottesville for saving the town in February. A mere three and a half months ago, only miles away from where he now stood, he had emerged victorious from a costly fight. But for what? His artillerymen, including the cavalrymen this time around, had to be called in to save the town again.

40

Boys, They Got Me This Time

Late June 1864 until the End of the Threat to His Love

James felt lackluster, and his artillerymen looked the same way. They were on the trail of the Federal cavalry, again; huntsman on their horses after the fox. Sometimes they changed roles, and the Confederates were the hunted. He looked at his men and smiled grimly. Man for man, they were good hunters and even better foxes; but he was tired. Their quarry was deep in his territory now, and this he could not tolerate. He had his cannon positioned at Ream's Station, south of the Petersburg defenses. James and General Fitz Lee waited patiently at the intersection of Hickford Road and the road to Stony Creek for their quarry to flush.

The hunt opened when the Federal cavalry arrived with scores of freed slaves in stolen buggies and carriages. He ran his cannon up the road as Fitz Lee's cavalry and Mahone's infantry opened fire on the Federals. He watched the Federal cavalry disperse into the woods. He was able to get off a few scattered shots from his guns, but the fire was mostly random and to no effect.

His artillerymen chased the Federal cavalry to Stony Creek where he ordered his cannon to be parked. He had not enough horses to keep the guns up anymore. James and a number of his men then joined in with the 6th Virginia Cavalry in a charge into what remained of the Federals and their contraband. James was at the head of the charge when, suddenly, a bullet knocked him out of his saddle. The dust created from the charge shrouded him in obscurity. The cavalrymen continued the charge as he grabbed his gut in extreme pain. His wound was oozing blood, rapidly staining his gray uniform. His gauntlets were covered in blood. Horses' hooves pounded the ground all around him. He thought he was done for.

It was not long before some of his artillerymen returned to find their fallen leader. They dismounted and stood around him in shock.

"Major, what can we do for you?" Private Matthews asked in a soft voice.

"Boys, they got me this time. Get me a surgeon!"

One man remounted and went for Dr. Leigh. When the doctor arrived, he removed James's jacket and shirt. Dr. Leigh poured some canteen water over his dirty fingers and explored the wound. Private Matthews propped up James's head and gave him a drink from a canteen.

"Major, I find no exit wound. I think the bullet is providentially lodged in the muscular stomach wall." Dr. Leigh diagnosed. "Get the major an ambulance and move him to a local home."

James was placed in a mule-drawn ambulance wagon by a number of his artillerymen. This was done gently and in silence. These men knew about gut wounds. Their cheeks were not dry. From the ambulance, James issued orders in a calm voice, "Privates O'Brien and Hopkins, I want you to ride on the road to Stony Creek and bring back the two captured wagons. They could be of some use to us. Understood?"

"Yes, sah."

James rode in the ambulance for a few miles to a small white clapboard farm house. He was helped into the house by Private Matthews and Dr. Leigh.

"Major Breathed, Mrs. Malone is a good woman, and she has agreed to take care of you until you're well enough to be moved to Richmond. I need to wash your wound and bandage it. Mrs. Malone, Major Breathed will need a dry warm place."

Mrs. Malone replied, "Doctor, we can put him in the side room off the kitchen where I can tend his needs."

Dr. Leigh turned to James, "I want you to take some laudanum to ease the pain."

He took the laudanum; his pain eased. The doctor washed the wound with warm water brought by Mrs. Malone. Dr. Leigh next applied compressive dressings to the wound and then wrapped his torso with bandages. By this time, James was becoming delirious. As they laid him on the bed, he mumbled, "Richmond, tell Dr. Macgill." He then passed out.

The next morning Mrs. Malone was sitting on a chair at his side with her knitting.

"Major, good to see you're back in the land of the living. Your cold sweats kept me up most of the night with a cool compress on your forehead. You had me worried for a while."

"Thanks for looking after me, Mrs. Malone."

"Do you feel like eating?"

"Yes, ma'am. Something easy on the stomach, of course," he said with a smile.

When she returned with the food on a tray, he could not help but think of Mollie. Mrs. Malone looked a good bit like Mollie with her black hair in a bun, bucksome figure, and pretty day dress. He eased over while she propped him up with two more pillows so he could eat his breakfast.

"Where's your husband?"

"He was in Jackson's Corps and was killed at Chancellorsville. He was in the 12th Virginia Infantry, best I remember, but I could be wrong."

"I was in that fight at the head of thousands of men with my horse artillery. We broke up the Yankees real good that day. But of course we lost General Jackson, and your husband."

"All I know is I wish this war would get over. The Confederates can't hold on much longer, and I don't think we can win anyhow."

"If I ever get to fight again, it'll be for the honor of our fallen comrades. Once a man starts something, if he is a real man, he needs to see it through to the very end. My end could have been yesterday, but God's providence spared me. I may have a bullet in me until the end, but I'll fight on!"

His excitement brought on the pain, and he asked Mrs. Malone for the bottle of laudanum. After a few swigs he felt the pain subside. He went back to his breakfast, mostly picking at it as he talked with Mrs. Malone. He soon tired and went back to sleep and did not awaken until evening.

Dr. Bill Murray, the horse artillery battery surgeon, and Private Matthews returned later that night to see how James was convalescing.

"Hello, Major," Dr. Murray said.

"Hello, Doc. After all these years of seeing you take care of my artillerymen, I never thought you would have to be taking care of me. My other wounds seem to have healed up, but this one is real dicey. It hurts like hell," he said.

"I came to take a look at it and change the bandages. Private Matthews is here to help me. A few more days of rest here and we'll get you moved to Dr. Macgill's home in Richmond. Private here tells me you've more interest there than simply seeing your old medical mentor."

Dr. Murray moved the lantern on the bed stand so that he could closely examine the wound after the bandages were removed. He looked at the stitched wound noticing it had stopped oozing blood.

"Private, hand me the new bandages. It looks like it is healing fine," Dr. Murray said as he reached for the wrap. "We'll have you to Richmond soon."

After a number of days passed, James was carefully taken on a stretcher from his bed and placed in an ambulance for his journey to Richmond. He was beginning to regain some strength.

"Good-bye, Mrs. Malone, and thanks," James said as she held his hand in the ambulance.

"Hope you're back in the fight soon, as you wish to be, to the very end," Mrs. Malone responded.

His thirty-plus-mile trip to Richmond would be a jarring one. The soldier who drove him was told by Dr. Murray to take it slow. The ambulance pulled onto the Old Stage Road and then headed north on the Halifax Road toward the capital city.

He tried to sleep with the help of the laudanum, and after a day in the ambulance, he finally arrived at 316 East Franklin Street.

"James, oh my dear, are you badly hurt?" Mollie exclaimed when she reached the rear of the ambulance.

"I'll be fine, now that I've you to nurse me back to health," James said to her with a smile as the soldier and Dr. Macgill prepared to lift the stretcher from the back of the ambulance.

"One, two, three, lift," Dr. Macgill said to the soldier.

Mollie held his hand as he was moved into a downstairs bedroom. When they had him in the bed, she pulled up a chair, took hold of his hand, and caressed his forehead. The trip had brought on the cold sweats again.

"Mollie, get some cool water. Bring some compresses for his forehead. We have to get him out of this fever and his sweats," Dr. Macgill said to her.

She soon returned and applied the compresses to his forehead. Dr. Macgill needed to see the wound. When the two of them took the bandage from his torso, they saw that the wound had started to seep. Mollie and Dr. Macgill cleaned and then re-bandaged it.

"Let him rest now, Mollie. He's had a long day. You may stay here with him and continue to apply the compresses, but let him rest," Dr. Macgill said.

She spent the next few days at his bedside. Finally, her loving care brought his fever down. One afternoon she came to his room with a letter. She sat down in the chair next to the bed and read it to him:

Hdqrs. Army of Northern Va.
Richmond, Va. July 7, 1864

Major James Breathed—I have heard with great regret that you were wounded and incapacitated for active duty. I beg to tender to you my sympathy and to express the hope that the army will not be deprived of your valuable services. The reports that I have received of your gallantry and good conduct on several occasions have given me great satisfaction, and, while they increase my concern for your personal sufferings, render me desirous that your health will soon permit you to resume a command that you have exercised with so much credit to yourself and advantage to the service.

Very respectfully, your obt. Servant,
R. E. Lee, General

"James, I hope this letter makes you feel a little better? Not too many soldiers hear directly from General Lee when they're wounded," she said.

"That certainly is a fine missive," he allowed. "I hope to meet the general in person someday."

"James, there's something I've been meaning to tell you. I've waited until you were feeling better. I know how you can get riled up. Back in the middle of March, President Davis sent me on a covert mission, which led Alfred and me into the Church Hill District. From the carriage, I was able to spy through my opera glasses, a suspected Yankee spy passing a missive to a Miss Van Lew."

"Yes, and then what happened?"

"Alfred and I were somehow observed by a darky on a horse. When I told Alfred to drive faster to get away, the darky followed us almost all the way to Franklin Street. Then before the house he turned down an alley and was gone. Ever since that night I've felt like I'm being watched. I can't tell you who is watching me or why I feel that way, but it scares me."

Patting her hand, he said, "Mollie, I can't have my girl threatened by Yankee spies. In a week or so, when I'm strong enough, here is what we're going to do . . ."

⁂

The night finally arrived when they were going to execute their plan. James entered the carriage while it was still in the barn and crouched down on the floor with his revolver in his hand. Alfred pulled the landau carriage out front of 316 East Franklin Street as Mollie came out the front door of her home. She was dressed as if she were going somewhere important and had donned the same bonnet that she had worn that night back in March. She had told Alfred the plan. He had agreed to drive them back into the Church Hill District, by the Van Lew mansion, with her as the bait to draw out the darky horseman.

"Are you sure this is the right thing to do, James?" she asked of him looking straight forward in the carriage.

"Don't worry. If he is stalking you and you go back down Twenty-fourth Street and turn onto East Grace Street in front of the mansion, he'll come after you again. We have to draw him out."

"Alfred, drive on."

Alfred drove the carriage southeast up Broad Street, heading for the district. There was a full moon and not a cloud in the sky. She had perfect visibility with her opera glasses. The carriage rumbled over the road until they arrived at 23rd Street. Alfred turned the carriage onto the street and slowly drove to East Grace Street. He turned the carriage and drove it past the Van Lew mansion.

Suddenly, forty yards behind the carriage appeared a darky on a horse. Mollie leaned forward and pounded on the glass. Alfred reined the horses and they took off.

"James, it's him. I can see his face well with my opera glasses," she said frantically. "He has pulled a revolver! Do something!"

James needed to hear no more. He sprang up off the floor of the carriage, opened the door, stepped out, and planted one boot onto the door footing. He hung onto the carriage, and with his free hand raised his revolver. The darky, now within twenty yards of the back of the carriage, raised his revolver and pointed it at the carriage.

Bang!

The darky came tumbling off his horse, hit the ground, and then rolled a few times in the street. Alfred brought the carriage to a halt. He saw that James had done what he said he would do, which was shoot the man.

James jumped off the carriage and ran back to the darky in the street. He grabbed the man by the collar of his shirt. A heavy flow of blood drained from a chest wound.

"Who are you! Tell me now or I'll put another bullet in your leg!" James exclaimed.

"I'm the husband of Mary who your lady outed," the darky said as he breathed his last and expired on the spot.

James released the darky. He left the body lying in the street and walked back to the carriage.

"Home, Alfred," James said as he stepped back in the carriage. He closed the door and looked at Mollie. "Darky said you outed his wife. Does that put two and two together for you?"

"Yes, I exposed Mary who was a servant in the Executive Mansion. She was passing information off of President Davis's desk to Yankee agents. But her real name was Mary. The darky you just killed was her husband."

"You know, if you aren't careful, this Mary whatever-her-name-is will think you bear her a grudge," James said. He tried to chuckle, but it ended in a grimace of pain.

Molly looked at him, started to speak, but said nothing.

41

War as the Continuation of Politik

CHRISTMAS SEASON 1864

MOLLIE AND HER SISTERS had decorated the home on Franklin Street, but there was not much Christmas cheer in the house as times were difficult in Richmond. Since the summer siege had begun, it became increasingly difficult to get even the bare necessities. Stores were open; however, there were no goods on the shelves.

Mollie heard a tinkle of the bell above the door, "Yes, may I help you," she said as the door opened.

"I've an official military correspondence for you, if'n you're Miss Mollie Macgill."

"I'm Miss Macgill."

The courier soldier handed her the correspondence and then tipped his hat.

"Good day, Miss Macgill."

"Good day to you."

She closed the door, walked across the parlor, and sat on the love seat. She opened the correspondence and read it:

Winter Camp – Stuart Horse Artillery
21st inst. December, 1864
Near Waynesboro, Va.

Dearest Mollie,

I will be on furlough from the Stuart Horse Artillery; coming to Richmond for Christmas. Expect my arrival December 24th at # 316 East Franklin Street.

Love,
Jas.

She dropped the paper and began to cry. Putting her hands over her cheeks, the tears ran down her face. Her sad feelings in relation to Christmas in Richmond dissipated. They were replaced with joyful feelings in anticipation of seeing him. She reached for her handkerchief in her sleeve, dried her eyes and face, and then sought out family members.

"Father, Ellen, Elizabeth! Come quickly! I've news to share with you!"

They came from different parts of the house and gathered around her. She read the note aloud to them.

"My daughter, I'm so happy for you!" Dr. Macgill said as he gave her a big hug.

"Sister, guess you won't be going to the Spotswood Hotel Christmas Day Party alone after all. You'll be on your lovie-dovie Major's arm all night long," Elizabeth said in a chiding manor.

"Well, we must do more to the house. Can we bring more Christmas decorations out of the attic? I know there are no holly trees to be found, but maybe a wreath on the door?" Mollie exclaimed with renewed vigor. "And everything must be cleaned from top to bottom. Tell Miss O'Shaunsay. We don't have much time. He'll be here tomorrow!"

⊷⊙⊶

James rode his black stallion into town from the west and traversed the streets, making his way to 316 East Franklin Street. He rode around back to the stable, where he found Alfred tending to the carriage horses.

"Marse James, goods ta sees ya! Miss Mollie is so excited yous comin'. She done the house up special for ya."

"Any further trouble from darkies bothering her?"

"Notta one. Ya got the right darky that night! Sure nough as I'sa standin' here."

"Alfred, you did a fine job that night. We both owe you a debt of gratitude for what you did. Take my stallion and brush him down and feed him some oats. We had a long journey around the Yankees to get here."

"Yessa, Marse James. Them Yankees got this here city surrounded north, east, and south with their trenches fulla guns and soldiers. We a been sufferin' something terrible here."

"Alfred, the Yankees haven't got this city yet."

He left Alfred and exited the stable toward the front of the house. When he came to the front porch, he rang the bell and pulled his jacket, straightening it out. He slicked his hair back, a bit nervous, as if he were a teenager coming to pick up his date for the first time.

The door swung open, "James! You're here, thank God!" Mollie cried. She leaped from the floor into his awaiting arms.

They embraced and hugged without a word being said. Then he looked into her eyes and kissed her like he had done so many years ago in George Carter's garden at Oatlands Plantation. He felt as if the war had never taken place and all those battlefield memories were magically erased for the moment their lips touched so passionately. She began to weep. The moment she had been waiting for had finally arrived. As she embraced her man, she felt their souls once again connect. Her emotions consumed her as if she was ablaze.

"My love, don't cry. I'm here now," James said as he caressed her neck and her back. "I've missed you and thought about you every day."

"James, I've also missed you. Every day I worry about your safety. But today God has brought you back to me alive and well!"

They stepped into the home, hand-in-hand, and sat on the love seat. The odors of food being cooked mixed with the rustic and musty odors of the old home. These odors reminded James of Bai-Yuka and the many pleasant memories he shared with her there.

"Remember the time before I enlisted when your family came to Bai-Yuka for that picnic? We danced and then sat under the tree and held hands. Would you ever have believed then what this war has done to our country and to us?"

She moved closer to him. His major's uniform positively shone. She said, "James, I remember like it was yesterday the time Alfred drove me around those country roads so that I could get the #191 Order information to South Mountain. I was so surprised to discover you there. We held hands and then you kissed me over the little dinner table. This war has been so terrible for our relationship."

"I remember your coming down from Hagerstown to meet me at George Carter's Oatlands Plantation. I kissed you at the old fountain in the gardens and you were a little taken aback by it, as I recall."

"I never did tell you how much I enjoyed that kiss or why I left the next morning without saying good-bye."

"Why did you leave without saying good-bye?"

"Lige inspired me unto another spying mission that night. I was so excited to get started the next morning, I was up and off like a shot. I was remiss in leaving and not bidding you adieu."

"I thought it might have been the kiss?"

"Oh, how could you think that?"

"What else could I think?"

"How is the wound, healed?"

He unbuttoned his jacket and pulled the flask of laudanum.

"It still troubles me, but this helps get me through the day."

Dr. Macgill entered the parlor, followed by Mollie's two sisters.

"Dr. Breathed I presume? Or are we now more comfortable with Major Breathed?" Dr. Macgill stated.

James stood to shake his mentor's hand.

"Please sit down," Dr. Macgill said.

"James Breathed, it is so good to see you again. Your wound fully healed I hope?" Ellen said. Both she and Elizabeth walked over to him to have their hands kissed.

"We're so glad you were able to get furlough and come to Richmond to celebrate Christmas with us," Dr. Macgill said as he sat in a chair close to James.

"It's good to be back. It seems ages ago that I left in early August to rejoin the horse artillery. I've been in a great deal of terrible fighting since then in the Shenandoah Valley. The valley has been destroyed by General Sheridan, despite what our small Confederate army under General Early tried to do to stop him. Our breadbasket is no longer and, coupled with the siege, I'm sure that is why Richmond and her people are suffering. General Sherman has almost arrived at the sea in Georgia. He is waging the same total war on the people of that state."

"They're criminals for what they're doing, every last Yankee, including Lincoln!" Elizabeth proclaimed in disgust.

"We need not make all this talk of war. James hears enough of that out in the field. Let us talk of Christmas, for the Yankees can try and starve us, but they'll never break our spirits and our will to celebrate the birth of Christ! Right father?" Mollie said.

"Yes, you're right, my dear. Elizabeth, ask Miss O'Shaunsay how long until supper. I'm getting hungry, and I'm sure James is ready for some home cooking," Dr. Macgill said.

❧ ⦿ ☙

The next day Mollie, her sisters, and Dr. Macgill were all dressed in their finest Christmas apparel. James helped the ladies into the landau carriage.

"Alfred, to the Spotswood Hotel, Main Street and 8th," Dr. Macgill said as he climbed in the carriage.

James looked out the carriage window and saw that they were approaching a five-story brick building, which was the finest hostelry in Richmond.

"James, the Mallorys, MacFarlands, Randolphs, Chesnuts, Clays, Carys, and even Dr. Minnigerode, the rector at St. Paul's Church, will be at the Christmas party tonight. I'll be so proud to introduce you to the best families of Richmond," Mollie said as the carriage rumbled toward the hotel.

"Mollie, remember all those fine people also have family members serving the cause who maybe have even died for it. Don't get me raised up on too high a pedestal," James humbly replied.

Alfred brought the landau to a halt in front of the columned entrance. When Mollie exited the carriage, James extended his bent arm to her and the two proudly walked into the lobby of the hotel. He observed the elegantly furnished and decorated interior as they made their way to the party.

"Good evening and welcome to the Macgills," said William Corkley, the proprietor, as he greeted them at the door.

"Good evening and Merry Christmas," Mollie responded as she slightly lifted her skirt to curtsy.

They walked to the center of the room where she introduced James to the "Cary Invincibles": Hetty and Jennie, who were sisters, and their cousin Connie.

"Major Breathed, we've heard all about you from Mollie, not to mention what my fiancé, General John Pegram, has told me about you," Hetty said as James took her hand and kissed it.

James could not help noticing her classic face, her beautiful auburn hair curled about her shoulders, pale complexion, and shapely figure. He thought she was indeed the "belle of the South." She was just as so many people had described her.

"Has the date been set for your wedding," James inquired.

"Yes, January nineteen, a little over three weeks away," Hetty responded with a cheerful smile.

Mollie unconsciously flinched her arm, which was tucked away in his, when she heard the conversation had turned to a wedding. At that moment the two lovers were approached and then surrounded by the men and women of the fine families Mollie had spoken of on the ride over. The gentlemen in the group motioned to James to follow them to a more private room for brandy and cigars.

"Major," a voice rang out. "Tell us what happened in the valley."

"I've returned from defending the Shenandoah Valley against General Sheridan. My Stuart Horse Artillery soldiers fought in September at Winchester, but we did not fare well. We fell back to Fisher Hill and my three batteries and I moved south, because we were heavily outnumbered. General Custer outflanked General Rosser's cavalrymen when we redeployed at Tom's Brook, and we lost eleven of our guns. It might have gone differently if I had had my Maryland artillerymen, but they had all left to join the Maryland line. Our horses, equipment, and ordinance supplies have all broken down. I'm afraid the Stuart Horse Artillery is a broken unit in need of refurbishing. General Early has been defeated and General Lee has nothing more to send him."

"Major," another gentleman called out, "we're suffering here in Richmond. Flour is eight hundred dollars a barrel. Beef, poultry are sky high in price. The siege is strangling us into starvation. Dr. Minnigerode has formed the Richmond Soup Association to try and ease food shortages. What are we to do?"

"I've studied the work of Major-General Clausewitz who was a Prussian in the Napoleonic Wars," James said. "I have concluded from his work *On War* that 'war is merely the continuation of policy by other means.' What I saw of General Sheridan's 'total war' in the valley is now involving the entire Southern population, which includes the citizens of our Confederate nation. I witnessed the Yankees destroying thousands of barns full of wheat and mills and implements needed to farm. They drove out thousands of cattle and sheep for either their own army's consumption or they shot them dead and left them. General Sherman is doing the same in Georgia. This is why Richmond suffers at the hands of the aggressors. I'm sorry I could not do more to stop it."

"It's not your fault. There're many extortionists among us who are making vast profits from the war. We curse these Yankee-like unprincipled speculators who are our fellow citizens," one of the gentlemen said.

"You've done your best, Major. That's all a man can do in times of war," another of the gentlemen in the crowd around James said as he patted him on the shoulder.

James and the gentlemen brought their brandies and cigars with them from the room and rejoined the women who themselves had become rather inspired in conversation.

"We, the women of Richmond, plan a holiday feast to be delivered to our men in the trenches on January first," Hetty Cary proclaimed as she raised her fist in the air in defiance.

"Yes! We've just begun to fight these Yankees here in Richmond," Mollie spoke out. "We need to reach a peace without surrender!"

"So much serious talk of war. It is Christmas Day. Let us celebrate the coming of the Christ child," Dr. Minnigerode exclaimed as he made his way toward James.

"Yes, James, so much talk of war. Let's celebrate Christ with Frankincense, myrrh and dance," Mollie responded.

"Mollie, could I have this dance," James asked.

"You most certainly may," she responded.

⁓⊙⊙⁓

James prepared himself to return to his unit in what promised to be a bad winter. Alfred brought the stallion around to the front of the home.

"James, I'll pray for you every day until this terrible war ends. My only hope is that you'll come back to me safe in the end, which I fear is near," Mollie said as she stood by the door to see him off.

"My dearest, I've you in my heart and that will keep me warm. Whatever this war may bring, God's providence will be with us."

They embraced. He kissed her, and then he swung his duster long coat over his shoulders. He walked out the door, and, as he did, he checked that his revolver was firmly in place at his waist.

"Godspeed, Alfred."

"Sames to you, Marse James," Alfred responded as he handed James the reins.

42

High Bridge & the Surrender

BY NOON, JAMES AND the remnant of the 8th Virginia Cavalry were dispatched to High Bridge to keep the Yankee forces from either burning it or using it to cross the Appomattox River.

James shivered. The day was overcast and raw. The dampness penetrated to his bones, so he kept his troopers moving even without the enemy in sight. He observed the hilly and treeless terrain. It would not make for easy fighting, but his men had fought in worse.

Suddenly, he saw Federal infantry ahead, hundreds of them. He ordered his troopers off the road and to form a line of battle. He awaited the command from Colonel Munford he knew must come. Then he saw mounted blue cavalry. He raised his field glasses and observed the 4th Massachusetts Federal Cavalry charging from behind the infantry. He looked again, not too many of them, he thought. The command came from his colonel.

"Forward at a trot—Charge!" James cried out as he repeated the officer's command.

James led his men forward at the trot, and then they broke into a gallop. They struck hard into the small number of blue horsemen. It was a melee, the dust flying, horses neighing, sabres of steel slashing through the air and striking flesh and bone, cursing, death cries; it was the chaos James had grown accustomed to.

James was like a bee honing in on the sweet smell of nectar, searching for his next target in blue, and when he found one he flew to it bringing with him his deadly skills. He pulled his revolver as a Federal cavalryman's lathered horse kicked its front hooves in the air—an easy target. He fired two quick shots, one into the horse's front loin and the second into the Federal man as the horse came down to its knees. The cavalryman pitched over the horse's head. He finished his foe off with a shot to the chest, so close that powder blackened the Federal's uniform. James cursed. The man had already been dead with a hole between the eyes; he had wasted two bullets.

The dust and sulfur-laced powder smoke was so thick that James felt as though he was floating in purgatory. Suddenly, out of the smoke emerged a Federal with an arm raised high, sabre brandished. The foe let loose with a mighty, wild sabre thrust.

"Green," James murmured as he ducked to avoid the slash of the blade.

The Federal passed by. James reined his black stallion in a tight circle and fired off a round into the cavalryman's side. The impact of the bullet knocked the trooper to the ground, his sabre falling free from his hand. The blue cavalier was kicked bloody by another cavalier's horse.

Back in the direction where the charge had commenced, a bugler rallied the 8th Virginia Cavalry on the guidon.

"Reform," James cried out.

He spurred his stallion to the rear to see a welcome sight. More regiments of Confederate cavalrymen were coming onto the field. After his troopers had fallen into the line of battle, James trotted quickly over to the guidon of the 35th Virginia Cavalry.

"Glad to see you, cousin Lige. We're having a hell of a fight here today, and we're just getting started. They're the Fourth Massachusetts Cavalry—Harvard men. Care to join us?"

"Dammit, Jim. Harvard men? Let's get the bastards."

James smiled as he switched cylinders on his revolver. Generals Dearing and McCausland rode up alongside the two cousins.

General Dearing inquired, "I hope we're not too late? Looks like the Blue Bellies are having trouble getting untangled. Been busy?"

"A mite," James replied. "But I thought we should save you a few."

General McCausland replied with a gruff look, "Tolerable kind of you, Major. What say we get about it? Right smart number of Yankee infantry a few miles back, so let's make some blue hay now. It's time to share the wealth."

General McCausland gave the necessary orders. James reined his stallion back to the front of the troopers who had reformed on the 8th Virginia's guidon.

When James was positioned to the front of his men, he saw McCausland drop his sabre from on high, farther down the line of posed cavalrymen, and nod.

James cried out, "Charge!"

All around him he heard a keen, eerie rebel yell as the cavalrymen surged forward. He had his sabre extended over his stallion's head as he galloped his black beauty straight toward the blue cavalrymen. The second charge was loosed. He was knee to knee with his fellow troopers at a full thundering gallop when they crashed the ragged Federal line coming to meet them. The impact was terrific. Horses smashed into each other, throwing riders to the ground in the maelstrom.

James slashed his sabre into the upper arm of a Federal cavalryman, who dropped his sabre from his limp and bloody arm. James parried a sabre away from his own head, returned his sabre to its scabbard, and drew his revolver. At point blank range, he fired shots into the torsos of a number of Federal cavalrymen swirling around him.

He experienced cottonmouth and dehydration. He was used to it, but he knew fatigue would set in before long. Fatigue dulled his reflexes.

Again he yelled out, "Reform! Rally to the guidon!"

James rode back with the guidon, leaving the dead and wounded where they lay. He drank half a canteen as he trotted back.

"Dismount, and fight on foot!" James ordered his cavalrymen as a private rode up to him.

"Sir, I'm Private Bronaugh. General Dearing has fallen, and I just removed Major Thomson's body from the field. Thought you'd want to know."

"Thank you, Private."

The private's report moved him deeply. Thomson and he had fought together throughout the course of the war. Suddenly, his old stomach wound began to hurt. He sat his stallion in utter anguish. He unbuttoned his jacket, removed the flask, and took a long swig of laudanum. His body dehydrated, the laudanum took effect almost immediately. With the pain gone, his thoughts harkened back to something Claverhouse had said, *When I think of death, as a thing worth thinking of, it is in the hope of pressing, one day, some well-fought and hard-won field of battle, and dying with the shout of victory in my ear—that be worth dying for, and more, it would be worth having lived for!*

His thoughts grew strangely calm as he reined his stallion in the direction of the reformed Federal line of cavalrymen and spurred him on. He pulled his sabre, waving it over his head in a taunting manner. When he had gotten a hundred yards away from his troopers' line of battle, two officers emerged from behind what was left of the Federal cavalry line.

"Mano-a-mano! Come out and fight!" James challenged at the top of his lungs.

The two officers in blue spurred their horses toward this seemingly suicidal attack.

They met halfway between the two astonished lines. He was mentally at Killiecrankie in Perthshire with Claverhouse. He slashed his sabre to parry a blow from one of the Dutch king's officers. The second officer's sabre struck James in the arm ripping open his jacket. A nasty flesh wound, but he didn't feel it. When he had ridden by them, he wheeled his stallion about and pulled his reloaded revolver. The William of Orange usurper's officers had also wheeled their horses and spurred straight for him.

When they encountered each other this time James cried out, "Fight like real soldiers! Two on one is a fair fight! This is for Jeb Stuart!"

He was parrying their sabre blows, protecting himself with his tightly gripped .44 caliber revolver, when one of the officers was able to knock James from the saddle. One of his boots came off in the tussle, and he crashed to the ground on his back. At the moment James hit the ground, he fired two quick shots. Each shot found its target in the torsos of the Federal cavalrymen. Down they tumbled, one of them onto him, the man's blood smearing his face.

James got to his feet, stood over the two dying men, tipped his kepi in respect, mounted his stallion, and rode back to the Confederate line. The cheers went up and down the line as he rejoined his dismounted cavalrymen.

"Cousin, I always thought you were a sumbitch, but who do you think you are, William Wallace?" Lige asked.

"No," he replied. "I was John Grahame."

Lige looked at him sideways for a second, "Well, whoever ya're, that strategy worked. Both armies stopped to watch your single combat and morale is high."

James wiped the blood from his face and said nothing.

General McCausland and Colonel Munford rode over to him.

"Major, splendid horsemanship," Colonel Munford said.

"Gentlemen, all we've left is our honor! If we're to die on the field of battle, we should die honorably and well," James responded to no one in particular.

General McCausland broke the silence, "Lieutenant Colonel White, I want you to take the 6th Virginia Cavalry and finish off those Yankee infantry on the hill. We'll round up or scatter the rest of these Yankee troopers to the winds."

⚬⚬⚬

James awoke outside the Federal lines the next morning. Colonel Munford's 2nd Virginia troopers were bivouacked around him. His gloom had become overwhelming since High Bridge. The beast, he thought, was General Grant, head of the Federal legions, tearing apart his beloved Southland. Now those legions had the Army of Northern Virginia surrounded. He felt surrender was but a matter of time, though the place for the surrender he could not know. He realized he didn't care.

When he heard the news that General Lee had written a note, late in the morning, asking for an interview with General Grant, James knew it was over. He did not know quite how to feel. He knew he would have to take some time to think about paroling and taking the oath of allegiance to the United States of America.

James was saddling his black stallion when the quartermaster of the 2nd Virginia, Captain Trent, told him Colonel Munford wished that he would join him and a few other men of the regiment later in the afternoon.

At the appointed time, James joined the gathering of Confederate cavaliers mounted in a circle. James positioned himself next to Colonel Munford.

"Major, I suspect you heard that General Lee surrendered to Grant," Colonel Munford said.

"Yes, sir, I got the word," James responded.

"We're riding to Lynchburg. We're not ready to parole. You coming with us?"

"Yes, sir."

James and a few of Munford's men rode a mile or so on the James River Road when they came across some Federal cavalrymen. There would be no avoiding a fight, but the Federals didn't look like they wanted to fight. James realized he didn't either.

"Colonel, do you know of a spring nearby?" the Federal officer asked.

James reined his stallion next to Colonel Munford, and the Confederate troopers soon formed up behind them.

"No, but here's some old peach brandy a friend of mine gave me this morning—if you could make that do," Colonel Munford responded to the Federal officer.

No one reached for a weapon, but there was a strange silence on both sides.

"Well, it's not often soldiers meet under such circumstances. I believe I could," the Federal officer replied.

Colonel Munford handed the canteen of brandy to the Federal officer and then the colonel offered, "Gentlemen, you're welcome to it!"

The canteen went around to all the Federal troopers, as both blue and gray were now intermingled in a loose circle. He thought there was something reconciling to the very act of sharing liquor. Oh, they had shared liquor with Yankees before, but that was when they were either prisoners or dying in the field.

This was different. Here were numerous Federal officers sharing from the same cup as he had drunk from while, days earlier, he was killing them on the battlefield. It became a cathartic moment for him; he suddenly realized the war was truly over and these men were no longer his enemy. He knew it was time to go home.

"Thank you, sir," the lead Federal officer said as he handed back the emptied canteen to Colonel Munford.

The Federal officers reined their horses out of the circle and rode back toward Appomattox Court House. James, Colonel Munford, and the other men rode on to Lynchburg and bivouacked there for the night.

⌒⊙⌒

James stayed a few days in Lynchburg before making his solitary journey north toward Winchester, Virginia. He rode his stallion carrying his sabre, revolver, and his thoughts with him. He did not have a penny to his name. He stayed in Southerners' homes during the journey north, but the farther down the valley he got the fewer homes he found. Sheridan had not left many whole. When he arrived in Winchester, toward the end of the month, he decided to parole himself. He took the oath.

Early one morning, riding a ways out of Winchester, he came to a fork in the road. One direction led him back to his boyhood home, his father at Bai-Yuka, and maybe Mollie. The other fork in the road led him to his sister Priscilla, now Priscilla Bridges, living in Hancock, Maryland. He halted his stallion and pondered for a moment.

He knew he was no longer the man he was before the war started. His wound from Reams Station had never healed. He knew it never would. Pain was now his constant companion when he wasn't taking laudanum. What chance would Mollie have with a dying man? He thought too much of her to put her to the test. He could not even propose in his state. If she said "Yes," would it be love or pity? If she said "No"? . . .

His stomach wound gave him a sudden, sharp pain. He recalled the Christmas party at the Spotswood Hotel in Richmond and how joyful Hetty Cary was talking about her January wedding to Brigadier General John Pegram. Three weeks later Pegram lay dead in the snow, killed in battle. Hetty would grieve, but could recover. How could he chain Mollie to a wretched wreck, and then leave her a sad and lonely widow after he died of his wound? How many years of hell would he put her through?

He chose the fork to Hancock.

43

_____

Who You Been, Ain't Who You Have To Be

AUGUST 1865

JAMES AND PRISCILLA, AFTER breakfast, sat in rocking chairs on the front porch, which ran the length of the Bridges home on Main Street in Hancock. He looked across the street at the Hancock Presbyterian Church and beyond it to the Chesapeake and Ohio Canal, and farther toward the Potomac River. The thunderstorm that had passed left Main Street muddy, and he noticed the morning mist rising from the canal and the river. Priscilla held her first child, Ann Macgill, in her arms and she was four months pregnant with her next child. The mist reminded him of the early morning on September 17th outside the town of Sharpsburg. It wafted in an eerie manner, which he equated with the ensuing death that he knew he and his artillerymen were then about to inflict on the Federals.

"Priscilla, thanks for breakfast and for you and Robert's putting up with me."

"You're welcome here as long as you'd care to stay. It's not like we don't have a room or two for you. You need to rest and let time pass between you and the war."

"I remember the morning that opened the battle outside of Sharpsburg. My battery of guns was perfectly deployed on Nicodemus Heights. When the Yankees began to move into Mr. Miller's cornfield, we opened fire. Every shot seemed to send ten or more men to their Maker. The Yankee artillery couldn't reach us, so we had a turkey shoot. The stranger memory I have about the Miller cornfield is when I was a boy making rounds with Dr. Macgill. I recall these seemingly blue-feathered vultures ripping apart a dead gray fox at the edge of the cornfield. I wanted to run down and throw rocks at the vultures, for the bloodshed sickened me. Mysteriously, years later, here I was ripping apart blue clad Yankees with my shot and shell and laughing hysterically."

"Do you really think that you derived pleasure from killing? That certainly isn't the brother I knew before the war."

James paused to realize that he had begun to rock his chair vehemently. He also realized that this was the first time he had shared a story of the war with his family. He noticed the rain dripping from the roof of the front porch as he felt lost for a moment in time past. He was not able to respond to his sister directly, and so instead decided to tell more.

"I also remember the time when we were sent to stop General Sheridan from attacking Richmond. General Stuart rode over to me and ordered me to hold the road at all cost. I gathered up what cavalrymen I could and we charged down the road into the Federals. With my sabre, I fought a pretty Yankee with golden ringlets. Turned out it was Custer. Then I was shot in the side. Then from behind I took a sabre slash in the head and fell unconscious. When I woke up I spied a Federal on a fine saddle. Same one I now ride. I pulled him out of the saddle and rode back into the Confederate line." He was rocking more easily now. "It was all to no avail. Next thing I remember, I was gathering troopers to head off Custer. Stuart was down and that golden-haired Yankee was trying to capture him. I didn't know Stuart's wound was mortal, not 'til later. That night, after my wounds were dressed, I was in a state of deep despair. I knew that the Confederacy was in great danger of failing. Our best generals were gone. Jackson, Longstreet, and now Stuart. Leastwise I thought Longstreet was gone. Our stepmother's brother performed a miracle to save him. Incredible piece of doctoring."

His words trailed off. He was rocking gently now.

"James, I hear pain and suffering in your words. You'll suffer this terrible war the rest of your life. And your wounds will be a constant reminder. Have you ever thought about what you might have accomplished as a doctor? A cure for pneumonia? After all, your School of Medicine thesis was on the subject. Your research on that was just beginning. You might have found a cure for this disease which has taken hundreds of thousands of lives. And will take God knows how many more."

James observed a rugged looking mountain man riding on Main Street in front of the house, heading west out of town. Full satchels were slung over the back of the mule he rode. The man looked strangely familiar to James.

"Mornin', Mrs. Bridges," the man said. "Good day to you. Reckon I wanted to justa thank Mr. Bridges fur keepin' my credit open til I gets some more pelts to pay it off."

"Morning to you, Mr. Hill. I see you've purchased your monthly supplies from our store. I'll tell him you stopped by," Priscilla responded as she waved to him good-bye.

"Who was he?" James asked.

"Robert Lee Hill, a distant relation to your General Robert E. Lee. He didn't want to fight so he came here and settled the Woodmont Estate on Sidling Hill Mountain. He has a small ramshackle cabin out there where he hunts and traps. Good man, but a bit eccentric."

"Bridges & Henderson Merchants and Proprietors of Round Top Hydraulic Cement Company keeps this town vibrant," James allowed.

"That they do. James, have you thought about going to visit with father?"

"Father and I didn't see eye to eye on the war. He took the oath, yet Dr. Macgill spent fourteen months as a political prisoner because he would not take the oath. I'm not ready to talk with him yet."

James took a small flask from his pocket and drank a swig.

"The war is over. Don't you think it is time you and father ended your personal war as well? Besides, you've never been to mother's grave at St. Mark's Church."

Priscilla rubbed her rounding belly, and James began to think about what she was proposing. He knew his sister well, so he preempted her next conversation.

"I know where you're going with this, Sis. And before you say it, yes, I need to talk with Mollie. I fear I'll break her heart. But I don't think I'm long for this world."

"James, stop that kind of talk! You're doing fine as long as you don't let that laudanum take over your life."

"My pain is my business and I have to deal with it the best I can."

"But there is still a life for you to live, and your family will always love you. You aren't the only one who lived through this war," Priscilla said as she looked sternly at him. "Robert plans to take you to Round Top today to show you the works. Explain the business to you. I need to tend to baby Ann. You should saddle your stallion. He'll be here shortly."

"I'll do that. I look forward to seeing the works."

"Morning, Mr. Corbett," Priscilla said as she waved to another man who had, like Mr. Hill, been buying supplies at the mercantile for his log cabin at the village of Round Top.

As James was about to get up, he saw a lean, dapper, athletic gentleman walking toward the porch. James recognized the full-bearded man, when he approached nearer, as being Captain W. T. Thompson. Thompson had been working in the telegraph office, but recently took a clerk position in the Bridges & Henderson Merchants and Proprietors General Store on Main Street.

"Captain, come sit a spell," James said. "Now that you're working for the family, spec we should get to know each other a bit better." James beckoned the captain to sit in the rocker Priscilla had vacated.

"Don't need to be clerking 'til eight. It'd be splendid to have a veteran to kibitz with. I been meaning to stop by. Your reputation from the war precedes you."

"Mighty kind of ya to say; trying to put it all behind me. Where'd you serve?" James responded. He stood to shake the captain's hand.

"I was born in Clarke County, Virginia," Captain Thompson replied, "and the family settled in St. Louis when I was ten. I was attending University of Virginia when the war got started, and I went west to find my folks. I mustered in June of '61 and, after eight months in the infantry, my feet told me it was time for a horse. During '62 through '63 I was Aide-de-Camp to my uncle, cavalry Brigadier General M. Jeff Thompson, known as 'the Swamp Fox of the Confederacy,' one of the best damn pistol shots in the West Virginia, of course," the captain said as he smoothed his beard with his fingers. "I'm a bit prosy and academically minded, which made for a good aide."

"You carry yourself well; I'm sure Mr. Bridges wouldn't have given you a clerkship if you weren't capable. I heard that General Thompson was fully imbued with the doctrine of Southern chivalry, but never made himself ridiculous by brash, ostentatious displays. Wasn't he mayor of St. Joseph, Missouri?"

"Yes, he was elected mayor in '59."

"'Bout the time I got out there," James said. "I settled in Rushville just down the road to set up my practice of medicine. Border Wars were at a pitch back then."

"I was also fightin' for General Marmaduke's division of the Trans-Mississippi, Eighth Missouri Cavalry, Company D. I surrendered June ninth in Shreveport and came to Hancock to operate the telegraph, and then Mr. Bridges offered me a position a few weeks ago."

"Why'd you fight?" James asked.

"I didn't fight the United States because I hated the United States; I didn't fight the North because I hated the North; but I fought for what I conceived to be the honor, the safety, and the material interests of the Southern people. Although, I'm a Scotsman, and I enjoyed the fierce exhilaration of the headlong charge. I 'spec my Revolutionary War ancestors did, too."

"I enjoyed the exhilaration of the roar of the cannon, too," James said. "Don't miss it now; glad it's over and I can get back to livin' peacefully."

They both rocked happily on the porch as they shared their stories. Off in the distance, across the river, a train passed on the way to Baltimore City.

"I was in some of the heaviest fightin' the Trans-Mississippi got inta all over Arkansas," Captain Thompson said. "I admired General Marmaduke."

"I'm kin to him!" James exclaimed. "He's a proud West Pointer, ya know. His uncle is Governor Claiborne Jackson of Missouri, a virulent secessionist who hated Lincoln. He married Jane Breathitt Sappington; when she died he married her sister Louisa. All my western Breathitt kin are also related to Kentucky Governor John Breathitt, elected in '32. Somewhere over the years the line changed the spelling of our name to end in *itt*. I journeyed out west to St. Joseph, and then settled in Rushville, partly because of my kinfolk out there."

"General Marmaduke was a fierce fighter," Captain Thompson said. "In September of '63 he accused his immediate superior officer, Major General Lucius 'Marsh' Walker, of cowardice and not being present with his men on the battlefield. Walker challenged him to a duel; complicating the quarrel there was an issue of rank."

"Where were you?"

"You see, it was in Federal Steele's advance on Little Rock, and we had been fightin' all day, and the sun and dust were intensely disagreeable. General Price, the corps commander, had advanced Walker above Marmaduke, and it was necessary to get instructions from General Walker. Marmaduke sent out courier after courier, but could get no intelligence on the whereabouts of Walker."

"So what happened next?" James inquired, leaning closer to the captain as the suspense of the story heightened.

"Well, finally, when on the retreat, he found Walker stationed about five miles in advance of the line, and in the irritation naturally occasioned, denounced him a coward. Walker responded with a challenge to him. They met and fought with pistols on a sandbar in the Arkansas River, below Little Rock. Walker was shot through the loins and died the next day," Captain Thompson shared with exuberance.

"You saw all this?"

"We all gathered on the banks of the river to watch. Afterwards Marmaduke was placed under arrest by General Price. But at Bayou Meto, with the Federal General Steele pressing upon our line, the soldiers of Marmaduke's division refused to fight without their general. He was accordingly released. I well remember how he was cheered as he passed down the line."

"I had heard he was a lieutenant colonel by '62, commanding the First Arkansas Battalion, then a brigadier promotion," James said.

"He was a brave man, and a fine strategist, but too cautious for the cavalry," Captain Thompson said as he reached for his elbow to massage it. "In October of '64, I took this wound from a bullet below my elbow. The doc wanted to cut her off, but I drew my pistol and told him I would shoot him before I'd let him cut off my arm. Sumbitch still stings me; gettin' better with time."

"I cut off many arms and legs during the war," James said. "After Brandy Station we had no preparation for field hospitals and were scarce on docs; Yankees caught us napping. So I cut 'em off all night long after the battle, bloody mess. I might've taken a few off that could've been saved, never know; we had so many to tend we just kept cuttin'. After we got all our men taken care of, we started on the Yankees. Legs and arms of both blue and gray piled high."

"I'm glad I still got mine; lotta docs were butchers, not surgeons."

"We did our darnedest with what we had," James replied. He then changed the subject rather than defend his professional merit. "Working at the mercantile, have ya noticed Sarah Bridges?"

"Who wouldn't? Kinda takin' a liken' to her. I think she might be sweet on me," Captain Thompson said with a smile. "Certainly well-endowed, and smart, too!"

"Mr. Bridges is a staunch Calvinist and a good man. His faith takes precedence in his life; might rub off on you? Ya may have to profess Presbyterian doctrine before you get too sweet on Mr. Bridges' sister, Sarah," James chuckled with a wink.

"Presbyterianism suits me well, especially if I getta court her! I believe God's providence got me through four years of bloody fightin'; reckon it might just get me through the rest of my life as well."

"The war has broken me somethin' bad," James confided; "got me this O'-be-joyful flask that keeps me going. I figure this minie in my gut ain't got me long for this world, but Providence has carried me this far; maybe it'll get me a few more years."

"Sorry to hear of your suffering; our wounds, both physical and emotional, are with us to the end, 'spec?" Captain Thompson speculated. He quickly turned the subject. "You much on huntin'?"

"Done enough shootin' and killin' to last me. Robert Lee Hill was by here earlier. He says the game is plentiful out on the Woodmont Estate where he lives. You oughta get his take on huntin' in the area."

"I'll do that; thanks for the tip. I'll be moseying on now; need to get clerking for Mr. Bridges, and seeing to Sarah, if'n you know what I mean. Have a good day," Captain Thompson said as he stood to shake hands with James.

"Same to ya; good talkin' with ya. Most folk who weren't there don't really understand it all," James said with sorrow.

"Know what ya mean."

✥

James was adjusting the saddle on his stallion when Robert Bridges walked into the stable behind the house. James looked over at this man of means and considered his long, pointed hawk's bill-shaped nose, sideburns, and receding hairline. They both wore fine three-piece suits, which reflected their standing as proper professional men in the Hancock community.

"I'm looking forward to our ride out to the Round Top works. It'll be a pleasure to have you along for the short ride along the tow path. I'll certainly feel secure having an old cavalier by my side," Robert said as the stable boy handed the reins of his horse to him.

"Tally-ho, Robert! Let's mount up. Front into line as we used to say in the cavalry," James said now feeling better.

They moved out from behind the house and onto Main Street-National Pike.

"I helped to finance the building of this bridge over the canal," Robert said. "The citizens of the town and I really needed it to get out to the works. You know George Anthony lives here in town, and he is an employee of the works. He makes the ride every day but Sunday, when I close the plant for the Sabbath day. God took a day off from building the creation, so I figure man needs a day off from work. I'm a strict Sabbatarian, as you well know."

"Very admirable quality you have there, Robert. Your Calvinist Presbyterian doctrines have always interested me, especially the one on providence. I'd like to learn more about this theological concept," James said. The horses' hooves clattered on the iron bridge as they crossed it.

"The providence of God has always been a big part in my life," Robert said. "I'm a firm believer in his providence. In fact so many of the blessings I have in my life I try to share with others. God's divine blessing, I believe, is a sign of my predestination. I do feel chosen by God, and I try to help the hundred or so men at the works also prosper so they too will feel the blessings of God in their lives. I try to live by the Golden Rule, I guess you could say."

James thought a moment about what this implied for his life. He could have concluded he was not among the elect, for he did not have a penny to his name. But warriors are not mercenaries. He had fought under the conviction that he was serving his country. But now he felt he needed to exonerate himself from the moral guilt he carried with him.

"Speaking for the Breatheds," James said, "we're certainly pleased to be now allied with the Bridges clan. It appears you and Priscilla are doing your part to multiply the family."

"The Lord commanded men and women to be fruitful and multiply, so in that we're doing our part."

James reined his horse beside the canal to the west, and the two meandered slowly toward the works.

They had traveled only a few hundred yards when Robert said, "James, the future of America is in commerce. Billy Henderson and I've owned the mercantile store since 1850. You see the back of it to your right. We service the National Pike out the front door and the canal barges out the back door. My success with the business enabled me to buy the Shafer Cement Company in '63. Now the works are booming, and I'm thankful to God for my prosperity."

James felt the moist, cool air. He saw that the sun was beginning to break through the very clouds that had brought the thunder and rain. As they rode farther, James noticed the lush vegetation to the right of the tow path ahead. Then he saw a canal boat being pulled by a mule on the tow path. He observed the rope from the canal boat to the mule tighten and then slacken into the water.

"Morning, sir. Looks as if you have a barge full of my cement. Be careful. That's valuable cargo you're carrying," Robert remarked to the man directing the mule.

"Yes, sir. Doing the best I can to get it to Georgetown safely," the man responded with a smile.

While Robert conversed with the canal man, James's thoughts wandered back to what Priscilla had said to him on the front porch. She was a little out of touch with his warrior thoughts, but her naivety made him happy. He had seen so many soldiers die from pneumonia, which he himself had diagnosed during the course of the war. Had he done research and found a cure for the awful disease, as she suggested, he certainly could have saved a lot of lives. But instead of peering in a microscope, he peered down an artillery tube and went to killing.

It was not much longer before they came to the giant works sitting on the canal. He observed four large wooden structures along the canal and a water wheel, which he assumed was used to power the mills. Back behind these buildings were eight kilns, and the tunnels for mining the limestone were nearby. He also saw where they were bringing down the silica sand from the heights of the crest of Round Top.

"James, welcome to Round Top Hydraulic Cement Company. Let's stable our horses, and I'll give you a tour."

"I'm all ears," James said, but his thoughts returned to him in relation to medicine and the war. Even if he had gone into the Confederate medical corps, he would not have been spared the horrors of war. Priscilla simply did not understand that he was not the sort of man to sit out history with a microscope in a laboratory. He felt he had made the only decision consistent with honor, whatever that word meant anymore.

They rode around back of the works and tied up their horses. Then they walked toward the back door of one of the buildings.

"We produce four hundred barrels in a twenty-four hour period," Robert said. "We start by mining the limestone. Once it's brought to the surface, we kiln it at one thousand degrees and then mill it on our four pairs of grindstones powered by the water wheel. We have twenty men in the copper shop making barrels for the shipping of the cement. As you saw on the way here, some of it goes by barge on the canal and some goes across the river on a cable to the warehouse on the other side. The Baltimore & Ohio Railroad makes a stop across the river to move the product we don't ship on the canal."

"This is a more elaborate operation than I had imagined," James allowed.

"Yes, it's fortuitous that Mr. Shafer sold out in '63. We've dramatically increased production since we bought the works. Follow me to my office and you can see the inside of the works."

James followed Robert and observed the mill with the grinding stones in motion. He had never been exposed to such industry. As he was about to sit in Robert's office, the steam whistle of a B&O engine blew, signaling its approach on the other side of the river.

"What you hear across the river is the future of this country, the railroad. Henderson's and my trust company are dependent on the railroad to move our product. The railroad will continue to move west, and with it will go the trust and industry. If this war did nothing else, it gave birth to a new industrial America and our continuing expansion west. James, you need to let go of the past and move forward with your life."

"That may take some time, Robert."

"You know you're welcome to stay in my home as long as you like. I'm prepared to offer you a position here at the works. You can begin to rebuild your life and get in on the future of America, the trust, industry, and the railroad. A lot of Confederate officers are going into railroading. The ways of the old South are over and the agrarian plantation economy is going to take years to recover. It never will be the same. Overseas markets found new sources of cotton in Egypt and India, cheaper, too. There is no slave labor here at the works and there never will be under my ownership. These men are all free laborers and I treat them with the Golden Rule."

"Robert, I know you've never owned another man. Priscilla has told me that you felt this was against your moral consciousness, and I respect that. I did not fight the war over freeing the darkies. But the Yankee trust, industry, and the railroad won the war. I'll have to think about your offer. I served the Confederacy and in the back of my mind I now feel I need to serve my fellow man, be they Yankee or Confederate, so I have not ruled out going back to medicine. What I took to be honor called me to service, and duty drove me through the war. I need time to discern my next call of service."

"I fully understand. You'll make the right decision."

"Priscilla was right about a few other things we discussed this morning. Although I'm not ready to see our father, I must write Mollie and set a date to go and see her."

"James, you're carrying a heavy load. I know it must be difficult living in this end of Maryland, where you're looked down upon in many circles for serving the Confederacy. But understand I'm honored to have you as a guest in my home."

"Thank you. I'll let you know my decision."

44

Maybe, if You Learn One Another's Story,
You Don't Kill Each Other

SUMMER 1866

JAMES LEFT THE BRIDGES' home midday in their carriage to travel to Bai-Yuka. He arrived later in the afternoon. Even though he had not been home since before the war, his
mission was not to reminisce. He knocked on the front door and the judge opened it. He
greeted his father with a firm handshake, and then stepped into the home.

"It's good to see you," his father said as he invited James into the parlor.

"I've come to say hello and to visit Mother's grave," James said in a formal manner.

"Would you like some tea?"

"Yes, that would be fine."

"Ortelia, James is here; come and meet him," his father called as he went toward
the kitchen to order that the tea be served.

Ortelia Cullen Breathed, James's stepmother, entered the parlor with a young
child in her arms. Then James's younger brother Edward came into the room.

"I've heard so much about you, Major. It is a pleasure to finally be able to meet
you," Ortelia said.

James greeted her with a kiss on her hand. "And I've heard good tidings of you
from your brother. Pleased to meet you." Turning to Edward, James said, "Edward, I've
not seen you since you were two! Tell me how old you are now?"

"I'm seven, and could whip ten Yankees at once, just like you did during the war."

"The war is over, so there'll be no more talk of whipping Yankees," he said as he
roughed the hair on Edward's head.

The judge returned. A servant James had never seen before followed with a
steaming service that featured three cups. Ortelia poured a cup of tea for James and
her husband, but refrained from taking one herself. As the men sipped the tea, the

heat of the day made for an oppressive silence. James felt uneasy as to what he would say, even though he had thought about it the whole carriage ride from Hancock.

His father broke the ice, "Will you stay the night?"

"No, I've made plans to stay at the Macgills' tonight. I'm taking Mollie to the basin in the morning to catch a steamer to Galveston. Father, may I speak with you on the porch."

"Certainly. Please excuse us, Ortelia."

They walked through the front door and sat on the front porch. James stoically looked at his father and began to get off his chest what he had come to express.

"I never understood how it was that you were able to take the Federal oath. Dr. Macgill couldn't take the oath, and as a result he spent fourteen months as a political prisoner. I now suffer a terrible gut wound which gives me great pain every day. My duty and honor were my motivation for four years of horrifying war."

"Before you go any further, I was very sorry to hear about your wound and I pray it'll heal completely," his father replied. "Now let me explain my position. Simply put, I was too old to fight when the war broke out, and I had a house full of children. But the truth of the matter was that when they approached me, I couldn't see myself locked up over a few words that I didn't care about. I saw this war as a matter of insincere words, hasty, angry, ill-conceived hypocritical words. And to what end?"

"We all had choices to make, and I chose to fight" James said. "I accept your explanation for your actions and inactions. But I saw Dr. Macgill, a man of unimpeachable integrity, refuse the oath. You know his reasons were based on integrity. You heard it right here on this porch. Was Dr. Macgill a hypocrite?"

"Well . . . I . . ."

James waved his hand to stop his father's faltering reply. "That's all in the past now. I've said what I needed to say. I must visit Mother's grave. Good evening, Father. Please give my apologies to your wife for my hasty departure."

James stood from his chair, placed his tea down on the table, and walked to the carriage. He climbed into the carriage driver's seat and reined the horses forward out the long drive back toward the abandoned College of St. James. When he reached the road he turned right, and never looked back.

When he arrived at the St. Mark's church he dismounted. He swung the black iron gates open, remounted, and drove the carriage to the front doors of his boyhood church. He climbed down and walked around the church to the cemetery. He looked over the family gravestones until he found the one marked *Ann Macgill Williams Breathed*. There he fell to one knee and rested one hand on the tombstone.

"Mother, I'm sorry I wasn't able to come to your funeral; I know you understand it was the war. I've thought about you so much, and I'm sorry it has taken me so long to come and see you. I've talked to Father, but I'm not sure I'll ever be able to forgive him."

Suddenly, the pain hit him hard in his gut. He reached in his coat breast pocket and pulled the flask. After a few swigs, the pain diminished.

"I've come to tell you about what I've done. I know you wanted me to become a great doctor and save lives. But I've done the opposite during the war. I've killed so many, and I don't know how to reconcile the killing with what you wanted me to become. I've prayed to God and asked for his forgiveness, but I need your forgiveness. I'm trying to pull my life together, but it is so hard. The nights haunt me, and I awake screaming in cold sweats. The horrors of my past are with me every day, and I don't know how to escape them."

He broke at that moment. Tears filled his eyes, flowed down his cheeks, and fell onto the grave.

"I'm going to make good and go back to the service of my fellow man. I think I can get my license for medicine back in Washington County. Then I'll go north and south bringing new babies into the world, helping ease the pain of wounded soldiers. Yankee, Southern, doesn't make any difference, new life does. Maybe if I do this I'll ease my conscience for all the killing I've done."

Suddenly, a wind blew. The leaves in the trees around the cemetery whistled. As the sun began to set, he saw that his shadow was cast over his mother's plot, perfectly covering the grave site. A warm feeling embraced him, and his tears flowed no more. He felt as if his mother was hugging his shadow.

"I must go now, Mother. I'm going to see Mollie and in the morning take her to catch a steamer to Galveston. She is going to take care of their family friend Letitia Cooper, now Mrs. Henry Rosenberg. She knows, Mother, that I'll not marry her because of my wound. I'm sad for us both, but I suspect I'll be with you soon. Good-bye, Mother. I love you."

⋅⊙⊙⊙⋅

The next morning they were up for an early breakfast. After loading Mollie's bags into the carriage and then saying good-bye to the Macgills, James pointed the carriage south on South Potomac Street on the road toward Williamsport.

"James, thank you for taking me to the steamer in Baltimore City. I've never told anyone what I am about to tell you. I feel compelled to confess it to somebody, and I believe you will understand," she said with a tentative smile, looking toward him.

"Mollie, you know your secrets are safe with me."

"I have killed a Yankee soldier. He was across the street from my home during the hand-to-hand cavalry fighting the same time you were retreating from Gettysburg. A bullet almost hit me through the window as I watched the fighting from the second floor. It made me angry, so I shot back."

"That's what happens in battles. It certainly has changed me; I am not the kind and caring doctor I was before the killing started. I suspect the war has transformed you also. I suspect it has transformed all it touched. I suppose every war does that," he responded.

"I just felt I needed to confide my secret to you."

"I understand better than you know." He slapped the reins on the horse's back to pick up the pace. They had a 1:30 train to catch out of Martinsburg.

As they approached Williamsport, he reflected upon his artillery actions. He and his artillerymen had protected the Confederate army hunkered down along the Potomac in the town. He drove through the town to the landing, paid his fee, and drove the carriage onto the ferry.

"Hedgesville isn't too far from here," James said. "Our artillery and cavalry were staged there before we crossed the Potomac on the way to Mercersburg. I was naive then, and still enthusiastic about the war. I had no idea how long it would go on in those days. Mollie, the war has broken us. Do you think we'll ever recover our souls and spirits?"

"Yes, I do!" she emphatically replied.

He pulled his laudanum flask from his coat to take a swallow.

"My pain seems to be worsening," he said. He tucked the flask back in his coat pocket.

The ferry docked on the West Virginia side of the river; the horse pulled the carriage up the ramp.

"You've both physical and emotional pain to heal. I believe God's providence will care for us both in the coming years. Our love for each other and God's love will restore our souls and spirits."

Pulling his pocket watch from his vest he noted the time, and then urged the horse down the road toward Martinsburg, hardly acknowledging her comment. He had learned to stoically disregard all his pains and consider them a consequence of his determination to fight the war. He supposed he had free will to act according to his convictions; he did not believe God was punishing or avenging him for his actions during the war.

Crossing the river jogged Mollie's memory back to the covert trip with Mr. Hollingsworth. She recalled how anxious she had been when she was doing her espionage work on the trip to Oatlands Plantation. The carriage sped along the road as she reflected in silence how motivated she had been to do her part for her beloved Southland. Or was she driven on by hatred against the Yankees who had persecuted her father?

She looked about at the farm fields and the corn waving in the breeze. Next to a barn, once painted bright red, which had since faded due to neglect, she saw horses and cattle grazing peacefully in a pasture. She wondered if simple serenity and peace of mind would ever return to heal her brokenness. Would James ever overcome his brokenness? Would he ask her to marry him? Would she accept?

 презентацияಬಿಸ಼

They arrived in Martinsburg, and after unloading her trunks on the platform of the Baltimore & Ohio train station, he left her to watch over her belongings while he drove the carriage to the livery stable not far away. He was walking back to the station when he heard the whistle blow, so he quickened his step. He regarded her standing on the platform and marveled at her beauty, but he was instantly stricken by a sadness in his heart. He knew she could never be his. The pain and the emotional wounds were too deep in his soul. The train arrived and rolled to a halt.

"Miss, may I help you with your trunks?" the heavyset conductor inquired.

"Thank you, yes."

James and the conductor grabbed the end handles of the first piece and lifted it from the platform and into the car. Mollie followed behind them and took a seat by a window while the men went back out to retrieve the other trunk. She had always enjoyed the train ride to Baltimore, she mused.

James sat down next to her. The whistle blew and the train lurched forward, headed east.

It was not long before they passed the road that lead to Shepherdstown.

"Mollie, I came down this road the next day after the bloody battle at Sharpsburg. My artillerymen certainly stacked them up in the cornfield that day."

"I remember the days that followed your cannonading. My brother, John Augustus, and I were left to care for the many soldiers of both sides whose lives would never be the same," she responded with an air of regret for what he had left for them to clean up.

"I was simply doing my duty to God and country. I hardly gave it a thought during the fight. I even tried to help a Yankee soldier after the battle. I gave water to him as his lower jaw was left dangling from a minie wound. I remember Pelham asked me why I did that, and I told him it was my Hippocratic oath that made me do it."

The train rolled on, and jarred them both side to side.

"I saw such horror in the ensuing days," Mollie said. "The first day I had to ask my brother to pull the carriage over so I could vomit. I couldn't understand how men visited such destruction on one another. I could've walked across the cornfield, from body to body, never touching the ground. I had never seen such suffering as I saw in the aftermath of that battle."

"Such is the travesty of war," James said. "Someday I hope we'll discover a better way to resolve our differences. I have nightmares to this day, waking up in cold sweats, as a result of the horror I caused and saw. I did a lot of killing, and the whole time I kept asking myself why I was doing it. I was trained to save life, not take it," he said with regret. "Mollie, I'm determined to redeem myself for what I did, if the providence of God allows me to live long enough to do so."

"You must learn to forgive yourself, for Christ has already. Our fallible and broken sinfulness points us to a cross, and Christ will forgive a contrite heart that's truly repentant."

"Tickets, tickets please!" the conductor cried out as he walked down the aisle toward them.

"Here you are, sir. We're going to Camden Station. Are we on time to arrive at 6:40?" James inquired as he passed the tickets to the conductor.

"Yes, we should have you there on time."

The train rumbled over the Harper's Ferry bridge going into Maryland. They were both staring out the window at the Potomac River below the bridge; the waters were running gently over rocks and past logs caught between the boulders.

"I suppose it may have really got going here with John Brown. General Stuart told me what he did to get that rascal. He thought Brown became a martyr for the Yankees at Harper's Ferry and further sparked the war cry in the North. There were so many causes of the war; the Yankees always point to slavery. I guess the victors will write the history according to their justifying all the bloodshed," James reflected.

But she was not listening very closely. "We'll never really know what all the true causes of the war were. I lament it ever happened. What might have become of us if we hadn't been pulled into that tragic war?" Mollie said aloud, but she was talking to herself more than to him.

He responded, "Maybe we'd have had a clutch of youngsters if the war had not happened; maybe I'd have found the cure for pneumonia by now, hard to tell. How war doth break people and nations in two."

She wondered if he knew what he had just said.

They held hands as the train stopped at Monocacy Junction outside of Frederick. She looked affectionately at him, but never caught his eyes staring back at her. He seemed to be stoically removed from her touch and her gentle eyes. She believed the laudanum had him in its dark depths of depression and despair. There was nothing that her love could do to bring him to her, and she felt he was lost to her, but she could not bring herself to totally believe it.

"I found the 191 Orders right up the road from here. I think Alfred and my race to South Mountain was my most valiant act of the war. When I was helping the wounded after the battle, I couldn't help but blame myself for all the bloodshed of that day."

"I helped add to the carnage. We both had a hand in that day's apocalypse."

She continued looking out the window as he spoke. He gazed on her profile with an agony of emotion; she watched the countryside roll by as the train steamed east.

∾◌◌⌒

During the last half of the trip they were both melancholy and subdued. She was lamenting the parting, which was soon to come at the dock. She had only hoped it would work out between them, but she knew now, deep down in her heart, that he was too broken for her love to repair. She still believed that in due time he would come back to her, provided that wound and the laudanum did not take him first. The thought gave her a sudden chill.

He thought that their parting would break her heart. He was adhering to a chivalric Southern code by leaving her love behind. He hated that code; it broke his heart as well as hers. He knew the wound would take him; he could not bear the thought of having her love for him buried with him in the ground. She was young and she had character and she would prosper, in time.

He looked at his pocket watch to see it was 6:40 as the train pulled into Camden Station, not far from the dock. Her steamer departed at 8:00, and he had wired ahead to have a coachman meet them at the station. The coachman appeared amongst the disembarking passengers. A white ribbon was tied around his muscular black arm, just as James had instructed.

James helped the coachman unload the two trunks onto a cart, and Mollie and James followed the coachman to the carriage. They then traveled to the basin where Mollie's steamer awaited in the twilight of early evening. The coachman drove the carriage close to the dock, and then sprang down to help Mollie out. He signaled for a porter to come and get her trunks.

"We've arrived in time, Mollie. Your steamer boards shortly."

"Thank you, James, for making the trip." Yet, she almost wished that the train had been late and she had missed the steamer; the thought passed. "I shouldn't be long in Galveston, but I need to see to Tish. She's like family to me, and she's not well."

"I understand. Don't worry yourself about me. Take as much time as you need in Galveston. I'll have things straightened out by the time you get back."

James walked her to the gang plank. She gazed into his beleaguered eyes with love. He could not pull away from the passion he knew remained between them, and they kissed and embraced as star-crossed lovers often do. Then she turned and walked the lonely plank onto the steamer. When she was on board she walked to the railing to wave good-bye. He was mounting the carriage, and from the corner of his eye he saw her wave. But he was unable to make himself look back. The steamer whistle blew, signaling that its departure was imminent. The coachman reined the horses and the coach was off to the Fountain Inn.

After travelling a few blocks from the dock, James could not help himself from looking back, one last time, in order to arrest his emotions. The steamer swung out into the darkness heading toward the Chesapeake Bay, south and then west to Galveston.

❧❧❧

James walked into the bar of the two-story brick inn on Light Street. In the bar was the colonel he had written and invited to go crabbing with him in the morning.

"Colonel Pennington, it's a pleasure to see you without having to hear your dogs barking."

"Major, it's infinitely more pleasant to see you here than to hear the ominous cadence of your batteries on the battlefield, knowing that your iron calling cards would be delivered to my doorstep in the next few seconds," the colonel responded. "Can I buy you a drink?"

James noted Pennington's gaunt face and tired eyes staring at him, as if trying to comprehend what his arch nemesis actually looked like in real life as a man.

"I'm a bourbon man."

"That'll do me just fine."

"Bartender, two bourbons," Pennington called out. "You know this hotel has been here since 1773. Old George Washington used to come here and run up incredible bar tabs at civic receptions in his honor," the colonel said.

James realized suddenly, with a force that hadn't struck him before, that the war was indeed over.

"I didn't know that," James replied, but in his mind he was not certain what exactly it was he didn't know.

"You've fine tastes, Major. Were you able to get your lady friend to the steamer in time?"

"Yes, I just let her off at the basin. The ship was departing as I left. She's heading to Galveston to see to the health of an old family friend."

After a pause, Pennington continued, "I remember thanking you once for saving me from drowning in the Potomac River when we were young boys. I'm equally thankful to God for sparing my life over the course of the war."

"It's not as if I didn't give you my best shots. I suspect we're both lucky we're here talking today, and I'm thankful it's as friends. It was good of you to accept my invitation to crab. I wasn't sure if you would."

"I owe you thanks, and I've a great deal of respect for your talents in artillery. I'm a West Pointer, but they tell me you're a doctor. How did you acquire your expertise in artillery? No West Pointer was ever taught some of the astounding talents you displayed as the war progressed. I shudder to think what the outcome of the war would have been if all Confederate artillerists had fought like you."

"I guess you could say it was on-the-job training. Pelham was a West Point man, and he did a lot to get me started in the right direction. After Kelly's Ford, I was forced to develop my own strategies and tactics manual."

"If you ever set those tactics in print, I believe West Point could learn a lot from your manual. I certainly did. Though, often the classroom was not to my liking."

Although he was speaking these words with a certain lightness, James could see that Pennington was both reliving moments of horror and at the same time expressing sincere admiration. James's own mind was in some turmoil, and he looked Pennington in the eyes in silence for a time, not knowing what to say. But Pennington seemed to see something in James's face that conveyed a deeper understanding than words could frame.

⁂

The next morning the two artillerists were up for an early breakfast together. They went to the Lexington Market to acquire the needed chicken necks for bait. Then they drove a carriage south on Light Street far enough to where he could turn east over to the fishing piers on the basin. When they arrived at a pier that had been recommended by the bartender, they negotiated the price for a small sail-rigged launch with oars and a live box. They stowed the chicken necks, a sizable bottle of bourbon, and some sandwiches into the launch. The sun already beat down upon them, and there was not a cloud in the sky.

The day promised to be a hot one, James thought. They would have to work together, he believed, and that would be a shift from their historic roles during the war. He raised the sail and Pennington began to row the rig out of the dock. The wind caught the sail and soon they were moving at a steady clip around Fort McHenry.

"We whipped the British twice," James said. "But our second revolution was abated by your forces."

"You know as well as I do the Confederacy never really stood a chance of winning that war," Pennington said as he saluted the American flag that flew in the fort. "But I'll give you Rebs credit for giving it a try. Now crack open the bourbon, Major, and pass me a cup of it, all this rowing is getting me thirsty."

"Aye, aye sir!"

They sailed the rig south toward Curtis Bay. Pennington enjoyed his bourbon and James enjoyed his laudanum. It was not long before they were feeling rather mellow.

"Major, get some of them necks tied off. I'll move us on a right oblique toward the shore. Fire them necks over at three degrees elevation."

"Aye, aye sir," James replied with a salute as he went to work on the strings and the necks, which he tied about twelve regular intervals to the light wooden lathing that ran along the inside of the launch, six to a side. Then he looked over to Pennington, who had his cup of bourbon to his lips.

"Battery loaded, ready to fire! Sir!"

"Fire them over, right front into line!"

They sat for a while, but nothing seemed to be happening. They looked over the sides at the lines, but the water was too murky to see very far down.

After a while James said, "Let's retire one slowly by prolong to see if anything is nibbling on them." He pulled up a line slowly, hand over hand.

As the chicken neck came into view, he could just make out a crab holding on to the neck with one claw and pulling pieces of chicken neck to its mouth.

"Man the net!"

Pennington stumbled to the bow, grabbed the net, and then went to the port side.

"Steady, Major. Wait til he's in range! I'm ready with the net," Pennington said.

The long-armed colonel positioned the long-handled net carefully in the water, then in one swift but splashless motion swept up the crab. James freed the chicken neck from the net and Pennington kicked the cover off the live box and deposited the crab. A few buckets of bay water were added to the live box, and the crab scuttled to a corner. James quickly replaced the lid.

"Reload, Major."

James slowly lowered the chicken neck over the side. They moved around the launch clockwise. Sometimes the crab got away, but not often. Sometimes they got two crabs on the same neck. Once, three. And so it went. And so did Pennington's bottle.

"You know, Major, I been noticin'. I don't see how as a one-clawed crab can eat. Maybe that's how come you all lost the war. You tried to fight with too many one-gun batteries."

"Yeah, but I remember many a fight when our outnumbered one-barrel gave you hell on earth!"

Pennington chuckled, "Reckon you're right there, leastwise when you were on that gun." Pennington said as he noticed James's countenance changed for a split second.

"Like on the Brock Road," James said in a low voice, almost to himself.

Then Pennington's voice was playful again, "Front-inta-line, Major. I'll admit I always knowd when it was you who I was a firing at. You always had a certain cadence of firing. Accurate as all get out. Wilderness you drove us from the Brock Road, I remember that!"

"Damned if I shouldn't have let you drowned when we was kids. I woulda pushed ya under if'n I had know you'd going to have been shootin' at me all war."

"If I'd know ya was going to keep that damned war going for four years, I'd have pulled you back in the river with me!"

"Battery forward—into line and reload that net, Colonel. Damn it we got crabs to get!"

"Yes, sir!" Pennington said.

They went on pulling and netting until the live box was so full that crabs were crawling out before they could get the lid closed again.

"Major, we got too many prisoners. Time to take 'em to the rear for close questionin'."

They took another swig and broke out the sandwiches.

"Major, even if'n you're a Reb, you aren't so bad. Maybe, if you learn one another's story, you don't kill each other. Whadda you think?"

"Wish ya woulda told Lincoln that years ago. Coulda avoided a lot of bloodshed. How're your nights, Colonel?"

"Not good. I keep havin' this haunting dream I'm with my battery on an exposed ridge. The cavalry has charged off and there's no infantry to protect us. To make it worse our ammunition chests are empty. All our horses are dead. I wake up in a cold sweat and can't get back to sleep. You got troubled dreams like that?"

"Ya, I sees my men loadin' canister and waves of Yankees coming. Then the pink mist explodes in the dream. I awake screaming in cold sweats. When I'm awake during the day, if'n I hears a loud noise go off, I duck. People look at me funny."

"Ya, got the same problem. What're doing now with yourself."

"Thinkin' about doctoring again. Gotta get something goin'. Livin' with my sister in Hancock. Her husband offered me a job in his hydraulic cement company, but I think I'd let 'im down. I'm either high or depressed due to this gut wound. Goin' to kill me."

"I could talk to the people at West Point. Sure they could use a man teaching horse artillery."

"Had enough of war."

45

Yankee Baby and Reconciliation

SUMMER 1868

JAMES SAT IDLY IN his rocking chair on the front porch of the Bridges' home. He heard the whistle of the Baltimore & Ohio steam engine approaching the Alpine Station across the Potomac River. It reminded him of his upcoming trip to Baltimore to meet with one of his men, Henry Matthews. James had been relicensed by the Washington County Medical Society and Robert had loaned him $1,200 to buy his apothecary kit and needed accoutrements. Now he was called Dr. Breathed, except when he encountered a veteran of the Army of Northern Virginia. He was taking a day off from home calls.

"Dr. Breathed, I need you to come quick! My wife is in labor and her sister said to come and fetch you to help with the delivery," Mr. Mellott exclaimed as he reined his lathered horse to a halt in front of the Bridges' home.

"How far along is she? Are her contractions constant or random?" James asked as he sprang from his chair and walked to the street.

"I don't know! But come quick!" Mr. Mellott said as he swung his one arm, with reins in hand, to follow him to the stable.

James saddled his stallion and then came around to the front of the home.

"Hold him; I need to get my doctor's bag inside. I'll be right out."

"Hurry!"

They rode west on the National Pike out of town, and then headed north towards the Mason-Dixon Line. They rode through the town of Warfordsburg, Pennsylvania, and continued on north paralleling Sidling Hill Mountain.

"I'm outside of the village of Dott. We still have a ways to go."

"Where did you lose your arm?" James asked trying to get the man's mind off his worries about his wife.

"I got hit in the Wilderness in '64. The minie shattered my upper arm and those butchers sawed her off. It's tough being a one-armed farmer."

He looked at the Yankee and felt a deep sense of sorrow. Mr. Mellott's long black beard reminded him of many Federals he had seen across the deadly lines, and others he had discovered dead on battlefields. Mellott dropped his reins with his one hand and removed his blue kepi. He wiped the sweat from his brow onto his sleeve and replaced the kepi, then picked up the reins again.

"I was there in that hell on earth with my horse artillery," James said. "That was some of the worst fighting I saw during the war."

"We both have bad feelings about that campaign. Your reputation as a horse artillery commander is well known in these parts. Let's hurry!"

The way Mellott said "reputation" caused James to glance at his companion's face. He saw no hate exactly, but Mellott's features were stern. He knew there must be some folk in these hills who resented his presence . . . or worse.

They quickened their pace to a trot through the rolling hills, and soon were passing through Dott. James observed a few Federal veterans, some with faded blue jackets, some with kepis, sitting on the front porch of the country store. Their eyes followed his progress with what he felt was open hostility. He heard words that, in another time and place, would have meant someone was likely to die—fighting words. He heard one caution a hot-heated youngster in civilian clothes, something about "careful" and "Old Jim Breathed."

James felt no emotion, nothing at all.

They made their way out of the village to a farm lane and followed it to a small rustic log cabin. Mr. Mellott's tall corn studded the fields. A pig pen, next to an old barn, reeked that distinct and familiar odor of mud mixed with hog manure.

They rode up to a hitching rail and dismounted. James unstrapped his medical bag from the back of his stallion. He walked toward the front porch of the cabin and under it saw a number of flea-ridden coon dogs. The dogs began to howl and bark when he came closer to the porch. He entered the cabin behind Mr. Mellott and saw a simple wooden dining table, a stone fireplace, and some chairs scattered around the wooden floor. The patchwork quilt over the sofa was finely hand stitched. He followed Mellott into the bedroom off the main room of the cabin.

"I done fetched the doctor, darling. Doc, this's Sarah Jane and her sister Phoebe."

"Pleased to make your acquaintance, Phoebe. How have the contractions been coming?"

"They're more regular now."

"Sounds like it's time. Mr. Mellott, warm some water on the fire and bring some clean cloths," James said as he opened his medical bag. He set a forceps out of sight of the expectant mother, just in case; then he bent the expectant mother's knees into a "V" position on the bed. "Now, Sarah Jane, I need you to push as hard as you can. I know it's painful, but you're dilated and the baby is ready to be born."

James kept sending Mr. Mellott on useless errands to keep him out of the room and asked Phoebe to hold Sarah Jane's hand and talk to her.

"Push, now—like you never have before! Push, push hard!"

Sarah Jane's screams deafened his ears as she strained to get the baby born. He saw the top of the baby's head as the cervix opened, and he reached forward to hold the head. He pulled gently as the whole head appeared. Then came the shoulders and the whole child came out with a gush of blood, followed by the afterbirth. He picked up the child, held her by her feet, and spanked her. The little girl let out a mighty cry. Then he reached for a scalpel. He cut the cord a few inches from the belly. Setting the baby on the end of the bed, he tied off the umbilical cord and sutured it at the end. He washed off the child with warm water and toweled her dry.

"She's a healthy girl!" James told Sarah Jane with a smile on his face. He gave the little girl, bundled in a swaddling towel, to her mother.

"Oh, she's so beautiful!"

"Mr. Mellott, come meet your new daughter," James said as Mr. Mellott was already walking into the room. James shook the hand of the new father.

"She's a spittin' image of ya Sarah Jane. Don't look much like me does she? Speck that's good for her. Doc, how can we thank you enough? Can I give ya some salted hog ribs to take with ya?"

"No, thank you. Just makes me feel good knowing I brought a new life into the world. But I'll have a few pieces of that home-cooked cornbread. Then I'll come back after your crops are harvested and you can pay me something then, if the harvest is good. I need to get back to Hancock before the sun sets."

"Mighty kind-a-ya to be delivering my child. Your reputation from the war is wrong, and I'll let all the folks around here know it!"

James reflected unhappily that his war reputation was based on rumor; he mused the truth was worse.

"I'll be takin' my leave. Congratulations, Mrs. Mellott; she sure is a pretty little girl."

Mr. Mellott walked James to the hitching rail and thanked him again. When James got to the end of the farm lane he turned and waved good-bye.

As the sun began to set behind Sidling Hill Mountain, he made his way back through the village of Dott slowly, single-footed, saving his horse. The scent of the fresh mountain air filled his nostrils, and he breathed it in feeling good about what he had done. He was back to his duty of serving his fellow man, he thought, and it gave him a certain sense of satisfaction.

When he got to the country store the cluster of men were still sitting on the porch. He passed by them and nodded. One of them spit his tobacco juice onto the street in his direction. He got to the end of the village main street and he heard a musket crack. The minie whistled by his ear. The old war horse never changed gait and James never moved.

"War's over, boys! Ya couldn't kill me then, and ya ain't goin' to get me now!" James called back in a level voice.

He and the old horse proceeded onward. There were no more shots; not that it would have mattered to him.

⁂

A few days later, James awoke in his room at the Bridges' home and he felt more at peace with himself. After a fine breakfast, he said good-bye to Priscilla and Robert.

"Ann Macgill, you take care of your brothers Robert and John. I'll be back in a few days."

"Where ya going, Uncle Jim?" Ann Macgill asked.

"I'm going to see a friend from the war."

"Is he a Yankee friend like Colonel Pennington or a Confederate like us?"

"He fought with me as a gunner in my battery. But remember there is no Confederacy any more. We're all Americans again."

"Alright, but you'll always be a Confederate hero to me."

"I can never forget my comrades and their many sacrifices, but, in years to come I hope you remember me best as Dr. Jim."

James patted his two nephews on their heads. He waved good-bye to Priscilla and Robert as he walked to the ferry. He carried only a small bag with him.

He paid the ferryman the toll to cross the Potomac River. Once across the river to the West Virginia side, he walked to the Alpine Station of the Baltimore & Ohio Railroad. When the train arrived he climbed aboard and settled into a seat for the ride into Baltimore City.

Later in the afternoon he arrived at Camden Station. He departed from the station, walked to Light Street, and turned north toward the Fountain Inn. He checked into the inn, and then ambled down to the bar to wait for Henry.

"Bourbon, Major Breathed?" the barkeep asked.

"Yes, and you can now call me doctor. I'm practicing again. I even delivered a baby a few days ago."

"Congratulations! I guess the war is over for you."

James smiled, but realized that for him the war would never be over. He had a painful wound that he suspected, as a doctor, would never heal properly. At night he had dreams, terrible dreams, full of dead friends and dead strangers. Sometimes he was killing them, sometimes they were killing him. He woke up in cold sweats and sometimes thought he was back on one of the terrible fields of carnage. It often took hours for him to come back to the present. And always in the back of his mind was the struggle between his duty to the dead and his duty to the living; he could confide in no one. No one who had not been in the deadly space for years could understand, and those who had were fighting their own demons and did not wish to be reminded of them. He realized that he was still at war. But with whom? His father? Her?

He took his drink and turned to see Private Matthews walk into the bar. Matthews looked fit and trim as ever. He always was a spindly and wiry man, tough in battle.

"Henry, good to see you old friend!" James said as he stood and shook Matthew's hand.

"Major, I've been looking forward to catching up with you for some time. I'm so glad you wrote me and proposed a meeting."

They sat together at a table much as they had sat around a campfire back in the days of the war. He felt comfortable with Henry and trusted him like a brother. Combat does that, he thought.

"Ya heard from any the other boys in the old battery?" Henry asked as he signaled the barkeep for a drink.

"I've been to see Colonel Chew in Jefferson County, Virginia, now, of course, West Virginia. He returned home to his family estate called the Heritage with a couple of mules and a few dollars. He's turned the farm around and is doing well for himself. I hear Major Johnston has been living in Lexington, Kentucky, and has been studying law. Major McGregor fought his way down to Joe Johnston's army without being captured; he always was a stubborn Scotsman when it came to the war and fightin'. He married in '65 and moved to Talladega. I heard he was practicing law too."

"What ever happened to Captain Shanks."

"I heard he went back to Southern Maryland and took up farming. He's married and has a family."

"I want to get in touch with him, Major. I think he has most of the Breathed battery records from the war archived. Someday I'm going to write about what we did; I think the world needs to know about you and the battery."

"Henry, the war is over. Let it rest. Hell, I even went crabbing with Colonel Pennington a few years ago. He isn't such a bad guy after all."

"He certainly gave us a hard time for all those years. I'm surprised you'd fraternize with a Yankee."

"We buried the war, at least for a while. I was glad I met him again. I'm now practicing medicine in Washington County. In fact a few days ago I delivered a Yankee baby. I figured I killed enough Yankees that I needed to bring some new ones into the world. Although, a Yankee shot at me when I rode out of Dott, Pennsylvania, after I delivered the little girl."

"Did ya shoot back?"

"No, I wasn't even carrying a revolver. They didn't get me over the course of four years, so I figure by the providence of God I must be here for a reason. I've got a mission now, Henry. I'm going to deliver Yankee babies or anybody else's for that matter."

"You see God as the one who was and is keeping you alive. I mean that wound you got at Ream's Station should've killed you right then and there."

"I've had my faith shaken by the war and doubted a lot. I figure God's providence has kept me alive, but I'm still unsure why he let the war go on as it did."

"Well, Doc, that's what ya was preaching to us during the war."

"War changes men. I saw too much to believe the horror of war was allowed by God. I don't see how a benevolent God could've let all that evil happen like it did, but maybe he knows the purpose of the war. Why I'm alive with a minie in my gut, I don't know. The pain I suffer keeps me from doing more, but the laudanum helps with that. I've redeeming work to do in delivering Yankee babies, healing old wounds from old soldiers—this I know. Sometimes, when I'm helping a legless Federal veteran I feel like we've more in common than I do with my own kin."

"You're a better man than I. I still have hate in my heart. I suspect I'll take it to my grave. I have flashbacks in my dreams—nights are hard on me still."

"We all suffer that, but have to bear it like real men. I don't talk about it. I've the same dreams. If that makes you feel any better, you're not alone. Even Pennington told me about his terrible nights."

James asked for another round of bourbons and the barkeep brought them over.

"You were certainly the greatest commander of horse artillery in the war," Matthews said. "I bet we were in some eighty battles and skirmishes. All for what? Scalawags and carpetbaggers are now roaming all over the South and taking advantage of our people. The Freedman's Bureau is taking the ex-Confederates lands and giving it to the darkies. That certainly isn't working out well, for whites or darkies! The "Black Republicans" are trying to give the vote to the darky, so they can reshape the South into the Northern image of free labor. Hell, they haven't even let Virginia back into the Union!"

"I know how you feel. It disgusts me that they have impeached President Johnson for 'usurpation of power' because he has been in opposition of the Republican reconstruction programs. Why they're trying to impose 'negro rule' on the South I don't know. Now we've got the *beast*, General Grant, running for the Republicans as their candidate for president. He'll beat Horatio Seymour, hands down. Grant is the most popular man in the country. But keep an eye on old Wade Hampton. He knows more about real politics than any Black Republican. He'll get South Carolina straightened out. Mark my words."

"Makes me sick. I don't want to talk about it anymore. Remember the time when we tied the bloody chicken head over Creole's nose? He woke up terrified. He believed it was an omen for his death. Strange thing about that was his omen turned out to be true."

"Wonder what ever happened to his wife and kids," James said.

"Don't know? We should send them some money, if we could locate them."

"Saddest day in the war for me was when the 'old boys' were transferred out of the battery in August of '64. You boys went to the Maryland Line. The battery was never the same. We got whipped pretty badly in the valley after that. The fresh fish couldn't fight like you boys could. I lost eleven cannon to Custer at Tom's Brook. It might've been different if you boys were there."

"We'll never know," Matthews said.

"Let's get some dinner."

"Sounds good to me."

⁂

The next morning they parted and James went to see his cousin, Reverend John Augustus, at the Chatsworth Independent Methodist Episcopal Church on the corner of Franklin and Pine Streets. James was shown around the church that Mr. Baker had help to build. It was an impressive church, he thought.

"Might I meet Mr. Baker?" James asked.

"Certainly, cousin. He's a major supporter of Reconstruction in Virginia. He has always been a Southern sympathizer, and the Federal occupiers never figured out all the things he was doing for the South. You two would get along famously," John replied with a certain smile of spite.

They made their way to Athol, Mr. Baker's large estate home west of Baltimore City. When John knocked at the door it was opened by one of the house servants. James stood next to his cousin.

"Could you please tell Mr. Baker that Reverend John Augustus Williams is here with a friend to see him."

"Reverend, is he expecting you?" the servant asked.

"No, but I'm sure he'll see me."

"Very well, come in and wait here."

They entered the mansion of the prominent glass manufacturer magnate, now a financier of stature in Baltimore City. They did not wait long before Mr. Baker appeared, dressed impeccably in his three-piece suit.

"Reverend Williams, it's always a pleasure to see you. How are things at the church?"

"It's all going according to plan. I preach to a full congregation every Sunday. Allow me to introduce you to my cousin, Major, and now doctor again, James Breathed. He was a commander with the Stuart Horse Artillery during the war."

"A pleasure, Doctor. Your reputation precedes you. I've only heard good things about your valor and bravery during the war. Anything I can do to aid you, please don't hesitate to ask. Will you have a seat in my reading room?"

James shook his hand, and then sat himself down next to a table that had the *Baltimore Sun* open on it.

"Doctor, I know you're a Virginian by birth. I've been doing what I can to aid that state in fighting off the carpetbaggers that plague the South. But these damn Republicans continue to block my efforts to get the state back on its feet," Mr. Baker said as he sat himself down.

"Yes," James said. "I understand the efforts in Virginia are being thwarted by many. I'd like to see the state get back in the Union and on the road to a smoother reconstruction."

"Please excuse me a moment," Mr. Baker said. "I need to see to a telegraph which has just come in. I'll be back in a moment."

James did not take the departure of Mr. Baker personally. He knew he was speaking to an important and very wealthy man. He took the opportunity to pick up the *Sun* paper and read a bit. He looked up to see that John had reclined in his chair and noted that John did not look well.

James's eyes gravitated to an article about Von Bismarck, the Prussian, who was trying to consolidate the confederations of independent Prussian states into a future unified Prussia. The article read as if it was right out of the administration of President Lincoln's during the war, he considered. From what he read about Von Bismarck, he thought the chancellor seemed to be trying to consolidate power for a unified Prussian empire. This article was witness to history repeating itself. He knew this to be the truth from all the classical literature he had read earlier in his life.

"Gentlemen, excuse me for that interruption," Mr. Baker said. "Now how can I be helpful to you two today? And by the way, how is Mollie Macgill? Did you ever hear about the time she came to Baltimore back in '62?"

46

The Requiem

JAMES AND THE BRIDGES family sat together at the dining table for the midday Valentine's Day dinner. Ann Macgill, Robert Willis, John William Breathed, and the newest addition to the family, two-month-old Helen Mar, where excited about the day. The three oldest children exchanged cards with their uncle. It was a happy occasion for the children, but James was not feeling well. His stomach wound had been increasingly painful and simply taking more laudanum did not seem to help him.

"Let's bow our heads and return thanks," Robert said as they all held hands around the table. *Thank you, God, for the blessings of this day. Help us to be mindful of the love we share around this family table. The cards we exchange are a symbol of this love. May your providence be with us and keep us strong. Bless this food to our bodies, minds, and spirits. Amen.*

"James, this letter came for you today," Priscilla reported. She handed him the letter, and he placed it in his pocket.

After dinner James excused himself from the table. He told Priscilla he was not feeling well and that he thought he would rest and not be down for supper.

"I hope you feel better. We'll not disturb you. Get some rest," Priscilla said to him as he went upstairs to his room.

When he got to his room he closed the door behind him. He coughed and some blood came out. He took his handkerchief from his coat pocket and wiped the blood from his mouth. Then he pulled the letter from his pocket and lay upon the bed. The large bottle of laudanum was next to his bed. He rolled over on his side, uncorked it, and filled a cup to the brim. He took a large swig and lay back on his pillow to open the letter:

Fort Laramie, Wyoming
7th Regiment of Infantry, Co. B
6th inst., February, 1870

Dear James,

Your kind letter of the 1st inst. I've read. I'm delighted to hear from you. As a soldier, you had no superior. I saw you upon many a hard fought field, and I have always thought you were, without exception, the most valiantly brave man in the Army of Northern Va. or any other Army for that matter. For the Army of Northern Va. was confessed of the best materialized that was stepped into a line of battle. No other Army in the world accomplished what they did, under similar circumstances.

I remember well, a day about a week after the great battle of Gettysburg had been fought, when Gen'l Lee was forming his line of battle on the banks of the Potomac, near Williamsport, Md. I was riding up a road, alone towards Hagerstown when approaching a fenced house a little off the road with a yard in front, I noticed quite a group of our Officers sitting around a map which was spread out upon the grass. And a tall fine-looking Officer pacing up & down the yard approached me in really deep meditation, who when I got about opposite to the gate faced me & asked how far down the road I had been. I saluted & answered "about three miles, Sir!" "Did you see anything of the enemies pickets?" "Yes! Sir! I exchanged shots with them!" "How old are you?" "Seventeen years of age, Sir!" "What is your name?" "Breathed!" "Are you related to Capt. Breathed." "Yes! Sir! A brother!" He reached over the gate and grasped my hand & said, "You may well be proud of being a brother of Capt. Breathed's, he is one of the most gallant & bravest Officers of My Army! You are very young, but please be careful of yourself & never expose yourself unnecessarily!" This was Gen'l Robert E. Lee, and the Officers sitting around the map were his trusted Lieutenants Gen'ls Longstreet, Ewell, A.P. Hill and last, but not least, Gen'l J.E.B. Stuart, his indefatigable Cavalry leader.

James, I've wanted to tell you this story for a long time. I'll always be proud to call you brother!

I'm fighting the Sioux Indians now and the Federal Government's Manifest Destiny Policy to expand west and exterminate the Indians, like they tried to exterminate the Confederates, is now in full-plan.

I am well and I hope you're doing well, too!

Love,
Isaac

His mind drifted back to the war, but he did not want to recall it, so he took another large swig of the opiate. He wondered what had ever happened to Sergeant

Shaw. He thought he might have gone back to Prussia. Shaw was a fighting man and he bet he was going to get involved in Chancellor Otto Von Bismarck's continued attempts to unify the Prussian principalities into a nation-state.

With the next large swig of laudanum James was feeling no pain, and the room began to get fuzzy. Then he saw her at the end of the bed. She was a beautiful Prussian woman garbed in a traditional dress with an Empire waist. He beckoned her to his bedside, and he believed she pulled a chair next to him.

Would you like some?

No, James, he believed she said.

I like your accent!

You know, I'm a cousin of Sergeant Shaw's. He asked me to come see you. He regrets he couldn't come himself. But he's getting ready to fight again.

He lifted his cup and took another long swig.

Helps with the pain you know. Your Von Bismarck is going to do the same thing our Lincoln did. They tried to kill Von Bismarck, shot him five times, and he still lives. I've read about him. "Iron and blood," just like our Lincoln. He destroyed our confederation of states, killed a lot of my friends to do it! Bismarck will provoke France into a war, just like the South got provoked into our war by Lincoln. You know—Fort Sumter.

He believed the beautiful Prussian loved him, and he felt a warm sensation run through his body. He thought she was caressing his forehead as he took another drink.

I think a lot about Oedipus Rex in the Sophocles play. He never knew he did anything morally wrong. He would sacrifice himself to serve his people. I fought for duty and honor. The really strange thing about me is that I medically helped the Yankees after the battles, when hours earlier I had been trying to kill them. . . . Now I'm serving the people again. Trying to redeem myself—killed so many Yankees. . . . Now I'm delivering Yankee babies by the providence of God . . . bringing new Yankee life to earth.

He drifted off for a moment and then came back to the room.

You did what your heart told you to do. You're a man of integrity. Now why did you never marry Mollie, he believed she asked.

I couldn't leave her a widow. She deserved better—a husband for life rather than a wreck for a few years. My blasted code of the gentleman's conduct! I hope her life has been good. I still think about her.

You did right by her. I'm sure she'll grieve your passing.

Where am I going? . . . Look over there: I see the faces of Major Pelham and General Stuart. I loved those two men. They were great warriors! . . . You know they're now killing the Indians. My brother, in this letter, says so!

Major Breathed, front-into-line, it's time for you to cross the River and be with your brothers-in-arms!

He smiled and peacefully drifted away.

47

The Families Remember

OCTOBER 15TH, 1900

MOLLIE ARRIVED BY TRAIN at Camden Station from a hurricane-ravaged Galveston City, Texas. She had been in a depressed mood since September 8th when she had found herself hunkered down on the second floor of her home at 1306 Avenue D in the Strand District. The storm had ripped the cupola off the roof, destroyed the front porch, and broken nearly all the windows in her and Henry's home. She had always been a survivor, and she felt it was providential that she did not count herself among the more than eight thousand dead in the ruined city. She told herself she needed to see her family. She was going on sixty-two and felt the past was calling to her.

Her brother, the now prestigious Dr. Charles Griffith Worthington Macgill, had driven from his home in Catonsville, Maryland. After scanning the arrival area, she saw him sitting, waiting for her. She hoped her face did not betray the wistful sadness she felt. She was struck by how much he had aged since their last meeting. As she walked toward him, he stood and came toward her; they embraced. They had always been close, and the look in his eyes made her feel young again.

"Hello, Charles, I feel like I've been through another war, this time brought by nature's wrath. It's so good to see you," she said. She kissed him on the cheek and gave him another hug.

"You're a survivor, Mollie! And you look wonderful. We were so concerned about you when we got news about the hurricane hitting Galveston. They said the winds were in excess of one hundred and forty-five miles an hour! How did you make it?" he asked as they made their way to his Duryea Motor Wagon.

"I just prayed! Our home is eight blocks into the island, and the fifteen-foot surge was softened by the time it got to our sturdy brick home. The downstairs was flooded, but the waters didn't come upstairs where I was holding on for dear life. I had gathered food and water, but they didn't give us much warning at all. If they had, I might have gotten off the island, but by the time I heard that it was going to be such an awful storm, it was too late."

Charles opened the passenger seat door for her. He walked around to climb into the driver's seat.

"No more horses and carriage for you, I see! How long have you had your horseless carriage?"

"They've been out for a while. Duryea Motor Company has produced one of the first really practical automobiles. I bought it a year ago," Charles said. They rode along in silence for a while. "I know you plan on visiting James's grave, and I know it's going to be difficult for you. You'll stay at the Bridges' in Hancock, I understand."

"Yes, I've not been east since Father's and Mother's funerals. In '98, I dedicated the windows at St. Paul's Episcopal Church in Richmond. Mother and Father would be so proud to know that I donated a second window after Mother died. I'm sure you would also be interested to know I've kept Mother's wedding dress in the Macgill Memorial Hall I built on Henry's and my estate. My Galveston Jefferson Davis Chapter of the United Daughters of the Confederacy meets there monthly. I still support the fallen of the 'lost cause' after all these years. Henry was a Confederate artillerist, and he would've wanted me to. I even gave money to build the Confederate Monument in Central Park. I've not seen how it survived the storm, yet."

"You've done so much good with the money Henry Rosenberg left you. He loved you for many reasons, but your taking care of his invalid wife, Letitia, from '66 for over twenty years would have won the love of Henry in a deeper way than youth can know. You told us about the Rosenberg Library that was built in Galveston City. Did the library make it?"

"I'm afraid to know how many of their papers were washed out to sea. I gave all of James's papers to the library."

"Well, I wouldn't worry myself about his reputation as a soldier. It has long outlived him. He doesn't need papers to prove what he did for the Confederacy."

"We've a good little drive to get to Hancock. These new autos don't move as fast as the trains. But there's so much to catch you up on, particularly about the Bridges. Priscilla and Robert have prospered. Robert was always known as the most honest businessman in Western Maryland, and his son Henry Percival is now reckoned the smartest."

And so their long journey began.

৵৩৬৵

They arrived late in the evening at the Bridges' home; Charles parked his auto in front of the house on Main Street. They walked to the door and knocked. They were warmly welcomed by the family, given a fine dinner, and put to bed.

After a good night's rest, she, Charles, Robert, and Priscilla had breakfast together the next morning. On the previous day's ride she had noticed that the leaves had begun to turn their beautiful amber and orange colors. The morning had brought a dense mountain fog and the air was cool, which was not conducive to sitting on the front porch, and so the four gathered in the parlor.

She had never been in the Bridges' home as she had not returned for James's funeral. She looked around the parlor and admired the fine wood-paneled walls. She noticed the bookshelves, a picture of George Washington on the wall, a cylinder phonograph player, ornate globed light fixtures, and lush oriental carpets on the floor. Priscilla wound up the phonograph and played some Beethoven as background music. Robert, with his well-groomed four-inch-long white beard and vested three-piece suit, sat in his black leather chair. She and Charles sat on a sofa; Priscilla next to them in a chair.

"Mollie, we're sorry about what has happened to your city. We know you've been so generous in Galveston City. We hope all your work has not been destroyed," Priscilla said as she looked at Mollie with her soft caring eyes.

"Thank you for your concern, Priscilla. My marriage to Henry Rosenberg was for only four short years after Letitia died in '88. He gave me great responsibilities and trusted me with his estate. Now, more than ever, I'll be needed by the people of Galveston City to help them rebuild their lives. I'm on many boards there, and I'll work with them to find the best way to help."

"Let me know how I can help, too," Robert said. "I want to give you a check to take back with you. It's the least I can do."

"I needed to get back to my family roots for a time, Robert. The city after the hurricane reminded me of the war. I saw corpses piled onto horse-drawn carts that were being taken to the sea for burial. But when the bodies started washing back onto the beaches, they began funeral pyres which burned for weeks. The odor reminded me of the time Charles and I were on the Sharpsburg battlefield a few days after that terrible fight.

"They built a 'White City on the Beach' with U.S. Army tents for the survivors. I saw one dredge boat three miles inland from the coastline. There's so much suffering there. I hope President McKinley will do what he can and quickly."

"On the 12th, we experienced the winds here. That must have been some storm you got if the winds were still blowing four days after the storm's eye hit ground," Charles said while patting her hand.

"After some rest in Catonsville with Charles, I'll head back. But there's nothing more I can do now. That is kind of you, Robert, to offer your aid," Mollie said, turning her eyes to him.

"In '81, we got word of your father's death at Mineola in Chesterfield County, Virginia," Priscilla stated.

"In '80, Father suffered a paralyzing stroke. He had to stop practicing then. Mother passed in '97; God rest their souls," Charles said.

"Whatever happened to John Augustus Williams?" Robert asked. "Last I heard he was preaching at Chatsworth independent Methodist Episcopal Church in Baltimore City. He was a gifted man of God's word."

"He was on a second voyage for his health in '73 when he passed. He had never enjoyed robust health. Probably his lungs gave out, but I never heard for certain," Mollie replied.

"I've always had a place in my heart for gifted men of the word. In '45, my father founded the Presbyterian Church across the street or *kirk*, as he called the church. My elder's roots go back to John Knox in Scotland. By God's providence I've been an elder at our Presbyterian church for many years," Robert said.

"The Bridges always have been good Scots Presbyterians. The Whites, Williams, Macgills, and Breatheds have always been good Episcopalians. I support Grace Episcopal in Galveston," Mollie said.

"Do you know where Lige Viers White is these days?" Priscilla asked. "James always spoke so highly of his cousin. He even told me that his 35th Battalion of Cavalry came to get him out of a few rough spots during the war."

Mollie could have shared her own secrets about the work she did for Lige, but just smiled and said, "Charles, you'd know more about him than I."

"He retired back to the family plantation called Selma in Loudoun County, Virginia. He's a Primitive Baptist preacher. He had a stint of being the county sheriff and then became president of the Peoples National Bank in Leesburg. He ran Conrad's Ferry on the Potomac and changed the name to White's Ferry. He seems to be doing well for himself," Charles said.

"What became of Judge Breathed?" she asked Robert.

"He sold Bai-Yuka after James died. In '72, I helped him buy Dungeness plantation on the James River in Goochland County, Virginia. He farmed it until '76, but never made a real go of it. I sold it for eighteen thousand dollars ,and he moved on to Lynchburg to retire. He became a magistrate there. He really enjoyed seeing his many children, of course with the exception of James, who was gone by then. They didn't seem to ever patch up their relationship after the war. He died in '93."

The tall entryway clock chimed after Robert finished his thought. Priscilla stood and approached Mollie, a letter in her hand.

"My dear, James would've wanted you to have this letter. We found it resting on his chest the day he passed. You know it was Valentine's Day of '70 when he died."

"Yes, I know it was. I remember feeling rather sad that day, even before I heard the news a few days later," she said to Priscilla.

"Would you like to go now and do what you came to do, see his grave at St. Thomas Episcopal Church cemetery?" Charles asked.

"Yes, I'm ready to see his grave."

They all bundled up in their warm clothes and overcoats. Mollie exited the house holding Priscilla's hand. They all walked up the street to the church, around to the left of the church building, and found the limestone marker. The pious Robert stepped next to the gravestone while the other three looked on.

"Shall I have a word of prayer?"

"Yes, please do," Mollie replied as she closed her eyes.

Gracious and Almighty God, we've come to remember a faithful man and a fallen soldier before thee. His death and election was foretold by thee in thine eternal predestined wisdom. He could no longer suffer his emotional and physical wounds on this earth. Now he is with thee and his other fallen brothers-in-arms. We remember him as a passionate fighter for the cause, in which he believed, and a compassionate doctor who bound the wounds of his fellow soldiers, be they men in gray or blue. He sought to redeem himself in thine eyes and his eyes by delivering babies in the north. Give him rest from thy judgments and his own. Bless him with thy grace and peace forevermore. We'll always remember him as a man of courage, bravery, and gallantry—one of thy own. Amen.

"Thank you, Robert," Mollie said. She walked over to Robert and gave him a hug.

Priscilla and Charles hugged her, and then in silence the three departed the cemetery leaving Mollie alone at the graveside.

She could see only about ten feet from the gravestone for the fog had grown very dense. The cool air made her grasp her shawl. A slight breeze swirled the thick fog around her and enshrined the two souls for the moment.

She stood, dignified and calm, before the stone. Then she pulled out from under her shawl a small Confederate battle flag mounted on a wooden dowel. She leaned forward, placing one hand on the stone, and then she firmly planted the flag in the soil with her other hand.

She spoke aloud in the stillness of the moment, "James, I hope you're resting peacefully. Now your soul is with God's loving unbroken circle. I want you to know that, after all these years, I've loved no other man with the passion I felt for you. You're in my thoughts and prayers daily. The violent times broke our circles of love and deprived us of our dreams. Full as my life has been, it's just a footnote to what we were deprived of."

Her tears began to run down her cheeks.

"My heart has been yours since we were children, even when we tested our wills against each other."

Her heart was too full to continue. Standing there at his grave released a deep sense of regret in her heart, almost to wildness. "I now understand why your feelings, as a gentleman and as a man who loved me, wished to spare me the lingering death you knew was your future. But I'll always lament that we never married after the war, even if it would have been only for five short years."

Tears now burst forth from her eyes and washed over his gravestone. After a while, she pulled her handkerchief from her sleeve and dried her eyes.

"Good-bye, my love."

Confederate Medal of Honor

Citation

Doctor/Major James Breathed

Stuart's Horse Artillery Battalion

BATTLE OF SPOTSYLVANIA COURT HOUSE,
OVERLAND CAMPAIGN, VIRGINIA

8 May 1864

Attacked by General Gouverneur K. Warren's V Corps of enemy soldiers, Major James Breathed faithfully manned his cannon at the Alsop House. Ordered by General Fitzhugh Lee to hold his position at all costs and knowing that failure to hold his battery on the knoll until reinforcements arrived would lead to the Union Infantry's arriving first at Spotsylvania Court House, he remained stalwart with total disregard for his own safety. As General Winfield Scott Hancock's II Corps flanked his position, the Union soldiers marched into his withering artillery fire from all sides. He reported, "My support having given back, I was obliged to run the risk of losing one gun to save the other three." He limbered four horses and, as he rode the lead horse, with Minie balls flying around his head, it was shot from under him. He cut the traces and mounted a second lead horse. It was shot from under him as he heard the Union soldiers crying out, "Come on, men! Get that gun!" Finally, he mounted one of the two remaining horses and rode the gun from the field. Major James Breathed is hereby awarded the Confederate Medal of Honor for extraordinary heroism at great personal peril.

CPSIA information can be obtained
at www.ICGtesting.com
Printed in the USA
FFHW010103200319
51140337-56604FF